REFLECTIONS ON THE ICE AGE IN SCOTLAND

An Update on Quaternary Studies

Edited by John E. Gordon

SAGT General Editor: John May

Scottish Association of Geography Teachers

Scottish Natural Heritage

Glasgow

Published by:
The Scottish Association of Geography Teachers and Scottish Natural Heritage

First published 1997

ISBN 0 9524210 11

Copies of this publication are available from Alan Doherty, Senior Editor, SAGT, Linlithgow Academy, Linlithgow EH49 6EH

Printed by S.K.I. Graphics (Scotland) Ltd, 89 James Street, Bridgeton, Glasgow G40 1BZ

CONTENTS

LIST OF CONTRIBUTORS

C.K. Ballantyne, *Department of Geography, University of St Andrews, St Andrews, Fife KY16 9ST.*

D.I. Benn, *Department of Geography, University of Aberdeen, Elphinstone Road, Aberdeen AB9 2UF.*

C.M. Clapperton, *Department of Geography, University of Aberdeen, Elphinstone Road, Aberdeen AB9 2UF.*

R. Crofts, *Scottish Natural Heritage, 12 Hope Terrace, Edinburgh, EH9 2AS.*

K.J. Edwards, *Department of Archaeology and Prehistory, University of Sheffield, Northgate House, West Street, Sheffield S1 4ET.*

A.M. Hall, *Department of Geography, University of Edinburgh, Drummond Street, Edinburgh EH8 9XP and Department of Geography, University of St Andrews, St Andrews, Fife KY16 9ST.*

N.F. Glasser, *School of Biological and Earth Sciences, Liverpool John Moores University, Byrom Street, Liverpool L3 3AF.*

J.E. Gordon, *Scottish Natural Heritage, 2 Anderson Place, Edinburgh EH6 5NP.*

J.M. Gray, *Department of Geography, Queen Mary & Westfield College, University of London, Mile End Road, London E1 4NS.*

R. Holmes, *British Geological Survey, Murchison House, West Mains Road, Edinburgh EH9 3LA.*

J.J. Lowe, *Department of Geography, Royal Holloway, University of London, Egham, Surrey TW20 0EX.*

L.J. McEwen, *Department of Geography and Geology, Cheltenham and Gloucester College of Higher Education, Francis Close Hall, Swindon Road, Cheltenham, Gloucestershire GL50 4AZ.*

A.P. McKirdy, *Scottish Natural Heritage, 2 Anderson Place, Edinburgh EH6 5NP.*

C. Mitchell, *Scottish Natural Heritage, Junction Road, Kirkwall, Orkney KW15 1AW.*

D.E. Smith, *Centre for Quaternary Science, School of Natural and Environmental Sciences, Coventry University, Priory Street, Coventry CV1 5FB.*

M.J.C. Walker, *Department of Geography, University of Wales, Lampeter, Dyfed SA48 7ED.*

COVER PHOTOGRAPHS

Front:

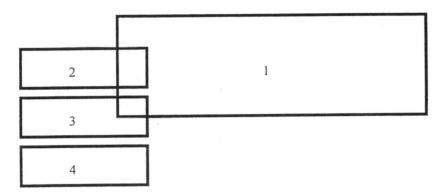

1. Glacier La Pleine Morte, Switzerland. The photo shows how parts of the Scottish Highlands may have looked during the Quaternary ice age. (Photo: A.W. Doherty).

2. Moreno Glacier, Argentina. The view shows how Glen Roy may have appeared during the Loch Lomond Stadial (c. 11,000-10,000 years ago) when glaciers dammed a series of lakes in the glen. (Photo: J.E. Gordon).

3. Pine stump revealed in eroding blanket bog in the Cairngorms represents a remnant of the great Caledonian forest that covered much of Scotland during the middle Holocene. (Photo: A.W. Doherty).

4. Loch Garry occupies an ice-deepened glen in the west Highlands. (Photo: A.W. Doherty).

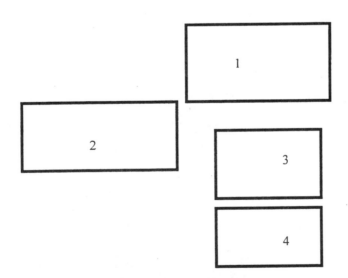

Back:
1. Lochan na h-Achlaise and the hills of the Black Mount, near Rannoch Moor. This area, with its high precipitation, lay at the centre of ice sheet development during the Quaternary. (Photo: J.E. Gordon).

2. Erratic block on the surface of the Glacier de Cheilon, Switzerland. Glaciers act as giant conveyor belts transporting eroded rock debris both on their surfaces and at their beds. (Photo: A.W. Doherty).

3. The Parallel Roads of Glen Roy, one of the classic ice age landforms in Scotland. The 'roads' are the shorelines of a series of ice-dammed lakes that formed during the Loch Lomond Stadial. (Photo: J.E. Gordon).

4. The River Quoich, near Braemar. The modern gravel fan of the Quoich is set within an older alluvial fan, illustrating different episodes of valley floor activity during the Holocene (Photo: J.E. Gordon).

NOTE ON ABBREVIATIONS AND TERMS

Abbreviations

- Ages in this volume are generally cited using the convention Ma and ka (*e.g.* 2 Ma for 2 million years and 50 ka for 50,000 years).

- Rates are expressed in a variety of units, *e.g.* glacier flow in m a^{-1} (metres per year) or km a^{-1} (kilometres per year); precipitation in mm a^{-1} (millimetres per year); sediment transport in t km^{-2} a^{-1} (tonnes per square kilometre per year); river discharge in m^3 s^{-1} (cubic metres per second).

- Gradients (*e.g.* of shorelines) are expressed as m/km (metres per kilometre).

- Radiocarbon (^{14}C) dates and ages are given in years BP (before present *i.e.* AD1950).
  These are equivalent to calendar years (see Chapter 9).

Terms

As far as possible, the more technical terms have been explained in the text. However, a useful source of reference is:

- Goudie, A. 1990. *The Encyclopaedic Dictionary of Physical Geography*. Blackwell, Oxford.

Foreword

Roger Crofts

For many classroom teachers of my generation, their experience of the Quaternary from the other side of the desk was no doubt limited to certain types of erosional and depositional landforms described in the basic textbooks. If, like me, you were lucky enough to experience at first hand some of these landscapes, then your interest may have been kindled, although your knowledge-base not particularly extended. Certainly, this was the case for me when my first visit to Scotland included the classic Glen Rosa glacial trough, much exemplified in many classroom textbooks of the late 1950s and early 1960s. Even my geomorphological teaching at university tended to focus on the variety of forms resulting from ice sheets and valley glaciers.

I was fortunate enough to arrive in Scotland to work in 1966 at a time of great debate on Quaternary issues. Heated arguments raged about the nature of deglaciation: whether the ice was stagnant or active, the juxtaposition of ice limits and marine limits in eastern Scotland, the tilting of shorelines and outwash plains, and the interpretation of controversial deposits. However, as in many things, what struck me most of all was to go back in time and to read the seminal works of previous generations. How was it that T. F. Jamieson, an estate factor from Ellon, managed in the mid-19th century to describe the fundamental process of glacio-isostasy, a process that has great significance for our understanding of the Scottish Quaternary? And how did the classic observations of Alexander Bremner in north-east Scotland, half a century later, prove to contain so many truths which are still being debated today? As with most budding geomorphologists, and I still hope classroom geography teachers and their pupils, visits to the field are a vital component in aiding understanding, alongside the modern interpretations provided by specialists in the subject. My introduction through the seeing eye of Francis M. Synge took me into a new world of careful observation of forms and features, of stratigraphy, and of landform interrelationships.

What intrigues me most, therefore, in looking through the papers in this splendid volume, is that some of the arguments which raged 30 years ago have been rekindled as a result of the application of new techniques and the application of new minds to the challenges of understanding the Quaternary.

That there has been such a tremendous amount of scientific and intellectual endeavour on the Quaternary of Scotland should be of no surprise. The diversity of features, the speculation of the impact of inherited topography and geological structures and rock types, the rapidly changing climatic conditions and Scotland's geographical location all excite tremendous interest. What is also intriguing is that researching the Quaternary of Scotland in isolation tells only a small part of the story. Much of what we know is gained by reasoned inference from research endeavours elsewhere, particularly on the Greenland ice cap and from deep-sea cores, and from wider climate modelling studies. Without the application of that knowledge, our understanding of the Quaternary of Scotland would have been the poorer. But the flipside of this is that our knowledge of the final ice retreat period is now so extensive that it provides a context for studies of the Quaternary in adjacent parts of Europe.

There are a number of major shifts which, as a lapsed Quaternary geomorphologist and equally lapsed classroom geography teacher, I consider to be most important for the classroom teacher.

The understanding of the climatic driving forces for the whole of the Quaternary period has revolutionised our approach to interpreting the landform evidence. We are now able to create the big picture of climatic patterns and the implications for the growth, distribution and topography of glaciers and ice sheets in a way that enables us to get some sort of handle on the relative age of the associated landform evidence. Whilst we have long understood the fluctuations of temperature in the Quaternary period, the more detailed evidence uncovered in recent decades has shown that the changes can be very rapid indeed. Far from a steady progression from glacial to interglacial or interstadial and back, there can be very rapid changes which release energy in the form of glacier advances and meltwater events which are then recorded in the stratigraphy and landforms.

Far from our knowledge of the Quaternary being founded on landforms and deposits, a major development has been in the understanding of the processes which have created them. Without awareness of analogues and comparators in present glaciated areas, we would not have been able to interpret the complex mix, often over small areas, of erosion, protection and deposition resulting from the activity of the ice itself and the meltwater regimes. Those who have visited modern glaciated areas have probably been surprised, like I was in Vest Spitzbergen and Iceland, to note the inherent fragility of glaciofluvial landforms such as eskers, and moraines and to reflect how, after 10 or 20 millennia, they are still intact. Such visits also enabled me, amongst others, to recognise that some marine deposits on land were most likely to have been derived from ice sheets carrying the material from the offshore area, rather than from stranded icebergs, as previously suggested.

Out of the process studies and the more detailed investigation of deposits, has come the confirmation that much of the topography of eastern Scotland was little modified by the activities of ice sheets and glaciers. Our knowledge of glacier bed temperature conditions obtained from high latitudes and the Alps has been a formative influence in confirming earlier views. The widespread remnants of deeply weathered rock, and the exhumed warm climate forms of tors, are ample evidence that ice sheets do not always erode.

In recent decades, significant advances in identifying the extent of periglacial deposits and their use in interpreting glacial limits have occurred. The practical implications of this work are, in my view, wide ranging as we seek to exploit the mountain terrain in Scotland without a full knowledge of the geotechnical properties of the landforms and their deposits.

Most intriguing to me, in my current day to day work with my colleagues in Scottish Natural Heritage of disentangling natural processes from human intervention, is the work on the changing pattern of surface vegetation. Even now, arguments continue as to the relative significance, or otherwise, of rapid and longer-term climatic shifts, compared with the impact of humans in chopping down the native forest and cultivating the land. And yet these are important questions if we are to address the retrieval of lost habitats, and in so doing, restore the diversity of the landscape.

It is paramount that the scientific community translate their knowledge into a form which is accessible to future generations of citizens and Quaternary geomorphologists. Teachers and pupils need to understand modern thinking, including current and ongoing controversies. The authors of the chapters in this volume are the experts in their fields and I hope that all readers will be grateful to them for setting down, in such an accessible form, the current extent of our knowledge of the various aspects of the Quaternary of Scotland. We should be proud that these authors, and the work of their colleagues which they are reporting here, follows the very fine tradition of investigation of the Scottish Quaternary begun in the last century.

In educating future generations on the Quaternary of Scotland, we should not forget two things. First, there is our intellectual inheritance and therefore the sites which have been formative in the development of new ideas. Second, we must secure the ability of future generations to apply new ideas and increase understanding. Both of these can be assured by properly conserving those key sites and areas which have been critical in the development of ideas to date and which will give the new enquiring minds of future generations an intellectual challenge.

I hope that the members of SAGT, like myself, will benefit from this volume, and will be stimulated into introducing new material to their pupils in the classroom and exposing it to them in the field. You might also be looking forward to other ways of portraying this information: when will we have the CD-ROM on the palaeogeography of the Scottish Quaternary?

1. Introduction: Recent Advances in Quaternary Studies

JOHN E. GORDON

The key themes covered in this chapter are:

- the Quaternary timescale;
- the scope of Quaternary studies;
- the role of Scotland and Scottish geologists in the development of Quaternary studies;
- summary of recent advances in Quaternary studies.

1.1 Introduction

The last two decades or so have seen major advances in understanding the history of environmental change and landscape evolution during the Quaternary, the recent period of geological time which spans the Ice Age. These advances have followed from major technological developments which have allowed, for example, coring of the ocean floor sediments, coring of the Greenland and Antarctic ice sheets, applications of new dating methods, improvements in the resolution of existing dating methods, new analytical techniques assisted by greatly enhanced computer power and better awareness of the characteristics and behaviour of modern glaciers and ice sheets. Numerical modelling of the Earth's climate system has emphasised the global scale of links between the atmosphere, oceans and cryosphere (the frozen realms of the world). The associated conceptual developments in Quaternary science have also greatly changed earlier ideas and understanding, for example concerning the frequency and rapidity of climate changes. Many of these exciting developments have a direct bearing on the interpretation of the evolution of Scotland's landforms (cf. Gordon and Sutherland, 1993; Haynes, 1995), but lie hidden in the scientific literature or in academic textbooks. The first purpose of this volume is therefore to bring these developments to a wider audience through a series of up-to-date overviews and particularly to attempt to bridge the gap between school and university teaching, in effect to provide a 'state of the art' resource for teachers in Scotland. The second purpose is to raise awareness of the significance of Quaternary studies in terms of understanding the present landscape of Scotland and its past evolution. The third purpose is to highlight the importance of Scotland for Quaternary studies in an international context. By virtue of its location on the extreme oceanic western margins of Europe, Scotland provides a vital location and source of field evidence for developing and testing models that link terrestrial and offshore evidence (Sutherland and Gordon, 1993). There is also an important historical dimension, in that Scottish geologists have played a crucial role in the development of Quaternary science. Finally, the fourth purpose of this volume is to emphasise the important natural heritage value of Scotland's Ice Age landforms.

In this first chapter, the scope of Quaternary studies is outlined and a basic time framework for the Quaternary is introduced. The important historical role of Scotland and Scottish geologists in the early development of Quaternary studies is then described as a backcloth against which to view recent advances, both to demonstrate the rich veins of scientific and cultural inheritance as well as the continuing relevance and value of our earth heritage. Finally, there is

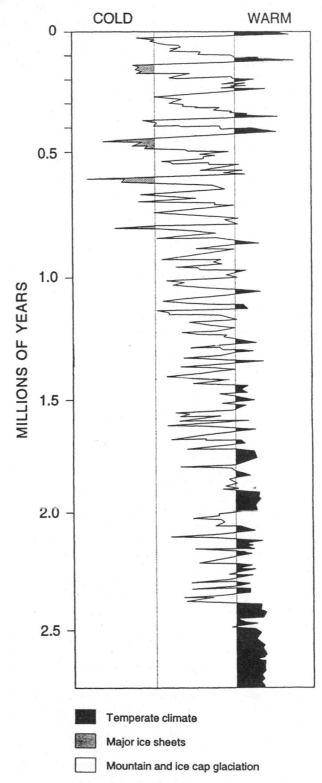

Figure 1.1 Climate record for the North Atlantic area over the last c. 2 Ma derived from the oxygen isotope record in deep sea cores. The figure shows an interpretation of the probable occurrence of periods of major ice sheets and mountain and ice cap glaciation in Scotland. (After Haynes, 1995).

1

an overview of the recent advances presented in the following chapters.

1.2 The Quaternary timescale

The Quaternary forms part of the late Cenozoic Era of geological time. The base of the Quaternary is formally defined in geological terms as beginning at approximately 1.8 Ma. Conventionally, the Quaternary is divided into the Pleistocene (the period up to 10 ka), and the Holocene (comprising the last 10 ka). However, we now know that the climate has fluctuated many times between glacial and interglacial conditions during the Quaternary and that the Holocene is merely another interglacial. The terms Pleistocene and Quaternary have often been used as synonyms for the Ice Age, but there is now evidence from many parts of the world of significant glacier expansion before the start of the Quaternary as formally defined. For example, studies of ocean floor sediments in the North Atlantic have shown that significant climatic deterioration occurred about 2.4 Ma (Figure 1.1), accompanied by the initiation of major glaciation on the mid-latitude continents in the Northern Hemisphere (Shackleton *et al.,* 1984; Ruddiman and Raymo, 1988). In this volume the term 'Quaternary' is therefore used in a broader sense to include the period of time beginning with the intensification of global cooling at 2.4 Ma. This cooling was abrupt and may be explained in part by changes in the global configuration of the continents and their relative relief and in the form of the ocean basins (see Chapter 2). Although changes in insolation associated with the orbital periodicities of the Earth (eccentricity of the planet's orbit, tilt of its axis and the precession, or 'wobble', of its axis) are now established as the driving forces of climate changes (Imbrie and Imbrie, 1979), additional factors are required to amplify the radiation changes to produce climate fluctuations of the required magnitude and rapidity. These factors involve physical, biological and chemical interactions and feedbacks between the atmosphere, oceans and the ice sheets, as well as possible variations in solar activity. In particular, the world's oceans may play a crucial role through major changes, or reorganisations, in their circulation patterns or through changes in the interchange of carbon dioxide with the atmosphere (Broecker and Denton, 1990). Recent work has focused on the North Atlantic 'conveyor' (Chapter 5) which carries warm surface water northwards and cold deep water back southwards. It appears that this circulatory system can undergo sudden changes that have a major impact on the climate of Europe and the North Atlantic region, but the 'switching' mechanism and its links to the solar radiation changes remain unclear.

Studies of the geochemistry and micropalaeontology of ocean-floor sediments have revealed that climatic conditions fluctuated many times during the Quaternary and that the climate system appears to switch rapidly between different modes (Figure 1. 1), probably linked to the changes in ocean circulation. The cold episodes are known as glacials, the relatively brief warmer interludes as interglacials. Typically the glacials lasted for c. 100 ka, the interglacials for 10 ka (Figure 1. 1). The glacials, however, were not uniformly cold, but were characterised by fluctuations between extremely cold conditions (stadials or stades) and relatively warmer interludes (interstadials or interstades). C.M. Clapperton (Chapter 5) describes the detailed pattern of stadial/interstadial fluctuations and, developing the work of Price (1983), infers the changing pattern of glaciation in Scotland through the last glacial cycle. Between about 2.4-0.75 Ma the climate oscillations followed a periodicity of 40 ka. During this time mountain glaciers were probably present in Scotland in the colder phases. After 0.75 Ma, the amplitude of the cycles increased and the frequency changed to 100 ka. The source of this change may lie in the uplift of the Tibetan plateau and the western USA, which significantly altered the pattern of atmospheric circulation, favouring the development of large standing waves (Ruddiman and Kutzbach, 1990). The resulting deflection of storm tracks allowed cold polar air to be pulled southwards, facilitating ice sheet growth during times of reduced solar insolation. This would have given rise to more extensive ice sheet glaciation in Scotland. The main conclusions from this work are that glaciers existed in Scotland in one form or another during most of the Quaternary (Figure 1.1) and that the landscape we see today is the product of many episodes of glaciation by corrie glaciers, mountain icefields and ice sheets.

Given the inferred frequency of glaciation in Scotland, it is not surprising that the terrestrial record of these events is fragmentary (Figure 1.2): later glaciations have removed much of the evidence for earlier events. British stratigraphy (the naming and correlation of series of events and stages based on the geological evidence) has therefore depended heavily on evidence from East Anglia where more extended suites of deposits have survived. As far as Scotland is concerned, most evidence relates to the last cold stage (the Devensian) and the preceding interglacial (the Ipswichian), although some older deposits are present locally in NE Scotland (Chapter 6). In contrast, the deep-sea cores provide continuous sedimentary records through the Quaternary and have allowed the development of a complete stratigraphy based on the oxygen isotope analysis of marine micro-fossils preserved in the sediments (Chapter 5). These oxygen isotope stages now provide a standard means of subdividing the Quaternary timescale. Figure 1.2 shows some of the named stages and their correlation with the oxygen isotope stages of the ocean cores and with stages on the NW European mainland. The informal term 'Late-glacial' (for Devensian late-glacial) is frequently used in the literature in Scotland to refer to the period of transition between the Devensian cold stage and the present Holocene interglacial, that is between 13-10 ka BP (see Chapter 9). Ages in this volume are generally cited using the convention Ma and ka *(e.g.* 2 Ma for 2 million years and 50 ka for 50,000 years). Radiocarbon dates and ages are given in years BP (before present–AD 1950); calendrical equivalents (cal BP) are variable through time, for example being almost 2000 years younger at 13 ka BP.

1.3 The scope of Quaternary studies

Although the broad outlines of the Scottish landscape owe much to long-term geological and tectonic controls (Chapters 2 and 3), the finer details reflect the imprint of successive ice ages and the dramatic shifts in geomorphological processes that accompanied them (Figure 1.2). These process shifts operated both spatially and through time as the glaciers advanced and retreated, and their interaction with the variable geology and pre-existing relief have produced the striking diversity of the present landscape. Within the ice limits, processes of glacial and meltwater erosion remodelled the landscape, while upon deglaciation the corresponding deposits left a characteristic signature on the lowlands and in many upland glens. Beyond the ice limits, the rates and intensity of geomorphological processes and sediment transfer patterns changed as periglacial processes disrupted the regolith and destabilised slopes, major shifts in coastline position occurred, river regimes and baselines altered and vegetation cover varied.

In Britain the extent of the area covered by glaciers and ice sheets varied during different glacial periods. During the last glaciation, ice extended as far south as the north Midlands and impinged on the north coast of East Anglia. During some earlier cold periods, ice extended farther south but never beyond the Thames valley. In Scotland, despite over 150 years of investigation, much uncertainty still remains over the limits of the last ice sheet, and even more for those of earlier glacial events (Chapters 6 and 7).

A fundamental feature of the Quaternary is the predominance of climatic change, and as the climate fluctuated, so too did environmental conditions. Particular types of environmental change have left a strong imprint in the landforms, fossils and recent sedimentary deposits of Scotland. By studying these features and by making comparisons with modern analogues, Quaternary scientists have made considerable progress in unravelling the past. They have shown that a wide range of landforms and sediments produced by ice erosion and deposition distinguish the glacial periods (Chapters 8 and 13). During the melting of the great ice sheets, the liberation of vast volumes of meltwater produced an equally characteristic suite of waterlain glaciofluvial landforms and deposits. In the areas that lay beyond the ice sheets, and also during less severe cold stages when glaciers were either restricted in their distribution or absent altogether, periglacial conditions prevailed. These are characterised by frost-assisted processes and by a range of frost and ground-ice generated landforms and deposits (Chapter 14). Mass wasting (downslope movement of soil on both large and small scales) and increased wind action were prevalent and also produced a range of diagnostic features. In parts of upland Scotland, periglacial processes are still active today. As reflected in the fossil record, the flora and fauna of the cold periods show restricted diversity of species and, not surprisingly, the predominance of cold-tolerant types.

Interglacials are characterised by the absence of glacial, periglacial and glaciofluvial features in the geomorphological and sedimentary record. They are often recognisable by periods of chemical weathering, soil formation or the accumulation of organic material. Changes in the amount and types of pollen preserved in organic deposits have been used to define systems of pollen zones, each zone being characterised by particular vegetation types, from which climatic and environmental conditions are inferred (Chapters 9 and 11). Progressive changes in vegetation through time can be reconstructed through sequences of pollen zones. Environmental conditions have varied during different interglacials, and the presence of particular types of pollen can be diagnostic of particular interglacials. Similarly, different mammal faunas characterise glacial and interglacial periods, and some species are diagnostic of particular glacials or interglacials. Both terrestrial and marine molluscs and coleoptera (beetles) are also useful in reconstructing past environmental conditions by analogy with their present environments.

In parallel with the growth and decay of ice sheets, significant changes have occurred in the coastal zone of Scotland, associated with a complex interplay of changing land and sea levels (Chapter 12). World sea level has varied according to the volume of water locked up within the world's ice sheets, being lower during glacials than interglacials (glacio-eustasy). The level of the land has also varied, sinking under the weight of advancing ice sheets and rising up again when they melted (glacio-isostasy). Such changes are evident in beaches, shore platforms and marine sediments now raised above present sea level. Submerged shoreline features and drowned valleys also point to

relatively lower sea levels in the past. Changes in river courses and channel patterns have followed from changes in discharge, sediment supply and sea level (Chapter 10). There have been times when rivers built up large thicknesses of glacially derived debris on their floodplains; others when they eroded down into their floodplains. The resulting effects on the landscape are staircases of terraces in many river valleys.

Change through time is therefore a fundamental aspect of the Quaternary. Very often traces of successive environments are recorded in layers of sediment preserved on top of one another; for example, glacial deposits may overlie interglacial beach deposits and in turn be succeeded by periglacial slope deposits and later sand dunes. The establishment of correlations between sequences of deposits at different sites forms part of a methodology known as stratigraphy. Change, too, is apparent in the present landscape on river floodplains, along the coast and on hill slopes, as geomorphological systems respond to perturbations of varying magnitude and frequency. Although a temporal theme has been emphasised, it is also the case that Quaternary environmental changes and associated processes have not been uniform in their operation throughout Scotland and, allied with the variety of the geology, this has produced a remarkable regional diversity in surface landforms and deposits.

The essence of the Quaternary is therefore its dynamism, driven by climate change. This dynamism is reflected in the responses of geomorphological processes, vegetation and faunas, together with the associated environmental changes. The record of these changes is preserved in a variety of forms which Quaternary scientists seek to explain. The aims of Quaternary science are to interpret and explain the evolution of the landscape during the Quaternary, the history of geomorphological events and processes, climatic and environmental change and the development of the flora and fauna, and to set contemporary processes and environments into their longer term perspective. Understanding is also sought of the relationships between each of these aspects and how they have varied both spatially and through time. Quaternary studies are therefore multidisciplinary and address three principal areas of evidence:

- geomorphology (landforms);
- clastic sediments and sediment sequences (*e.g.* till and other glacigenic sediments);
- biogenic sediments and fossil remains (*e.g.* plant and pollen remains in peat bogs and lakes).

This evidence is investigated using a wide array of analytical techniques and dating methods which are described in standard textbooks (*e.g.* see list of general reading).

1.3 Historical developments in Quaternary studies: a Scottish perspective

Scotland has produced a long line of eminent geologists who have played a crucial role in the development of the subject and its concepts and theories. This is equally true of the Quaternary. The glacial theory itself is little more than 150 years old and the realisation that large areas of northern Europe and North America were formerly covered by extensive land-based ice sheets was one of the major scientific advances of the 19th century. The birth of the glacial theory lay in the Alps and the Alpine foreland, where granite erratics resting on the Jura limestones could be traced to sources in the Alps, indicating a formerly greater expansion of the Alpine glaciers. Although the eminent Scottish geologists, James Hutton and John Playfair, among

Age (ka BP)	Oxygen Isotope Stage	Chronostratigraphy — Britain				NW Europe
		Holocene				Holocene
— 10	1	Devensian	Late Devensian	Late-glacial	Loch Lomond Stadial	Younger Dryas (s)
— 11					Late-glacial (Windermere) Interstadial	Allerød (i)
— 12	2					Early Dryas (s) Bølling (i)
— 13				Dimlington Stadial		Weichselian
— 24						
— 26	3		Middle Devensian			Denekamp (i)
— 30						
— 40						Hengelo (i)
— 50						Glinde (i)
— 59						Oerel (i)
— 71	4		Early Devensian			
	5a			Brimpton (i)		Odderade (i)
— 85	5b					
— 92	5c			Chelford (i)		Brørup (i)
— 105						
	5d					
— 116	5e	Ipswichian				Eemian
— 128	6					Saale (Warthe)
— 186	7					
— 245	8					Saale (Drenthe)
— 303	9					
— 339	10					
— 362	11					Holsteinian
— 423	12	Anglian				Elsterian
— 480						
	13-19	Cromerian 'complex'				
— 780	20 -					
— 2400						

late Quaternary
middle Quaternary
early Quaternary

Main Glacial Events and Other Landscape Changes

- river channel changes; flood events; formation of river terraces; debris flows; solifluction; periglacial activity on higher summits;
- relative sea-level changes; formation of Main Postglacial Shoreline and other raised shorelines; formation of carselands, machair and sand dunes; tsunami event; formation of 'drowned' coastlines in Northern Isles and Outer Hebrides;
- soil stabilisation and pioneer phase of vegetation; spread and expansion of tree species; development of Caledonian pine forest; deforestation; increasing impact of human activity;

- mountain glaciers; formation of moraines, Parallel Roads of Glen Roy; widespread periglacial activity;
- relative sea-level changes; formation/re-occupation of Main Rock Platform; Main Late-glacial Shoreline;
- vegetation and soil revertence;

- development of soils and pioneer vegetation, then closed vegetation cover;

- relative sea-level changes; formation of raised beaches in eastern Scotland and Inner Hebrides;
- deglaciation of last ice sheet; formation of moraines, till, meltwater channels and deposits; nearshore glaciomarine deposits (Errol Beds and Clyde Beds);
- (?) ice sheet readvances/stillstands;
- ice sheet nunataks;
- formation of moraines on floor of North Sea (Bosie's Bank and Marr Bank) and on shelf edge west of Hebrides;
- reshaping of major features of glacial erosion;
- development of last ice sheet and expansion across floor of North Sea and west of Hebrides; (?) confluent with Scandinavian ice sheet prior to c. 22ka;

- (?) ice sheet advance before c. 30ka;
- fluctuating mountain glaciers and icefields;

- (?) ice sheet glaciation extending west of the Hebrides and Shetland and in outer Moray Firth;
- (?) till in NE Scotland

- pine-birch woodland in NE Scotland and heath and grassland on Shetland during interstadials;

- last interglacial; pine trees growing on Shetland;

- ice sheet extends over floor of North Sea and west of Shetland and the Hebrides (?);
- glacial deposits in NE Scotland and in outer Moray Firth;

- sequence of glacial and interglacial stages; no clear evidence preserved;

- interglacial deposits in North Sea;

- extensive ice sheet glaciation; ice sheet extending to shelf edge west of Outer Hebrides; Scottish and Scandinavian ice sheets coalescent in the North Sea;
- glacial deposits in NE Scotland;

- sequence of glacial and interglacial stages; ice sheet in Forth Approaches and North Sea;

- early Quaternary glaciations;
- initiation of major features of glacial erosion - corries, glacial troughs, glacially breached watersheds; stripping of regolith deeply weathered during the Tertiary.

Figure 1.2 Abbreviated timescale and terminology used to subdivide the Quaternary. The main glacial events and other landscape changes are also indicated. Note that the timescale shown is not linear. s: stade; i: interstade.

others at the end of the eighteenth century, had recognised the role of glaciers in the transport of these boulders, it required a major conceptual advance to extend the glacial theory more widely to areas where glaciers were no longer present or far from high alpine mountains. Scotland, however, provided not only a pivotal area in which to test and develop the ideas formulated in the Alpine foreland, notably through the work of Louis Agassiz, but also a receptive intellectual climate (Gordon, 1995).

Although Agassiz is widely credited with the origin of the glacial theory, his ideas were a development of earlier work by de Charpentier, Esmark and others. Agassiz developed and promoted the concept of continent-wide glaciation as part of wider climatic changes that affected the whole of Europe and the northern hemisphere. In Scotland, Robert Jameson was aware of the new ideas emerging from Europe and their potential significance, and as editor of the *Edinburgh New Philosophical Journal*, he was influential in their wider dissemination. Also, in his lectures at Edinburgh University in the 1820s, as recorded in the lecture notes of James Forbes, Jameson expressed the view that former glaciers might once have existed in Scotland, but regrettably he did not publish his own ideas. It was therefore Agassiz who was the first to assemble detailed field evidence that glaciers had once existed in Britain, far from any modern glaciers and obvious high mountain source areas. During the course of a visit to Scotland in 1840, Agassiz found clear evidence for glaciation in the deposits around Glasgow. As he travelled north through the West Highlands with William Buckland, the evidence accumulated, and following a visit to Glen Roy and Glen Spean, Agassiz wrote to Robert Jameson about his discoveries. Jameson passed the information to Charles Maclaren, editor of *The Scotsman* and himself a geologist. Thus on 7 October 1840 that newspaper announced to the world the former existence of glaciers in Scotland. The significance of the Scottish evidence and its influence on the development of his ideas was clearly recognised by Agassiz (Agassiz, 1842).

For some 20 years after Agassiz's visit, the arguments for and against the glacial theory continued to be debated. In the absence of knowledge about the nature of the Greenland and Antarctic ice sheets, the idea of continental-scale glaciers proved a difficult concept for many geologists to embrace, particularly in areas without present-day glaciers. From a philosophical viewpoint, the glacier theory confronted not only conventional thinking on uniformitarianism but also biblical teaching. Generally, the idea of mountain glaciers was more readily accepted perhaps because the field evidence was so striking, as described for example by James Forbes in 1842 in the Cuillin (Forbes, 1846). However, difficulties were encountered in explaining the origins of lowland deposits, the so-called drifts, which often contained marine shells. Although more modern studies have demonstrated that this material was dredged from the sea floor by glaciers, the idea of marine submergence and rafting of debris by icebergs persisted until the early 20th century.

Despite the reservations made in some quarters, the announcement of the glacial theory was made in a receptive intellectual climate in Scotland and the field evidence continued to accumulate, notably through the early work of Charles Maclaren and Thomas Jamieson. The officers of the Geological Survey added significantly to knowledge about the glacial geology and geomorphology of Scotland. Archibald Geikie, later Director General of the Geological Survey, published a seminal paper on the glacial drifts of Scotland in 1863, followed in 1865 by the first edition of his book on *The Scenery of Scotland*. His younger brother, James,

later published in 1874 the first of three editions of *The Great Ice Age,* in which he assembled a considerable body of evidence for the glacial theory. James Geikie's books, with their international perspective and recognition of multiple phases of glaciation, effectively established the scientific basis of the ice age paradigm.

Other 19th century Scottish geologists, through painstaking fieldwork and conceptual insights, contributed to the development and elaboration of the glacial theory, for example Charles Maclaren, James Forbes, Thomas Jamieson, Andrew Ramsey, John Smith of Dalry, James Smith of Jordanhill, James Croll, Benjamin Peach and John Horne. Charles Maclaren (1842) established the principle of glacio-eustasy, the idea that global sea level varied as ice sheets expanded and melted. He also identified geomorphological links between glaciation and raised shorelines, although it was Thomas Jamieson (1865) who later formally developed the corresponding theory of glacio-isostasy, that the level of the land changed through crustal depression by ice sheets. The discovery of fossil marine shells of cold water (arctic) affinity in raised marine deposits by James Smith (1838) gave rise to a series of papers on the fossil molluscan remains in Scottish Late-glacial and Holocene deposits and provided the foundation for modern biostratigraphic studies of marine deposits. The concept of multiple ice-sheet glaciation was developed by James Croll (1875) and James Geikie (1894). Croll (1867, 1875, 1885), in particular, established the foundation of the astronomical theory of ice ages - that orbital variations of the Earth around the Sun were the principal driving forces of climate change. This theory was later developed by Milankovitch (1941) and finally confirmed by the results of ocean floor drilling described above (see Imbrie and Imbrie, 1979). In recognising that the ocean currents played a key role in global climate processes through the transfer of heat from the tropics to the polar areas, Croll also anticipated modern ideas in this field *(e.g.* Broecker and Denton, 1990).

The period of the mid- late-19th century and the early 20th century saw a great expansion in knowledge about the Quaternary deposits and landforms of Scotland. Although detailed interpretations may now have changed in the light of new concepts and analytical techniques, the meticulous field observations and descriptions of many of the early field workers still stand the test of time. Pre-eminent among the field surveyors of the Geological Survey were Benjamin Peach and John Home who mapped extensive areas of the Highlands and Northern Isles; indeed their enthusiasm was such that they mapped Shetland during their annual leave from the Survey! The realisation that glaciers were powerful agents of erosion, capable of moulding entire landscapes, was convincingly demonstrated by Andrew Ramsay, a Scottish geologist working for the Geological Survey. Ramsay's work, in North Wales and Switzerland, effectively dispelled earlier doubts about the efficacy of glacial erosion in shaping the landscape of Britain (*e.g.* Ramsay, 1862). Also notable was the later work of W.B. Wright who recognised the significance of a glaciated raised shore platform in the Inner Hebrides (Wright, 1911); in addition, he was the first to recognise that the age of shorelines in glacio-isostatically uplifted areas would vary along their lengths (Wright, 1934). In north-east Scotland, Alexander Bremner produced a series of key papers describing in detail the Quaternary deposits and landforms of the region (*e.g.* Bremner, 1934). Further afield, James Forbes made a significant pioneering contribution to the understanding of modern glaciers through his work in the Alps (*cf.* Cunningham, 1990).

A final Scottish contribution from this period is to the terminology of glacial geology and geomorphology through the adoption of Scots words such as 'till', 'kame', 'kettle' and 'drumlin' as standard terms.

1.4 Recent advances

Recent advances span major developments in understanding the Earth's climate system, with their implications for interpreting the Quaternary of Scotland, to the application of new approaches and techniques to the analysis of the stratigraphic and palaeoenvironmental records. In summary, significant advances have been made in the following areas:

- in understanding the role of geological forces in driving long-term climate cycles (over timescales of greater than 10^6 Ma) and in controlling macro-scale and meso-scale landform evolution over large areas of Scotland;
- the construction of detailed and continuous proxy climate records from analyses of cores from the ocean floors, covering the whole of the Quaternary, and from the Greenland and Antarctic ice sheets, covering shorter timescales (up to 250 ka);
- in understanding the role of orbital parameters as the prime underlying forcing mechanism of climate change over timescales less than 1 Ma;
- awareness of the importance of physical and biogeochemical feedbacks between the atmosphere, oceans and ice sheets in amplifying the insolation changes into the climatic responses of the magnitude observed in the geological record;
- awareness of the frequency and rapidity of climate fluctuations;
- correlation of the terrestrial stratigraphic record with the records from the ocean floor and ice sheet cores;
- in field and theoretical knowledge of the behaviour of glaciers, allowing the development and application of mathematical models of former ice sheets and their application to explain the patterns and processes of landform and landscape genesis and to develop and test palaeoclimate reconstructions;
- development of new models describing the form, extent and activity of the last ice sheet, based on offshore mapping, mathematical modelling and the palaeoclimate results from the Greenland ice sheet cores and North Atlantic Ocean cores;
- improved understanding of the processes of formation of glacial and periglacial landforms and deposits;
- improved palaeoenvironmental reconstructions based on multi-proxy data for terrestrial, offshore and nearshore marine environments;
- recognition of the heritage and conservation value of earth science features.

1.4.1 Long-term landscape evolution

In Chapters 2 and 3, C. Mitchell and A.M. Hall, respectively, review recent advances in the understanding of the longer-term geological controls of landscape evolution and the development of the preglacial relief. Mitchell outlines the 'journey' of Scotland from a position south of the Equator to its present northerly latitude against a background of plate tectonic processes. Such large scale earth movements have determined the broad outlines of the landscape of Scotland, the distributions of the different rock types and the changing climatic processes. In turn, the changing climatic processes have driven the different geomorphological systems that have shaped the detailed landforms of Scotland. Mitchell also points out that factors such as the changing global distribution of the continents, the form of the ocean basins and continental uplift were fundamental in determining long-term climate changes, including the initiation of the Quaternary ice ages, although their tempo is modulated by orbital parameters. These geological factors largely determine the patterns of global atmospheric circulation and ocean circulation, and hence heat transfer from the equator to the poles; for example ice sheet expansion in Antarctica followed the poleward drift of the continent, the opening of the Southern Ocean and the development of a circumpolar ocean current which isolated Antarctica from warmer waters to the north. Geological controls on the form of the pre-glacial relief also strongly affected the patterns of glaciation and glacial erosion, the basic west-east distribution of high and low ground and the fault-line control of some West Highland glens.

Hall (Chapter 3) draws attention to the survival of pre-glacial landform elements in the landscape of Scotland. Important conclusions are the relatively limited amount of erosion in eastern Scotland since the Devonian, and the Mesozoic origins of the major relief features of Scotland. Geological events during the Tertiary had a significant impact on the landscape through major igneous activity and uplift in western Scotland, followed by intensive local erosion. Uplift elsewhere also formed the main mountain masifs that we see today. Overall, some 600-800 m of rock may have been removed from the land surface during the Tertiary, a relatively low rate of erosion. Observant hillwalkers will notice the summit accordances of our highest mountains which, according to Hall, define a surface perhaps only a few hundred metres below the sub-Cretaceous surface. The Tertiary period also saw other major changes in relief development. Under warm, humid climatic conditions, extensive covers of chemically weathered bedrock developed, remnants of which have survived today in Buchan. Their survival is a strong indicator of the limited impact of glacial erosion in this area (see Chapter 4). A range of further features reflects landscape inheritance from the Tertiary, and in some areas earlier. Particularly in eastern Scotland there is the form of the drainage pattern which reflects ancient structural controls; in the west, more intense glacial erosion has produced a more dissected landscape. Also there are topographic basins, inselbergs, tors, scarp slopes and erosion surfaces. The most striking and least modified of the pre-glacial landscapes is in NE Scotland.

1.4.2 Modern glaciers and glacier theory

The detailed form of the landscape of Scotland reflects the action of glacial processes and the spatial variations in their character and intensity. Understanding of glacier processes and behaviour has advanced significantly, based both on field observations and measurements on modern glaciers and ice sheets, and on the development of glacier theory (Paterson, 1994). N.F. Glasser (Chapter 4) reviews these advances and highlights their relevance for interpreting the patterns of landform development in Scotland described by D.I. Benn (Chapter 13). The significance of basal ice temperatures in explaining patterns of glacial erosion is emphasised: areas of basal melting are associated with extensive glacial erosion, whereas areas of basal freezing show little modification of the preglacial landscape. The development of fast flowing streams of ice within ice sheets can in part explain the origin of deeply eroded glens; deformation of subglacial sediments may explain the form and sedimentary architecture of subglacial deposits. One notable development (see also Chapter 13) has been the recognition of the importance of the character of the glacier bed, whether rigid or deformable, in influencing the ice flow.

Glaciers on 'soft' beds, such as sediments or weak rocks, may have a significant component of their flow sustained through deformation of the bed and may present lower ice surface profiles than glaciers on hard rock beds.

Modern glacier theory also allows the characteristics of former glaciers in Scotland to be reconstructed and their behaviour to be modelled, and a significant area of recent advance lies in the development and testing of such models against the field evidence. Relatively simple models have been used to test ideas about glacial erosion and glacier thermal regime (Gordon, 1979; Glasser, 1995); others have been used to reconstruct the form and dynamics of the last ice sheet (Boulton *et al.,* 1985; Boulton *et al.,* 1991). Mathematical models have also been developed to simulate the build up of the Loch Lomond Readvance icefield in the West Highlands (Payne and Sugden, 1990; Hubbard, 1996). When tested against field evidence, such models can be used to draw inferences about palaeoenvironmental conditions. For example modelling by Hubbard (1996) has shown that a drop in mean July temperature of 8°C, together with enhanced precipitation gradients, is required to simulate the build-up of the icefield to its maximum size and that this could have occurred within a period of some 550 years; the model also suggests that the onset of extremely arid conditions is required to halt the build-up of the ice at its observed limits. This combination of glacier modelling, studies of existing ice sheets and of the glacial geology and geomorphology of the beds of former ice sheets provides a potentially powerful approach (Sugden, 1988). Scotland, in particular, provides an ideal test area in view of the detailed field evidence available for the Loch Lomond Readvance and the Late Devensian ice sheet.

1.4.3 Ice cores and ocean floor cores

One of the most important areas of recent advance has involved the analysis of ice cores and deep-sea cores. C.M. Clapperton (Chapter 5) reviews the far reaching developments in this area and their implications for the pattern of glaciation and deglaciation in Scotland during the last glacial cycle. Clapperton places the changes in Scotland in the wider context of ocean circulation in the North Atlantic which exerts a fundamental control on climate changes in Scotland. The detailed climate records from the Greenland ice cores are remarkable in two respects: for the magnitude and frequency of fluctuations which they reveal during the last glacial cycle, and the rapidity of the changes; for example at the end of the last ice age *c.* 10 ka BP, mean annual temperatures increased by 7°C over a period of 20-50 years (Dansgaard *et al.,* 1989). Recent work has revealed that the ocean floor records correlate with the ice core data. The challenge now is to assess to what extent the climate fluctuations might be represented in the terrestrial geomorphological and palaeoenvironmental records in Scotland. As pointed out in Chapter 6, the terrestrial record is incomplete and its interpretation, until recently, has been dominated by models of rapid ice sheet downwasting (Chapter 5). Clapperton's analysis leads to the conclusion that glaciers of varying size would have been present in Scotland for most of the interval between 75 ka and 10 ka BP. He also suggests that the ice core data provide a new framework from which to reinterpret the terrestrial evidence and that the time is now appropriate to critically review the evidence for ice sheet readvances in this light. His suggestion that the last Scottish ice sheet actively retreated, but with periodic readvances in response to climate changes in the North Atlantic area, represents a return to earlier views. A reassessment of the field evidence,

combined with improved resolution in dating sediments and landforms may lead to exciting new developments in our understanding of the behaviour of the last ice sheet.

1.4.4 The stratigraphic record

Despite the incomplete record, A.M. Hall (Chapter 6) notes the significant advances which have been made in terrestrial and nearshore stratigraphy through the discovery of new sites and re-investigation of older sites with organic deposits. These sediments have been studied by multidisciplinary methods, including sedimentology and analysis of organic remains (pollen, beetles and marine molluscs), supported by the application of new dating methods. He records the progress made towards matching the limited terrestrial stratigraphy with the offshore and ice core isotopic records as well as with continental stratigraphic records. The oldest terrestrial glacial sediments are preserved at Kirkhill in NE Scotland and appear to date from the Anglian cold stage (*c.* 480-423 ka). The most detailed, although nevertheless fragmentary, sedimentary records are for the period spanning the last interglacial-glacial cycle and it is here that the greatest progress has been made in matching the terrestrial and marine/ice core evidence. However, while incontrovertible evidence for Early and Middle Devensian glaciation remains elusive in the absence of firm stratigraphic evidence and dating, the isotopic data suggest the presence of glaciers at this time (Chapter 5). The overall picture of the Devensian that emerges is one of rapidly fluctuating climatic and environmental conditions.

Ice sheet glaciation during the Late Devensian left a strong imprint on the landscape of Scotland. However, as Hall points out, there are still major unresolved questions about the timing and extent of ice sheet advances and possible readvances. The conventional wisdom of maximum ice extent at *c.* 18 ka BP has now been questioned. From the offshore data, the last ice sheet may have rapidly built up after 29 ka BP and involved a double maximum, with the main peak at 22 ka BP and followed by a smaller peak at 18 ka BP (see also Chapters 5 and 7). The lateral extent of the ice sheet also continues to be hotly debated (compare the maps of ice limits in Chapters 5 and 6); according to one school, several areas, including parts of NE Scotland, Caithness, Orkney and northern Lewis, were unglaciated at the maximum of the last ice sheet; another view holds that the ice covered all these areas, extending to near the edge of the continental shelf west of the Outer Hebrides. Taken together, various lines of evidence summarised by Hall tend to support the latter view. The vertical extent of the last ice sheet has also been debated and whether or not it covered all the summits or left some areas exposed as nunataks. Recent work by C.K. Ballantyne and colleagues (*e.g.* Ballantyne, 1997) has demonstrated the existence of a trimline in parts of Wester Ross, Skye and Harris associated with the last ice sheet (Chapter 15). However, it remains to incorporate this trimline into an integrated ice sheet model, reconciling it with offshore ice limits and ice surface profiles on hard and soft beds.

The pattern of wastage of the last ice sheet has seen major shifts in interpretation. The work of the Geological Survey during the late-19th and early-20th centuries established a model of active ice sheet decay, involving a series of valley glaciers retreating into the glens and corries of the Highlands (*e.g.* Peach *et al.,* 1913). Various readvances that were later proposed were actively debated during the late 1960s and early 1970s. Reinterpretation of the field evidence, against a background of the introduction of Scandinavian ideas of downwasting glaciers, led to a rejection of the putatative Perth and Aberdeen-Lammermuir readvances (Paterson, 1974; Sissons, 1976) and the establishment of a ruling hypothesis that the ice sheet areally stagnated rather than actively retreated. Other events, the Loch Lomond Readvance, the Elgin Oscillation (Peacock *et al.,* 1968) and the subsequently identified Wester Ross Readvance (Robinson and Ballantyne, 1979) and Otter Ferry Stage (Sutherland, 1984), have remained largely unchallenged. Sutherland (1984) proposed a model of active retreat, in places accelerated by calving in sea lochs and estuaries, but with halt stages determined by topography. More recently, various authors have questioned the ice sheet stagnation model based on reinterpretation of the geomorphological evidence in the Dee valley (Brown, 1993), the Inverness area (Merritt *et al.,* 1995), in the Cairngorms (Brazier *et al.,* 1996), and in western Scotland (Benn, 1997). Current ideas are now returning to active recession based on interpretation of the fluctuating climatic record in the Greenland ice cores. Further reinterpretation of the field evidence seems likely to be driven by a search to relate the pattern of ice wastage to the ice core and ocean core records (*cf.* McCabe, 1996; Peacock, 1997) and by future developments in ice sheet modelling. The detailed resolution of the deglacial behaviour of the last Scottish ice sheet, a small ice sheet likely to have been sensitive to climatic fluctuations, would have wider significance for constraining models of ocean-climate-ice sheet interactions in the North Atlantic area. However, the two main problems remain that have bedevilled earlier investigations: 1) the largely geomorphological nature of the field evidence and the lack of clear stratigraphic evidence; and 2) the lack of dateable materials and dating techniques that can be applied to landforms and inorganic sediments. In addition, given that sea level was relatively high during deglaciation, calving processes and controls may have been significant determinants on ice margin behaviour, unrelated to wider climate changes (*e.g.* Merritt *et al.,* 1995). The pattern of ice sheet recession may therefore have been both spatially and temporally variable.

The glacial periods saw major eustatic lowering of sea level, possibly by as much as *c.* 140m, so that the Scottish ice sheets extended offshore, reaching at their maximum extent to near the edge of the continental shelf west and north of the Outer Hebrides, and to the middle of the North Sea. Therefore a considerable part of their geological record is represented in thick sediment sequences offshore (Chapter 7). However, much of our understanding has been based on the terrestrial part of the record alone. It is only in the last *c.* 20 years, through the use of geophysical surveying, combined with sedimentological and palaeontological analyses of sediment cores, that the great wealth of offshore evidence has become accessible and allowed a better overview of the wider picture, as explained by R. Holmes (Chapter 7). Also, because the offshore areas include the peripheral zones of the ice sheets, there is a greater potential for the preservation of earlier events in the sedimentary record. Nearshore and offshore studies have therefore seen major developments in two related areas, namely in the lithostratigraphy and biostratigraphy of sediment sequences on the sea floor. Some important results (see Chapters 6 and 7) include: possible evidence for ice sheet glaciations of the northern North Sea and adjacent shelves during the early Quaternary, and evidence in variable detail for ice sheet glaciation of Scotland and adjacent shelves during the Cromerian (Isotope Stage 16), the Anglian (Isotope Stage 12), the Saalian (Isotope Stage 6), the Early Devensian (Isotope Stage 4) and the Late Devensian (Isotope Stage 2)

(Figure 1.2). Inevitably, there is considerable uncertainty about the interpretation, dating and correlation of events pre-dating the Late Devensian. Studies in the northern North Sea (Sejrup *et al.,* 1994) have suggested a double peak to the Late Devensian glacial maximum (*c.* 22 ka BP and 18 ka BP), and work on the Hebridean shelf has identified ice limits on the West Shetland Shelf (Stoker *et al.,* 1993) and *c.* 75 km west of North Uist (Peacock *et al.,* 1992). Macro- and micro-palaeontological studies of sediment cores have allowed reconstruction of palaeoenvironmental conditions, including changes in sea level, water temperatures and water circulation, during the Late-glacial (*e.g.* Peacock, 1989; Peacock and Harkness, 1990; Peacock *et al.,* 1992). Important advances are likely to arise from a closer integration of the offshore and terrestrial evidence to build up a more integrated picture of Quaternary events and environments. Thus Ross (1996) has combined both offshore and onshore evidence to reconstruct an integrated model of the dynamic pattern of deglaciation of the last ice cap on Shetland and the adjacent shelves.

Interest in the nearshore marine environment has been sustained since the 19th century work on the fossil shells contained in the raised silts and sands of Scotland's major estuaries (the Errol Beds and Clyde Beds). These deposits (Chapters 5 and 12) are now recognised to be partly glaciomarine and partly marine/estuarine in origin and they have yielded much information on the character of the nearshore environment during deglaciation (*e.g.* Peacock, 1981; Peacock and Harkness, 1990; Peacock, in press).

1.4.5. Late-glacial environmental changes

The Late-glacial was a period of intense environmental change reflecting marked and rapid shifts in climate. Two papers in this volume, by J.M. Gray (Chapter 8) and by M.J.C. Walker and J.J. Lowe (Chapter 9), review the geomorphological changes and the changes in vegetation, respectively. Gray describes the patterns of landforms formed during the wastage of the last ice sheet, that shaped much of the topographic detail of lowland Scotland, and refers to the newly emerging ideas and evidence concerning active ice sheet recession. He concludes that the field evidence at present implies active recession during the earlier phase of deglaciation (*c.* 18-14 ka BP), followed by large-scale stagnation *in situ* (14-13 ka BP).

Relatively little is known about geomorphological changes during the Late-glacial interstadial, but the bare, unvegetated slopes left behind after deglaciation must have been rapidly modified by soil erosion, mass movement and river processes. The subsequent climatic deterioration and readvance of glaciers during the Loch Lomond Stadial has been intensively investigated through studies of glacier limits, palaeoclimate reconstructions, periglacial features (see also Chapter 14) and coastal evolution (see also Chapter 12). Recent mapping studies of the so-called 'hummocky moraines' produced by the glaciers show that in many areas the features have a strong pattern of organisation, representing former ice margin positions (see also Chapter 13). Like the last ice sheet, it now appears that the Loch Lomond Readvance glaciers retreated actively, before final stagnation in some areas (*cf.* Bennett, 1994). Other important developments have included resolution of the formation of the Parallel Roads of Glen Roy (Sissons, 1981), involving the drainage of ice-dammed lakes through catastrophic floods and elaboration of the early interpretations of Agassiz and Jamieson last century.

Walker and Lowe describe recent advances in palaeoecological studies that allow reconstruction of the vegetation history and climate change during the Late-glacial and early Holocene. Following the climatic warming at c. 13 ka BP, pioneer open tundra communities were replaced by closed grassland and heathland, with some scrub and woodland. Although summer temperatures during the Late-glacial Interstadial briefly reached similar values to those of today, woodland development was largely confined to scattered stands of birch, and the regional tree-line probably did not reach Scotland. During the Loch Lomond Stadial, there was a return to a tundra landscape. Following the early Holocene warming, a succession of tree species migrated into Scotland, culminating in an extensive forest cover. Various lines of evidence, for example from pollen and fossil insects, show that climatic conditions fluctuated markedly and rapidly during the Late-glacial and early Holocene, with significant changes in temperature occurring within a matter of a few dacades around 13 ka BP and 10 ka BP. Particularly notable is the close correspondence between the terrestrial, marine and ice-core records, allowing the changes in Scotland to be placed in a wider North Atlantic and European context (Walker *et al.*, 1994). Walker and Lowe emphasise the international significance of the detailed palaeoenvironmental records available from Scottish sites for future multidisciplinary studies of the climate changes at the last glacial-interglacial transition and the responses of the terrestrial biota to such changes.

1.4.6 Holocene environmental changes

During the early Holocene, geomorphological processes continued to modify the landscape under conditions of abundant debris supply and unstable slopes (L.J. McEwen, Chapter 10). Rivers actively reworked their floodplains forming suites of terraces, and rockfalls, debris flows and other mass movements modified the steeper slopes (Ballantyne, 1991 a). Little is known about geomorphological activity during the middle Holocene, but it seems probable as soils stabilised and vegetation cover developed (see Chapter 9) that process thresholds increased, so that higher magnitude storm events were required to produce significant landscape changes. Proxy climate data suggest a number of wetter episodes during the Holocene, c. 7.3 ka BP, 6.2-5.8 ka BP, 4.2-3.94 ka BP and c. 3.3 ka BP (Dubois and Ferguson, 1985) and these may well have been accompanied by increased landscape instability. Although there have been a number of detailed local studies (*e.g.* Tipping, 1995), there is generally inadequate data to establish broader regional contemporaneity of events.

During the last c. 5 ka, human activity has increasingly interacted with natural processes and extensively modified the natural vegetation cover of Scotland; this is reflected in the pollen and sediment records preserved in peat bogs and lochs and is described by K.J. Edwards and G. Whittington (Chapter 11). A major problem lies in deciphering the causes of the changes observed in the palaeoenvironmental records and disentangling the effects of human activity and those of climate change. This is the case, for example, in relation to the initiation and expansion of peat over large areas of the country at different times during the Holocene. Extensive evidence of prehistoric farming activity in the uplands reveals that such areas were once more productive and attractive for settlement, and that woodland clearance and agricultural activities were associated with landscape instability, as reflected in river terrace aggradation and accelerated soil erosion (*e.g.* Tipping, 1992). Perhaps one of the most striking changes was the demise of pine forest in Caithness c. 4 ka BP, which has been variously attributed to climate deterioration, podzolisation, acid rain deposition associated with Icelandic volcanic activity and human

activity (*e.g.* Gear and Huntley, 1991; Charman, 1994). Also, the last few hundred years have seen an apparent increase in geomorphological activity both in terms of river changes (Chapter 10) and soil erosion and periglacial activity in the uplands (Chapter 14). Climate change and extreme flood events associated with the Little Ice Age have been proposed as possible underlying causes, but again the effects may have been enhanced or moderated by land-use changes. More detailed local studies are required before broader generalisations can reliably be made about cause and effect.

1.4.7 Sea-level changes

The advance and retreat of the ice sheets during the Quaternary was accompanied by major changes at the coastline arising from glacio-isostatic and glacio-eustatic processes. These changes have left a remarkable legacy on the geomorphology of Scotland's coastline, as described by D.E. Smith (Chapter 12). The study and reconstruction of Quaternary sea-level changes is now based on an array of techniques that relate not only to the geomorphology of the features but also to the lithostratigraphy and biostratigraphy of associated sediments onshore and offshore. Smith reviews the large body of evidence that has been painstakingly pieced together over the last 30 years. Major outstanding problems concern the conflicting evidence between sites in the west and in the east for an early Holocene transgression, the ages and processes of formation of pre-Devensian shore platforms (see also Chapter 8) and detailed chronologies for sea-level changes in areas peripheral to centres of isostatic uplift. Future advances seem likely to involve geophysical modelling (*e.g.* Lambeck, 1995), combined with detailed field studies.

1.4.8 Glacial and periglacial landforms

In Chapter 14, D.I. Benn reviews recent advances in the study of glacial landforms in Scotland. Erosional features, such as corries and glacial troughs, represent the cumulative effects of the many episodes of mountain and ice sheet glaciation now inferred to have affected Scotland during the Quaternary (Chapter 5); two implications are 1) that most large-scale erosional landforms were probably initiated earlier during the Quaternary and in large part pre-date the last glaciation (see Chapter 6); and 2) that mountain glaciers (corrie glaciers and small icefields) shaped the mountain landscape of the Highlands during extended periods of restricted glaciation throughout Quaternary.

The main developments in the study of glacial deposits have followed from the theory of deforming beds: where a glacier is underlain by weak, saturated sediments, these deform under the stress imposed by the ice, so that the glacier moves on the bed of deforming sediment. Such a mechanism, which has been reported from modern glaciers (*e.g.* Alley *et al.*, 1986; Boulton and Hindmarsh, 1987) has important implications for understanding the formation of subglacial depositional landforms such as drumlins and flutes. It has also been inferred that glaciers flowing over deformable beds have lower ice surface profiles, which has a significant bearing on matching glacier reconstructions with field evidence, such as glacier limits and trim lines as discussed above (*e.g.* Ballantyne 1989, 1990). A second important development has been in the interpretation of 'hummocky moraine'. Formerly believed to be a form of ice stagnation deposit, detailed mapping for Loch Lomond Readvance glaciers has revealed that in many areas of this type of deposit the individual mounds have clear alignments believed to have formed at the ice margin (*e.g.* Benn *et al.*, 1992; Bennett and Boulton, 1993), which has allowed reconstruction of the patterns of ice wastage (see above). Finally, the application of detailed sedimentological studies has revealed the sedimentary architecture of depositional landforms, allowing a detailed interpretation of their genesis and sedimentary environment of deposition (*e.g.* Benn, 1989, 1996a; Benn and Evans, 1993, 1996).

During the cold episodes of the Quaternary when glaciers and ice sheets were of limited extent, periglacial processes shaped the landscape, as described by C.K. Ballantyne (Chapter 14). In lowland areas, traces of former permafrost are evident in the form of ice-wedge polygons, ice-wedge casts, involutions, indurated soil horizons and solifluction deposits. Many such features relate to the period of recession of the last ice sheet before 13 ka BP, although some are older. The mountains of Scotland are likely to have experienced periglacial conditions for long periods during the Quaternary (see Chapter 5) and frost weathering has produced a mantle of weathered rock debris on the higher summits. The nature of the weathered bedrock relates closely to the rock type, but the age of the weathering appears to be variable; in places the mantle may be quite ancient, as indicated by the clay mineralogy of the detritus, having survived burial by cold-based ice. Recent work by Ballantyne and colleagues has revealed the existence of a periglacial trimline cutting across the weathered bedrock, which they have used to infer the maximum altitude of the last ice sheet (see above).

A variety of periglacial landforms is widespread on Scottish mountains ranging from small-scale solifluction lobes to large-scale rockfall-related features. An important development has been the use of such features to draw inferences about palaeoclimates. For example, from the distribution of protalus rock glaciers during the Loch Lomond Stadial, Ballantyne (Chapter 14) has inferred that precipitation was significantly reduced and there was an even more marked SW-NE gradient than at present, so that NE Scotland would have been an arid tundra with precipitation possibly only of 100-200 mm a^{-1}. Periglacial processes continued to shape mountain slopes during the Holocene and remain active today, although under wet and windy maritime conditions rather than cold, dry conditions. Landforms relating to frost action and nivation processes, wind and debris flows are described by Ballantyne. An important but unresolved question concerns whether an increase in slope instability and soil erosion documented over the last few hundred years relates to changing climatic conditions or the effects of land use (see above) (Ballantyne, 1991b).

1.4.9 Earth heritage conservation

In the final chapter of the volume, J.E. Gordon and A.P. McKirdy recognise the conservation value of Scotland's Quaternary landforms and deposits as a fundamental part of our natural heritage. A major development in this area has been the identification of a network of sites for the Geological Conservation Review (Gordon and Sutherland, 1993). However, through their underpinning of habitat diversity and landscape character, Quaternary landforms, deposits and palaeoenvironmental records also have much wider significance in helping to understand the physical basis of the natural heritage zones that will form the basic units for the future management of Scotland's natural heritage.

1.5 Conclusion

The chapters in this volume reflect the breadth of scope of Quaternary studies in Scotland and the recent level of interest and scientific activity in this area of our natural heritage. Significant advances in understanding the climate history and accompanying palaeoenvironmental changes have followed from developments in a number of areas, most notably in ocean floor coring and ice sheet coring. The results of this work have shed new light on the pattern and rapidity of climate change and the associated environmental changes preserved in the geological record. They have also revealed a fascinating record of a dynamic landscape, its evolution driven by geological processes and climate change; what we see today is the product of that ongoing evolution.

The recent advances described in this volume convey the dynamism and something of the excitement in Quaternary science, reflected in changing ideas, paradigms and interpretations of the palaeoenvironmental record. They have taken place in an international context, and the evidence from Scotland must now be seen in the wider frame of events in the North Atlantic arena, in turn linked to global-scale processes in the Earth's climate system. Equally, the field evidence from Scotland, in the form of landforms, sediment sequences and the detailed palaeoclimatic signals that they contain, has an important bearing on testing wider regional palaeoclimate models for the North Atlantic area and in bridging the offshore evidence with that from continental Europe, work that may ultimately help to elucidate the climate 'switching' mechanism.

Future developments are likely to include advances in glacier modelling that will allow testing of glaciological scenarios against the field evidence (both onshore and offshore), improvement of links between terrestrial evidence, offshore records and ice cores, the wider application of multidisciplinary approaches to palaeoenvironmental reconstruction and the greater temporal resolution of events recorded in the geological evidence. This should allow answers to increasingly detailed questions about climate change, and the responses of glaciers, geomorphological processes and biotas, to match the detail from the ice core records. The speed of such developments will depend crucially on improved dating methods and other analytical techniques; methods such as luminescence dating (*e.g.* Duller *et al.,* 1995), tephrochronology (*e.g.* Dugmore *et al.,* 1995; Hunt *et al.,* 1995) and exposure dating using cosmogenic isotopes (*e.g.* Stone *et al.,* 1996) hold encouraging promise. However, it should not be forgotten that Quaternary science has a fundamental field basis, and equally important is the continued availability of key reference sections and deposits, ensuring a vital role for earth heritage conservation. Much will also depend on the discovery of new sites, and it should also be remembered that crucial sites are often found by chance or through excavations for commercial or infrastructural developments. It is therefore unfortunate that there are now so few 'amateur' enthusiasts, compared with the 19th century, to identify and record temporary exposures. The papers in this volume thus have an important role to help stimulate such wider interest, as well as to bear a testimony to the value of our Quaternary heritage.

Acknowledgements

I am grateful to Professor J.D. Peacock for reviewing the manuscript and to Alan Doherty, John May and Alan McKirdy for their enthusiasm, support and encouragement during the preparation of this volume.

References

Agassiz, L. 1842. The glacial theory and its recent progress. *Edinburgh New Philosophical Journal,* **33**, 217-283.

Alley, R.B., Blankenship, D.D., Bentley, C.R. and Rooney, S.T. 1986. Deformation of till beneath Ice Stream B, West Antarctica. *Nature, 322,* 57-59.

Ballantyne, C. K. 1989. The Loch Lomond Readvance on the Isle of Skye, Scotland: glacier reconstruction and palaeoclimatic implications. *Journal of Quaternary Science,* **4,** 95-108.

Ballantyne, C.K. 1990. The late Quaternary glacial history of the Trotternish escarpment, Isle of Skye, Scotland, and its implications for ice-sheet reconstruction. *Proceedings of the Geologists' Association, 101,* 171-186.

Ballantyne, C.K. 1991a. Holocene geomorphic activity in the Scottish Highlands. *Scottish Geographical Magazine,* **107,** 84-98.

Ballantyne, C.K. 1991b. Late Holocene erosion in upland Britain: climatic deterioration or human influence? *The Holocene, 1,* 81-85.

Ballantyne, C.K. 1997. Periglacial trimlines in the Scottish Highlands. *Quaternary International, 38/39,* 119-136.

Benn, D.T. 1989. Controls on sedimentation in a Late Devensian ice-dammed lake, Achnasheen, Scotland. *Boreas,* **18,** 31-42.

Benn, D.I. 1996. Subglacial and subaqueous processes near a glacier grounding line: sedimentological evidence from a former ice-dammed lake, Achnasheen, Scotland. *Boreas,* **25,** 23-36.

Benn, D.I. 1997. Glacier fluctuations in Western Scotland. *Quaternary International, 38/39,* 119-136.

Benn, D.I. and Evans, D.J.A. 1993. Glaciomarine deltaic deposition and ice-marginal tectonics: the 'Loch Don Sand Moraine', Isle of Mull, Scotland. *Journal of Quaternary Science, 7,* 279-291.

Benn, D.I. and Evans, D.J.A. 1996. The interpretation and classification of subglacially-deformed materials. *Quaternary Science Reviews,* **15,** 23-52.

Benn, D.I., Lowe, J.J. and Walker, M.J.C. 1992. Glacier response to climatic change during the Loch Lomond Stadial and early Flandrian: geomorphological and palynological evidence from the Isle of Skye. *Journal of Quaternary Science, 7,* 125-144.

Bennett, M. R. 1994. Morphological evidence as a guide to deglaciation following the Loch Lomond Readvance: a review of research approaches and models. *Scottish Geographical Magazine,* **110,** 24-32.

Bennett, M.R. and Boulton, G.S. 1993. A reinterpretation of Scottish 'hummocky moraine' and its significance for the deglaciation of the Scottish Highlands during the Younger Dryas or Loch Lomond Stadial. *Geological Magazine,* **130,** 301-318.

Boulton, G.S.B. and Hindmarsh, R.A.C. 1987. Sediment deformation beneath glaciers: rheology and geological consequences. *Journal of Geophysical Research,* **92,** 9059-9082.

Boulton, G.S., Peacock, J.D. and Sutherland, D.G. 1991. Quaternary. In: Craig, G.Y. (Ed.), *Geology of Scotland.* 3rd ed. The Geological Society, London.

Boulton, G.S., Smith, G.D., Jones, A.S. and Newsome, J. 1985. Glacial geology and glaciology of the last mid-latitude ice sheets. *Journal of the Geological Society,* **142,** 447-474.

Brazier, V., Gordon, J.E., Kirkbride, M.P. and Sugden, D.E. 1996. The Late Devensian ice sheet and glaciers in the Cairngorm Mountains. In: Glasser, N.F. and Bennett, M.R. (Eds), *The Quaternary of the Cairngorms. Field Guide.* Quaternary Research Association, London, 28-53.

Bremner, A. 1934. The glaciation of Moray and ice movements in the north of Scotland. *Transactions of the Edinburgh Geological Society,* **13,** 17-56.

Broecker, W. S. and Denton, G.H. 1990. What drives glacial cycles? *Scientific American,* **262**(l), 43-50.

Brown, I.M. 1993. Pattern of deglaciation of the last (Late Devensian) Scottish ice sheet: evidence from ice-marginal deposits in the Dee valley, northeast Scotland. *Journal of Quaternary Science,* **8,** 235-250.

Charman, D.J. 1994. Late-glacial and Holocene vegetation history of the Flow Country, northern Scotland. *New Phytologist,* **127,** 155-168.

Croll, J. 1867. On the eccentricity of the Earth's orbit, and its physical relations to the glacial epoch. *Philosophical Magazine,* **33,** 119-131.

Croll, J. 1875. *Climate and Time and in Their Geological Relations. A Theory of Secular Changes of the Earth's Climate.* Daldy, Isbister & Co., London.

Croll, J. 1885. *Climate and Cosmology. Adam* & Charles Black, Edinburgh.

Cunningham, F. 1990. *James David Forbes. Pioneer Scottish Glaciologist.* Edinburgh, Scottish Academic Press.

Dansgaard, W., White, J.W.C. and Johnsen, S.J. 1989. The abrupt termination of the Younger Dryas climate event. *Nature,* **339,** 532-534.

Dubois, A.D. and Ferguson, D.K. 1985. The climatic history of pine in the Cairngorms based on radiocarbon dates and stable isotope analysis, with an acccount of the events leading up to its colonization. *Review of Palaeobotany and Palynology,* **48,** 55-80.

Dugmore, A.J., Larsen, G. and Newton, A.J. 1995. Seven tephra isochrones in Scotland. *The Holocene,* **5,** 257-266.

Duller, G.A.T., Wintle, A. G. and Hall, A.M. 1995. Luminescence dating and its application to key pre-Late Pleistocene sites in Scotland. *Quaternary Science Reviews,* **14,** 495-519.

Forbes, J.D. 1846. Notes on the topography and geology of Cuchullin Hills in Skye, and on the traces of ancient glaciers which they present. *Edinburgh New Philosophical Journal,* **40,** 76-99.

Gear, A.J. and Huntley, B. 1991. Rapid changes in the range limits of Scots Pine 4000 years ago. *Science,* **251,** 544-547.

Geikie, A. 1865. *The Scenery of Scotland Viewed in Connection with its Physical Geology.* Macmillan, London.

Geikie, J. 1894. *The Great Ice Age and its Relation to the Antiquity of Man.* 3rd ed. Edward Stanford, London.

Glasser, N.F. 1995 Modelling the effect of topography on ice sheet erosion, Scotland. *Geografiska Annaler,* **77A,** 67-82.

Gordon, J.E. 1979. Reconstructed Pleistocene ice-sheet temperatures and glacial erosion in northern Scotland. *Journal of Glaciology,* **22,** 331-344.

Gordon, J.E. 1995. Louis Agassiz and the Scottish connection. *Geology Today,* **11,** 64-68.

Gordon, J.E. and Sutherland, D.G. (Eds) 1993. *Quaternary of Scotland.* Chapman & Hall, London.

Haynes, V.M. 1995. Scotland's landforms: a review. *Scottish Association of Geography Teachers' Journal,* **24,** 18-37.

Hubbard, A. 1996. High resolution modelling of glaciers. Unpublished PhD thesis, University of Edinburgh.

Hunt, J.B., Fannin, N.G.T., Hill, P.G. and Peacock, J.D. 1995. The tephrochronology and radiocarbon dating of North Atlantic, Late-Quaternary sediments: an example from the St. Kilda Basin. In: Scrutton, R.A., Stoker, M.S., Shimmield, G.B. and Tudhope, A.W. (Eds), *The Tectonics, Sedimentation and Palaeoceanography of the North Atlantic Region.* Geological Society of London, Special Publication, No. 90, 227-248.

Imbrie, J. and Imbrie, K.P. 1979. *Ice Ages. Solving the Mystery.* Macmillan, London.

Jamieson, T. F. 1865. On the history of the last geological changes in Scotland. *Quarterly Journal of the Geological Society of London, 21*, 161-203.

Lambeck, K. 1995. Late Devensian and Holocene shorelines of the British Isles and North Sea from models of glacio-hydro-isostatic rebound. *Journal of the Geological Society, 152*, 437-448.

Maclaren, C. 1842. The glacial theory of Prof Agassiz. *American Journal of Science and Arts, 42*, 346-365.

McCabe, A.M. 1996. Dating and rhythmicity from the last deglacial cycle in the British Isles. *Journal of the Geological Society, London, 153*, 499-502.

Merritt, J.W., Auton, C.A. and Firth, C.R. 1995. Ice-proximal glaciomarine sedimentation and sea-level change in the Inverness area, Scotland: a review of the deglaciation of a major ice stream of the British Late Devensian. *Quaternary Science Reviews, 14*, 289-329.

Milankovitch, M. 1941. Kanon der Erdbestrahlung und seine Andwendung auf das Eiszeitproblem. *Royal Serbian Academy, Special Publication, 133*. (Also published in 1969 as *Canon of Insolation and the Ice Age Theory*. Israel Program for Scientific Translations, Jerusalem).

Paterson, I.B. 1974. The supposed Perth Readvance in the Perth district. *Scottish Journal of Geology, 10*, 53-66.

Paterson, W.B. 1994. *The Physics of Glaciers*. Pergamon/Elsevier Science Ltd, Oxford.

Payne, A.J. and Sugden, D.E. 1990. Topography and ice sheet growth. *Earth Surface Processes, and Landforms, 15*, 625-639.

Peach, B.N., Horne, J., Hinxman, L.W., Crampton, C.B., Anderson, E.M. and Carruthers, R.G 1913. *The Geology of Central Ross-shire*. Memoirs of the Geological Survey of Scotland. HMSO, Edinburgh.

Peacock, J.D. 1981. Scottish Late-glacial marine deposits and their environmental significance. In: Neale, J. and Flenley, J. (Eds), *The Quaternary in Britain*. Pergamon Press, Oxford, 222-236.

Peacock, J.D. 1989. Marine molluscs and late Quaternary environmental studies with particular reference to the Late-glacial period in northwest Europe: a review. *Quaternary Science Reviews, 8*, 179-192.

Peacock, J.D. 1997. Was there a readvance of the British ice sheet into the North Sea between 15 ka and 14 ka BP? *Quaternary Newsletter, No. 81*, 1-8.

Peacock, J.D. in press. Ice rafted sediments of Loch Lomond Stadial age in western Scotland. *Scottish Journal of Geology, 33*.

Peacock, J.D. and Harkness, D.D. 1990. Radiocarbon ages and the full-glacial to Holocene transition in seas adjacent to Scotland and southern Scandinavia: a review. *Transactions of the Royal Society of Edinburgh: Earth Sciences, 81*, 385-396.

Peacock, J.D., Berridge, N.G., Harris, A.L. and May, F. 1968. *The Geology of the Elgin District*. Memoirs of the Geological Survey of Scotland. HMSO, Edinburgh.

Peacock, J.D., Austin, W.E.N., Selby, I., Graham, D.K., Harland, R. and Wilkinson, I.P. 1992 Late Devensian and Flandrian palaeoenvironmental changes on the Scottish continental shelf west of the Outer Hebrides. *Journal of Quaternary Science, 7*, 145-162.

Price, R.J. 1983. *Scotland's Environment During the Last 30,000 Years*. Scottish Academic Press, Edinburgh.

Ramsay. A.C. 1862. On the glacial origin of certain lakes in Switzerland, the Black Forest, Great Britain, Sweden, North America, and elsewhere. *Quarterly Journal of the Geological Society, 18*, 185-204.

Robinson, M. and Ballantyne, C.K. 1979. Evidence for a glacial readvance pre-dating the Loch Lomond Advance in Wester Ross. *Scottish Journal of Geology, 15*, 271-277.

Ross, H. 1996. The last glaciation of Shetland. Unpublished PhD thesis, University of St Andrews.

Ruddiman, W.F. and Kutzbach, J.E. 1990. Late Cenozoic plateau uplift and climate change. *Transactions of the Royal Society of Edinburgh: Earth Sciences, 81*, 301-314.

Ruddiman, W.F. and Raymo, M.E. 1988. Northern hemisphere climate régimes during the past 3Ma: possible tectonic connections. *Philosophical Transactions of the Royal Society of London, B318*, 411-430.

Shackleton, N.J. *et al.*, 1984. Oxygen isotope calibration of the onset of ice-rafting and history of glaciation in the North Atlantic. *Nature, 307*, 62-623.

Sejrup, H.P., Haflidason, H., Aarseth, I., King, E., Forsberg, C.F., Long, D. and Rokoengen, K. 1994. Late Weichselian glaciation history of the northern North Sea. *Boreas, 23*, 1-13.

Sissons, J.B. 1976. *Scotland*. Methuen, London.

Sissons, J.B. 1981. Ice-dammed lakes in Glen Roy and vicinity: a summary. In: Neale, J. and Flenley, J. (Eds), *The Quaternary in Britain*. Pergamon Press, Oxford, 174-183.

Smith, J. 1838. On the last changes in the relative levels of the land and sea in the British Islands. *Memoirs of the Wernerian Natural History Society, 8*, 49-88.

Stoker, M. S., Hitchen, K. and Graham, C.C. 1993. *United Kingdom Offshore Regional Report: the Geology of the Hebrides and West Shetland Shelves, and Adjacent Deep-water Areas*. London, HMSO for the British Geological Survey.

Stone, J., Lambeck, K., Fifield, L.K., Evans, J.M. and Cresswell, R.G. 1996. A Lateglacial age for the Main Rock Platform, western Scotland. *Geology, 24*, 707-710.

Sugden, D.E. 1988. Perspectives on the glaciation of Scotland. *Scottish Association of Geography Teachers' Journal, 17*, 4-10.

Sutherland, D.G. 1984. The Quaternary deposits and landforms of Scotland and the neighbouring shelves: a review. *Quaternary Science Reviews, 3*, 157-254.

Sutherland, D.G. and Gordon, J.E. 1993. The Quaternary in Scotland. In: Gordon, J.E. and Sutherland, D.G. (Eds), *Quaternary of Scotland*. Chapman & Hall, London.

Tipping, R. 1992. The determination of cause in the generation of major prehistoric valley fills in the Cheviot Hills, Anglo-Scottish border. In: Needham, S. and Macklin, M.G. (Eds), *Alluvial Archaeology in Britain*. Oxbow Monograph 27. Oxbow Books, Oxford, 111-121.

Tipping, R. 1995. Holocene landscape change at Carn Dubh, near Pitlochry, Perthshire, Scotland. *Journal of Quaternary Science, 10*, 59-75.

Walker, M.J.C., Bohncke, S.J.P., Coope, G.R., O'Connell, M., Usinger, H. and Verbruggen, C. 1994. The Devensian/Weichselian Late-glacial in northwest Europe (Ireland, Britain, north Belgium, The Netherlands, northwest Germany). *Journal of Quaternary Science, 9*, 109-118.

Wright, W.B. 1911. On a preglacial shoreline in the Western Isles of Scotland. *Geological Magazine, Dec. 5, vol. 8*, 97-109.

Wright, W.B. 1934. The isokinetic theory of glacially controlled shorelines. *Comptes Rendus du Congres Internationale de Geographie, Varsovie*, Section II, 534-553.

General reading

Several recent textbooks provide a good introduction to Quaternary studies:

Andersen, B.G. and Borns, H.W. Jr 1994. *The Ice Age World*. Scandinavian University Press, Oslo.

Bell M. and Walker M.J.C. 1992. *Late Quaternary Environmental Change: Physical & Human Perspectives*. Longman, London.

Bennett M.R. and Glasser, N.F. 1996. *Glacial Geology. Ice Sheets and Landforms*. Wiley, Chichester.

Ballantyne C.K. and Harris C. 1994. *The Periglaciation of Great Britain*. Cambridge University Press, Cambridge.

Dawson, A.G. 1992. *Ice Age Earth. Late Quaternary Geology and Climate*. Routledge, London.

Ehlers, J., Gibbard, P.L. and Rose, J. (Eds) 1991. *Glacial Deposits in Great Britain and Ireland* A.A. Balkema, Rotterdam.

Hambrey, M.J. 1994. *Glacial Environments*. London, UCL Press Ltd.

Jones R.L. and Keen D.H. 1993. *Pleistocene Environments in the British Isles*. Chapman & Hall, London.

Lowe J.J. and Walker M.J.C. 1996. *Reconstructing Quaternary Environments*. 2nd edition. Longman, London.

An overview of the Quaternary of Scotland and a description of key localities is provided by: Gordon, J.E. and Sutherland, D.G. (Eds) 1993. *Quaternary of Scotland*. Chapman & Hall, London.

Several specialist journals publish papers on Quaternary research. Among these are *Journal of Quaternary Science and Quaternary Science Reviews*. *Scottish Geographical Magazine* also publishes a series of articles on classic Scottish landform examples.

Further information

The Quaternary Research Association is an organisation for all interested in the Quaternary and problems of Quaternary research; membership includes professional scientists and interested amateurs. The Association regularly holds field meetings and discussion meetings throughout Britain and its publications include a newsletter, journal and field guides. Information about the Association is available from the Secretary, currently Dr P. Coxon, Department of Geography, Trinity College, Dublin 2, Ireland.

2. The Geology of Scotland

Clive Mitchell

The key themes covered in this chapter are:

- plate tectonics;
- the major geological divisions of Scotland;
- outline geological history of Scotland;
- climate change through geological time;
- plate tectonics and climate change.

2.1 Introduction

Geology and geological processes have played a fundamental role in shaping the landscape of Scotland. In general, the major role of geology lies in providing the foundation on which geomorphological processes work; most strikingly, geology controls the form of topography and its altitude, and exerts a profound control on the development of soil types and hence habitats. The aim of

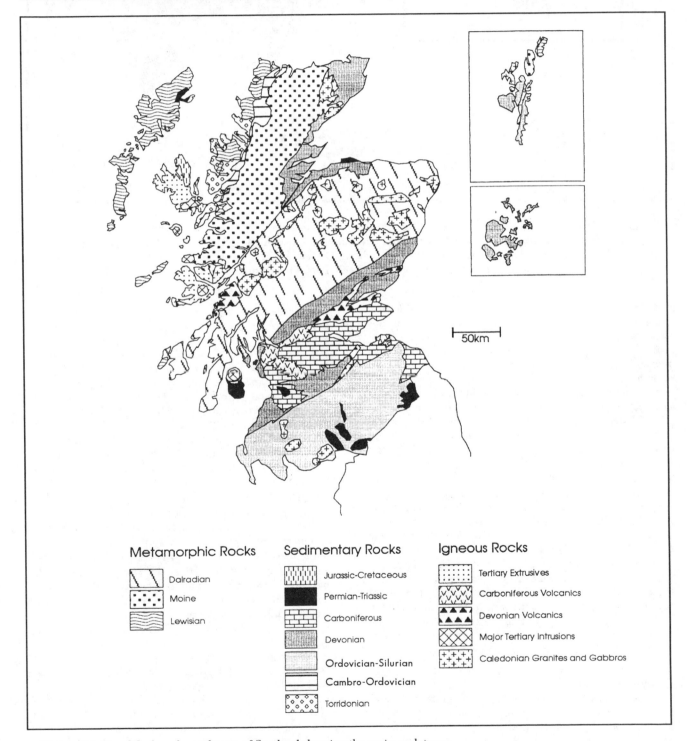

Metamorphic Rocks
- Dalradian
- Moine
- Lewisian

Sedimentary Rocks
- Jurassic-Cretaceous
- Permian-Triassic
- Carboniferous
- Devonian
- Ordovician-Silurian
- Cambro-Ordovician
- Torridonian

Igneous Rocks
- Tertiary Extrusives
- Carboniferous Volcanics
- Devonian Volcanics
- Major Tertiary Intrusions
- Caledonian Granites and Gabbros

50km

Figure 2.1 Simplified geological map of Scotland showing the main rock types.

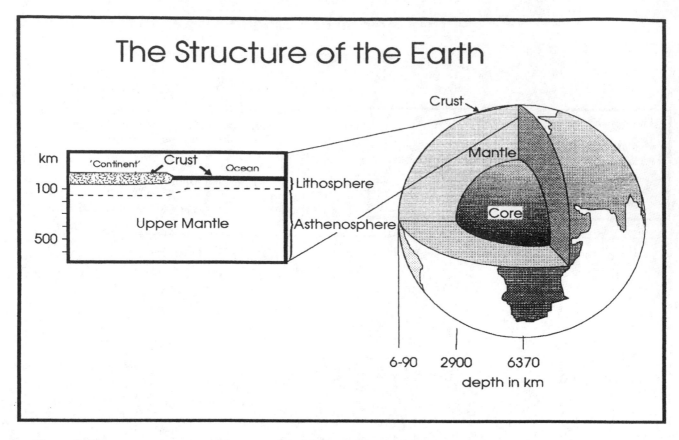

The Structure of the Earth

Figure 2.2 Diagrammatic section of the structure of the Earth, showing the core, mantle and crust. The crust is too thin to show to scale in the main diagram, but is detailed in the enlargement on the left. The crust and the uppermost part of the mantle together make up the relatively rigid lithosphere. The lithosphere comprises a series of plates which move over the 'softer' asthenosphere, part of the upper mantle underlying the lithosphere. (Modified from Wilson, 1994).

this chapter is to present an overview of the geological processes that have led to the formation of Scotland as it is today, and in so doing to account for the distribution of the major rock groups. These processes have operated across a range of scales from global to local. At a global scale they include episodes of mountain building, the formation of supercontinents and continental breakup, but these same large-scale processes, driven by plate tectonics, have given rise to local variations in rock type and structure. Global scale processes have also exerted a profound influence on climate change through time. In particular, the intensification of Northern Hemisphere glaciation 2.4 Ma ago reflects a longer-term rearrangement of the continents that has influenced global cooling during the last 55 Ma.

Scotland is blessed with an immensely rich geological record that spans a vast amount of geological time, beginning with the 3,300 Ma old rocks of the Lewisian Gneiss (Figure 2.1). These are among the oldest rocks in Europe, and compare with the oldest rocks in the world (3,900 Ma old Acasta Gneiss from northwest Canada), and the age of the Earth at 4,600 Ma. The geological record of Scotland is more or less continuous from 3,300 Ma to the present, and the study of Scotland's geology has made, and continues to make, important contributions to our understanding of the evolution of the Earth.

2.2 Plate tectonics

Developed in the 1960s, the theory of **plate tectonics** completely revolutionised geological thinking. The scope of the theory is vast and it can be applied to virtually all geological phenomena. Broadly, it explains how the Earth works at least at the present, and most likely throughout most of its history; it is probably fair to say that most geologists accept that even very ancient rocks (older than, say, 1000 Ma) were formed by processes similar to those operating today. Furthermore, in determining how the outer shell of the Earth is constructed and recycled, plate tectonic processes exert a profound influence on the composition and circulation of the oceans and atmosphere, and therefore on the biosphere.

Plate tectonic theory is primarily concerned with the outermost 670 km of the Earth, an outer shell comprising the **upper mantle**, and the **oceanic** and **continental lithosphere** (Figure 2.2). (To give some idea of the size of the Earth, the deepest borehole into the Earth, drilled over several years on the Kola Peninsula in Russia, currently reaches a depth of 12 km, barely penetrating half the continental crust: put another way, if the Earth were shrunk to the size of a half-metre beach ball, the deepest borehole would not have punctured the ball). The **lithosphere** is that part of the mantle permanently attached to the oceanic or continental crust, and is divided up into a series of **plates** which fit together like parts of a jigsaw (Figure 2.3). Plate tectonic theory explains geological phenomena in terms of large-scale horizontal movements of these plates about the surface of the Earth (Figure 2.4).

The movement of the plates about the surface of the Earth is driven by heat escaping from the Earth's interior: most of this heat is produced by radioactive decay of certain elements, mainly potassium, rubidium, uranium, and thorium, largely in the mantle and crust. Earlier in the Earth's history (older than about 1,000 Ma) it is likely that

16

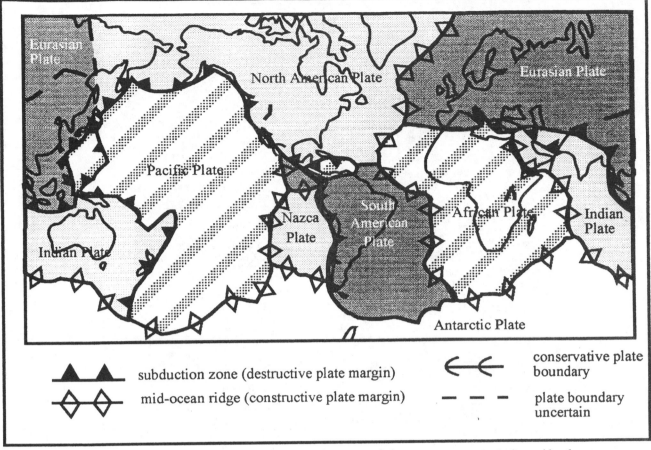

Figure 2.3 The current distribution of crustal plates. The directions of plate movements are indicated by the arrows or teeth according to the type of plate boundary. (After Wilson, 1994 from original source in Wyllie 1976).

more heat was produced than today, and the style of plate tectonics may have differed.

One of the most important aspects of plate tectonics is the way in which oceans are created and destroyed (Figure 2.5), because this accounts for most of the formation of both continental and oceanic crust.

2.2.1 The birth of oceans: rifting and mid-ocean ridges

If the continental crust is stretched, it will thin and rift (Figure 2.5a). Continued stretching will cause the continent to break apart, and a new ocean will grow as the two continents separate. This process can be accelerated by a hot jet, or **mantle plume**, rising from deep in the Earth

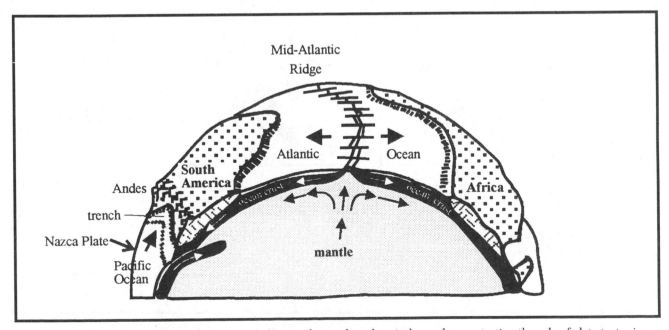

Figure 2.4 The relationships of three crustal plates in the southern hemisphere, demonstrating the role of plate tectonics in driving major geological processes. The subduction of the Nazca Plate (see Figure 2.3) beneath South America gives rise to the Andes. The thickness of the crustal layers is not to scale. (After Wilson, 1994 from original BGS source).

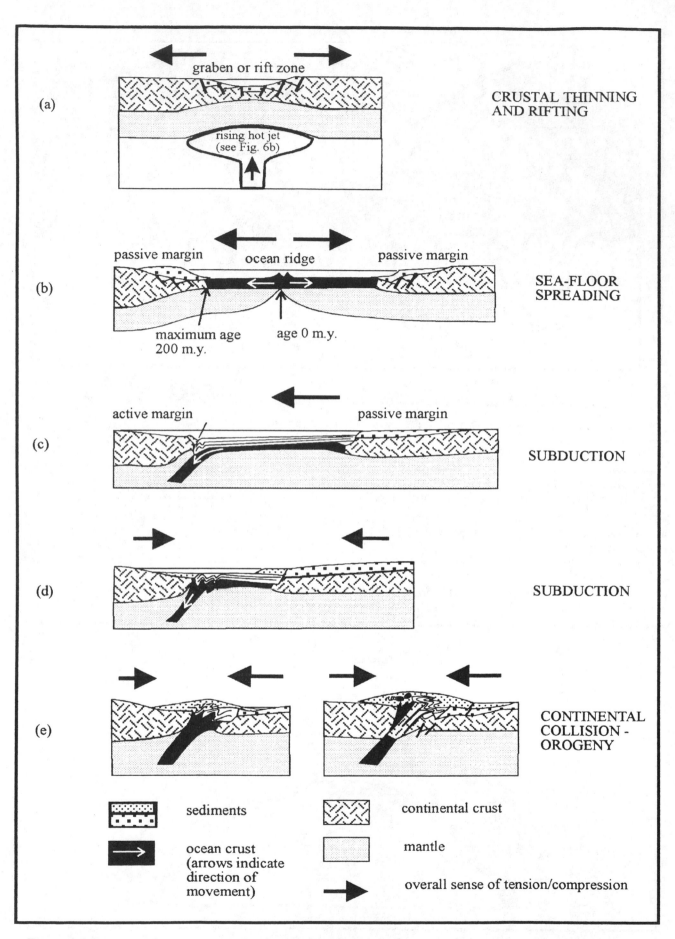

Figure 2.5 Sequence of events in a cycle of ocean opening and closing, culminating in continental collision. It is possible for both margins of an ocean to be subjected to subduction, although this is not shown here. (Modified from Wilson, 1994).

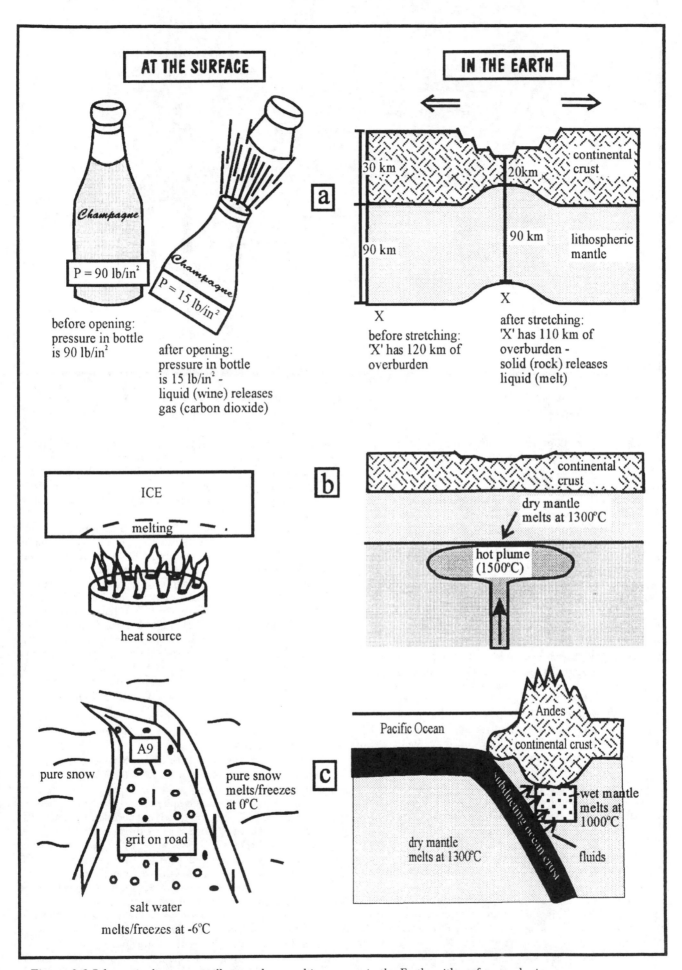

Figure 2.6 Schematic diagrams to illustrate how melting occurs in the Earth, with surface analogies.

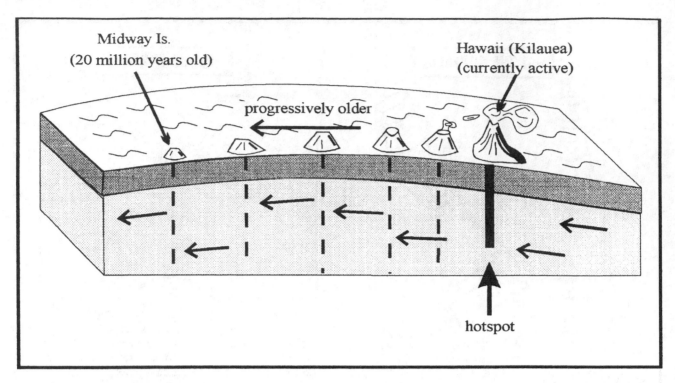

Figure 2.7 Generation of the Hawaiian Island chain as the Pacific Plate migrates over a hotspot. Arrows indicate the movement of the Pacific Plate.

impinging on the continent that is being stretched (Figure 2.6b). Melting above such **hotspots** results from heating of the mantle under the plate by the deep-seated mantle plume (Figure 2.6b). The melts produce, broadly, igneous rock called **basalt**. The best known example today is the Hawaiian Islands where the Pacific Plate moves like a conveyor belt over the Hawaiian Hotspot, producing volcanoes (Figure 2.7). The volcanoes (attached to the Pacific Plate) expire as they move away from the hotspot, and new volcanoes are formed in their place. Thus the age of the islands in the Hawaiian Chain increases away from the currently active volcano of Mauna Loa (Figure 2.7).

The Hawaiian Hotspot rises under the middle of a plate, but in the past similar hotspots have risen under plate margins that were being pulled apart. Where this occurred, the stretching process was accelerated, and huge volumes of lava were erupted at the surface. The resulting lava fields are found on all the continents today - the area of these **continental flood basalt** provinces is usually measured in terms of hundreds of thousands (or millions) of square kilometres, and they are usually a few kilometres thick. Examples include the Deccan Traps of India, the Paraná of South America, the Karoo of southern Africa, the Siberian Traps of Russia, and the North Atlantic Tertiary Province. The North Atlantic Tertiary Province, formed between 64 Ma and 52 Ma, heralded the opening of the North Atlantic Ocean at 55 Ma, and is related to the currently active hotspot under Iceland. In Scotland, the North Atlantic Tertiary Province is dramatically represented today by the Cuillin of Skye and Rum, as well as other ancient volcanic centres on Mull, Ardnamurchan and Arran, and the plateau lavas of Skye and Mull.

New oceanic crust is formed at **mid-ocean ridges** (*e.g.* the Mid-Atlantic Ridge). Here, two plates are pulled apart. By this action the mantle moves closer to the surface and starts to melt. Melting occurs as a result of the release of pressure (Figure 2.6a). The process is rather like removing the cork from a bottle of champagne: in the case of

champagne the release of pressure causes the liquid (wine) to release gas (carbon dioxide); in the case of the mantle, the solid (rock) releases liquid (molten rock, or **magma***)*. The liquid rises to the surface where it solidifies to form a type of basalt and becomes part of the ocean crust (Figure 2.5b).

The plates continue to be pulled apart (typically at rates of a few cm/year) and the melting process is continuous. Thus, new crust is continually pulled away from the mid-ocean ridge, and the age of the oceanic crust varies from zero at the mid-ocean ridge to a maximum of about 200 Ma at the transition to continental crust (Figure 2.5b). The reason for this maximum age is that as the new crust moves away from the mid-ocean ridge, it gets older, colder, and more dense, causing it to sink (this is why the depth of an ocean increases away from the mid-ocean ridge). Eventually the old oceanic crust becomes unstable and sinks back into the mantle. The zone of sinking is called a **subduction zone**, and the plate margin is called an **active margin** (Figure 2.5c).

2.2.2 The death of oceans: subduction and the growth of continental crust

As the oceanic crust sinks back into the mantle it encounters a warmer environment and begins to lose any fluids it collected at the surface. The fluids baked off the subducting slab are driven into the wedge of mantle between the subduction zone and overlying continent (Figure 2.5c). These fluids act as a flux and cause the mantle to melt (Figure 2.6c). The process is the same as gritting the roads in the winter-salt water freezes at a lower temperature (about -6°C) than fresh water (0°C); likewise 'wet' mantle melts at a lower temperature than dry mantle. Some of the melts that are produced in this environment will migrate to the surface and erupt to form volcanoes, such as those forming the 'Ring of Fire' around the Pacific Ocean today. The volcanoes here erupt magmas of a different composition to those produced at mid-ocean ridges, tending to be richer in silica and forming **intermediate** and **acid** igneous rocks - examples

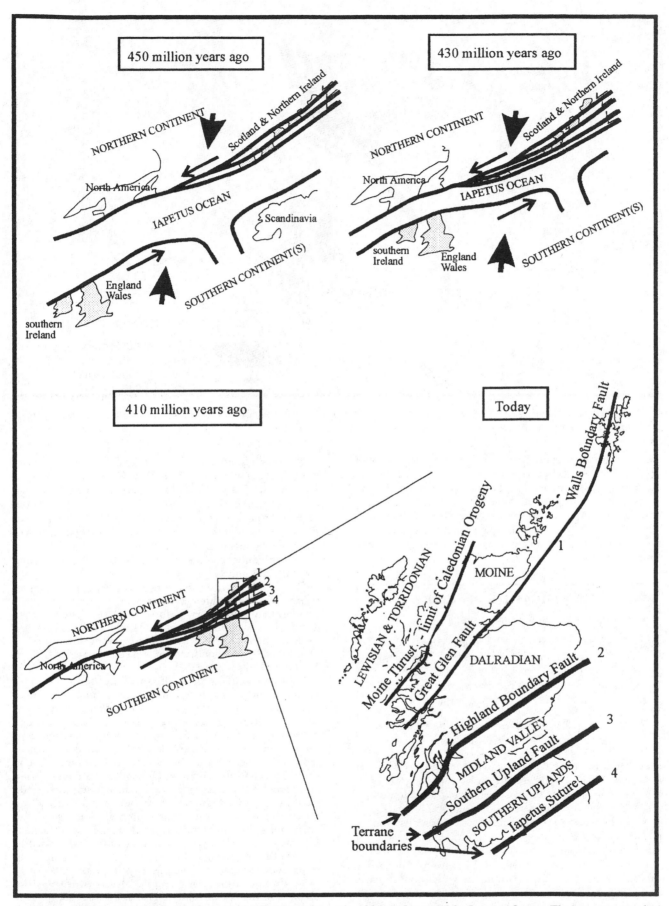

Figure 2.8 How Scotland was constructed. The figure shows the oblique closure of the Iapetus Ocean. The compressional forces (heavy arrows) and the forces from the plates sliding past each other (thin arrows) produced a complex mountain belt. Note that the shear zones are sinistral, *i.e.* looking across the fault, the continental blocks moved to the left with respect to each other. In the lower right diagram, the short arrows indicate the movement of blocks that finally came together to form the present landmass of Scotland.

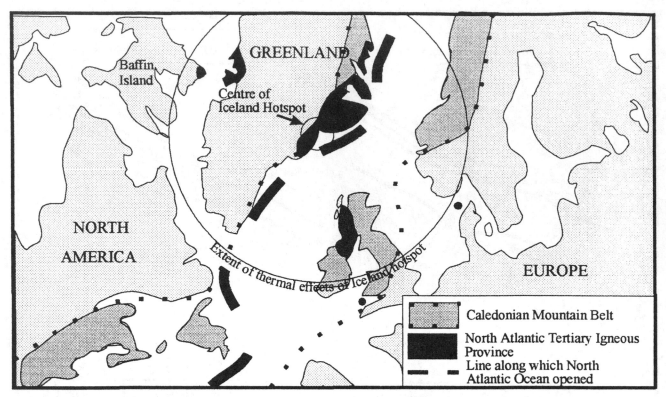

Figure 2.9 The opening of the North Atlantic Ocean. The positions of the continents at 55 Ma are shown as the North Atlantic Ocean opened along the line of the Caledonian Mountain Belt.

include **andesites** (named after the Andes), and **rhyolites** (the extrusive – see Box 1 – equivalent of granite). Many of the granites of the Scottish Highlands were formed in this type of environment about 450-400 Ma ago (*e.g.* Cairngorm and Rannoch Moor), and the Lewisian Gneiss, the bulk of which formed 3,300-2,000 Ma ago, probably represents the deep roots of an ancient active continental margin that has since been eroded.

Box 1   CLASSIFICATION OF ROCKS

Rocks are divided into 3 main groups:

• **Igneous** rocks are formed through the crystallisation of molten rocks (**magma**); magma that reaches the surface is called **lava** and cools to form **extrusive** igneous rocks, and magma that cools below the surface forms **intrusive** igneous rocks.

• **Metamorphic** rocks are formed when existing rocks are altered by heat and/or pressure.

• **Sedimentary** rocks are formed by: the transportation and deposition of rock fragments created by erosion and weathering (*e.g.* sandstones); the accumulation of material of biological origin (*e.g.* shelly limestones); precipitation of chemicals dissolved in water (*e.g.* rock salt).

Eventually the entire ocean will be consumed at such a subduction zone, and two continents will approach each other (Figure 2.5d). In this case, neither continent will subduct because both are too buoyant to sink into the dense mantle. The two continents will collide and produce a mountain belt (the process of **orogenesis**, Figure 2.5e). For example, the Himalayas are the result of the collision of India with Asia, when an ocean closed 40 Ma ago: the

mountain building caused by this collision still continues today. The mountains of Scotland (the Caledonian Mountain Belt) are the result of a collision between North America and Europe 400 Ma ago when the closure of the **Iapetus Ocean** brought together the early North American and European continents (Figure 2.8). Scotland lay on the North American continent, and England and Wales on the European continent - a line along the Solway Firth marks the probable suture.

The story is not quite that simple. Scotland, for example, did not exist as a single mass, but rather as several separate fragments, or **terranes**, before being brought together during the Caledonian Orogeny. The boundaries between these fragments now form major geographical boundaries in Scotland (*e.g.* the Southern Upland Fault and the Highland Boundary Fault (Figure 2.8)).

Most continental crust is produced in subduction zone environments. Prior to collision, magmas build mountain chains such as the Andes (on continental crust, Figure 2.4) or huge volcanic island arc complexes (on oceanic crust, *e.g.* west Pacific). During collision, the volcanic islands and intervening sediments are scrunched-up to form new mountain belts, such as the Caledonian Mountains. The Ochil Hills and the Pentland Hills in the Midland Valley are examples of volcanic island arcs added to the continental crust in this way. Mountain belts, running roughly along the sites of former oceans often represent weak lines in the crust, and new oceans tend to open along the lines of ancient mountain belts. However, the new crust that was added to the continents during the mountain building episode remains on the continent; in this way the continents slowly grow through time. An example of this process is the opening of the North Atlantic Ocean 55 Ma ago, roughly along the line of the 400 Ma old Caledonian Mountain Belt running through Norway, Greenland, Britain, Ireland, eastern Canada and the USA (Figure 2.9).

With this background, we can now look at the geology of Scotland in more detail.

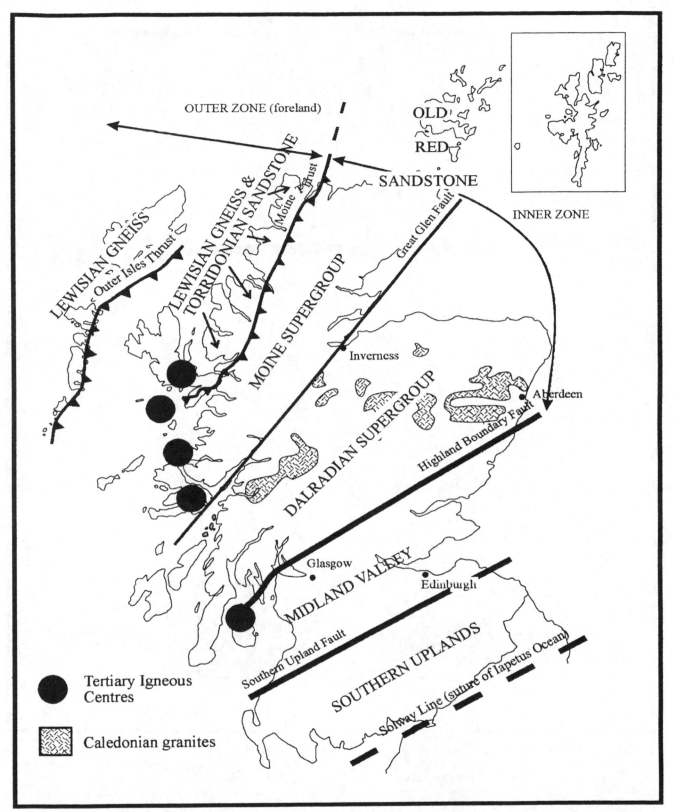

Figure 2.10 Simplified geological map of Scotland, showing the distribution of the major rock groups. Major faults are also shown - heavy lines indicate terrane boundaries (see text for details). The 'inner' and 'outer' zones of the Caledonian Oregeny are also indicated (see also Figure 2.11).

2.3   Scotland: a story of continental collision and continental break-up

The geology of Scotland may be described in terms of five main belts, bounded by major SW-NE oriented faults (Figure 2.10). Figure 2.11 shows how the major geological divisions and rock-groups fit into an idealised cross-section through an orogeny. In very general terms the geology of Scotland can also be divided into five major time periods (Figure 2.12) (note these do *not* necessarily correspond to the 5 main belts above).

1. *Before 600 Ma:* ancient rocks (the Lewisian Gneiss) formed by early mountain building processes, and the

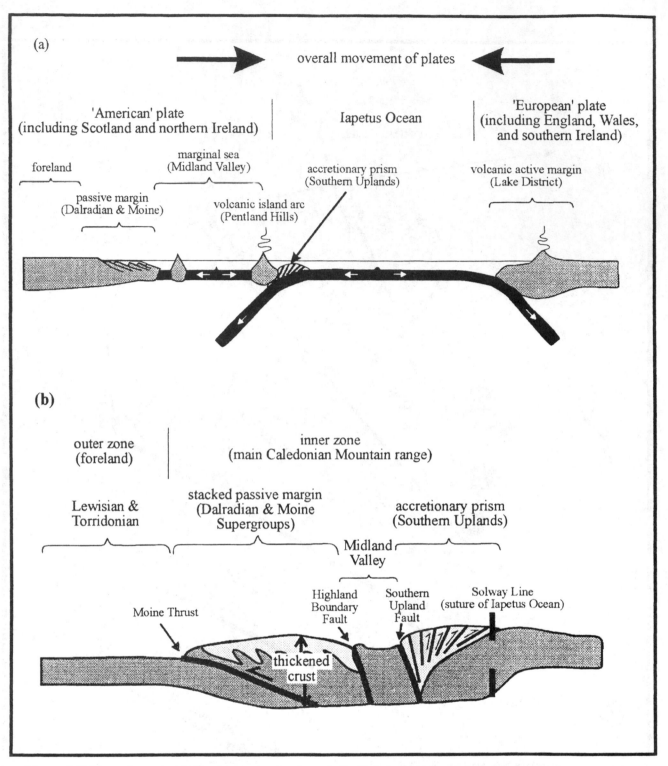

Figure 2.11 Very schematic, idealised cross-section through the Caledonian Mountain Belt in Scotland.
A. The situation prior to collision, with the subduction of ocean crust, the formation of an accretionary prism (a wedge of ocean sediments scraped off the subducting plate) and the generation of volcanoes.
B. The mountain belt after collision. The crust has been shortened and thickened, especially in the old passive margin (site of Dalradian and Moine sedimentation). Some major faults and main rock groups have been marked, and the current distribution of the rocks is shown in Figure 2.10.
 Note that the geological history of the Midland valley is complex, and the intention here is only to outline the position of the valley in the scheme of the Caledonian orogeny. (Similar considerations apply to other crustal blocks).

Torridonian Sandstones (about 1000 Ma old) subsequently formed by erosion of the Lewisian Gneiss.

2. *600-400 Ma:* the opening and closing of the Iapetus Ocean. The opening is recorded by rocks of the Dalradian Supergroup (forming the southern Highlands), and the closing of the ocean is recorded by the deformation of rocks

(e.g. Dalradian, Moine) and the intrusion of numerous granites (*e.g.* Cairngorm, Rannoch Moor).

3. *400-350 Ma:* Scotland was part of a growing supercontinent, as all the continents on Earth welded together to form **Pangaea**.

4. *350-55 Ma:* stretching and small-scale rifting within

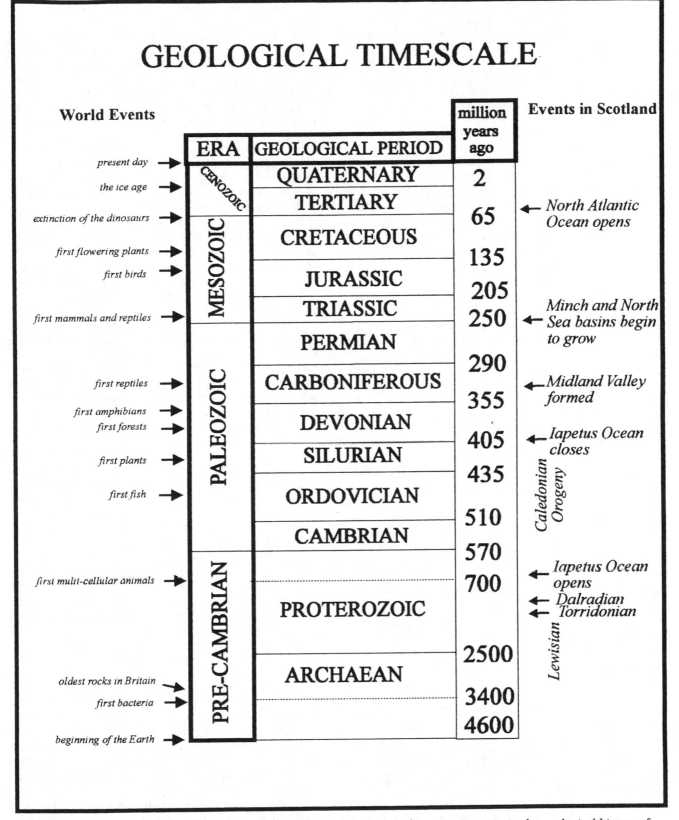

GEOLOGICAL TIMESCALE

World Events	ERA	GEOLOGICAL PERIOD	million years ago	Events in Scotland
present day →	CENOZOIC	QUATERNARY	2	
the ice age →		TERTIARY		← North Atlantic Ocean opens
extinction of the dinosaurs →	MESOZOIC	CRETACEOUS	65	
first flowering plants →			135	
first birds →		JURASSIC	205	
first mammals and reptiles →		TRIASSIC	250	← Minch and North Sea basins begin to grow
	PALEOZOIC	PERMIAN	290	
first reptiles →		CARBONIFEROUS	355	← Midland Valley formed
first amphibians →		DEVONIAN		
first forests →			405	← Iapetus Ocean closes
first plants →		SILURIAN	435	
first fish →		ORDOVICIAN	510	Caledonian Orogeny
		CAMBRIAN	570	
first multi-cellular animals →	PRE-CAMBRIAN		700	← Iapetus Ocean opens ← Dalradian ← Torridonian
		PROTEROZOIC	2500	Lewisian
oldest rocks in Britain →		ARCHAEAN	3400	
first bacteria →				
beginning of the Earth →			4600	

Figure 2.12 A chart of the geological timescale, indicating the timing of important events in the geological history of Scotland with respect to major events in the history of the Earth.

Pangaea formed sedimentary basins and igneous rocks. Most of the igneous rocks formed between 350-250 Ma, and occur in the Midland Valley; most of the stretching and basin formation occurred during the Mesozoic (250-65 Ma), forming basins such as the North Sea and the Minch. This latter period can be viewed as a series of failed attempts to open the North Atlantic Ocean.

5. *55 Ma – present:* opening of the North Atlantic Ocean, with dramatic effects on the geology along the west coast of Scotland (*e.g.* the formation of the igneous rocks of Arran, Mull, Rum, and Skye).

In the following section the geology of the 5 main belts is described mainly in terms of its influence on the topography and relief of each area. The term *relief* is used in the following way:

- high relief refers to areas in which there is a marked variation in altitude, from high summits to low valleys;
- low relief refers to areas where there is little variation in altitude, leading to subdued topography.

It is important to note that areas of low relief can occur at any altitude; both Orkney and the Cairngorm plateau are areas of low relief. Likewise, high relief is not confined to high altitudes (many areas of the seafloor have high relief).

2.3.1 Belt 1: west of the Moine Thrust

This area was not greatly affected by the Caledonian Orogeny, as it lies on the **foreland** (Figures 2.10 and 2.11), away from the collision zone. The coastal geology of the mainland is dominated by Torridonian Sandstone and Lewisian Gneiss; the Torridonian Sandstones rising to form the high peaks towering over low-lying cnoc-and-lochan topography underlain by Lewisian Gneiss, especially between Loch Maree and Loch Broom.

The Western Isles are separated from the mainland by the Minch; this sea began to open about 250 Ma, and, along with other Mesozoic basins around Scotland (*e.g.* North Sea), represents initial attempts to break up the European - North American continent and open the North Atlantic. On land, the Jurassic sediments of Raasay, Skye, Eigg, Muck, and Mull were deposited in basins resulting from this stretching.

The Western Isles themselves almost entirely comprise Lewisian Gneiss. The hill ranges of Harris and Uig are formed by intrusions of granite, injected during orogenic activity associated with the formation of the Lewisian Gneiss. These hills rise sharply over the low-lying subdued topography of the bulk of the Lewisian Gneiss. In the southern islands, the hills along the east coast are produced by the Outer Isles Thrust, while the characteristic lowlands of the west coast are a result of the flat-lying structures in the Lewisian Gneiss. The Outer Isles Thrust is a major long-lived geological fault, along which movement has occurred on a number of occasions since about 1,100 Ma: movements on the fault caused instantaneous friction-melting of the rock, which subsequently froze to form a hard glassy rock very resistant to erosion - hence the relationship between the thrust and upland areas.

Much of Skye, except parts of the Sleat Peninsula and Strath, escaped the effects of the Caledonian Orogeny. The most important topographic features are the jagged peaks of the Black Cuillin and the more rounded summits of the Red Cuillin. The rocks forming both ranges were produced about 55 Ma ago, as the Iceland Hotspot rose and generated large volumes of igneous rocks associated with the opening of the North Atlantic Ocean. The peaks of the Black Cuillin are formed of **gabbro**, the intrusive (see Box 1) equivalent of basalt; the Red Cuillin, of granite. North of these hill ranges the topography is dominated by the plateau lavas, also formed during the early stages of the opening of the North Atlantic Ocean.

The Moine Thrust marks the western limit of the effects of the Caledonian Orogeny in Britain (Figures 2.10 and 2.11). The thrust is a low-angle fault along which rocks of the Moine Supergroup (about 800 Ma old) were carried westward on to the foreland, overriding Cambrian rocks (about 500 Ma old). Along the Moine Thrust itself are important outcrops of Cambrian-Ordovician strata, mainly quartzites and limestones (the Durness Limestones); the latter are often conspicuous in giving rise to lush vegetation on nutrient-rich, neutral pH soils.

2.3.2 Belt 2: between the Moine Thrust and the Great Glen Fault

This belt lies in the **inner zone** of the schematic orogeny shown in Figures 2.10 and 2.11. The rocks in this area were disrupted and deformed during the Caledonian Orogeny. The Moine Supergroup comprises sandstones and finer-grained sedimentary rocks that have been changed by heat and pressure into **metamorphic** rocks (Box 1), as well as having been disrupted by a number of thrusts and faults. Rocks in the group have been folded, usually more than once and in different directions, so that complex fold interference patterns have developed, and the structural grain inherent in the rocks is not simple. On the whole, the rocks in the group are quartz- and mica- rich metamorphic rocks that are fairly resistant to erosion.

In the west, the relief of the region is still characterised by high summits and deep glens - the glaciations of the last 2.4 Ma have accentuated strengths and weaknesses in the rocks of the Moine Supergroup, gouging out corries and glens to produce dramatic scenery, *e.g.* Lochaber north of the Great Glen. By contrast, in the east the relief is generally low, and rocks of the Moine Supergroup underlie large areas of the flow country of Sutherland and Caithness.

Not all of the rocks in this belt bear the mark of the Caledonian Orogeny. The lowland areas of Caithness and Orkney are dominated by the Old Red Sandstones. These sandstones were deposited about 380 Ma ago in desert and salt lake environments when Scotland lay south of the equator, in the desert belt roughly equivalent to that at the latitude of the Atacama - Namibia - Australia today. These rocks form subdued topography and this, together with their poor drainage characteristics, has contributed to the formation of blanket bog in the flow country of Caithness.

The conspicuous rings of hills of Ardnamurchan and Mull represent the remnants of Tertiary volcanoes (active about 60 Ma ago), associated with the opening of the North Atlantic Ocean. In Mull the hills punched through Jurassic sediments (associated with the Minch basin), but these are largely blanketed by the plateau basalts that dominate the low-lying areas of the island.

The most striking feature of Shetland is its north-south elongation and the presence in the eastern half of the islands of smooth N-NE trending ridges with intervening partly drowned valleys. Here, the underlying geology comprises schists (quartz- feldspar- mica- rich metamorphic rocks) in which the minerals are aligned to produce a structural grain that trends N or NE. The western part of the group is separated geologically by the Walls Boundary Fault, a continuation of the Great Glen Fault. In the west the relief is higher than in the east, reflecting the varied bedrock geology of the area, including several masses of granite, belts of schist, some highly folded sandstones, and andesite and basalt lavas - all associated with the Caledonian Orogeny.

The Great Glen Fault forms a prominent topographic feature bisecting Scotland from Inverness to Fort William. Geologists continue to argue about the sense and timing of movement along it. It is clear that there has been a long and complicated history of movement, starting during the Caledonian and continuing to the Jurassic. Furthermore, although the Great Glen Fault is a prominent topographic feature, it is *not* a terrane boundary. Rocks of the Moine Supergroup are found on both sides of the fault, and the Lewisian Gneiss probably underlies both the Moine and Dalradian supergroups (Figure 2.10): thus the blocks to the north and south of the Great Glen Fault do *not* have markedly different geological histories.

2.3.3 Belt 3: between the Great Glen Fault and the Highland Boundary Fault

This belt lies in the **inner zone** of the Caledonian Orogeny, and is characterised by intense deformation of rocks belonging, mostly, to the Dalradian Supergroup (Figures 2.10 and 2.11). This supergroup comprises a diverse range of rock types - from quartz- and mica- rich metamorphic rocks, through fine-grained metamorphosed sedimentary rocks, to limestones and metamorphosed basalts. The sequence as a whole represents a developing sedimentary basin that eventually opened to form the Iapetus Ocean shortly after 590 Ma. The sediments and basalts of the Dalradian Supergroup were later intensely deformed during the Caledonian Orogeny as the Iapetus Ocean closed: this deformation led to geological structures that run in a zone from Islay to Aberdeen, and the rocks have a strong inherent SW-NE structural grain. This grain is especially evident in the trend of many of the local hill ranges in Argyll and Bute, in the SW Grampian Highlands.

Many new rocks were injected during the Caledonian Orogeny. These are mostly the granite masses of Ben Cruachan, Ben Starav, Rannoch Moor and the Cairngorms. Many of these granites were intruded into quartz- and mica-rich rocks of the Dalradian Supergroup, and where there is not much difference between the resistance to erosion of these rocks and the granites, this has contributed to the formation of high plateaux with low relief, as in the Cairngorms.

In the west, the Mull of Kintyre, and the isles of Colonsay, Islay, and Jura are underlain by Dalradian rocks. The Mull of Kintyre is 'separated' from the mainland by the isthmus at Tarbert, formed by erosion along a geological contact in the Dalradian Group.

Arran can be divided into two areas: granites form the northern hills, whereas sandstones and other Permian rocks, with occasional limestones, and the remnants of a volcano (granitic rocks) form lower lying ground in the south. The northern granite is about 58 Ma old and was formed during the early stages of the opening of the North Atlantic Ocean.

The southern part of this belt is delineated by the Highland Boundary Fault, an important geological feature that separates the Midland Valley from the Highlands. The fault is defined by a prominent break of slope from Stonehaven in the east to Helensburgh in the west. The dramatic change in the landscape is seen near Callander or by Balmaha at Loch Lomond. The fault marks a terrane boundary: the rocks on either side had different geological histories until they were joined 400 Ma ago during the closing stages of the Caledonian Orogeny.

2.3.4 Belt 4: the Midland Valley

The Midland Valley is a low-lying geological block (a rift valley) that has slipped down between the southern Highlands and the Southern Uplands. During the Caledonian Orogeny the area was characterised by chains of volcanic islands (island arcs) feeding lavas and sediments into the surrounding seas. Later, from about 350-250 Ma (the Carboniferous and Permian periods), the area was downfaulted by movements on the Southern Upland and Highland Boundary Faults and was characterised by warm shallow tropical seas punctuated by isolated volcanoes. At this time, Scotland lay in equatorial regions and, in environments similar to the Caribbean today, limestones accumulated in the warm shallow seas, and large coal deposits in lagoonal swamps near the shore. Despite subsequent earth movements, this simple geology is reflected in the topography of the belt today: most of the low-lying areas are underlain by Carboniferous limestones and coal

sequences and are punctuated by isolated hills (laws) that are the remnants of ancient volcanoes (e.g. Arthur's Seat and Castle Rock in Edinburgh, Traprain Law, North Berwick Law and the isolated 'Green Hills' of Ayrshire). The remains of the ancient volcanic island arcs form more extensive upland areas of the Ochil Hills and the Pentland Hills.

Much of the solid geology of this belt is hidden beneath a thick blanket of drift deposited during the Quaternary by glaciers and ice sheets emanating from the surrounding upland areas. The glaciers also shaped many classic features, such as the crag-and-tail of Castle Rock and Arthur's Seat in Edinburgh.

The Southern Upland Fault forms a prominent break of slope from Dunbar to Girvan, and is a terrane boundary separating the Midland Valley from the southern Uplands.

2.3.5 Belt 5: the Southern Uplands

The rocks in this belt can be divided into two main groups. Those older than 400 Ma comprise a thick sequence of sediments that filled the Iapetus Ocean, mainly poorly sorted quartz-rich rocks, mudstones, lavas, and volcanic ashes. During the Caledonian Orogeny these sediments were scraped-off the subducting plate and piled on to the continental crust, creating an **accretionary prism** (Figure 2.11), that forms most of the upland areas in the Southern Uplands today.

The second group of rocks formed after the Caledonian Orogeny. Some areas in this belt were centres of deposition for Carboniferous limestones, and Carboniferous basalts were erupted to form the upland areas south and east of Coldstream.

2.4 Scotland: a tale of northward drift and changing climate

In the preceding paragraphs, the geology has been described mainly in relation to major topographic features. In this section the geological history is described in terms of its relation to the climatic history of Scotland as reflected in the variations in rock type through time (Table 2.1).

Table 2.1 Simplified geological history of Scotland indicating the relationship between certain rock types, environment of deposition and palaeolatitude during the last 600 Ma.

Age in millions of years	Geological Period	Rock Type	Environment of deposition	Palaeo-latitude
600	Dalradian	various including tillites	various (glacial for tillites)	70°S
400-360	Devonian	red sandstones	arid/desert	15°S
350-250	Permian-Carboniferous	limestones, coals	warm shallow seas, lagoonal swamps	equatorial
250-225	Triassic	red sandstones	arid/deserts	15°N
2.4 - present	Quaternary	tills	glacial	57°N

27

The source of information for the palaeolatitudes in Table 2.1 is **palaeomagnetism** (see Box 2). Given these data, we might be forgiven for assuming that changes in Scotland's climate through geological time are the result of Scotland's northward drift through the Earth's climate belts. Thus, at 600 Ma, Scotland was near the South Pole, and then drifted north through the southern desert belt (*e.g.* current Australian desert), the equator, the northern desert (*e.g.* current Sahara) belt to our current latitude of 57°N. However, the story is not that simple, and the geological record is a little more complex. This complexity is illustrated well by the example of laterites on Skye and Mull.

Box 2 PALAEOMAGNETISM

Paleomagnetism is the investigation of the history of the Earth's magnetic field recorded in the rock record. The Earth can be thought of as a giant bar magnet with poles at the top and bottom; the magnetic field intersects the Earth's surface vertically at the poles and is parallel to the surface at the equator. When rocks form containing minerals capable of recording magnetism, the magnetic minerals align themselves with the magnetic field of the Earth, recording the latitude on the Earth at which they formed. Analysing such information in rocks often reveals a mismatch between the position of the magnetic poles recorded in the rock and the location of the present-day poles. The easiest way to explain this discrepancy is to invoke large-scale movement of the plates over the surface of the Earth. The alternative, that the magnetic poles have wandered as recorded in the rock record, is far more difficult to substantiate given current observations and our knowledge of physics.

At 55 Ma, just as the North Atlantic Ocean was beginning to open, basalt lavas were pouring out on to the land surfaces of Skye and Mull. Between eruptions, soils developed on some of the basalt flows, and, more importantly, some of the basalts were chemically weathered to form **laterites**. Laterites today form in tropical environments, but 55 Ma ago Scotland's latitude was similar to that of today, about 50-60°N, and Scotland's climate today could hardly be described as tropical. Similar observations on the geology around the world lead to the conclusion that the world's climate belts, as well as the continents themselves, have shifted during geological time. At times, global climate was warmer than at present, there were no polar ice caps, and equatorial belts shifted north (as at 65-55 Ma). Other times were characterised by similar conditions to today, with polar ice caps, well-defined climate belts, and a strong thermal gradient from the equator to the poles.

Research in Quaternary geology has shown that the most likely mechanism driving the shifts between glacial and interglacial periods during at least the last 2.4 Ma is changes in the Earth's orbital parameters. These changes include the eccentricity of the orbit around the sun (how far the orbit deviates from a pure circle), the precession and the amount of tilt away from the rotation axis. These variables change on a cyclical basis and are called Milankovitch cycles (Chapter 5). However, it is likely that similar shifts in the Earth's orbital characteristics have occurred throughout its history, and Milankovitch cycles alone cannot explain the long-term onset and termination of ice ages through geological time. Another mechanism is required to explain why the Earth's climate changes from warm to cool, and this is plate tectonics. Plate tectonic processes control global climate in two main ways:

- Plate tectonic processes control the cycling of carbon dioxide through the various carbon reservoirs of the Earth (mainly carbonate rocks, organic carbon (including coal and oil), the oceans and the atmosphere). The amount of carbon available in the ocean and atmosphere, and the interchange between the different reservoirs, controls the CO_2 content of the atmosphere which, as a greenhouse gas, affects global temperatures by preventing re-radiation of in-coming solar radiation to space. Of the reservoirs, carbonate rock holds about 5,000 times as much carbon as the oceans and atmosphere at any time, although it is taken-up and released (*i.e.* cycled) far more slowly than carbon in the oceans and atmosphere. Nevertheless, its sheer magnitude ensures that plate tectonic processes (volcanic activity and metamorphic processes in particular) acting on the carbonate reservoir are fundamental in controlling global climate. Thus, while the atmospheric content of CO_2 has increased by 1.28 times in the past 150 years (at current rates of growth the CO_2 content of the atmosphere will be double that of pre-industrial levels by 2050) due to human use of fossil fuels (coal and oil), plate tectonic processes have caused atmospheric CO_2 to vary by 3-100 times current values over periods of 10s to 100s of millions of years.

- Plate tectonics also determines the distribution of land and sea areas, including large scale surface topography, so controlling circulation in the atmosphere and oceans.

The relationship between plate tectonics and mean global temperature is shown in Figure 2.13. One of the best illustrations of the key role of plate tectonics in determining global climate is the example of global cooling during the last 55 Ma.

2.5 Global cooling during the last 55 Ma

The pattern of global cooling during the last 55 Ma (the Cenozoic era, Figure 2.12) involves a complex, and poorly understood, interplay of positive and negative feedbacks. The main components include:

- the positions of the continents, and in particular the increasing isolation of Antarctica over the South Pole;

- the opening and closing of ocean gateways, particularly the establishment of the circum-polar current around Antarctica, the closing of the circum-equatorial current by the collision of Africa with Europe and the raising of the Panama isthmus;

- plateaux uplift, especially in Tibet and the western USA;

- Milankovitch cycles, mainly in their role in driving shorter-term fluctuations in global climate.

The onset of global cooling began 55 Ma ago as Australia and Antarctica begin to rift apart at high southern latitudes. The rifting process continued with the opening of the Drake

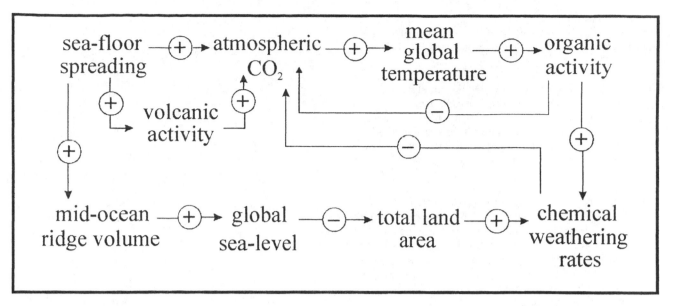

Figure 2.13 The relationship between plate tectonic processes and mean global temperature. Positive signs indicate a positive relationship between two variables; negative signs, an inverse relationship. For example, an increase in seafloor spreading produces increased volcanic activity and increased atmospheric CO_2, leading to an increase in mean global temperature and increased organic activity and so increased rates of chemical weathering, in turn causing a decrease in atmospheric CO_2 and therefore a decrease in mean global temperature. (Modified from Summerfield, 1991).

Passage (between South America and Antarctica) 25 Ma ago (isolating Antarctica) and the establishment of the deep water circum-polar current 22 Ma ago. This current isolated Antarctica from the warming effects of tropical waters and so accelerated cooling of Antarctica. As a result of this continuing isolation, ice on Antarctica reached the sea by 30 Ma and thickened rapidly after 22 Ma.

Meanwhile, 40 Ma ago the Alpine and Himalayan orogenies were underway as Africa collided with Europe, and India with Asia. In the western USA the pace of orogenic processes accelerated, with uplift of the western plateaux. While narrow, sharp mountain ranges have a dramatic effect on local climates, their ability to affect global climate is more limited. In this respect, the uplift of large areas of land has a more profound effect, deflecting the flow of air currents upward above the plateaux and changing the hemispherical circulation pattern. Thus, the uplift of the Tibetan Plateau (mean elevation 5 km above sea level) and the western plateaux of the USA affected air circulation markedly as they reached half their current height by 5-10 Ma ago, and their full heights 2.5 Ma ago. The changes in wind directions associated with uplift of these plateaux led to increased aridity at mid-low latitudes (establishment of the Prairie and Steppes of North America and Eurasia, and growth of the Saharan, Gobi, and Californian deserts).

Continued mixing of the Indian and Atlantic Ocean waters through equatorial currents was prevented by collision of Africa and Europe 40 Ma ago. Similarly, the elevation of the Panama isthmus 15 Ma ago prevented ready mixing of Atlantic and Pacific Ocean waters, and intensified the Gulf Stream in the North Atlantic. Large-scale ocean currents began to resemble those of today. Shortly after this, between 14-12 Ma, there was a marked build up of Antarctic ice, causing further cooling, particularly in the Southern Hemisphere.

About 5 Ma ago glaciers in the Arctic expanded, although there is evidence for localised glaciations at high latitude much earlier than this in the Northern Hemisphere. Mainly because of the huge increase in volume of the Antarctic Ice Sheet and the corresponding fall in global sea-level, the Mediterranean Basin was isolated from the Atlantic Ocean, and dried up. The basin refilled as global ice volumes later decreased, giving rise to what must have been the grand-daddy of all waterfalls over the Straits of Gibraltar! The periodic evaporation from the basin produced thick salt deposits which now underlie the Mediterranean Sea.

Intensification of glaciation in the Northern Hemisphere occurred about 2.4 Ma ago as ice sheets expanded on the continents and adjacent shelves. A possible explanation is that the plateaux of the western USA and Tibet reached their full height and various feedback mechanisms took marked effect. For example, increased uplift led to increased chemical weathering, which drew-down CO_2 from the atmosphere (chemical weathering has the net effect of transferring CO_2 from the atmosphere to the carbonate rock reservoir), leading to further global cooling. Also, ice is more reflective than land so that more of the Sun's radiation was reflected away from the polar regions, causing further cooling.

From 2.4 Ma, Milankovitch cycles are clearly recorded in the deep-sea sediment records. This marks the point in time when cooling reached a particular threshold, allowing the Milankovitch cycles to 'kick-in', and dominate global climate. In particular, the global ice volume began to vary on a 100 ka cycle (Chapter 5), corresponding to a subtle variation in the eccentricity of the Earth's orbit. This causes variations in the amount of incoming solar radiation as the Earth moves closer to, and further away from, the Sun. However, the actual deviation of the Earth's orbit from a pure circle is only slight, and the mechanism by which this causes such enormous changes in ice volume is unclear, although various feedbacks between the atmosphere, oceans and ice sheets appear to be involved (Chapter 5). Similar cycles are superimposed on c. 40 ka and c. 22 ka timescales (controlling how the incoming amount of solar radiation is distributed), driving the cyclic variations in ice volume and extent described in Chapter 5. A major outstanding issue is to discover the precise mechanisms by which climate responds so profoundly to such small changes in orbital characteristics.

2.6 Conclusions

The geomorphology and Quaternary history of Scotland have been influenced by the longer-term geological history in two key ways.

- The building of Scotland by the amalgamation of several terranes during the Caledonian Orogeny, and the formation of new rocks during the early stages of opening of the North Atlantic Ocean, have determined the pre-glacial topography and materials on which Quaternary glaciations (and other processes) have operated.

- The conditions necessary to trigger extensive Northern Hemisphere glaciations c. 2.4 Ma ago were brought about by long-term plate tectonic processes; specifically, changes in the distribution of the continents (especially the isolation of Antarctica over the South Pole) and changes in the topographic features of the continents (especially the orogenic uplift of large plateaux).

Although plate tectonic processes operate on timescales of tens of millions of years, they cannot be ignored in attempts to understand the mechanisms that drive climate change. While the broad pattern of climate change during the last c. 2.4 Ma is a complex one produced mainly by the interaction and superimposition of orbital cycles operating on timescales of 100 ka or less, the underlying causes of warm and cool periods during the longer history of the Earth must be understood in terms of the interaction and superimposition of cycles operating on all scales, from thousands of years to hundreds of millions of years.

Acknowledgements

Many thanks to Mike Bentley for detailed comments on an early draft of this chapter and to Nic Odling for compiling and drawing Figure 2.1. Figure 2.4 is based on a BGS source and is reproduced by permission of the Director, British Geological Survey.

Further Reading

Craig, G.Y. 1991. (Ed.) *Geology of Scotland*. 3rd ed. The Geological Society, London.

Frakes, L.A., Francis, J.E. and Syktus, J.I. 1992. *Climate Modes of the Phanerozoic*. Cambridge University Press, Cambridge.

Ruddiman, W.F. and Kutzbach, J.E. 1990. Late Cenozoic plateau uplift and climate change. *Transactions of the Royal Society of Edinburgh: Earth Sciences,* **81,** 301-314.

Summerfield, M.A. 1991. *Global Geomorphology*. Longman Scientific and Technical, Harlow.

Wilson, C. 1994. *Earth Heritage Conservation*. The Geological Society in Association with the Open University, Milton Keynes.

Wyllie, P.J. 1976. *The Way the Earth Works*. Wiley, Chichester.

3. Landform Evolution in Scotland Before the Ice Age

Adrian M. Hall

The key themes covered in this chapter are:

- the early geological and geomorphological evolution of Scotland;
- tectonic events during the Tertiary;
- landscape evolution during the Tertiary;
- landscape inheritance from the Tertiary;
- Buchan case study.

3.1 Introduction

Three generations of landforms can be recognised in Scotland. The youngest comprises the postglacial landforms, created by mass movement and rivers since the end of the Ice Age. The most spectacular landforms are the glacial features, created by the ice sheets and smaller glaciers during the Ice Age. The oldest generation, the pre-Quaternary landforms, is the least understood. Yet old landforms dominate the scenery of large parts of Scotland and were a major influence on patterns of glacial erosion. This paper reviews the evolution of Scotland's scenery before the Ice Age.

Investigating the pre-Quaternary landscape is not an easy task. Scotland is a mainly erosional landscape, with few correlative sediments on land, and erosion leaves little evidence as to the origins of landforms. Yet there are rewarding lines of enquiry. Evidence about Tertiary environments comes from the sedimentary basins in the North Atlantic and the North Sea, in which material denuded from Scotland accumulated. Cover rocks, sedimentary layers which overlie the ancient crystalline basement terrains, also provide important evidence of levels of denudation over periods of tens of millions of years. Weathering covers and ancient landforms, relics from before the Ice Age, provide information on how the relief developed and how deeply the Quaternary ice sheets eroded.

3.2 Deep time: geology and geomorphology before the Tertiary

3.2.1 In the beginning

The oldest rocks in Scotland are truly venerable. The gneisses of the Lewisian belt stretch back in time to about 3000 Ma, just 1500 Ma after the formation of the Earth. These rocks form the Hebridean craton, a fragment of the Laurentide (North America-Greenland) Shield detached by the opening of the North Atlantic in the late Mesozoic (Chapter 2). The oldest landforms are significantly younger, though still ancient, and date from around 1000 Ma. These are hilly terrains cut in Lewisian gneiss, which were deeply buried by sandstones, gravels and screes of the Torridonian (Godard 1965). At this time, north-west Scotland lay at around 15°N to 45°S and was a hot desert, with ephemeral rivers and playa lakes. This fossil landscape has been locally exhumed by erosion and moulded into 'cnoc-and-lochan' topography (areal scouring) by Quaternary ice sheets (Chapter 13).

3.2.2 Late Palaeozoic and Mesozoic

The low-angle Moine Thrust separates the Hebridean craton from the schists and granites of the Caledonides. These rocks were formed during the cataclysmic Caledonian mountain building period which culminated around 500 Ma ago (Chapter 2). Closure of an ocean basin brought together the Hebridean craton and the rest of the Highland terrain. Intense folding, thrusting and metamorphism of trapped sediments created the Moine and Dalradian series of schists and gneisses. In the south, a second ocean, the Iapetus, was consumed as Scotland was welded to northern England. Faulted wedges of weakly-metamorphosed ocean floor sediments were piled up in the area of the present Southern Uplands. Uplift associated with intrusion of granite masses across the Highlands created mountains of alpine proportions. During the Caledonian orogeny some 25 km of rock was removed by intense erosion and no landforms east of the Moine Thrust can predate this period.

There is a lot of evidence, however, that levels of erosion since about 400 Ma have been relatively modest. The level of the Devonian landsurface can be fixed across most of the eastern Highlands because of the many outliers of Old Red Sandstone which rest on Moine and Dalradian metamorphics. Several Newer Granites, emplaced around 400 Ma, were exposed within 10-20 Ma of their formation, and the retention of roof rocks or other near-surface effects means that subsequent' denudation has been modest. Moving forward in time to the Carboniferous and Mesozoic, there are numerous near-surface volcanic vents or weathering effects which survive in many parts of Scotland and which testify to limited post-Devonian erosion. In terms of basement rocks, levels of erosion have probably not exceeded 1.5 km in 300 Ma, a very low rate of long-term erosion (5 mm/ka). To this should be added an unknown thickness of former sedimentary cover rocks. It seems that during the Mesozoic, Scotland was a subdued terrain, with widespread marine transgressions at the close of the Triassic, Jurassic and Cretaceous periods. Intervening periods of uplift were of limited magnitude and the resultant sediment came mainly from the recycling of cover rocks. This means that the origins of the major relief elements in Scotland can be traced back to the Mesozoic and before.

The main Grampian watershed which today divides the waters which drain north to the Moray Firth (e.g. the Spey) from those which drain south to the Firth of Forth (e.g. the Tay) must have existed in the Devonian since Old Red Sandstone conglomerates, both north and south of the watershed, contain rocks derived from the Grampian area. The sedimentary basins of the inner Hebrides, Moray Firth and North Sea received detritus from adjacent uplands centred on the Long Island (the Outer Hebrides), the Shetland Platform, the Highlands and the Southern Uplands throughout much of the Mesozoic. This is because these are persistently buoyant structural elements which shed sediment to marginal basins which have a long-term tendency to subsidence.

3.3 Early Tertiary tectonics

In the Late Cretaceous, tropical seas covered most of Britain. Scotland had been reduced to an area of low relief (Figure 3.1). We know this because surrounding sedimentary basins, which earlier in the Mesozoic had been receiving lots of clastic sediments, were starved in the Late Cretaceous, and only the calcareous oozes of the Chalk accumulated.

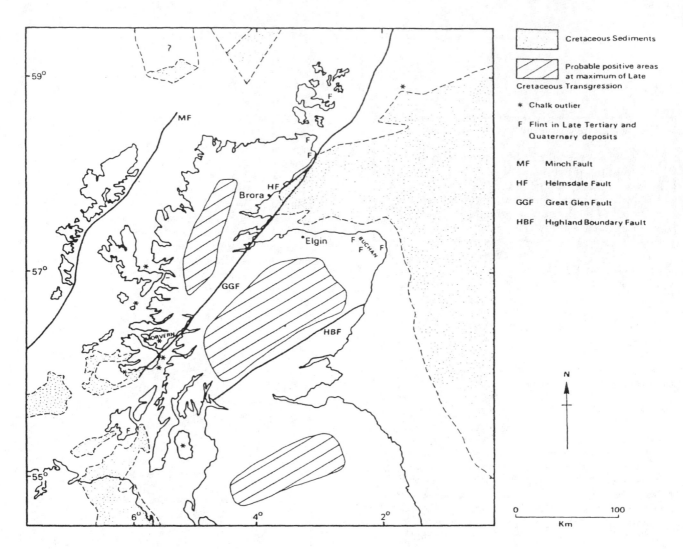

Figure 3.1 Late Cretaceous palaeogeography. (After Hall, 1991. Reproduced by permission of the Royal Society of Edinburgh from *Transactions of the Royal Society of Edinburgh: Earth Sciences* 82(1) (1991), pp. 1-26).

At around 60 Ma there was an extraordinary burst of tectonic and igneous activity in western Scotland (Chapter 2). Scotland was uplifted by 1 km or more and tilted towards the North Sea. There were major block movements along pre-existing faults, and Scotland must have been a high-risk area for earthquakes. Huge Icelandic-type volcanoes poured flow after flow of lava to give accumulations many hundreds of metres thick. Ash falls covered Britain and are preserved today in the London Clay of southern England. The pile of igneous and volcanic rocks which was produced at this time is called the Tertiary or Hebridean igneous province and formed in response to the opening of the Atlantic and, in particular, rifting of the east Atlantic margin.

In the Hebridean area, there were impressive differential fault movements (Figure 3.2). Over the main igneous centres there was intense uplift, perhaps 2 km or more, within bounding ring faults. Erosion was intense, with 2 km of lava removed from Mull in 2 Ma. Yet in parts of Skye, less than 40 km from the main igneous centres, great thicknesses of lava are preserved, demonstrating huge differential movements. Elsewhere in the Hebridean region, the Chalk and earlier Mesozoic sediments were stripped away and the basement was exposed to erosion. A lot of this sediment was carried east by rivers draining the tilted block and dumped in the North Sea to form thick Early Tertiary sand sequences.

Away from the Hebridean province it is less easy to reconstruct styles of Early Tertiary uplift and denudation. It used to be thought that the Tertiary dyke swarms which radiate from the igneous centres must imply deep erosion, for the dykes are exposed on some of the highest tops of the western Highlands. This is wrong because many dykes represent the sites of Eocene fissure eruptions and the presence of features such as vesicles and amygdales suggest that the dykes cooled close to the Tertiary landsurface. Instead, it seems that subsequent erosion was rather limited.

Early Tertiary uplift pushed up the Cairngorms and created mountain walls at the western and eastern edges of the northern Highlands. The summits, like An Teallach, which now line the coast of the Minch did not exist in the Late Cretaceous. Similarly, along the north shore of the Moray Firth, the Helmsdale Granite was covered by Cretaceous rocks until differential movement across the Helmsdale Fault pushed up the line of hills (*e.g.* inland from Helmsdale and Brora) which now faces the Moray Firth.

One way to get crude figures of Tertiary erosion for Scotland as a whole is to calculate sediment volumes in the North Sea basin and to relate them to the Scottish source area. This indicates that about 600-800 m of rock was removed from Scotland during the Tertiary. Today, there is only 25% of Scotland lying above 300 m and yet many summits, the Munros, reach 900-1000 m. These summits

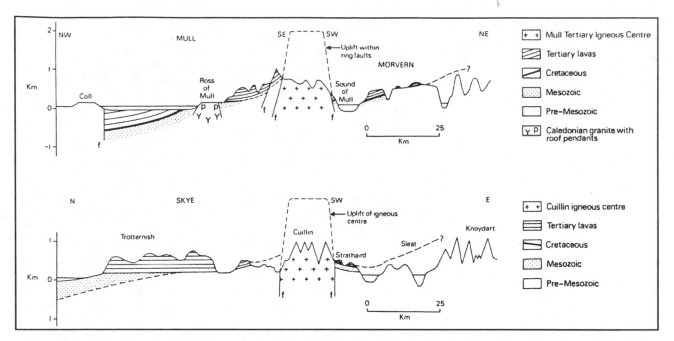

Figure 3.2 Early Tertiary fault movements in the Inner Hebrides. (After Hall, 1991. Reproduced by permission of the Royal Society of Edinburgh from *Transactions of the Royal Society of Edinburgh: Earth Sciences* 82(1) (1991), pp. 1-26).

define a surface whose elevation must lie within a few hundred metres of the sub-Cretaceous surface.

3.4 Tertiary environments

3.4.1 Tectonics

By 50 Ma, the Early Tertiary magmatism was at an end. In the North Sea, sedimentation rates dropped and sands were replaced by muds, and there followed a period of about 20 Ma when earth movements were rather limited. There was renewed uplift in the Late Oligocene, about 25 Ma, with formation of rift basins in western Britain from Devon to Stornoway and uplift of Fennoscandia. Uplift probably continued at a modest rate through the Miocene and Pliocene and into the Quaternary. Uplift probably was due to isostasy and continued subsidence of the North Sea basin, so that the tendency to tilt was continued. The depth of some of the west coast fjords may reflect the fact that Quaternary glaciers were cutting down into a still-rising Highland edge.

3.4.2 Climate

The Tertiary climate in Scotland was warm and humid. Humid-tropical conditions prevailed during the Eocene, but after a sharp drop in temperature in the Oligocene, the temperatures only recovered to sub-tropical levels. There is no evidence for aridity in Scotland after the start of the Tertiary. This is not surprising given the location of the country at the edge of a widening Atlantic Ocean.

3.4.3 Weathering

Hot and humid climates encourage deep chemical weathering. We know that intense weathering affected Scotland in the Tertiary because inter-bedded with Eocene lavas in Antrim and in western Scotland are laterites formed during phases of quiescence between eruptions. There are also sediments in the North Sea from the Palaeocene through to the Miocene which contain lots of kaolin clay and quartz sand and these materials can only have come from highly altered rocks. As far as we know, kaolin-rich weathering profiles are now preserved in only one region of Scotland,

the Buchan area, but through much of the Tertiary the terrain would have been underlain by weathering profiles many tens of metres deep and composed largely of kaolin and quartz. In other words, Scotland would have resembled areas of the humid tropics and sub-tropics today.

In the Late Miocene, the climate cooled to a more temperate regime and there was a fundamental change in weathering styles. Deep kaolinisation ceased and was replaced by deep grussification, where rocks were broken down to sandy regoliths in which lots of feldspar was preserved. These sandy weathering profiles are very widespread in Scotland and in pockets reach depths of up to 25 m. They represent a once continuous mantle of weathered rocks which covered Scotland in the latest Tertiary. In many areas this material was largely swept away by Quaternary ice sheets but enough survives to indicate that glacial erosion often has been limited to a depth of a few tens of metres at most (Chapter 4). In areas where this pre-glacial weathering survives, there is little doubt that the larger-scale landforms are basically of pre-glacial origin.

3.4.4 Valleys and drainage patterns

A remarkable feature of the Tertiary drainage lines in Scotland is how closely they correspond with present-day river valleys. In the Early Tertiary, a proto-Dee and Don river system fed sediment to the western North Sea (Figure 3.3). Around the Moray Firth, valleys once choked with Devonian sediments were cleaned out and re-utilised by the Tertiary rivers. The reasons for this persistence lie in the strong structural control on most valley alignments. For example, the new Keith by-pass crosses the River Isla where a section of the valley follows a Caledonian shear belt, a major line of weakness. Since patches of Old Red Sandstone occur in the valley, it must have been excavated by Devonian times. Beneath the valley floor, and causing major engineering problems, are highly altered schists that were weathered to a depth of over 30 m during the Tertiary. Similarly altered rock must have existed beneath many valley floors before the Ice Age and been cleaned out by Quaternary glaciers.

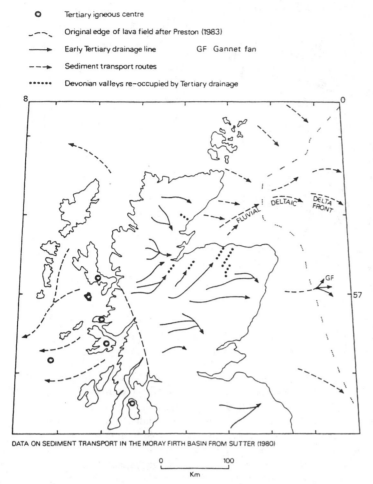

○   Tertiary igneous centre

⌒⌒   Original edge of lava field after Preston (1983)

⟶   Early Tertiary drainage line   GF   Gannet fan

⟶ - - Sediment transport routes

•••••• Devonian valleys re-occupied by Tertiary drainage

DATA ON SEDIMENT TRANSPORT IN THE MORAY FIRTH BASIN FROM SUTTER (1980)

Figure 3.3 Early Tertiary drainage and sediment transport. (After Hall 1991. Reproduced by permission of the Royal Society of Edinburgh from *Transactions of the Royal Society of Edinburgh: Earth Sciences* 82(1) (1991), pp. 1-26).

3.4.5 Topographic basins

Basins are a major feature of the scenery of the Highlands, large depressions strung out along the courses of the main rivers. Although the largest basins, like Rannoch Moor, have been scoured and modified by ice action, they nevertheless originated during the Tertiary. Some basins are even older and are exhumed features, uncovered from beneath a fill of Devonian sediments. The Cabrach basin, south-west of Huntly, is a good example. The key to understanding the formation of these basins lies in their relation to the underlying geology. Often the basins are located on outcrops of rocks susceptible to chemical weathering. In NE Scotland, many basins coincide with basic igneous intrusions. Elsewhere, biotite granites form the locus of basin development. As a result of Tertiary uplift and enhanced groundwater circulation, deep weathering has exploited compartments of weakness in such rocks and the loosened material has been removed by rivers.

3.4.6 Inselbergs and tors

In counter-point to basins are the inselbergs. These island mountains are often developed on resistant rocks, or at least rocks which are resistant to chemical weathering. Quartzite is an important inselberg-forming rock, as exemplified by the Paps of Jura and Schiehallion. Some inselbergs, however, do not correspond in any way with the margins of resistant

rock outcrops. The splendid chain of inselbergs which rise from the Lewisian basement north of Ullapool are formed in Torridonian sandstone which once covered this whole area. These hills are a result of parallel scarp retreat in near-horizontal, resistant sandstones as a consequence of warping (bending of a surface by uplift, without major dislocation such as faulting) of the western edge of the northern Highlands during the early Tertiary.

The small rocky knolls, or tors, which rise from the summits and slopes of the granite hills of the Cairngorms are related features. Here, joint density is the fundamental control on rates of weathering. The largest, monolithic tors on Ben Avon probably reflect a two-stage evolution, with deep weathering of surrounding fractured rock before glaciation and removal of this loose material by solifluction and related nival processes during the Ice Age (see Chapter 14). Smaller tors, with their encircling blockfields, may be simpler, younger features, created largely by differential frost action in the Quaternary. Although most tors show little or no signs of glacial erosion, a few have been disturbed and weakly moulded by the passage of ice and so demonstrate that an ice cap once covered the tops of the Cairngorms. The tors are therefore key landforms for determining the extent of cold-based, non-sliding glaciers (see Chapter 4) in the later stages of the Quaternary.

3.4.7 Scarps

Long, straight, steep slopes front many mountain and hill groups in Scotland. Examples include the Ochil escarpment east of Stirling and the edge of the eastern Grampians above the Mearns west of Brechin. In some cases, these are fault-line scarps, where movement along ancient faults has brought together rocks of unequal resistance and led to the weathering, erosion and lowering of the weaker rock and the formation of a linear depression. Elsewhere, scarps represent a stage in slope retreat, as in the Torridonian sandstone mountains north of Ullapool. In some cases, however, where rocks of low resistance form scarps and backing hills, it is reasonable to ask if Quaternary faulting has not been responsible for fault scarp development, especially as minor earthquakes continue today to affect faults such as the Great Glen Fault and the Highland Boundary Fault. In the Elgin area, for instance, faults which transect homogeneous lithologies are associated with scarps. If these block movements are not Quaternary in origin, then the only other possibility is that these are recently-exhumed Mesozoic horsts.

3.4.8 Erosion surfaces

Stepped erosion surfaces form level skylines which dominate the scenery of many parts of upland Scotland, at least in eastern areas. The standard model of erosion surface formation is that these erosional plains form close to sea level after a prolonged period of erosion and relief reduction and then are uplifted to form plateaux which are slowly dissected and destroyed. This cannot apply in Scotland as upland areas have been elevated since the early Tertiary and so these higher surfaces have evolved well above sea level. Many erosion surfaces are, in fact, etch surfaces where differences in rock resistance have been exploited by prolonged chemical weathering. The rock surface is lowered as the weathered material is stripped away. Landforms of differential weathering, like basins and tors, develop on the etch surface, but low relief is maintained until valley incision begins the process of dissection. Thus high-level surfaces which form major watersheds, like those of the Cairngorms, have been evolving by etch processes for the last 50 Ma.

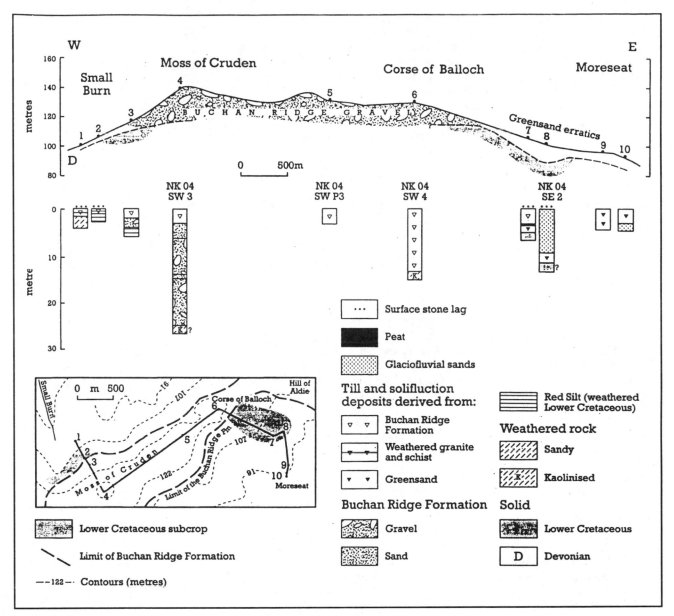

Figure 3.4 Long-term landscape evolution at Moss of Cruden, Buchan. (After Hall 1993).

3.5 The case of Buchan: the best preserved pre-glacial landscape in Scotland?

Probably the best preserved pre-glacial landsurface in Scotland is in Buchan. This is because Buchan experienced limited uplift in the Tertiary and little glacial erosion in the Quaternary (see Chapter 4). Here are found the deepest weathering profiles in Scotland, extending for 50 m or more below the ground surface. Here, also, are the most intensely altered rocks – kaolinised granites and metamorphic rocks. The whole landscape is made up of low hills, valleys and basins whose position in the topography reflects the relative resistance of the rocks that form them.

At Moss of Cruden, near Peterhead, there is a fascinating sequence of rocks (Figure 3.4). The Peterhead granite is overlain by a patch of Devonian sandstone, no more than a single field in area, but important because it shows that the granite was unroofed in the Devonian. Thus the landsurface at 400 Ma was at a similar level to that of today. Also resting on the granite is a small and highly weathered outlier of Lower Cretaceous greensand. This is the final remnant of the Mesozoic rocks which once covered this area and which preserved the underlying granite from erosion. Cut into the granite are 25 m deep river channels filled with flint gravels. The flint comes from a former cover of chalk, weathered away before deposition of the gravels. The gravels are full of kaolin and quartz sand and are clearly derived from a highly weathered landscape. Moreover, the few granite clasts in the gravels are themselves kaolinised, and so the gravels were intensely weathered after deposition. How old are these gravels? It is not clear for they contain no fossils, but the intensity of weathering indicates a Tertiary age. Since their deposition by some now-lost river flowing to the North Sea, the gravels have had a long weathering history and now cap low hills and ridges. It is possible that these gravels represent torrential deposits shed eastward from the newly-uplifted Cairngorms in the early Tertiary. What we see at Moss of Cruden is a continuity of landform evolution over 400 Ma, showing that in some parts of Scotland, landforms can be very old.

3.6 Conclusion

The form of the landscape of Scotland, particularly in the south and east, displays a series of distinct relief elements that strongly reflect an inheritance from pre-glacial times.

These include erosion surfaces, topographic basins, scarps, inselbergs and tors. Pre-glacial elements are also evident in the evolution of the drainage pattern and in the presence of chemically altered bedrock that weathered under warmer and more humid climatic conditions during the Tertiary. The survival of these features, the oldest of which may date back to the Devonian (400 Ma), reflects variations in the intensity of glacial erosion and emphasises the antiquity of significant parts of the present Scottish landscape.

Further reading

Andrews, I.J., Long, D., Richards, P.C., Thomson, A.R., Brown, S., Chesher, J.A. and McCormac, M. 1990. *United Kingdom Offshore Regional Report: the Geology of the Moray Firth*. British Geological Survey, HMSO, London.

Ballantyne, C.K. 1994. The tors of the Cairngorms. *Scottish Geographical Magazine,* 110, 54-59.

Craig, G.Y. (Ed.) 1991. *Geology of Scotland*. The Geological Society, London.

George, T.N. 1966. Geomorphic evolution in Hebridean Scotland. *Scottish Journal of Geology,* 2, 1-34.

Godard, A. 1965. *Recherches de Géomorphologie en Écosse du Nord-Ouest*. Masson et Cie, Paris.

Hall, A.M. 1985. Cenozoic weathering covers in Buchan, Scotland, and their significance. *Nature,* 315, 392-395.

Hall, A.M. 1991. Pre-Quaternary landscape evolution in the Scottish Highlands. *Transactions of the Royal Society of Edinburgh: Earth Sciences,* 82, 1-26.

Hall, A.M. 1993. Moss of Cruden. In: Gordon, J.E. and Sutherland, D.G. (Eds), *Quaternary of Scotland*. Chapman & Hall, London, 218-221.

Hillis, R.R., Thomson, K. and Underhill, J.R. 1993. Quantification of Tertiary erosion in the Inner Moray Firth by sonic velocity data from the Chalk and Kimmeridge Clay. *Marine and Petroleum Geology,* 11, 283-293.

Le Coeur, C. 1988. Late Tertiary warping and erosion in western Scotland. *Geografiska Annaler,* 70A, 361-368.

Lewis, C.L.E., Green, P.F., Carter, A. and Hurford, A.J. 1992. Elevated K/T paleotemperatures throughout Northwest England: three kilometres of Tertiary erosion? *Earth and Planetary Science Letters,* 112, 131-145.

Lewis, C.L.E., Carter, A. and Hurford, A.J. 1992. Low-temperature effects of the Skye Tertiary intrusions of Mesozoic sediments in the Sea of the Hebrides basin. In: Barnell, J. (Ed.), *Basins on the North Atlantic Seaboard: Petroleum Geology, Sedimentology and Basin Evolution*. The Geological Society, London, 175-188.

Thomas, M.F. 1994. *Geomorphology in the Tropics*. Wiley, Chichester.

Watson, J. 1985. Scotland as an Atlantic-North Sea divide. *Journal of the Geological Society of London,* 142, 221-243.

4. The Dynamics of Ice Sheets and Glaciers

Neil F. Glasser

The key themes covered in this chapter are:

- glacier mass balance;
- processes of ice flow;
- the role of basal ice temperatures;
- patterns and rates of ice flow;
- reconstructing former glaciers and ice sheets.

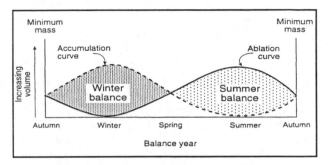

Figure 4.1 An accumulation curve (dotted line) and an ablation curve (solid line) for an ice sheet over one balance year. The winter balance is positive and the summer balance negative, but over the entire year the two are equal. In this situation the net mass balance is therefore zero and the ice sheet will neither grow nor decay.

4.1 Introduction

The aim of this chapter is to describe the main processes which operate beneath modern ice sheets and glaciers and to demonstrate the role these processes played in shaping the Scottish landscape during the ice ages of the Quaternary. The following topics are discussed: glacier mass balance, the mechanisms of ice flow within ice sheets and glaciers, the role of ice temperature and basal thermal regime, the patterns and rates of ice flow in glaciers, the methods by which former ice sheets and glaciers can be reconstructed, and the means by which all these processes have interacted to produce the various landscapes of glacial erosion and deposition which are found in Scotland today.

4.2 Glacier mass balance

A knowledge of glacier **mass balance** is vital to an understanding of how ice sheets work. Mass balance concerns the inputs to, and outputs from, the glacial system, and can be thought of as the net gain or loss of snow and ice across a glacier. A glacier forms whenever a body of snow accumulates, compacts and begins the transformation to ice. Glaciers can therefore form in any climatic zone where more snow accumulates annually than is melted, whether this is because the amount of annual snowfall is sufficiently high for some to survive warm summers (such as in the Southern Alps of New Zealand) or because low summer temperatures are insufficient to melt even a meagre winter snowfall (such as in Antarctica). The inputs to the glacial system are those which add mass and are collectively known as **accumulation**. They include fresh snow, hail, frost, avalanched snow and rainfall. The outputs from the system are known as **ablation** and include anything which removes mass from the glacier, such as direct ice melt, iceberg calving and sublimation. The rates at which these processes occur are known as the accumulation rate and the ablation rate, respectively. In climatic zones where there is high accumulation and high ablation (for example, in many Alpine areas), glacier ice can form relatively fast; but in climatic zones where there is low accumulation and low ablation (for example, Antarctica), the transformation of snow to glacier ice is much slower. In any area where accumulation is greater than ablation, a glacier can begin to grow and expand until such time as the ablation rate exceeds the accumulation rate, at which point it will begin to slowly shrink in size. This cycle of growth and decay has occurred many times in Scotland during the Quaternary, resulting in the growth of both large ice sheets which covered all but the highest mountains and the development of much smaller and more restricted corrie glaciers and mountain icefields (Chapter 5).

Mass balance is therefore concerned with the overall balance between accumulation and ablation across a glacier or ice sheet (Bennett and Glasser, 1996). It is largely dependent on the prevailing climate since this determines the accumulation and ablation rates. In general, ablation tends to dominate in the warm summer months and accumulation dominates in the winter months (Figure 4.1). The exception to this rule is where an ice sheet or glacier terminates in water, and where iceberg calving may occur at any time of the year. The rate of growth or retreat of a glacier is determined by the difference between the accumulation and ablation rates (called the **net mass balance**, and usually measured over the course of a year). When the two are equal, the glacier is said to be in balance and will remain constant in size, but when the accumulation rate is greater than the ablation rate (positive mass balance), the glacier will grow and expand in size. When the ablation rate is greater (negative mass balance), the glacier will begin to shrink in size and gradually disappear. Since accumulation and ablation are largely dependent on climate, they are not equal across the surface of a glacier. Ablation tends to dominate at the terminus where the climate is relatively mild and where iceberg calving may occur, whereas accumulation tends to dominate in the upper reaches where temperatures tend to be lower and precipitation (snowfall) higher. The point on a glacier where accumulation equals ablation is known as the **equilibrium line**, normally expressed as an altitude in metres above sea level. At present in Scotland, the equilibrium line lies above the level of the highest land and glacier ice cannot form. However, if the annual temperature were to drop several degrees or snowfall were to increase, it is conceivable that many of the highest mountain corries could support small glaciers (see Chapter 5).

4.3 Ice flow

Once a glacier is established, it flows primarily because the ice within it deforms under the influence of gravity. This gravitational force is a result of the fact that a glacier slopes downwards towards its terminus and because of the spatial imbalance between accumulation and ablation described above. As a rule of thumb, the greater the imbalance

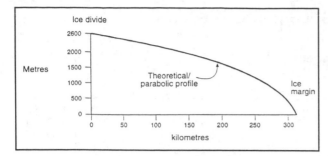

Figure 4.2 The parabolic surface profile observed on most ice sheets which flow over rigid beds. In this example, the distance from the ice divide to the ice margin is slightly over 300 km and ice sheet is 2600 m thick at the divide. This parabolic profile is commonly used in the reconstruction of former ice sheets, but note the absence of any basal topography to complicate the theoretical profile.

between accumulation and ablation, the greater the rate of ice flow and the steeper the surface gradient of the glacier. The flow of ice enables a glacier to transfer the mass accumulated in its upper regions to its lower regions, thus maintaining a relatively constant surface slope. If there is no surface slope or no imbalance between accumulation and ablation, a glacier will not flow. Glacial mass balance is therefore the overall driving force of a glacier. The physical mechanism responsible for flow is the deformation of ice under the influence of gravity (known as the **shear stress**). Although crystalline, ice behaves as a plastic material: it is brittle at very high imposed stresses but flows at lower and more slowly applied stresses. The level of shear stress beneath an ice sheet depends upon both the surface slope of the glacier and the thickness of the ice. The highest shear stresses are found in situations where the ice is both thick and steep. Since ice is a relatively plastic substance, it begins to deform under low values of shear stress and, partly because of this, the values of shear stress found beneath modern glaciers are relatively constant (usually between 50 and 100 kilopascals). Because of the latter, it follows that where an ice sheet is thick it must have a shallow surface slope, and that where it is thin it must have a steep surface slope. As a rule, most ice sheets and glaciers have a parabolic cross section when viewed in profile, with steep slopes near the margin and shallow slopes in the upper reaches (Figure 4.2). This is an important rule because it means that the approximate surface profiles of former ice sheets and glaciers can be reconstructed if their former margins are known.

Ice sheets and glaciers flow in response to the applied shear stress by three different mechanisms: internal deformation, basal sliding and subglacial bed deformation (Figure 4.3). They operate as follows.

4.3.1 Internal deformation

Internal deformation of a glacier is achieved in two ways: by the process of ice creep and by large scale folding and faulting. Ice creep is the mutual displacement of ice crystals relative to one another in response to the applied shear stress, causing a slow forward motion in the direction of the ice surface slope. The rate of ice creep is a function of the shear stress, so the greater the applied shear stress, the greater the rate of creep. This explains why the greatest deformation in glaciers is at the base because it is here that the highest shear stresses are found (because ice thickness is high). At a much larger scale, the internal deformation of ice can also be caused by folding and faulting. This is

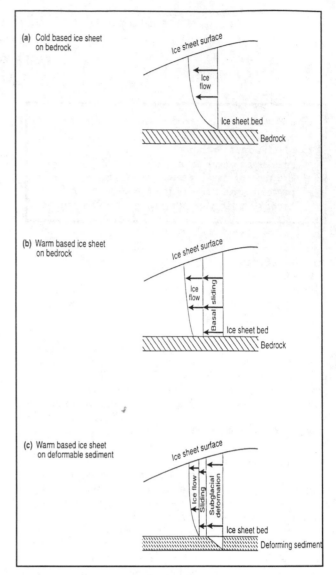

Figure 4.3 The velocity distribution for sections of three ice sheets with different basal thermal regimes and bedrock conditions. **A**: for a cold-based ice sheet resting on rigid bedrock, all movement is due to internal deformation (depicted as 'ice flow'), and velocity increases towards the ice surface. **B**: for a warm-based ice sheet resting on rigid bedrock, movement is due to a combination of basal sliding and internal deformation, and velocity again increases towards the ice surface. **C**: for a warm-based ice sheet resting on a deformable bed, movement can take place by all three flow processes – subglacial deformation, basal sliding and internal deformation.

especially common in situations where ice creep alone cannot adjust sufficiently fast to the stresses set up within the ice, causing folds and faults to develop. These structures are common in areas where a glacier encounters a sudden change in ice velocity, for example at topographic features such as bedrock steps or large constrictions.

4.3.2 Basal sliding

Basal sliding is the name given to the process whereby a glacier slides across its bed, often across a thin film of lubricating meltwater. There are two main processes responsible for this: enhanced basal creep and regelation (refreezing) slip. The first of these, **enhanced basal creep**, occurs as basal ice deforms around irregularities on the bed such as bedrock bumps or lodged boulders. As the ice moves against the obstacle, basal shear stresses increase sufficiently to cause an increase in the rate of ice creep (hence the name of this process). This allows the ice to move more efficiently around obstacles on the bed. The larger the obstacle, the greater the increase in basal shear stress and therefore the greater the rate of deformation. Theoretical calculations suggest that this process is most effective around obstacles which are larger than 15cm in size. The second mechanism of basal sliding, **regelation slip**, occurs when ice at its melting point encounters smaller obstacles on its bed. Basal shear stresses and ice pressures increase on the upstream side in the manner outlined above. This causes a layer of basal ice to melt, and the meltwater produced then flows around the obstacle before refreezing in its lee. This process is most effective around obstacles under 15cm in size because the latent heat released by the refreezing of the meltwater can be transferred from the downstream side of the obstacle, through the obstacle itself, to assist with ice melting on the upstream side. Glaciers which flow by basal sliding generally experience rates of ice flow an order of magnitude greater than those which flow by internal deformation alone.

4.3.3 Subglacial bed deformation

Subglacial bed deformation is the name given to the process by which unfrozen sediment beneath a glacier deforms under the weight of the overlying ice. It occurs when the water pressure in the pore spaces between sediment grains rises sufficiently to reduce the resistance between individual grains, allowing them to flow relative to one another as a slurry or deforming carpet of sediment. This is an important process beneath some modern glaciers (for example, it has been estimated that 90% of the velocity of Breidamerkurjökull in Iceland is due to subglacial bed deformation), and while its significance has yet to be fully assessed, it was probably important beneath the terrestrial parts of former Scottish ice sheets in areas of the lowlands where deformable sediments occur (Chapter 13), as well as in offshore areas (Chapter 7).

4.4 Basal thermal regime

Just as accumulation and ablation vary across a glacier, so the temperature of the ice both at its surface and at its base may also vary. The variations in temperature underneath a glacier constitute its **basal thermal regime**. The principles involved are complicated but they are vital to an understanding of the landscape produced by a glacier because the basal thermal regime is a primary control on the resulting patterns of erosion and deposition. For example, the temperature at the base of a glacier controls which of the above flow processes (ice creep, basal sliding and subglacial deformation) can occur and therefore the dynamics of the glacier. In terms of basal thermal regime, there are two fundamental types of glacier: cold-based and warm-based glaciers. Where a glacier is frozen to its bed, it is deemed to be **cold-based**; no meltwater is produced and basal sliding does not occur. Where a glacier is **warm-based**, however, basal ice is constantly melting and meltwater is produced. The lubricating layer of meltwater means that basal sliding is an important component of ice flow. Only glaciers which are warm-based can flow by basal sliding, whereas cold-based glaciers move by internal deformation alone (Figure 4.3). A glacier which is warm-based therefore has the potential for greater flow rates than one which is cold-based, and as a result has a greater ability to modify its bed.

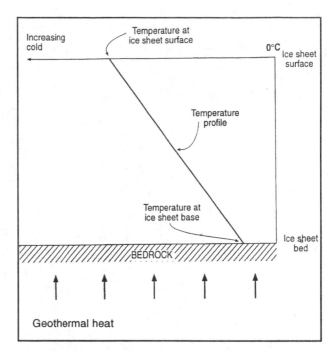

Figure 4.4 Schematic diagram to illustrate the temperature distribution in an ice sheet. Temperatures are highest near the base where geothermal heat flow from the Earth and frictional heat due to ice flow are greatest. They decrease towards the ice surface as heat can be conducted through the ice towards the relatively cold exterior.

4.4.1 Factors affecting the basal thermal regime of an ice sheet or glacier

The basal thermal regime of an ice sheet or glacier is determined by the balance between the heat generated at the base of the glacier and the temperature gradient within the ice, which determines the rate at which that heat is drawn away from the base towards the ice surface above. Heat is generated beneath a glacier by the geothermal heat which enters its base from the Earth below and by the frictional heat produced as a result of basal sliding and internal deformation (Figure 4.4). Many interlinked factors determine the basal thermal regime of a glacier but the most important are ice thickness, ice surface temperature, geothermal heat and frictional heat. The role of individual factors is as follows. Increasing ice thickness causes basal ice temperatures to rise since ice is a relatively good insulator, and the thicker the ice the more heat it can retain at its base. An increase in the atmospheric air temperature at the ice surface also causes the basal temperature to increase because it reduces the temperature gradient within the glacier. A low ice surface temperature means that annual layers of snow accumulate at low temperatures and as this snow is incorporated into the glacier and moves downwards, it causes a slow cooling of the basal layers. Increasing the amount of geothermal heat increases the basal ice temperature. The same is true of frictional heat production which is primarily a result of the overall ice velocity. Of these latter two variables, frictional heat production is quantitatively the most important since a glacier velocity of only 20 ma^{-1} is sufficient to produce the same amount of heat as the average geothermal heat flux.

It is possible to predict theoretically the situations likely to produce cold- and warm-based ice. Cold-based glaciers are likely to occur where a glacier is thin and slow moving,

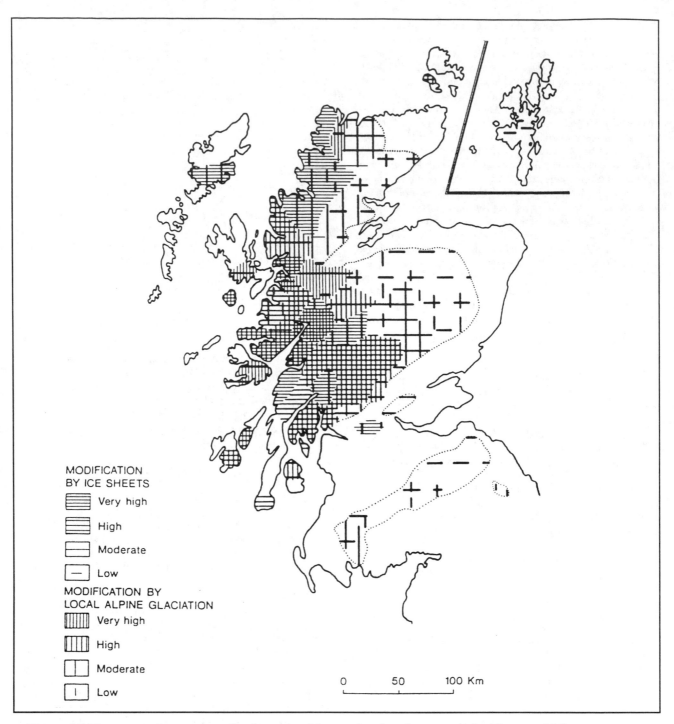

**MODIFICATION
BY ICE SHEETS**

▤ Very high

▤ High

▤ Moderate

▭ Low

**MODIFICATION BY
LOCAL ALPINE GLACIATION**

▥ Very high

▥ High

▢ Moderate

▢ Low

0   50   100 Km

Figure 4.5 Variation in the intensity of landscape modification by glacial erosion. (After Haynes, 1995).

and where the surface layers are cooled severely in winter. Warm-based glaciers are likely to occur where the ice is thick and fast moving. Although it would therefore seem a simple task to predict the basal thermal regime beneath a glacier, the interaction of many other variables makes this more complex than we might think. For example, increasing ice thickness will tend to cause a rise in basal ice temperature due to the insulating effect, but this will be offset by the occurrence of snow accumulation at an increasing altitude, and therefore lower temperatures, tending to cause a drop in basal ice temperatures. There is also a continuum between warm- and cold-based glaciers, as well as the potential for the basal thermal regime to vary both in time and space within a single glacier. For example, many glaciers in circumpolar areas such as Svalbard are polythermal, with a

zone of basal melting in their accumulation zones, a zone of basal freezing at their margins and a transition zone between the two. The basal thermal regime of a glacier may also change over time, for example due to a change in overall temperature or a change in accumulation rate.

The importance of basal thermal regime in determining the processes of landscape evolution beneath glaciers is now recognised, and it is acknowledged that warm-based ice is capable of erosion an order of magnitude greater than cold-based ice. Areas such as the Cairngorm Mountains, with their deep glacial troughs and little-modified plateau surfaces, illustrate very well that where an ice mass has a variable basal thermal regime it is possible to produce a highly selective pattern of glacial erosion. On a larger scale, calculations of the basal thermal regime of former Scottish ice sheets show that the pattern of basal ice temperatures can accurately predict the pattern of erosion across wide areas of the landscape, with a close correlation between areas of the former ice sheet which experienced basal melting and areas of intense glacial erosion. These calculations provide a basis for explaining the location of the different landscapes of glacial erosion that are found in Scotland, in particular the difference between the landforms indicating intense glacial erosion in western Scotland and the more selectively eroded eastern Highlands (Figure 4.5). In contrast, relatively little is known about the basal thermal regime of the small glaciers which have periodically occupied the Scottish corries or of the pattern of basal temperatures which characterised the Loch Lomond Stadial icefields (Chapter 8). Although the West Highland icefield was a relatively thin ice mass, it is tempting to suggest that, because of its location, the heavy precipitation and rugged terrain caused some or all of its outlet glaciers to be warm-based. Although further corroboration is required, certainly the volume of morainic material deposited by these glaciers suggests that they were capable of a great deal of erosion in a relatively short period of time.

4.5 Patterns of ice flow

The flow of ice within a glacier follows the direction of surface slope, because this corresponds to the direction of maximum shear stress. This explains why ice sheets and glaciers are capable of flowing against the grain of the underlying topography and even uphill in certain cases. In an ice sheet, flow is outward from the summit of the ice sheet (the ice divide) towards its margins. In the accumulation zone, this flow is downwards into the ice, counteracting the upward growth of the ice surface as new snow is added annually. In the ablation zone, flow is upwards towards the surface, counteracting surface lowering due to ablation. Similar patterns of ice flow are found in a valley glacier, except that the rates of movement are influenced by the frictional drag of the valley walls. Maximum ice flow is therefore in the centre of the glacier and near its surface, decreasing closer to the valley walls as the frictional resistance to flow increases. In most ice sheets or glaciers, overall rates of flow increase from the ice divide outwards to the equilibrium line, before decreasing towards the margin. This is because, if the glacier is in balance, all mass accumulated upstream of any point on its surface must be evacuated through that point. The rate of flow is therefore greatest near the equilibrium line because mass is continually being added to the glacier upstream of this point. The rate of flow then decreases downstream of the equilibrium line because increasingly mass is lost through the processes of ablation. This pattern is significant because it implies that there will be little or no geomorphological activity beneath ice divides, because of the low velocities there, and that most geomorphological activity will take place at the equilibrium line because of the fast rates of flow. The last ice sheet to cover Scotland probably had its ice divide located relatively far towards the more maritime west coast. In north-west Scotland, for example, reconstructions of the former ice sheet suggest that the ice divide lay at an altitude of over 900 metres above present sea level over the Beinn Dearg massif and the Fannich mountains (McCarroll *et al.*, 1995).

4.6   Rates of ice flow

Most glaciers have velocities in the range of 3 to 300 m a^{-1} but velocities of up to 1 or 2 km a^{-1} can be attained in steep terrain or where there is a high throughput of mass through the glacial system. This explains why glaciers in maritime areas with high annual snowfall tend to have the highest velocities and are able to descend from mountain ranges as far as sea level even in mild climatic zones. For example, the San Rafael Glacier in Chilean Patagonia is fed by an ice cap which receives up to 5 m of snow annually, and as a consequence it has been measured at a velocity of up to 19 m per day (7 km a^{-1}). These great velocities mean that it reaches sea level to calve icebergs at a latitude equivalent to that of southern France. Additionally, some outlet glaciers of the large Greenland and Antarctic ice sheets have velocities of as much as 7 to 10 km a^{-1} in situations where ice flow is channelled down large troughs. These glaciers are known as **ice streams** and are important because they drain large areas of these ice sheets. They are thought to be permanent or semi-permanent features since their fast rates of flow are not limited by the supply of ice accumulating upstream. It is likely that parts of the former Scottish ice sheet were drained by such ice streams, with present day valleys such as the Dee, Spey and Forth being major ice discharge routes. Further west, where the topography is more heavily dissected, the role of ice streams is less clear but it is probable that individual glens were still important in providing major routes for ice discharge.

Some glaciers also experience periodic **surges** in ice flow, when velocities of 10 to 100 times the normal have been recorded. Unlike the ice streams described above, these surges are usually limited by the amount of ice available in the accumulation zone, so that the increased flow rates cannot be sustained and the glaciers alternate between periods of accelerated flow (the surges) and periods of normal flow (quiescence). Only about 4% of the world's glaciers are prone to surging, and these are confined to certain geographical areas such as Svalbard and Alaska. One of the most famous surging glaciers is the Variegated Glacier in Alaska, which has surged several times this century alone. The mechanisms and precise controls on glacial surges are still not fully understood and this is an area of ongoing research. Surging glaciers produce a distinctive suite of landforms, including folded and thrusted sediments and moraines, but recognising these landforms in the record of former ice sheets is problematic and the importance of surges in Scottish glaciers is still not clear.

4.7 Reconstructing former ice sheets and glaciers

By studying modern glaciers we can learn the physical laws which govern the growth and movement of ice sheets and the processes which operate within them. Using the principle that former ice sheets behaved in the same manner as present day ice sheets, these physical laws can be extrapolated back in time to reconstruct the ice sheets which formerly existed in areas such as Scotland. Many techniques can be used to do this, but the most commonly used lines of evidence are the position of ice-marginal constructional features such as end moraines and lateral moraines, evidence from features of glacial erosion such as the orientation of striations, friction cracks or roches moutonnées, the position of meltwater features such as eskers or meltwater channels, erratic dispersal and transport paths, clast fabric analysis (the orientation of stones in glacial deposits), evidence from trimlines and theoretical models based on glaciological criteria. In the following section some of these features are examined using examples drawn from the Scottish Quaternary.

4.7.1   Evidence from glacial deposition

Probably the most common means of reconstructing former glaciers is by the mapping of the depositional landforms left behind as they grew, advanced and decayed

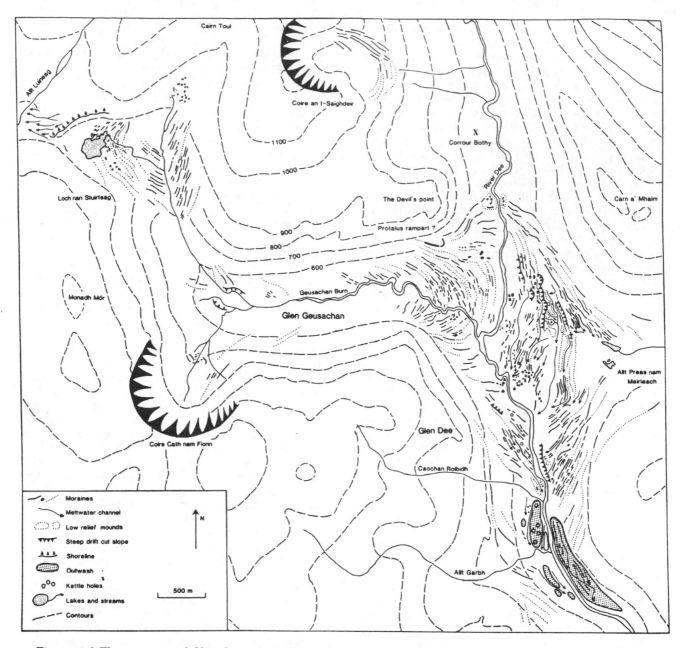

Figure 4.6 The moraines of Glen Geusachan. The moraines form a series of alignments and are interpreted as ice marginal landforms, representing the active recession of a glacier towards the head of the glen. (Reprinted from 'The glacial landforms of Glen Geusachan, Cairngorms: a reinterpretation' by M.R. Bennett and N.F. Glasser, from *Scottish Geographical Magazine,* 107, 1991, 116-123, by permission of the Royal Scottish Geographical Society.)

(see Chapter 8). In this category fall landforms such as end moraines, medial moraines, lateral moraines and glaciofluvial features such as eskers, kames and kettle holes. These landforms can be used to determine the position of a glacier and its change over time. This technique is especially powerful when used in conjunction with dating methods which can establish the time period in question and a relative sequence of events. It is, however, not without its controversy. This point is illustrated by the moraines of Glen Geusachan in the Cairngorms Mountains (Figure 4.6). Within the Cairngorms there are numerous glacial deposits of different ages. Some relate to the deglaciation of the last Scottish ice sheet, while others were deposited during the return to glacial conditions during the Loch Lomond Stadial (*cf.* Chapter 8). At this time an icefield existed in the Western Highlands (Bennett and Boulton, 1993a, 1993b) and small glaciers in the Cairngorms. The moraines of Glen

Geusachan were first mapped by Sugden (1970) who interpreted them in terms of the prevailing model of the time which stressed the importance of glaciofluvial landforms and ice sheet stagnation. He argued that most of the landforms pre-dated the Loch Lomond Stadial. This view was vigorously challenged by Sissons (1979). He dismissed the glaciofluvial interpretation and suggested that the landforms were best interpreted as hummocky moraine produced by the stagnation of a small valley glacier. In turn, this interpretation was challenged by Bennett and Glasser (1991). They agreed that the moraines were the product of a Loch Lomond Stadial valley glacier, but mapped them as individual ice-marginal landforms formed at an actively retreating ice margin (Figure 4.6). This example highlights the difficulty in interpreting the glacial landscape and the former glacier dynamics, in the absence of independent dating control.

4.7.2 Evidence from glacial erosion

The lines which separate glacially eroded bedrock in valleys from weathered or frost-shattered rock above are known as **trimlines**. They can be used in the reconstruction of former ice sheets because they mark the maximum level to which an ice sheet has eroded or 'trimmed' a pre-existing zone of frost-weathered rock or debris on a hillslope (*cf.* Chapter 14). Trimlines therefore mark the maximum surface altitude or vertical extent of former glaciers. When mapped across several mountains, they can also be used to reconstruct the horizontal and vertical dimensions of the glaciers and therefore their former surface profiles. For example in north-west Scotland, McCarroll *et al.* (1995) have mapped the distribution of frost shattered bedrock on mountain summits and found that the trimline this forms with glacially eroded bedrock can be used to calculate the surface gradient of the last ice sheet. They suggest that at its maximum the ice sheet was not thick enough to cover completely the highest mountains and that these summits would have stood above the ice surface as nunataks. Elsewhere, on Skye, Ballantyne (1994) found that many of the upper mountain slopes are mantled with gibbsitic soils (gibbsite is a clay mineral characteristic of soils weathered in a temperate climate) but that on the lower slopes the gibbsitic soils are uncommon or absent because they have been removed by glacial erosion. By mapping the vertical extent of these soils in a transect across several mountains, he was able to estimate the height and surface slope of the former glaciers. Both these studies show that the ice sheet had a comparatively low surface gradient, averaging 4.5 m/km (0.26°), and that across the NW tip of the Scottish mainland the ice surface altitude was probably less than 500 m above present sea level. In particular, this work also demonstrates that at the time this area was last glaciated, the ice sheet was not sufficiently large to extend to the Outer Hebrides and that these islands must have supported an independent ice cap.

Erratic dispersal is the study of the transport routes of debris (especially larger 'erratic' rocks and boulders) beneath ice sheets and glaciers. The technique works in the following way. As an ice sheet flows over and erodes bedrock it can entrain a variety of different lithologies. By mapping the distribution of these erratics and matching them to their source areas, it is possible to reconstruct the former ice flow directions and ice flow patterns required to produce the pattern observed. This technique is particularly appropriate in areas with distinctive or varied bedrock lithology and was used by Thorp (1987) to reconstruct a distinctive radial pattern of flow of the last ice sheet outwards from the area around Rannoch Moor. Although erratic dispersal is a good indicator of former ice flow directions and ice flow patterns, it does not provide great insight into the physical dimensions of the ice sheet, changes in the configuration of the ice sheet over time or the age of events. A further example of the use of glacial erosional evidence to reconstruct former ice sheet dynamics, from North Wales, is given by Sharp *et al.* (1989). They used the location and depth of glacial striations and small scale features of glacial abrasion on bedrock to reconstruct former ice flow directions, basal ice pressures and velocities for a former ice sheet in the area. Their work illustrates the potential for using landforms of glacial erosion to reconstruct former ice sheet dynamics.

4.7.3 Glaciological modelling of former ice sheets

Glaciological theory is a useful tool in the reconstruction of former ice sheets. The most common means of doing this is to use mathematical models based on the known physical properties of glaciers to simulate the behaviour of an ice sheet. In this way, both the internal variables (such as flow rates or basal thermal regime) and external variables (such as climate) in the ice sheet system can be estimated and used to build a predictive model of a former ice sheet. For example, Payne and Sugden (1990) used a computer model to predict the extent of the Loch Lomond Stadial ice cap in Scotland. Their model used the prevailing temperature and precipitation as climatic inputs and the present day topography to represent the ice sheet bed. The output of the model is the extent of the ice cap at various time stages. When compared to the known ice limits, the model quite accurately replicates the geomorphological evidence. The model also demonstrates the sensitivity of this ice cap to topography, since it grew faster and more dramatically in basins than on topographic ridges. Such models, based on glaciological theory, are good for predicting the pattern of growth and dimensions of former ice sheets, although care must be taken since the models are only as good as the physical laws and input parameters on which they are based. A good example of this is the two models of the last British ice sheet produced by Boulton *et al.* (1977) and Boulton *et al.* (1991). In the first of these, the ice sheet was considered to have been sufficiently thick to cover even the highest of the Scottish mountains with hundreds of metres of ice (Boulton *et al.*, 1977). However, after the discovery that some former ice sheets that crossed areas of deformable sediment possessed much lower surface profiles than ice sheets' on rigid beds (Boulton and Hindmarsh, 1987), this model was revised. The later model of Boulton *et al.* (1991) therefore shows that some of the higher mountains of north-west Scotland remained above the last ice sheet as nunataks, which fits with the field evidence discussed above.

Glaciological models can also be used to reconstruct the dynamics of former ice sheets as well as simply their overall form. For example, both Gordon (1979) and Glasser (1995) have used models based on glacier theory to calculate the basal thermal regime of parts of former Scottish ice sheets. The results of these models show that a lot of the variation in the pattern of glacial erosion and deposition in Scotland can be explained by changes in the temperatures at the base of the ice sheets. In particular, areas of basal melting are associated with areas of intense erosion, whereas areas of basal freezing are associated with areas of limited glacial erosion. These types of models go a long way to explaining the patterns of area of scouring in northern Scotland, the spectacular landscapes of selective linear erosion developed in areas such as the Cairngorm Mountains (Sugden 1968) and the preservation beneath ice sheets of older pre-glacial landsurfaces in eastern Scotland (Hall and Sugden 1987) (see also Chapters 3 and 13).

4.8 Conclusions

By studying present day ice sheets and glaciers it is possible to learn a great deal about the processes associated with them. In this way a detailed body of knowledge has been built up concerning glaciological processes such as mass balance, ice flow and basal thermal regime. There is also a large literature concerning the types of landforms, both erosional and depositional, produced by present day ice sheets and glaciers. By the careful mapping and study of these landforms in formerly glaciated landscapes such as Scotland, it is therefore possible to make inferences about the processes operating beneath former ice sheets during the Quaternary. In this way we can learn a great deal about how the ice sheets modified the landscape. We can also use the landforms to reconstruct the physical dimensions and behaviour of the ice sheets, an important tool in predicting the possible future behaviour of present day ice sheets and glaciers.

Further reading

A general review of the principles of glacial mass balance and ice flow can be found in text books by Sugden and John (1976) and by Bennett and Glasser (1996). Paterson (1994) tackles the subject from a more theoretical angle and Drewry (1996) puts glacial mass balance into a more global perspective using examples from present day ice sheets. Andrews (1972) explains the significance of mass balance to geomorphological studies. Hooke (1977) explains the fundamentals of basal thermal regime, and Boulton (1972) illustrates its significance to glacial sedimentation. Gordon (1979) and Glasser (1995) both provide examples of how the basal thermal regime of former Scottish ice sheets can be calculated and the relevance of basal ice temperatures to studies of glacial erosion. The operation of ice streams is reviewed by Bentley (1987), whilst Boulton and Hindmarsh (1987) explain the fundamentals of bed deformation. The mechanisms of glacial surges are described in detail by Raymond (1987) and Sharp (1988), whilst Warren (1992) reviews the processes of iceberg calving. More specific examples of how the glacial landforms of Scotland provide insight into the dynamics of former ice sheets are given in the references cited in the text.

References

Andrews, J.T. 1972. Glacier power, mass balance, velocities and erosion potential. *Zeitschrift für Geomorphologie,* **13,** 1-17.

Ballantyne, C.K. 1994. Gibbsitic soils on former nunataks: implications for ice sheet reconstruction. *Journal of Quaternary Science,* **9,** 73-80.

Bennett, M.R. and Boulton, G.S. 1993a. Deglaciation of the Younger Dryas or Loch Lomond Stadial ice-field in the northern Highlands, Scotland. *Journal of Quaternary Science,* **8,** 133-145.

Bennett, M.R. and Boulton, G.S. 1993b. A reinterpretation of Scottish 'hummocky moraine' and its significance for the deglaciation of the Scottish Highlands during the Younger Dryas or Loch Lomond Stadial. *Geological Magazine,* **130,** 301-318.

Bennett, M.R. and Glasser, N.F. 1991. The glacial landforms of Glen Geusachan, Cairngorms: a reinterpretation. *Scottish Geographical Magazine,* **107,** 116-123.

Bennett, M.R. and Glasser, N.F. 1996. *Glacial Geology: Ice Sheets and Landforms.* John Wiley, Chichester.

Bentley, C.R. 1987. Antarctic ice streams - a review. *Journal of Geophysical Research,* **92,** 8843-8858.

Boulton, G.S. 1972. The role of thermal regime in glacial sedimentation. In: Price, R.J. and Sugden, D.E. (Eds), *Polar Geomorphology.* Institute of British Geographers Special Publication, **4,** 1-19.

Boulton, G.S. and Hindmarsh, R.C.A. 1987. Sediment deformation beneath glaciers: rheology and geological consequences. *Journal of Geophysical Research,* **92,** 9059-9082.

Boulton, G.S., Jones, A.S., Clayton, A.M. and Kenning, M.J. 1977. A British ice-sheet model and patterns of glacial erosion and deposition in Britain. In: Shotton, F.W. (Ed.), *British Quaternary Studies: Recent Advances.* Clarendon Press, Oxford, 231-246.

Boulton, G.S., Peacock, J.D. and Sutherland, D.G. 1991. Quaternary. In: Craig, G.Y. (Ed.), *Geology of Scotland.* 3rd ed. The Geological Society, London, 503-543.

Drewry, D. 1996. Ice sheets, climate change and sea level. *Physics World,* **9,** 29-33.

Glasser, N.F. 1995. Modelling the effect of topography on ice sheet erosion, Scotland. *Geografiska Annaler,* **77A,** 67-82.

Gordon, J.E. 1979. Reconstructed Pleistocene ice-sheet temperatures and glacial erosion in Northern Scotland. *Journal of Glaciology,* **22,** 331-344.

Hall, A.M. and Sugden, D.E. 1987. Limited modification of mid-latitude landscapes by ice sheets: the case of north-east Scotland. *Earth Surface Processes and Landforms,* **12,** 531-542.

Haynes, V.M. 1995. Scotland's landforms: a review. *Scottish Association of Geography Teachers' Journal,* **24,** 18-37.

Hooke, R. LeB. 1977. Basal temperatures in polar ice sheets: a qualitative review. *Quaternary Research,* **7,** 1-13.

McCarroll, D., Ballantyne, C.K., Nesje, A. and Dahl, S.O. 1995. Nunataks of the last ice sheet in northwest Scotland. *Boreas,* **24,** 305-323.

Paterson, W.S.B. 1994. *The Physics of Glaciers.* Pergamon/ Elsevier Science Ltd, Oxford.

Payne, A.J. and Sugden, D.E. 1990. Topography and ice sheet growth. *Earth Surface Processes and Landforms,* **15,** 625-639.

Raymond, C.F. 1987. How do glaciers surge? A review. *Journal of Geophysical Research,* **92,** 9121-9134.

Sharp, M. 1988. Surging glaciers: behaviour and mechanisms. *Progress in Physical Geography,* **12,** 349-370.

Sharp, M., Dowdeswell, J.A. and Gemmell, J.C. 1989. Reconstructing past glacier dynamics and erosion from glacial geomorphic evidence: Snowdon, North Wales. *Journal of Quaternary Science,* **4,** 115-130.

Sissons, J.B. 1979. The Loch Lomond Stadial in the Cairngorm Mountains. *Scottish Geographical Magazine,* **95,** 66-82.

Sugden, D.E. 1968. The selectivity of glacial erosion in the Cairngorm Mountains, Scotland. *Transactions of the Institute of British Geographers,* **45,** 79-92.

Sugden, D.E. 1970. Landforms of deglaciation in the Cairngorm Mountains, Scotland. *Transactions of the Institute of British Geographers,* **51,** 201-219.

Sugden, D.E. and John, B.S. 1976. *Glaciers and Landscape.* Edward Arnold, London.

Thorp, P.W. 1987. Late Devensian ice sheet in the western Grampians, Scotland. *Journal of Quaternary Science,* **2,** 103-112.

Warren, C.R. 1992. Iceberg calving and the glacioclimatic record. *Progress in Physical Geography,* **16,** 253-282.

5. Greenland Ice Cores and North Atlantic Sediments: Implications for the Last Glaciation in Scotland

Chalmers M. Clapperton

The key themes covered in this chapter are:

- the role of the Atlantic Ocean in climate change;
- oxygen isotopes and past climate;
- Greenland ice cores and past climate;
- North Atlantic sediments and past climate;
- Heinrich events;
- Scotland during the last glacial cycle;
- timing and patterns of deglaciation of the last ice sheet;
- climate and glacier changes during the Late-glacial.

5.1 Introduction

The concept that a great Ice Age had once embraced much of NW Europe evolved in the early decades of the 19th century. Field observations by eminent geologists like Louis Agassiz, William Buckland, Archibald Geikie and James Geikie, gave them a clear vision that polar-like ice sheets and alpine glaciers had covered extensive upland and lowland regions in recent geological times. The notion of a vast ice sheet burying the green and fertile glens and straths of Scotland must have seemed an incredible anomaly to the average lay person of these times. How could the climate have become so different as to generate polar conditions in this land endowed with comparatively mild maritime conditions?

Mean annual summer temperature in western Scotland is about 14°C, and the average winter temperature seldom falls below 4°C, making Scotland much warmer than the average for its latitude in the Northern Hemisphere. It has long been recognised that such comparative mildness occurs because prevailing air masses reaching Scotland originate and/or travel over the relatively warm North Atlantic Current, but realisation that this oceanic influence can change dramatically and rapidly has developed only within the last decade. The knowledge has come from detailed studies of Greenland ice cores and North Atlantic sediments. It has revolutionised our understanding of the coupled ocean-atmosphere system in the Northern Hemisphere, and how this undergoes spectacular reorganisation from time to time on the scale of decades to millennia (Broecker and Denton, 1990). Such reorganisations affect the climate of Scotland and the rest of Northern Europe, switching periodically from the extreme cold of glacial and near-glacial modes to the comparative warmth (like today) of interglacial and near interglacial conditions.

How does this happen, and what is the cause? This chapter addresses these questions, focusing on the large-scale circulation of Atlantic water, and on the proxy climatic records from the Greenland ice sheet and deep sea sediments from the North Atlantic. The implications of important recent discoveries in these fields for the pattern of glaciation and deglaciation in Scotland during the last glacial cycle (last *c.* 100 ka) are then examined.

5.2 The Atlantic conveyor

The Atlantic Ocean basin is still quite narrow because it is tectonically rather young (less than *c.* 200 Ma), and this

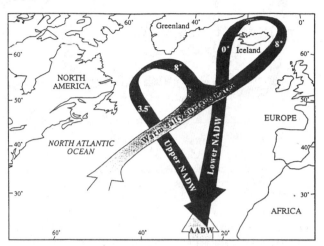

Figure 5.1a North Atlantic Deep Water (NADW) forms when warm salty water of the Gulf Stream/ North Atlantic Current cools, becomes increasingly saline due to evaporation, and descends to the ocean floor. The most dense water overtops the Greenland-Scotland submarine ridge and flows south as lower NADW. Less dense water forming between Greenland and North America (less salty in this colder environment) flows south as upper NADW overriding the lower, denser water. Because both water masses are less dense than northward-flowing Antarctic Bottom Water (AABW), they pass over it on their southward journey. (After Skinner and Porter, 1995).

focuses circulation of ocean water into well-defined currents at different depths. Atlantic water connects through to the Pacific Ocean basin by way of the Indian and Southern oceans, participating in a great conveyor-like cell of circulation (Broecker and Denton, 1990) which transports cold dense water at depth and warm less dense water at shallow and intermediate (800 m) depths (Figure 5.1a). Water at intermediate to shallow depths flowing north into the North Atlantic is warm and has a relatively high salinity. This is due partly to the influx of major rivers from surrounding continents, and partly because of the evaporation of so much 'fresh' water into the atmosphere in the tropical and temperate zones of cyclogenesis (where cyclonic depressions are generated). Every winter at about the latitude of Scotland to Iceland, this reservoir of heat is released as it warms the air masses travelling generally eastwards in the zone of cyclonic circulation along the atmospheric Polar Front. Release of this warmth cools the water from about 10°C to 2°C. This heat-loss is transferred to the air sweeping across Scotland and is equal to about 30% of the yearly input of solar energy to the surface of the North Atlantic. This staggering bonus of winter warmth largely explains why there are no glaciers currently in the Scottish mountains.

The Atlantic's high salinity together with the drop in temperature makes it exceptionally dense, and this cool highly saline water sinks to the ocean bottom to form what is known as North Atlantic Deep Water (NADW). This vertical circulation is on a huge scale, averaging 20 times the combined flow of all the world's rivers (Broecker and Denton, 1990). Likened to the vertical limb of a conveyor system, it drives the Atlantic bottom water current that

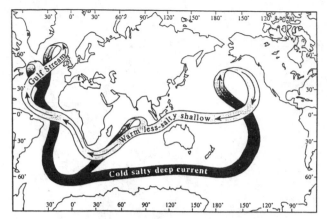

Figure 5.1b The major thermohaline circulation cells that make up the global ocean conveyor system are driven by exchange of heat and moisture between the atmosphere and ocean. (After Skinner and Porter, 1995).

sweeps southward, curves around the southern tip of Africa, and joins the deep water current circling Antarctica, which distributes deep water to the other oceans (Figure 5.1b). This great oceanic circulation system is strongly coupled to the atmosphere because two thirds of the Earth's surface, which imparts the properties of temperature and humidity to the troposphere, consist of ocean water. As will be demonstrated later, the Atlantic conveyor system is potentially unstable, and can develop different modes of operation. When it flows vigorously, as it has done for the past 10 ka, the global climate is warm. When it slows down and reduces in scale, the global climate is glacial. An in-between condition is characterised by rapid shifts from one state to the other, and typically this occurs during much of a glacial cycle (100 ka).

5.3 Stable oxygen isotopes and past climate

As long ago as the 1950s a significant break-through in knowledge about past climate change came from the analysis of tiny fragments of calcium carbonate (shell) that constantly accumulate on parts of the deep ocean floor. These are the shells of single-cell marine organisms called foraminifers (forams) which make up elements of planktonic life in the surface waters. At the time of their formation, the shells lock up key information about the ocean surface water in the stable isotopes present in the oxygen component of the carbonate. It was discovered by Emiliani (1954) that the ratio of the heavy isotope of oxygen(^{18}O) to the lighter one (^{16}O) can be interpreted to give an estimate of sea surface temperature (SST). Moreover, when ice sheets grew during

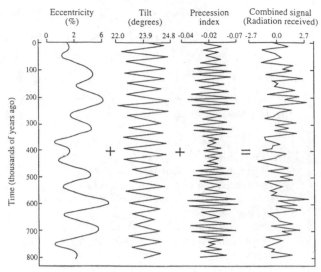

Figure 5.2a The three curves on the left represent variations in the amount of solar radiation arriving at the Earth's surface due to changes in orbital eccentricity, tilt and precession during the last 800 ka. The combined curve on the extreme right shows the amount of solar radiation received at about latitude 40-60°N. (After Skinner and Porter, 1987).

glacial times, the higher concentration of the lighter isotope in snow that fell to the ice sheets left the oceans relatively enriched in the heavier ^{18}O isotope. This means that the shells of forams growing during glacial times were relatively enriched in ^{18}O, whereas the oxygen locked in air bubbles in the growing ice sheets was relatively enriched in the ^{16}O isotope.

Thus, in the 1960s and 1970s, considerable progress was made in understanding the Earth's Quaternary and pre-Quaternary glacial history using the isotopic record from sediment cores taken in the deep ocean basins (Shackleton and Opdyke, 1973). The most important revelation was that the peaks and troughs in the isotopic curves, representing cold and warm variations in the Earth's ice volume and climate, matched the curve of cyclical insolation changes (Milankovitch cycles) due to the orbital geometry of the Earth around the Sun (Figure 5.2a). Deep sea records from the Pacific, Atlantic and Indian oceans demonstrated that the Earth's climate has underdone cyclical periods of warm and cold conditions over at least the last 3.5 Ma. Until about 760 ka, the change from cold to warm occurred about every 40 ka (Figure 5.2b), reflecting control on the Earth's radiation budget by the tilt of the planet's axis, going from a high to a

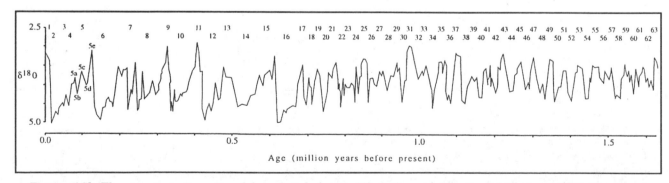

Figure 5.2b The oxygen isotope record from borehole site 607 in the mid-Atlantic at latitude *c.* 41°N. Numbered isotopic stages are shown at the top; even numbers indicate relatively cold conditions, and odd numbers relatively warm conditions. The amplitude and wavelength of the curve increase at around 760 ka from a periodicity of *c.* 40 ka to 100 ka. (After Bridgland, 1994, compiled from data in Ruddiman *et al.*, 1989).

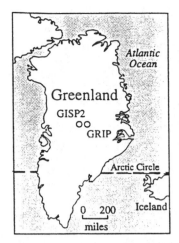

Figure 5.3 Location of the GISP and GRIP ice coring sites on the Greenland Ice Sheet.

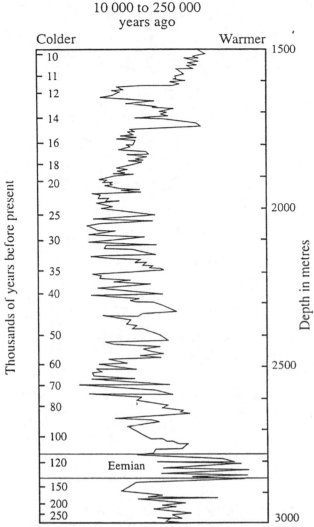

Figure 5.4 A generalised curve of warm-cold climatic fluctuations over the Greenland Ice Sheet during the last 250 ka, based on the $\delta^{18}O$ record from air bubbles in the ice. (After Dansgaard *et al.*, 1993).

low angle over this time scale. It is generally recognised that during the cold intervals, ice caps and glaciers in maritime mountain areas like Greenland, Alaska, Iceland and Scandinavia expanded to the coast, where they discharged icebergs laden with glacial debris that appears in the ocean sediment cores. It is not known if glaciers developed in Scotland during these 40 ka cycles of cooling, but it seems highly probable as higher parts of the Western Highlands are close to the glaciation threshold even today.

A major change in the orbital-insolation system occurred about 760 ka, enabling the build-up of much larger ice sheets in the Northern Hemisphere every 100 ka (Figure 5.2b). The cause of this change is still not known. Each so-called 'glacial cycle' of *c.* 100 ka duration ended abruptly and was followed by an interglacial interval lasting 10-15 ka. In addition, each glacial cycle was periodically punctuated by warmer intervals known as interstades, when the ice sheets and glaciers receded considerably without disappearing entirely. The interstades generally endured for a few thousand years, separating the colder stadial intervals (stades). Initially, climatic fluctuations during a glacial cycle were attributed to the precessional (every *c.* 22 ka) and tilt (every *c.* 40 ka) variations in insolation (Imbrie and Imbrie, 1979), but recent studies of the Greenland ice cores and North Atlantic sediments have shown that the Earth's climate was much more variable than this during the last glacial cycle, and that substantial temperature swings occurred also at the millenial scale.

5.4 Greenland ice cores and past climate

Between 1990 and 1992, teams from America and Europe drilled new cores to bedrock through the Greenland ice sheet, providing the most remarkable data about the Earth's climate for the past 250 ka. The two teams drilled at sites close to the summit of the ice sheet at latitude *c.* 73°N, where the rate of iceflow is least and depth greatest (Figure 5.3). Mean annual temperature here (Summit), at an altitude of 3238 m, is -32°C. The European project is known as GRIP (Greenland Ice-core Project), while the American one is called GISP (Greenland Ice-sheet Project). Core length at the GRIP station is 3028 m, and the basal ice is estimated to have formed about 250 ka (Dansgaard *et al.*, 1993). This means that the core contains ice and compressed bubbles of air that formed during the last two glacial cycles and the last three interglacial intervals. After recovery, the ice cores were studied in a number of ways to extract high resolution data about the Earth's past climate. These include analyses of stable isotopes, dust content, snow accumulation rates and greenhouse gas content.

Perhaps the most fundamental information has come from the stable isotopes present in the oxygen molecules trapped in the air bubbles throughout the cores, thus representing conditions in the atmosphere over 250 ka. In particular, the deviation of the heavier ^{18}O isotope concentration from that in standard mean ocean water (SMOW) gives important estimates of past temperature. The deviation is expressed as $\delta^{18}O$. It has been found that $\delta^{18}O$ in polar ice and snow depends mainly on the temperature of formation of the precipitation. As ^{18}O is the heavier of the two stable isotopes, rain or snow falling during warmer conditions contains more of this isotope in relation to the lighter one (^{16}O), and less of it during colder conditions. Thus the $^{18}O{:}^{16}O$ isotopic ratio gives a clear indication of warm-cold changes in the atmosphere.

Down-core analyses established continuous $\delta^{18}O$ profiles initially for the past 40 ka (Johnsen *et al.*, 1992) and then to core base over the past 250 ka (Dansgaard *et al.*, 1993). The age of the ice with depth was established by a combination of methods, including the counting of annual accumulation layers back to 14.5 ka (calendar years), extrapolation between dated volcanic ash layers, and estimation from an iceflow model. The general trends of the $\delta^{18}O$ curves from both the GRIP and GISP cores match each other closely and correspond well with the trend observed in earlier Greenland ice cores, and in the Vostok core from Antarctica

47

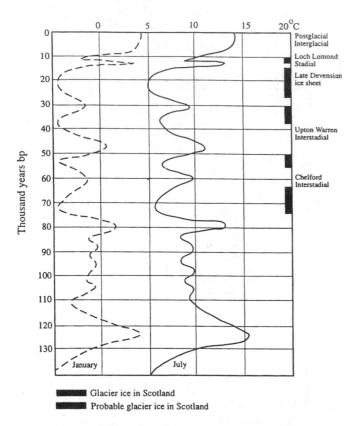

Postglacial
Interglacial

Loch Lomond
Stadial

Late Devensian
ice sheet

Upton Warren
Interstadial

Chelford
Interstadial

January   July

■■■ Glacier ice in Scotland
■■■ Probable glacier ice in Scotland

Figure 5.5 Estimated air temperature at sea level in west Scotland for January and July over the past 130 ka, and intervals when glacier ice probably was present in the mountains. (After Price, 1983, with permission from Scottish Academic Press).

(Jouzel *et al.,* 1987), suggesting that the major climatic fluctuations occurred worldwide (Jouzel, 1994).

The most outstanding feature of the GRIP and GISP core data is their high resolution, revealing frequent and substantial fluctuations in temperature over Greenland throughout the last glacial cycle. The long GRIP δ¹⁸O record (Figure 5.4) shows that 24 interstadial intervals punctuated the generally cold conditions of the last glacial cycle (Dansgaard, et *al.,* 1993). The seven of these that are identified also in the European pollen records are the longest and warmest of the series, each lasting for more than 2 ka (see figure 5.10). Many others were short-lived events, however, spanning no more than a century. Using a geographical relationship between δ¹⁸O and temperature, Dansgaard *et al.* (1993) found that stades at Summit during the last glacial cycle were 7°C colder than the interstades, and 12-13°C colder than modern conditions. This means that even the milder interstades had a climate 5-6°C colder than now. The high resolution data from these cores have also confirmed that cooling episodes occurred about every 2 ka, and these are known as Dansgaard-Oeschger cycles.

5.5 North Atlantic sediments and past climate

A flurry of sediment coring projects in the North Atlantic during the 1960s and 1970s led to the publication of several extremely influential papers on Quaternary palaeoclimate (*e.g.* McIntyre *et al.,* 1972; Sancetta *et al.,* 1973; Ruddiman *et al.,* 1977; Ruddiman and McIntyre, 1981). These marine biologists analysed the skeletons of marine forams that had accumulated over time in areas of stable sedimentation in mid-latitudes of the ocean basin. Two kinds of analyses gave

important palaeoclimatic information: the downcore change in stable isotopes (¹⁸O:¹⁶O, as in the ice cores), and the relative abundance of temperature-dependent species. The studies concluded that latitudinal shifts of the oceanic Polar Front, the boundary zone between cold polar water and warmer North Atlantic Drift water, had occurred during the last glacial cycle. In particular, Sancetta *et al.* (1973) estimated sea surface temperatures (SSTs) for various time intervals over the past *c.*100 ka from a core located about 1000 km south-west of Scotland (lat. *c.* 52°N). These data implied that North Atlantic water had chilled to 7-11°C colder than now several times after *c.* 70 ka, and that warmer conditions, when temperatures rose by 3-6°C, had occurred on at least three occasions. This information was used by Price (1983) in an innovative attempt to assess on-land conditions in Scotland during the last glaciation (Figure 5.5). This was most appropriate as Scotland's glacial climate was dominated by North Atlantic SSTs and must have been extremely sensitive to changing positions of the Polar Front.

It is now believed that latitudinal shifts in position of the North Atlantic Polar Front are caused by variations in thermohaline circulation. For example, when colder fresher water forms a less dense 'lid' over the North Atlantic, as during intervals of rapid glacier melting and when global climate cools significantly, the formation and sinking of deep ocean water is reduced. Weakening of this vertical limb of the conveyor system slows down the thermohaline circulation and enables the southward penetration of the Polar Front.

5.6 Heinrich events

Renewed interest in Atlantic sediments hit the scientific world in the 1990s, close in time to the sensational results emerging from Greenland ice core analyses. The initial impetus came from a paper by Helmut Heinrich (1988) who identified six unusual layers of coarse ice-rafted debris in sediment cores taken from the Dreizack Sea Mount area at latitude 47° 23'N, some 1300 km west of the Bay of Biscay. Heinrich concluded that these sediments had been released by the melting of large volumes of icebergs discharged by the Laurentide ice sheet covering North America, at times when the Atlantic Ocean had been cold enough to enable the icebergs to travel so far south. Because the interval of time between these iceberg rafting events appeared to average 11 ka, Heinrich explained the cooling with reference to the half-precessional solar cycle when there is reduced insolation in mid-high northern latitudes.

The full significance of Heinrich's findings was not appreciated until further cores from the North Atlantic were analysed in the early 1990s by American oceanographers and marine biologists. Not only have these studies revealed the nature of rapid fluctuations in marine sedimentation in the North Atlantic during the last glacial cycle, but also they have shown correlations with the Greenland ice core data, thereby demonstrating that a close atmosphere-ocean coupling existed during the last glacial cycle (Bond *et al.,* 1993; Bond and Lotti, 1995). Similar investigations in the North Pacific region subsequently revealed equivalent millennial-scale climate variability, and led Keigwin (1995) to conclude that such changes have affected most of the Northern Hemisphere during the past 100 ka. In a review paper discussing the possibility that these massive 'armadas' of icebergs were triggers for global climate change, Broecker (1994) emphasised the Canadian origin of the detritus found in the so-called Heinrich layers of the North Atlantic. This clearly tied the iceberg source to ice streams from the Laurentide ice sheet discharging through Hudson Bay and the St. Lawrence valley. Glaciologists quickly came up with a theoretical explanation for these quasi-cyclic iceberg events every 7-10 ka by suggesting that the Laurentide ice sheet underwent phases of stability and instability ('binge-purge' cycles) during the last glacial cycle (MacAyeal, 1993; Alley and MacAyeal, 1994). According to this model, long periods (c. 7.7 ka) of slow ice sheet growth (binge) alternate with short periods (c. 0.75 ka) of rapid ice discharge (purge) through ice streams when the ice has become thick enough to permit melting at the glacier bed. A remarkable implication of this model is that the Laurentide ice sheet may have driven the climate variabilty of the last glacial cycle in the North Atlantic domain (and possibly worldwide) by diminishing the production of NADW through the freshwater released by melting icebergs; this slowed down the Atlantic Conveyor circulation, thereby enabling a southward migration of the Polar Front.

This model of Laurentide ice sheet behaviour was initially believed to be the explanation for Heinrich cooling events which somehow impacted the global climate. For example, glaciers in New Zealand and southern Chile apparently advanced coevally with the Heinrich events (Lowell et al., 1995; Clapperton, 1995), but how the climate signal was transmitted between hemispheres remained unexplained. However, the role of the Laurentide ice sheet in driving such climate variability during a glacial cycle is now uncertain. Other sea-terminating ice sheets (Greenland, Iceland, Britain, Scandinavia) seem to have advanced and discharged icebergs also during Heinrich events (Bond and Lotti, 1995; Kotilainen and Shackleton, 1995; Fronval et al., 1995). As these ice sheets were of vastly different sizes, their internal dynamics were unlikely to have operated similarly and in unison (cf. the binge/purge cycles). Current opinion favours the view that global cooling was forced by some other mechanism (e.g. reduced solar radiation, variation in greenhouse gases like H_2O and CO_2), and that this occurred (and still does) every 6100 years (Lehman, 1996; Mayewski et al., in press). When glaciers and ice sheets were large, as during cold intervals of glacial cycles, their

response was correspondingly bigger - hence the iceberg 'armadas'. In Scotland, ice streams draining through the major firths of the west and east coasts would have advanced during each Heinrich event.

5.7 The Dansgaard-Oeschger and Bond cycles

As Broecker (1994) has pointed out, the glacial portion of the Greenland ice core record is dominated by cold-warm fluctuations averaging between one and three thousand years in duration, and these have been called Dansgaard-Oeschger (D-O) cycles. Bond et al. (1993) showed that these are bundled together in gradually declining (in temperature) sequences, each of which culminates in a Heinrich event. Dramatic warming followed each Heinrich cold peak within a decade or so (Figure 5.6). This pattern of cyclical climatic change has now been termed a Bond cycle, and evidence is rapidly accumulating that D-O cycles, Bond cycles and Heinrich type events all have global signatures. This firmly shifts the emphasis away from the Laurentide ice sheet, the North Atlantic and the Atlantic Conveyor as primary forcers for climate variability during the last glacial cycle, although they may have been involved in strong feedback mechanisms. An alternative explanation for the climate changes could involve secular variations in receipts of insolation at the Earth's atmosphere and surface due to periodic reductions in solar output superimposed on secular changes in solar radiation arising from the Earth-Sun orbital geometry. Recent results from the Hubble space telescope suggest the Sun undergoes considerable variations in its flaring activity, and this causes significant changes in the strength of the solar wind and in the intensity of radiation reaching the Earth. It is not yet known whether regular or random 'solar flickering' was a primary mechanism for causing climate variability during the last glacial cycle, superimposed on the effects of the Milankovich cycles. But if climate change has occurred globally and simultaneously, the finger of suspicion points at the Sun. The effect of fluctuations in sunspot cycle activity in causing distinct

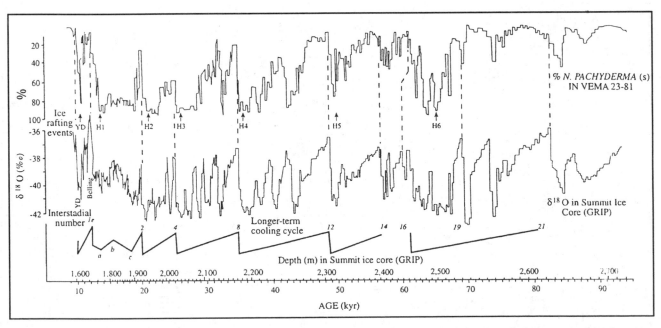

Figure 5.6 Correlation of the $\delta^{18}O$ record from the GRIP ice core at Summit, Greenland, with the percent abundance of marine foraminifera *(Neogloboquadrina pachyderma,* sinistral) at core V23-81 in the North Atlantic. The bundles of progressively cooling Dansgaard-Oeschger cycles form the longer-term Bond cycles, as shown in the bottom curve. Peaks in ice-rafting detritus (Heinrich events) are shown as H1- H6, along with the similar Younger Dryas (YD) event. (After Bond et al., 1993).

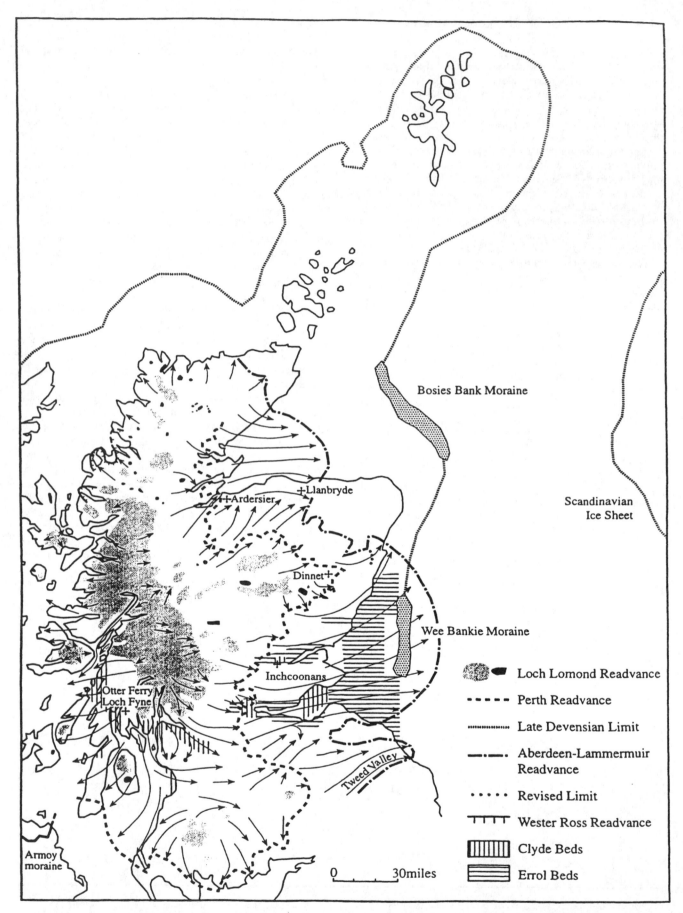

Figure 5.7 The original map of J.B. Sissons (1967) showing the Loch Lomond, Perth, and Aberdeen-Lammermuir Readvance limits. Other ice limits and place names mentioned in the text have been added; for example the possible limit of the ice sheet during the Late Devensian (after Hall and Bent, 1991) and the Wester Ross Readvance (after Robinson and Ballantyne, 1979). Arrows show directions of ice movement.

50

Figure 5.8a A sketch map of Europe as it was c. 29-22 ka BP, showing the confluent Scandinavian and British ice sheets inferred from North Sea seismic and core data (Sejrup *et al.*, 1994). Much of the land as far south as southern France was sparsely vegetated tundra. (After Andersen and Borns, 1994).

Figure 5.8b A sketch map of Europe as it was at *c.* 15-14 ka BP, showing the possible extent of ice in Scotland (and in Scandinavia, where the ice sheet readvanced to form the Pommeranian moraines in northern Germany) during the so-called Aberdeen-Lammermuir Readvance of Sissons (1967). It is likely that a readvance did occur in Scotland, but some of the limits are in need of revision. (After Andersen and Borns, 1994).

Figure 5.8c A sketch map of Europe showing the position of winter sea ice (a) during the period of interstadial warmth at *c.* 13 ka BP preceding Younger Dryas cooling, and (b) the position of the Polar Front (winter sea ice) during the Loch Lomond Readvance (Younger Dryas Stade) at 11-10 ka BP. (After Andersen and Borns, 1994).

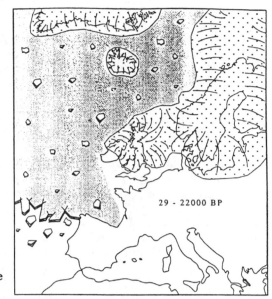

Figure 5.8a

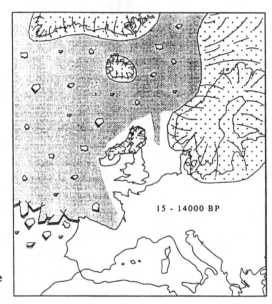

Figure 5.8b

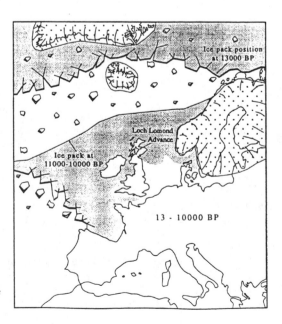

Figure 5.8c

cooling episodes during the last few centuries may be a 'smoking gun' that also points to a solar cause for climate change. For example, solar radiation is reduced when sunspots (solar flares) are absent, and such events between AD 1400-1510 (Sporer Minimum) and from AD 1645-1715 (Maunder Minimum) produced two periods of greatest climatic stress through cooling during the Little Ice Age of the last few centuries (Lamb, 1995). An alternative mechanism driving climate change could involve the periodic absorption and release, by the oceans and biosphere, of greenhouse gases like CO_2 and water vapour, but this is equally speculative.

5.8 Scotland during the last glacial cycle

5.8.1 Background and early views

Opinions about the nature of the last glaciation in Scotland have varied somewhat since the first detailed accounts by Jamieson (1865), A. Geikie (1865), and J. Geikie (1874). Much of the more recent literature has dealt with local and regional descriptions, and only Sissons (1967), Price (1983) and Sutherland (1984) had provided national overviews until recently (Gordon and Sutherland, 1993). Because of the dearth of stratigraphical evidence for glacial events prior to the last ice sheet maximum, most overviews have been concerned with the tail end of the last glacial cycle (the cycle having begun about 116 ka). As the last glaciation in Britain is known conventionally as the Devensian, it is referred to as such in the following discussion. Ages quoted are in radiocarbon years before present (BP). These do not correspond directly with calendar years, for example being some 1500 years 'younger' than calendar years at 10 ka BP.

A common perception of the last glaciation in Scotland is that an ice sheet grew and covered most of the land about 18 ka BP, that this had melted away by 12 ka BP and that a final cooling at 11-10 ka BP caused the advance of mountain glaciers and small ice caps (Figure 5.7). This advance is known as the Loch Lomond Stadial event (or Loch Lomond Readvance), which occurred coevally with the European Younger Dryas Stade. Earlier views that readvances had occurred during the deglacial phase of the last ice sheet, the Aberdeen-Lammermuir and Perth Readvances (Sissons, 1967), were abandoned as alternative explanations were proposed for the hummocky landforms and other features invoked as the readvance limits (*e.g.* Sissons, 1974;

Clapperton and Sugden, 1977). Nevertheless, firm evidence for a stillstand or readvance of the ice sheet was found in Wester Ross by Robinson and Ballantyne (1979). Known as the Wester Ross Readvance, it is clearly older than the Loch Lomond Readvance but its precise age remains uncertain; some believe it occurred at about 13.5 ka BP (Ballantyne *et al.*, 1987; Benn, 1997).

Price (1983) was first to appreciate the significance of the ocean sediment records for interpreting the history of glaciers in Scotland during the last glaciation. Estimating the likely July temperature at 600 m in the Scottish Highlands for various cold intervals identified in the marine record from Atlantic core V23-82 (Sancetta *et al.*, 1973), he inferred that glaciers had probably existed in Scotland at 78-65 ka BP, at 55-50 ka BP, at 45-32 ka BP, and at the last glacial maximum (LGM) of 25-14 ka BP, as well as briefly during the Loch Lomond Readvance. Of course sedimentary evidence is lacking for most of these inferred stages, other than the LGM and the Loch Lomond Readvance, although glacial deposits beneath organic beds in peripheral parts of Scotland were subsequently assigned tentatively to the Early Devensian (78-65 ka BP) by Sutherland (1984). At the time of Price's study, high resolution data from Greenland ice cores and North Atlantic sediments were not yet available. This makes a reappraisal of his views worthwhile.

5.8.2 New data and revised views

Interstades. The interpretation and radiocarbon dating of sediments extracted from the northern North Sea basin suggest that glaciers in Norway and Scotland were probably small during the Ålesund interstade, sometime before *c.* 29.4 ka BP (Sejrup *et al.*, 1994). Subsequently, ice sheets from Scandinavia and Scotland became confluent in the North Sea basin during the interval 29.4-22 ka BP, indicating a maximum expansion of ice for the later part of the last glacial cycle (Figure 5.8a). This contradicts earlier views based on the interpretation of seismic and sediment core data from the northern North Sea basin that the limit of Late Devensian deposits lies no more than 100 km off eastern Britain and that there was never any connection between British and

Scandinavian ice during the Devensian maximum (Cameron *et al.*, 1987). Partial deglaciation seems to have occurred around 19 ka BP before a readvance of the ice culminated during the Dimlington stade, when the north British ice sheet terminated in the Vale of York and close to the Vale of Pickering on the east coast of England. Accepting that the Wee Bankie-Bosies Bank moraines, located in the North Sea basin some 35 km east of eastern Scotland (Figure 5.7), and submerged moraines on the shelf west of the Outer Hebrides mark the offshore limits of this later phase of the Late Devensian ice sheet (Hall and Bent, 1991; Sutherland and Gordon, 1993; see also Chapters 6 and 7), it follows that all of lowland Scotland was probably ice-covered from (say) 25 ka BP to about 16 ka BP. However, some of the higher ridges and peaks in the west appear to have protruded above the ice sheet as nunataks, (Ballantyne, 1990, 1997; Ballantyne and McCarroll, 1995; McCarroll *et al.*, 1995). Organic sediments deposited prior to this ice sheet glaciation have survived only in a few peripheral lowland areas; they are generally dated to *c.* 30 ka BP and older, and pollen analyses suggest cool interstadial climates (Sutherland, 1984; Walker et *al.*, 1992).

Because of the erosive effects of the last ice sheet, there are no Early and Middle Devensian interstadial sedimentary sequences comparable to those of the southern half of England. Here, the palaeoecology of organic beds documents four warmer intervals during the Devensian glacial cycle: three during the Early Devensian (Wretton, Chelford and Brimpton) and the Upton Warren complex (*c.* 45 ka BP) of the Middle Devensian (Jones and Keen, 1993). However, it is clear that the Middle Devensian in Europe actually contained three interstades, and it is likely that these have been lumped together in the poorly dated Upton Warren complex of the British record (which probably contains equivalents of the Moershoofd, Hengelo and Denekamp interstades of the Netherlands). If so, these six interstades may well be land equivalents of the warm intervals that followed Heinrich-type events in the North Atlantic, during which the polar front migrated northwards, enabling warmer water to influence the British climate. Given the scale of these ocean-atmosphere changes, it would

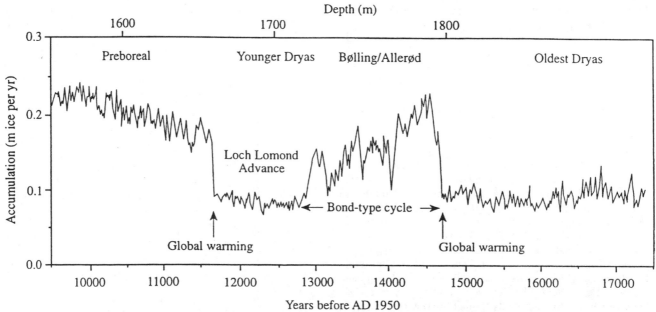

Figure 5.9 Graph of Late-glacial snow accumulation on the Greenland ice sheet at Summit (after Alley *et al.*, 1993). The steady, stepped cooling sequence typical of a Bond cycle took place through the two millennia preceding the Younger Dryas cold event, and it is likely that glaciers persisted in the highest catchments of the Scottish mountains during these conditions. Note that the timescale is in calendar years before AD 1950.

be remarkable if Scotland had not experienced interstadial conditions at the same time as those in England and the Netherlands, albeit with slightly cooler average temperatures.

Glaciers in Scotland. It has been estimated from modern climatic data that the topographic glaciation threshold for western Scotland lies at 1670-1735 m altitude (Lockwood, 1982; Benn, 1997), which is roughly 320-400 m above the highest summits. Assuming a vertical gradient in atmospheric temperature of 0.65°C per 100 m, and current precipitation totals, this means that a fall in summer temperature of about 2.5-3°C would be necessary for glaciers to form and survive in the higher catchments of the Scottish mountains.

A useful guideline for estimating climatic conditions suitable for extensive glacier development in Scotland is to reconstruct those known to have occurred during the Loch Lomond cold event at 11-10 ka BP. Prior to this cold event, warm North Atlantic water had pushed the Polar Front to the latitude of Iceland, so that cyclonic air masses reaching Scotland from southerly and westerly directions raised summer sea surface temperatures 5°C above those of the preceding glacial interval, possibly on three occasions (Haflidason *et al.*, 1995).

The Bond cycle that began c. 13.5 ka BP clearly shows a progressive cooling trend over the following two millenia before culminating in the Younger Dryas cold event at about 11 ka BP (Figure 5.9). Estimates of temperature for this interval, from marine, ice-core and palaeoecological records, suggest that mean July values in the North Atlantic region were 8-9°C lower than those of the present (Sissons, 1981; Ballantyne, 1989). Assuming that July temperature during the preceding Windermere interstade (at sea level in west Scotland) had been about 12°C, compared to the modern value of 15°C, it follows that the amount of summer cooling during the Loch Lomond Stade was 4-6°C.

Glaciers during the last glacial cycle. We can use the Loch Lomond Stade cooling as a model for other stadial events of the last glacial cycle with reference to the $\delta^{18}O$ graph of Dansgaard *et al.* (1993), shown in Figure 5.10. The mean $\delta^{18}O$ value for polar ice today is -35‰, and this changed to c. -43‰ when mean summer temperature fell by 12-13°C at the LGM. This implies that a -1‰ change in $\delta^{18}O$ represents a temperature fall of about 1.5°C. During the Loch Lomond Stade, mean July temperature at sea level in west Scotland is estimated to have been c. 6°C (Ballantyne, 1989), some 8°C lower than that of the present day. On Figure 5.10, a line representing the $\delta^{18}O$ value equivalent to this lower temperature (-40.5‰) is drawn to indicate when climatic conditions in Scotland during the last glacial cycle could have sustained icefields comparable to those of the Loch Lomond Readvance. This suggests that glaciers would have been present for much of the past c. 75 ka.

Accepting that glaciers could exist in Scotland if mean sea level temperatures were to lower by c. 3°C (corresponding to a $\delta^{18}O$ value of -37‰ on Figure 5.10), it appears that conditions warmer than this during the last glacial cycle (to the right of the -37‰ line on Figure 5.10), when Scotland may have been ice-free, occurred only during major interstades of the Early Devensian. Modelling experiments based on the Scottish ice sheet and the Loch Lomond ice cap (Payne and Sugden, 1990) concluded that a depression of 3°C in July temperature will initiate ice cap growth. A temperature lowering of 3-6.5°C creates small stable ice caps, whereas a lowering in excess of 6.6°C will create a large ice sheet because a critical threshold is crossed. Subsequent experiments by Hubbard (1996) demonstrate that the Loch Lomond Readvance icecaps could have

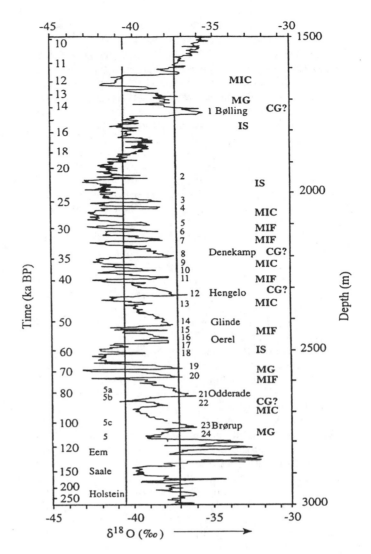

Figure 5.10 The GRIP Summit $\delta^{18}O$ record plotted from depths of 1500-3000 m, covering the interval 10-250 ka BP (after Dansgaard *et al.*, 1993). The timescale was determined by counting annual ice layers back to 14.5 ka BP, and beyond this it was estimated by ice flow modelling. The warmer interstades are correlated with the European pollen zones. Intervals when glaciers were probably present in Scotland are indicated by: MIC, mountain ice caps; MG, mountain glaciers; CG (?), corrie glaciers; IS, ice sheet; MIF, mountain icefields (smaller than an ice cap but with coalescing valley glaciers from common snowfields).

attained their maximum size within 550 years if the July temperature fell 8°C below modern values and W-E and N-S precipitation gradients were enhanced by 25% and 50%, respectively.

Testing theory with field evidence. Organic material in Scotland older than the Late Devensian glaciation occurs as fossiliferous marine sediments around some coastal areas, and as peat and mammalian fossils in lowlands peripheral to the main zones of glacial erosion at the LGM. These occurrences are documented in Gordon and Sutherland (1993) and appear to indicate at least two major interstadial events when ice in Scotland had vacated at least the coastal and lowland areas (see also Chapter 6). Although the dating of these deposits is relatively imprecise, the warmer conditions they imply seem to have occurred in the Early

Devensian (possibly *c.* 90-100 ka BP, corresponding to the Brørup Interstade of The Netherlands), and in the late Middle Devensian (at *c.* 35-28 ka BP, roughly coeval with the Denekamp Interstade of The Netherlands). However, pollen analysis of some deposits from both intervals suggests that the climatic conditions sustained only grass heathland and limited birch woodland, implying that mean annual temperature was significantly lower than now. Thus, even the warmest interstades of the last glacial cycle in Scotland, for which palaeoecological evidence exists, were probably more than 3°C colder than the modern climate. This implies that glaciers may well have existed in the West Highlands and possibly in the high catchments of the Central and Eastern Highlands even during the warmest intervals of the last glacial cycle.

Ice sheet glaciation in Scotland. The GRIP δ¹⁸O record indicates frequent warm-cold climatic oscillations throughout the last glacial cycle, but there were two occasions when the cooling endured much longer than during other intervals. The first was at *c.* 70-57 ka BP and was long enough to have been designated as a separate 'isotope stage' in the marine oxygen isotope record (Shackleton and Opdyke, 1973); it is known as Isotope Stage 4. The second, of course, was during Isotope Stage 2 and lasted from *c.* 25-14 ka BP, during which the global ice volume reached its maximum of the last glacial cycle (LGM). Both of these intervals corresponded to insolation minima in mid-high latitudes of the Northern Hemisphere due to the Earth's tilt and precession. During Stage 4, it is generally believed that the global ice volume reached only 75% of that achieved at the LGM. Both cold intervals lasted for about 10 ka, but whereas the Stage 4 stadial was preceded by lengthy interstadial conditions, the Stage 2 event followed on from about five millennia of relatively cold conditions. The point of this is that glaciers worldwide were probably quite large prior to the Stage 2 cooling, whereas they would have been small or absent prior to the Stage 4 cold event.

There is growing support for an ice sheet in Scotland during the Early Devensian (Isotope Stage 4) (*cf.* Chapter 6). Although firm dating is not yet established, till units in Caithness and Orkney (Bowen, 1989), the Inverness area (Merritt, 1990), Buchan (Hall and Connell, 1991) and Ayrshire (Jardine *et al.,* 1988) have been assigned tentatively to this interval. Also, glacial and glaciomarine sediments thought to date from this time have been reported from the outer Moray Firth and the Hebridean shelf (Chapters 6 and 7). As inferred sea surface temperature (SST) for January in the North Atlantic some 1000 km southwest of Scotland had fallen to 0°C during Stage 4, it is clear that the Polar Front had migrated far to the south. Price (1983) estimated that winter SST to the west of Scotland at this time would have been about -2°C (implying the presence of pack ice) and that July values were probably no higher than 3°C. Corresponding air temperatures at sea level in western Scotland were estimated as -6°C and 5°C. As these conditions endured for about 10 ka, it is inevitable that ice build-up in the Scottish mountains crossed the threshold for ice sheet growth (Payne and Sugden, 1990). Whether or not this Early Devensian ice sheet was as extensive, or more extensive, than that of the Late Devensian is not known, but the responsive maritime mountain glaciers worldwide appear to have reached close to, or beyond, their LGM limits during Stage 4 (Gillespie and Molnar, 1995; Clapperton, 1995).

Mountain glaciers, icefields, and ice caps in Scotland. Taken together, the δ¹⁸O GRIP and North Atlantic sediment records allow us to infer when southern excursions of the Polar Front took place during the last glacial cycle,

characterising the unstable glacial mode of operation of North Atlantic thermohaline circulation (the Conveyor). As these excursions caused severe cooling of air masses reaching Scotland, while moisture supply remained abundant, it is inevitable that glaciers would have formed and/or expanded during these intervals. On this basis, notations have been applied in Figure 5.10 to indicate the likely types of glacier build-up in Scotland in the course of the last glacial cycle. It is assumed that brief cooling intervals lasting less than two millennia probably produced corrie glaciers and some mountain valley glacier complexes in places. Bond-type cooling cycles of about 7-11 ka duration probably produced extensive mountain ice caps and many valley glaciers in Scotland, as during the Loch Lomond Stade. Other Dansgaard-Oeschger cooling events exceeding two millennia would also have caused the formation of ice caps and valley glaciers. Thus, it is unlikely that Scotland was entirely ice-free at any time during the last glacial cycle, because the global atmospheric temperature, judging from the polar and marine oxygen isotope records, seems always to have been at least 2-3°C cooler than now. Even during the warm Devensian Late-glacial (Windermere) interstade, when the North Atlantic Current brought warm water as far north as the latitude of Iceland, the Laurentide and Scandinavian ice sheets were still areally extensive and the global atmosphere was still depleted in its greenhouse gases. Although the Scottish ice sheet had disintegrated, receding initially due to reduced precipitation at the LGM, and then collapsing because of global warming around 13 ka BP, rising precipitation during the Late-glacial, combined with cooler-than-now mean annual temperatures, probably permitted the presence of glaciers in the highest catchments.

5.9 Deglaciation of the last ice sheet

It has been pointed out by Sutherland (1984) and Sutherland and Gordon (1993) that deglaciation of the Scottish ice sheet began while the climate was still cold. They attributed this apparent anomaly to the drier climate induced by polar continental conditions when the Polar Front was situated far to the south of Britain, causing extensive pack ice cover over the Atlantic west of Scotland. However, it is evident from the δ¹⁸O record from the GRIP ice core that a distinct warming occurred at *c.* 18-17 ka BP, prior to a severe cold oscillation coincident with the Heinrich (H1) event at *c.* 15-14 ka BP. This may have reactivated the slowly receding ice sheet, causing a readvance because of increased precipitation, assuming the Polar Front had shifted north of its glaciation maximum position.

Although radiocarbon dated stratigraphy for these intervals is lacking in Scotland, certain inferences can be made about the ice sheet status from assemblages of ice marginal landforms (see also Chapter 8). Good evidence exists in the west for a distinct readvance of the ice sheet margin prior to the Late-glacial warming and sea-level rise that led to its final disintegration. For example, the confluent Linnhe and Clyde ice streams advanced on to the Antrim coast of northeast Ireland to form the Armoy moraine prior to final deglaciation (Figure 5.7). The advance of ice over soft waterlogged sediments shaped drumlins behind this moraine, and possibly also those in the Clyde valley and Ayrshire. In eastern Scotland, parts of the limit drawn by Sissons (1967) for his Aberdeen-Lammermuir Readvance may mark ice marginal deposits formed at this time (although revision of the limit is required in places, as in the Aberdeen area). An impressive assemblage of such deposits, largely composed of glacifluvial sands and gravels and contiguous outwash plains, delimits the southern margin of the Moray Firth ice stream in the Lhanbryde area close to the mouth of the River Spey. Also, in the Aberdeen area, a 3 km wide belt of ice-marginal deposits curving across the lower Dee valley (Brown, 1993) is considerably older than c. 12.6 ka BP (the radiocarbon age of basal bog sediments near Braemar), but is younger than c. 15,370 BP, a minimum age for on-shore recession of the ice sheet in coastal Aberdeenshire (Hall and Jarvis, 1989). Recent investigation of the glacial features along the northern flank of the Cairngorm mountains in Strath Spey has concluded that significant readvances occurred during deglaciation (Brazier et al., 1996a, 1996b). The scale of these seems compatible with the readvance of Moray Firth ice to Lhanbryde. It is also possible that the belt of ice marginal deposits along the southern side of the Tweed valley in northernmost Northumberland, where the Bowmont and Till drainage was ponded to form a large ice-dammed lake (Clapperton, 1971) marks the limit of Southern Upland ice in south-east Scotland at this time.

Deglaciation from this stage in eastern Scotland allowed a marine incursion to the coastal lowlands and the deposition of glaciomarine sediments containing high Arctic fauna that show the sea was very cold. These deposits are known as the Errol Beds (see Sutherland, 1984 for a review) and indicate a substantial retreat of the eastern margin of the Scottish ice sheet to inner parts of the main firths. For example, the classic site at Inchcoonans in the Tay valley lies more than 25 km from the open sea (Figure 5.7). Recession of the main ice streams was probably rapid due to iceberg calving into the rising relative sea level, as indicated by clusters of ice-rafted boulders and gravel dropped into the finer sediments by the melting icebergs. It is remarkable that none of these deposits have been radiocarbon dated, except for those at St. Fergus on the Aberdeenshire coast, assuming these formed coevally with the Errol Beds. As the age of the St. Fergus glaciomarine deposit is c. 15 ka BP, it indicates that cold Arctic water was invading the Scottish coast by this time. Sutherland and Gordon (1993) have suggested these conditions lasted until c. 13.5-13 ka BP, when warmer water arrived with the northward migration of the Polar Front.

The age of the Errol Beds is crucial in providing a maximum limiting date for the next readvance of Scottish glaciers that incorporated and/or glacitectonised these glaciomarine deposits, as at Ardersier in the Moray Firth (Merritt et al., 1995). A readvance probably affected the whole Scottish ice sheet at this time. For example, it is speculated that the conspicuous moraine in Wester Ross (Wester Ross Readvance) formed at about 13.5-13 ka BP (Robinson and Ballantyne, 1979; Ballantyne, 1993), and also the Otter Ferry Stage limit in Loch Fyne (Sutherland, 1984). If this is true, then the glacier advance that formed these limits occurred when global temperature was rising rapidly. This means either that the glaciers readvanced because of increased precipitation, or that the event actually occurred more than a millenium earlier, during the Heinrich I cold interval. It may also be inferred that the ice marginal landform complexes in eastern Scotland used by Sissons (1967) to define limits of the Perth Readvance formed during this interval. As comparatively weak evidence was used in argument against the concept of a Perth Readvance (e.g. Paterson, 1974; Paterson et al., 1981), there is now incentive for detailed studies of the deposits and a reappreciation of earlier concepts of readvances during deglaciation. For example, Brown (1993) confirmed the ice marginal nature of deposits in the Dee valley near Dinnet - formerly known as the Dinnet Readvance (Bremner, 1931; Synge, 1956). Although these were reinterpreted as stagnant ice deposits

formed during overall ice sheet stagnation - without implying a glacier readvance (Clapperton and Sugden, 1972) - such a view now needs revision. If the radiocarbon dates from bogs in the Dee valley are correct, they indicate that the deposits at Dinnet are older than c. 12.6-11.5 ka BP (see Table 4.2 in Price, 1983) and thus may represent the limits of a Dee ice stream that readvanced about two thousand years earlier. These examples are quoted to encourage reinstatement of the concept that the Scottish ice sheet remained dynamically active during recession and periodically readvanced in response to climatic changes in the North Atlantic area prior to complete deglaciation, as suggested by the data from North Atlantic sediments and Greenland ice cores.

Such ice sheet activity in Scotland at c. 15-13 ka BP (cf. Figure 5.8b) is to be expected in view of the climatic signal from the isotopic record, and also because glaciers worldwide appear to have readvanced at this time (Broecker and Denton, 1990; Clapperton, 1995). For example, the Cordilleran ice sheet of north-west North America advanced to its maximum limits at 14.5-14 ka BP, while the Laurentide ice sheet readvanced along much of its margin close to its LGM morainic limits. Glaciers in the Alps readvanced (e.g. the Gschnitz moraines of the Eastern Alps), and the Scandinavian ice sheet formed the Pommeranian moraine belt south of the Baltic at this time. In the Southern Hemisphere, northern outlets of the Patagonian ice cap advanced close to their LGM limits at c. 14.9 ka BP (Lowell et al., 1995), while the Kumara III moraines of the New Zealand Southern Alps indicate a substantial readvance of glaciers in that region during the same interval (Clapperton, 1995). Thus, given the apparent worldwide response of glaciers and the oxygen isotope record to a climatic cooling during the millenia c. 15-13 ka BP, it would be remarkable and puzzling if the Scottish ice sheet had remained immune to it. Moreover, it is possible that reactivation of receding glaciers in Scotland occurred in response to increased precipitation as the Polar Front migrated northward at c. 13.5 - 13 ka BP, even although average temperatures were slowly rising.

Greenland ice cores and North Atlantic sediments reveal that a dramatic warming quickly followed the Late-glacial climate change that produced this readvance; its effect in Scotland appears to have been almost catastrophic. Immense volumes of sands and gravels deposited by torrential melt streams fill the glens and lowlands of many parts of Scotland, forming complexes of eskers and kame-and-kettle topography. These landforms document rapid disintegration of the thin Scottish ice sheet, which had vacated major highland valleys by 13-12 ka BP, according to the radiocarbon age of organic sediments forming in boggy hollows by this time. As mentioned earlier, it seems likely that small glaciers probably remained in the highest catchments, as the global atmosphere was still cooler than now due to the absence of greenhouse gases and due to the cooling influence of large ice sheets remaining over North America and Eurasia. Inferences that climate at 13-12 ka BP was as warm as modern conditions have been made from fossil beetles, but as these are probably more responsive to ground temperature, influenced by direct solar radiation, than by mean air temperature, such claims are probably over-estimates. Moreover, the beetle studies were made in England and SW Scotland, and do not accommodate the strong thermal gradient from north to south and from lowland to highland in Scotland.

5.10 Termination 1 and Late-glacial global warming

The abrupt warming at c. 13.5-13 ka BP appears to have been a global event as it is registered in ice cores and pollen records in both hemispheres. The event has been labelled as Termination 1, with the implication that it marks the end of the last glaciation. Oceanic evidence clearly shows that the North Atlantic Polar Front had moved north as far as the latitude of southern Iceland by *c.* 13 ka BP (Ruddiman and McIntyre, 1981). At least a millenium of warmth caused extensive decay of the last Scottish ice sheet, until even major Highland valleys had become ice-free. For example, the radiocarbon ages of organic sediments in bogs near the Cairngorm mountains (*c.* 13.1 ka BP at Loch Etteridge, upper Strath Spey, and *c.* 12.6 ka BP near Braemar) and in the NW Highlands (*c.* 12.8 ka BP at Loch Droma) (see Price, 1983) demonstrate that any glacier ice remaining in Scotland must have been confined to the highest catchments.

However, by *c.* 12.5 ka BP climate in Scotland had begun to cool again, a trend compatible with the palaeoclimatic record from Greenland (Figure 5.9). The cooling has been inferred from vegetational changes revealed by fossil pollen grains, for example in bogs in Skye (Walker *et al.,* 1988) and Fife (Whittington *et al.,* 1996) (see Chapter 9). Assuming that the trend of climatic deterioration between 12.5 ka and 11.5 ka BP indicated by the Greenland record reflects the progressive southward migration of the North Atlantic Polar Front, with occasional brief excursions north again (as during the Allerød interstade at *c.* 11.8-11.2 ka BP), it seems likely that glaciers would have started expanding again in the mountains of western Scotland. Thus, when the interval of sustained Loch Lomond Stade cooling began at 11.2 ka BP, substantial glaciers probably existed in the Scottish Highlands.

5.11 The Loch Lomond Readvance

The 1000-year long cold interval of the European/North Atlantic Younger Dryas Stade between c. 11 ka and 10 ka BP generated the major icefields and valley glaciers of the Loch Lomond Readvance (Figure 5.7) as January and July mean temperatures in western Scotland fell by at least 14°C and 7°C respectively below modern values (Gray and Coxon, 1991). This was caused by a rapid southward migration of the Polar Front (Bard *et al.,* 1987) to the latitude of northern Portugal (Figure 5.8c). The reason for this event has generated much speculation, including floods of freshwater from glacial lakes in North America (Broecker *et al.,* 1989) and iceberg discharge from the Laurentide ice sheet (the last Heinrich-type event); but as a cooling occurred coevally in the Southern Hemisphere (Denton and Hendy, 1994; Clapperton, 1995), it is apparent that it impacted the entire world synchronously and may not have originated simply in the North Atlantic region. The cause of the Younger Dryas Stade is still being investigated at the time of writing.

There is some evidence that glaciers fluctuated during this millennium of cold conditions due partly to shifts in position of the North Atlantic Polar Front, and partly to changing precipitation amounts. For example, precipitation probably decreased during the interval of extreme cold as formation of extensive pack ice over the Atlantic Ocean west and south of Scotland reduced the source of moisture for air flowing over the country (Benn *et al.,* 1992). Thus, slow glacier recession is believed to have set in while mean temperature was still low. As the North Atlantic Polar Front returned north towards the end of the Younger Dryas/Loch Lomond Stade, precipitation probably rose again over the Scottish mountains when open water developed offshore, and this would have occurred when atmospheric temperature was still relatively low. This might explain why the massive glacier in the Loch Lomond basin advanced to its maximum extent after *c.* 10.5 ka BP, the radiocarbon

age of peaty deposits covered by Loch Lomond Readvance glacial sediments at Croftamie near Drymen (Rose *et al.,* 1989).

By about 10 ka BP, global climate entered an interglacial mode, as temperatures worldwide rose and atmospheric composition (in terms of ^{18}O:^{16}O ratios and greenhouse gas content) became similar to that of today. The flux of warmth over Scotland as the North Atlantic Current was re-established caused rapid disintegration of the Loch Lomond Readvance glaciers, and the sequence of postglacial vegetation successions began, ultimately leading to the afforestation of much of the land (Chapter 9).

5.12 Conclusions

The following conclusions may be made about conditions in Scotland during the last glacial cycle.

1. While glaciers probably developed in Scotland during the two cold intervals of Isotope Sub-stages 5d and 5b in the Early Devensian, they may have melted away completely during the interstadial warmth of Isotope Sub-stages 5c and 5a.

2. From about 70 ka BP, the beginning of the Isotope Stage 4 cold interval, climate in the North Atlantic domain fluctuated frequently due to the unstable behaviour of the North Atlantic thermohaline system. Each stepped series of millenial-scale cooling events, giving lower and lower temperatures, endured *c.* 7-11 ka (Bond cycles) and each ended abruptly with rapid warming. As these climatic events imply latitudinal fluctuations in the position of the North Atlantic Polar Front, it is inevitable that the climate of Scotland and its glacier cover would have responded in harmony with the oceanic changes, because sea surface temperatures to the west of Scotland largely determine the mean temperature on land.

3. The $\delta^{18}O$ record of the GRIP ice core implies that climatic conditions in Scotland during the interval c. 70-10 ka BP may never have been warm enough for glaciers to have melted away completely. Thus the Scottish glaciers probably advanced and receded many times in unison with the vagaries of the North Atlantic Polar Front. This means that most corries and many valleys were constantly being eroded, and that glacial and glacifluvial sediments were constantly being reworked.

4. If similar fluctuations characterised earlier glacial cycles, it is evident that landforms of glacial erosion in Scotland have evolved largely through constant glacial activity during the glacial cycles, and are not simply a product of glacial maximum stages, as at *c.* 25-16 ka BP. Also, the frequent reworking of gravels by glacial and glacifluvial processes may partly explain the abundance of sub-rounded and rounded clasts in some morainic deposits.

5. As most of Scotland was covered by the last ice sheet at *c.* 25-16 ka BP, sedimentary evidence of earlier fluctuations will be scarce on the mainland due to glacial erosion, although a few sites have been found in peripheral areas. However, evidence of glacier fluctuations in Scotland prior to the Loch Lomond Readvance, may well exist in the eastern straths, as the ice sheet seems to have pulled back from its off-shore position early in the deglaciation because of dry conditions. The identification and dating of these (*cf.* Merritt *et al.,* 1995) is currently an exciting research goal.

Acknowledgements

Thanks are due to John Gordon and John S. Smith for helpful comments on an early draft of this paper.

References

Alley, R.B. and MacAyeal, D.R. 1994. Ice-rafted debris associated with binge/purge oscillations of the Laurentide Ice Sheet. *Paleoceanography,* **9,** 503-511.

Alley, R.B., Meese, D.A., Schuman, C.A., Gow, A.J., Taylor, K.C., Grootes, P.M., White, J.W., Ram, M., Waddington, E.D., Mayewski, P.A. and Zielinski, G.A. 1993. Abrupt increase in Greenland snow accumulation at the end of the Younger Dryas event. *Nature*, **362**, 527-529.

Andersen, B.G. and Borns, H.W. 1994. *The Ice Age World*. Scandinavian University Press, Oslo.

Ballantyne, C.K. 1989. The Loch Lomond Readvance on the Isle of Skye, Scotland: glacier reconstruction and palaeoclimatic implications. *Journal of Quaternary Science*, **4**, 95-108.

Ballantyne, C.K. 1990. The late Quaternary glacial history of the Trotternish escarpment, Isle of Skye, Scotland, and its implications for ice-sheet reconstruction. *Proceedings of the Geologists' Association*, **101**, 171-186.

Ballantyne, C.K. 1993. Gairloch moraine. In: Gordon, J.E. and Sutherland, D.G. (Eds), *Quaternary of Scotland*. Chapman & Hall, London, 103-106.

Ballantyne, C.K. 1997. Periglacial trimlines in the Scottish Highlands. *Quaternary International*, **38/39**, 119-136.

Ballantyne, C.K. and McCarroll, D. 1995. The vertical dimensions of Late Devensian glaciation on the mountains of Harris and SE Lewis, Outer Hebrides, Scotland. *Journal of Quaternary Science*, **10**, 211-223.

Ballantyne, C.K., Sutherland, D.G. and Reed, W.J. 1987. Introduction. In: Ballantyne, C.K. and Sutherland, D.G. (Eds), *Wester Ross Field Guide*. Quaternary Research Association, Cambridge, 1-63.

Bard, E., Arnold, M., Maurice, P., Duprat, J., Moyes, J. and Duplessy, J-C. 1987. Retreat velocity of the North Atlantic polar front during the last deglaciation determined by ^{14}C accelerator mass spectrometry. *Nature*, **328**, 791-794.

Benn, D.I. 1997. Glacier variations in Western Scotland. *Quaternary International*, **38/39**, 137-147.

Benn, D.I., Lowe, J.J. and Walker, M.J.C. 1992. Glacier response to climatic change during the Loch Lomond Stadial and early Flandrian: geomorphological and palynological evidence from the Isle of Skye, Scotland. *Journal of Quaternary Science*, **7**, 125-144.

Bond, G., Broecker, W., Johnsen, S., McManus, J., Labeyrie, L., Jouzel, J. and Bonani, G. 1993. Correlation between climate records from North Atlantic sediments and Greenland ice. *Nature*, **365**, 143-147.

Bond, G. and Lotti, R. 1995. Iceberg discharges into the North Atlantic on millennial time scales during the last glaciation. *Science*, **267**, 1005-1010.

Bowen, D.Q. 1989. The last interglacial-glacial cycle in the British Isles. *Quaternary International*, **3/4**, 41-47.

Brazier, V., Gordon, J.E., Hubbard, A. and Sugden, D.E. 1996a. The geomorphological evolution of a dynamic landscape: the Cairngorm Mountains, Scotland. *Botanical Journal of Scotland*, **48**, 13-30.

Brazier, V., Gordon, J.E., Kirkbride, M.P. and Sugden, D.E. 1996b. The Late Devensian ice sheet and glaciers in the Cairngorm Mountains. In: Glasser, N.F. and Bennett, M.R. (Eds), *The Quaternary of the Cairngorms. Field Guide*. Quaternary Research Association, London, 28-53.

Bremner, A. 1931. The valley glaciation in the district round Dinnet, Cambus o'May and Ballater. *The Deeside Field*, **5**, 15-24.

Bridgland, D. R. 1994. *Quaternary of the Thames*. Chapman & Hall, London.

Broecker, W.S. 1994. Massive iceberg discharges as triggers for global climate change. *Nature*, **372**, 421-424.

Broecker, W.S. and Denton, G.H. 1990. What drives glacial cycles? *Scientific American*, **262** (1), 43-50.

Broecker, W.S., Kennet, J.P., Flower, B.P., Teller, J.T., Trumbore, S., Bonani, G. and Wolfil, W. 1989. Routing of meltwater from the Laurentide Ice Sheet during the Younger Dryas cold episode. *Nature*, **341**, 318-320.

Brown, I.M. 1993. Pattern of deglaciation of the last (Late Devensian) Scottish ice sheet: evidence from ice-marginal deposits in the Dee valley, northeast Scotland. *Journal of Quaternary Science*, **8**, 235-250.

Cameron, T.D.J., Stoker, M.S. and Long, D. 1987. The history of Quaternary sedimentation in the UK sector of the North Sea Basin. *Journal of the Geological Society of London*, **144**, 43-58.

Clapperton, C.M. 1971. The pattern of deglaciation in part of north Northumberland. *Transactions of the Institute of British Geographers*, **50**, 115-127.

Clapperton, C.M. 1995. Fluctuations of local glaciers at the termination of the Pleistocene. *Quaternary International*, **28**, 41-50.

Clapperton, C. M. and Sugden, D. E. 1972. The Aberdeen and Dinnet glacial limits reconsidered. In: Clapperton, C.M. (Ed.), *North-east Scotland: Geographical Essays*. Aberdeen University Geography Department, Aberdeen, 5-11.

Clapperton, C.M. and Sugden, D.E. 1977. The Late Devensian glaciation of north-east Scotland. In: Gray, J.M. and Lowe. J.J. (Eds), *Studies in the Scottish Lateglacial Environment*. Pergamon Press, Oxford, 1-13.

Dansgaard, W., Johnsen, S.J., Clausen, H.B., Dahl-Jensen, D., Gundestrup, N.S., Hammer, C.U., Hvidberg, C.S., Steffensen, J.P., Sveinbjornsdottir, A.E., Jouzel, J. and Bond, G. 1993. Evidence for general instability of past climate from a 250-kyr ice-core record. *Nature*, **364**, 218-220.

Denton, G.H. and Hendy, C. 1994. Younger Dryas age advance of Franz Josef glacier in the Southern Alps of New Zealand. *Science*, **264**, 1434-1437.

Emiliani, C. 1954. Depth habitats of some species of pelagic foraminifers as indicated by oxygen isotope ratios. *American Journal of Science*, **252**, 149-158.

Fronval, T., Jansen, E., Bloemendal, J. and Johnsen, S. 1995. Oceanic evidence for coherent fluctuations in Fennoscandian and Laurentide ice sheets on millennium timescales. *Nature*, **374**, 443-446.

Geikie, A. 1865. *The Scenery of Scotland Viewed in Connection with its Physical Geology*. MacMillan, London.

Geikie, J. 1874. *The Great Ice Age and its Relation to the Antiquity of Man*. Isbister, London.

Gillespie, A. and Molnar, P. 1995. Asynchronous maximum advances of mountain and continental glaciers. *Reviews of Geophysics*, **33**, 311-364.

Gordon, J.E. and Sutherland, D.G. 1993. *Quaternary of Scotland*. Chapman & Hall, London.

Gray, J.M. and Coxon, P. 1991. The Loch Lomond Stadial glaciation in Britain and Ireland. In: Ehlers, J., Gibbard, P.L. and Rose, J. (Eds), *Glacial Deposits in Great Britain and Ireland*. Balkema, Rotterdam, 89-105.

Haflidason, H., Sejrup, H.P., Kristensen, D. K. and Johnsen, S. 1995. Coupled response of the late glacial climatic shifts of northwest Europe reflected in Greenland ice core: evidence from the northern North Sea. *Geology*, **23**, 1059-1062.

Hall, A.M. and Bent, A.J.A. 1991. The limits of the last British Ice Sheet in northern Scotland and the adjacent shelf. *Quaternary Newsletter*, **61**, 2-12.

Hall, A.M. and Connell, E.R. 1991. The glacial deposits of Buchan, northeast Scotland. In: Ehlers, J., Gibbard, P.L. and Rose, J. (Eds), *Glacial Deposits in Great Britain and Ireland*. Balkema, Rotterdam, 129-136.

Hall, A.M. and Jarvis, J. 1989. A preliminary report on the Late Devensian glaciomarine deposits around St. Fergus, Grampian Region. *Quaternary Newsletter*, **59**, 5-7.

Heinrich, H. 1988. Origin and consequences of cyclic ice rafting in the north-east Atlantic Ocean during the past 130,000 years. *Quaternary Research,* **29,** 142-152.

Hubbard, A. 1996. High resolution modelling of glaciers. Unpublished PhD thesis, University of Edinburgh.

Imbrie, J. and Imbrie, K.P. 1979. *Ice Ages: Solving the Mystery.* MacMillan, London.

Jamieson, T. F. 1865. On the history of the last geological changes in Scotland. *Quarterly Journal of the Geological Society of London,* **21,** 161-203.

Jardine, W.G., Dickson, J.H., Haughton, P.D.W., Harkness, D.D., Bowen, D.Q. and Sykes, G.A. 1988. A late Middle Devensian interstadial site at Sourlie, near Irvine, Strathclyde. *Scottish Journal of Geology,* **24,** 288-295.

Jones, R.L. and Keen, D.H. 1993. *Pleistocene Environments in the British Isles.* Chapman & Hall, London.

Jouzel, J. 1994. Ice cores north and south. *Nature,* **327,** 612-613.

Jouzel, J., Lorius, C., Petit, J.R., Genthon, C., Barkov, N.I., Kotlyakov, V.M. and Petrov, V.M. 1987. Vostok ice core: a continuous isotope temperature record over the last climatic cycle (160,000 years). *Nature,* **329,** 403-408.

Keigwin, L.D. 1995. The North Pacific through the millennia. *Nature,* **377,** 485-486.

Kotilainen, A.T. and Shackleton, N.J. 1995. Rapid climate variability in the North Pacific Ocean during the past 95,000 years. *Nature,* **377,** 323-326.

Lamb, H.H. 1995. *Climate History and the Modern World.* (2nd Edition). Routledge, London.

Lehman, S. 1996. True grit spells double trouble. *Nature,* **382,** 25-26.

Lockwood, J.G. 1982. Snow and ice balance in Britain at the present time, and during the last glacial maximum and lateglacial periods. *Journal of Climatology,* **2,** 209-231.

Lowell, T.V., Heusser, C.J., Andersen, B.J., Moreno, P.J., Hauser, A., Heusser, L.E., Schluchter, C., Marchant, D.R. and Denton, G.H. 1995. Interhemispheric correlation of late Pleistocene glacial events. *Science,* **269,** 1541-1549.

McCarroll, D., Ballantyne, C.K., Nesje, A. and Dahl, S-O. 1995. Nunataks of the last ice sheet in northwest Scotland. *Boreas,* **24,** 305-323.

MacAyeal, D.R. 1993. Binge/purge oscillations of the Laurentide Ice Sheet as a cause of the North Atlantic's Heinrich events. *Paleoceanography,* **8,** 775-784.

McIntyre, A., Ruddiman, W.F. and Jantzen, R. 1972. Southward penetration of the North Atlantic Polar Front: faunal and floral evidence of large-scale surface water mass movements over the last 225,000 years. *Deep Sea Research,* **19,** 61-77.

Mayewski, P. *et al.* (in press). *Reviews of Geophysics.*

Merritt, J.W., Auton, C.A. and Firth, C.R. 1995. Ice-proximal glaciomarine sedimentation and sea-level change in the Inverness area, Scotland: a review of the deglaciation of a major ice stream of the British Late Devensian Ice Sheet. *Quaternary Science Reviews,* **14,** 289-329.

Paterson, I.B. 1974. The supposed Perth Readvance in the Perth district. *Scottish Journal of Geology,* **10,** 53-66.

Paterson, I.B., Armstrong, M. and Browne, M.A.E. 1981. Quaternary estuarine deposits in the Tay-Earn area, Scotland. *Report of the Institute of Geological Sciences,* **81/7.**

Payne, A.J. and Sugden, D.E. 1990. Topography and ice sheet growth. *Earth Surface Processes and Landforms,* **15,** 625-639.

Price, R.J. 1983. *Scotland's Environment During the Last 30,000 Years.* Scottish Academic Press, Edinburgh.

Robinson, M. and Ballantyne, C.K. 1979. Evidence for a glacial readvance pre-dating the Loch Lomond Advance in Wester Ross. *Scottish Journal of Geology,* **15,** 271-277.

Rose, J., Lowe, J.J. and Switsur, R. 1988. A radiocarbon date on plant detritus beneath till from the type area of the Loch Lomond Readvance. *Scottish Journal of Geology,* **24,** 113-124.

Ruddiman, W.F. and McIntyre, A. 1981. The North Atlantic Ocean during the last deglaciation. *Palaeogeography, Palaeoclimatology, Palaeoecology,* **35,** 145-214.

Ruddiman, W.F., Sancetta, C.D. and McIntyre, A. 1977. Glacial/interglacial response rate of subpolar North Atlantic waters to climatic change: the record in oceanic sediments. *Philosophical Transactions of the Royal Society of London,* **B 280,** 119-142.

Ruddiman, W.F., Raymo, M.E., Martinson, D.G., Clement, B.M. and Backman, J. 1989. Pleistocene evolution: northern hemisphere ice sheets and North Atlantic Ocean. *Palaeoceanography,* **4,** 353 -412.

Sancetta, C.D., Imbrie, J. and Kipp, N.G. 1973. Climatic record of the past 130,000 years in North Atlantic Deep-Sea Core V23-82: correlation with the terrestrial record. *Quaternary Research,* **3,** 110-116.

Sejrup, H.P., Haflidason, H., Aarseth, I., King, E., Forsberg, C.F., Long, D. and Rokoengen, K. 1994. Late Weichselian glaciation history of the northern North Sea. *Boreas,* **23,** 1-13.

Shackleton, N.J. and Opdyke, N.D. 1973. Oxygen isotope and palaeomagnetic stratigraphy of Pacific core V28-239: oxygen isotope temperatures and ice volumes on a 10^5 year and 10^6 year scale. *Quaternary Research,* **3,** 39-55.

Sissons, J.B. 1967. *The Evolution of Scotland's Scenery.* Oliver & Boyd, Edinburgh.

Sissons, J.B. 1974. The Quaternary in Scotland: a review. *Scottish Journal of Geology,* **10,** 311-337.

Sissons, J.B. 1981. The last Scottish ice-sheet: facts and speculative discussion. *Boreas,* **10,** 1-17.

Skinner, B.J. and Porter, S.C. 1987. *Physical Geology.* Wiley, New York.

Skinner, B.J. and Porter, S. C. 1995. *The Dynamic Earth.* 3rd. Edition. Wiley, New York.

Sutherland, D.G. 1984. The Quaternary deposits and landforms of Scotland and the neighbouring shelves: a review. *Quaternary Science Reviews,* **3,** 157-254.

Sutherland, D.G. and Gordon J.E. 1993. The Quaternary in Scotland. In: Gordon, J.E. and Sutherland, D.G. (Eds), *Quaternary of Scotland.* Chapman & Hall, London, 13-47.

Synge, F.M. 1956. The glaciation of north-east Scotland. *Scottish Geographical Magazine,* **72,** 129-143.

Walker, M.J.C., Ballantyne, C.K., Lowe, J.J. and Sutherland, D.G. 1988. A reinterpretation of the Lateglacial environmental history of the Isle of Skye, Inner Hebrides, Scotland. *Journal of Quaternary Science,* **3,** 135-146.

Walker, M.J.C., Merritt, J.W., Auton, C.A., Coope, G.R., Field, M.H., Heijnis, H. and Taylor, B.J. 1992. Allt Odhar and Dalcharn: two pre-Late Devensian/Late Weichselian sites in northern Scotland. *Journal of Quaternary Science,* **7,** 69-86.

Whittington, G., Fallick, A.E. and Edwards, K.J. 1996. Stable oxygen isotope and pollen records from eastern Scotland and a consideration of Late-glacial and early Holocene climate change for Europe. *Journal of Quaternary Science,* **11,** 327-340.

6. Quaternary Stratigraphy: the Terrestrial Record

Adrian M. Hall

The key themes covered in this chapter are:

- the glacial record during the Quaternary;
- environmental change during the last interglacial-glacial cycle;
- the last ice sheet glaciation - timing, vertical extent, ice limits, patterns of flow, and timing and pattern of deglaciation.

6.1 Introduction

A key feature of the Quaternary is the frequency and rapidity of climate change (Chapter 5). Some 50 major 'warm' and 'cold' oscillations are recognized over the last 2.4 Ma (Figure 6. 1). Most of these 'interglacial' and 'glacial' periods were abruptly interrupted by interludes of a few hundreds to thousands of years of colder or warmer temperatures. These fluctuations are driven by small, orbitally-controlled variations in solar radiation which are amplified through complex interactions between the atmosphere, oceans, ice sheets and global tectonics. A key challenge is to determine to what extent these fluctuations

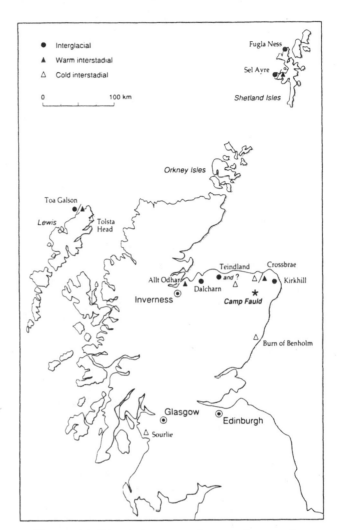

Figure 6.2 Sites with organic deposits that pre-date the Late Devensian. (Reprinted from 'A pre-Late Devensian pollen site from Camp Fauld, Buchan, Grampian Region' by G. Whittington, A.M. Hall and J. Jarvis from *New Phytologist,* 125, 867-874, 1993, by permission of Cambridge University Press).

in climate have left a recognisable signature in the geological record of landforms, sediments and fossil floras and faunas.

Significant advances have been made in understanding Quaternary environmental change in Scotland over the last 20 years. The timing and pace of climate change in Scotland can now be seen as part of broader patterns affecting the whole North Atlantic region (Boulton *et al.,* 1991). Evidence of regional events is found in deep-sea sediment cores, in cores from the Greenland ice sheet spanning the last 250 ka and from European continental stratigraphy (Chapter 5). Moreover, although the stratigraphic record on land in Scotland is poor, the sedimentary sequences offshore in the North Sea and along the Atlantic shelf are more complete and allow identification of key events in the Early and Middle Quaternary (Chapter 7). On land, important Late Quaternary sites which include organic sediments have been discovered or re-investigated (Figure 6.2). Integrated studies of such sites, involving sedimentology and analysis of

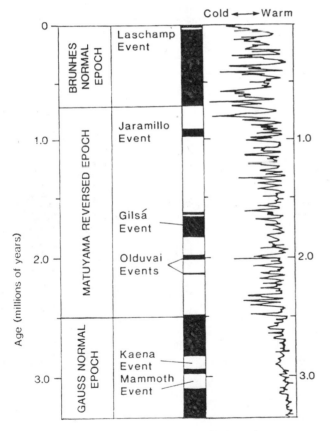

Figure 6.1 The climate record of the North Atlantic region during the last *c.* 3 Ma based on oxygen isotope analysis of ocean floor sediments. The principal geomagnetic epochs and events are shown on the left; periods of normal magnetisation are shown in black, reversed magnetisation in white. (After Boulton *et al.,* 1991).

organic remains, such as pollen, beetles and marine molluscs, has provided much new information on Quaternary environments. Finally, new dating techniques have been developed, for example, based on chemical changes through time in the amino acids in mollusc shells, on decay of Uranium isotopes and on reversals of the earth's magnetic field. Crucially, these techniques go beyond the 60 ka range of radiocarbon methods and allow resolution of older events.

6.2 Early Quaternary

Ocean floor sediments indicate that the climate of the North Atlantic was warmer than at present until around 2.4 Ma. The first appearance of dropstones at this time marks the onset of iceberg calving from ice masses, such as the Greenland ice sheet, around the North Atlantic. Temperatures before about 1 Ma were generally as warm as today but may have been low enough during cold stages for small glaciers to develop in the Scottish Highlands (Chapter 5).

In the central North Sea, thick Early Quaternary sediments were deposited on a huge, northward-advancing delta complex. Most of the sediment came from the major river systems of the European mainland, including the Baltic River and the ancestral Rhine. There is no clear evidence of direct glacial sedimentation in the basin during this period, although arctic marine microfauna are recognised as early as about 2 Ma (Gatliff *et al.,* 1994). Termination of delta formation may reflect the first regional glaciation of NW Europe at about 1 Ma and the consequent disruption and southward shift of pre-existing drainage patterns. (Chapter 7).

Early signs of an ice margin extending beyond the present Scottish coast are given by deposits of glaciomarine mud and lodgement till in the Forth Approaches. These sediments date from the Early - Middle Quaternary boundary at around 0.8-0.75 Ma and mark the first of a series of cold stages in which ice sheets covered Scotland (Gatliff *et al.,* 1994).

6.3 Middle Quaternary

The Early-Middle Quaternary boundary roughly corresponds with an intensification of cold stages and a strengthening of a 100 ka periodicity (corresponding to variations in the Earth's orbital eccentricity) of glacial-interglacial cycles. We know little of what was happening in Scotland between about 750-500 ka but the oxygen isotope record of North Atlantic sediments indicates that conditions were periodically suited to glaciation, and the stratigraphy of the North European Plain records extensive glaciations of Fennoscandia. There were also long temperate stages, including the Cromerian Interglacial around 500 ka. Sediments of this age from Boxgrove, Sussex, have yielded the oldest hominid remains in Britain.

Probably between about 480-420 ka, there occurred the most extensive of the North West European glaciations. In Britain, this is termed the Anglian glacial phase, after the widespread and thick glacial deposits of this age found in East Anglia. In Europe, this stage is named the Elsterian. In Scotland, the ice sheet was probably the first to reach the continental shelf edge west of the Hebrides and form a tidewater margin, with iceberg calving (Stoker *et al.,* 1993). To the east, Scottish ice crossed the floor of the North Sea to join up with the Scandinavian ice sheet. There was extensive erosion of older sediment from the bed of the North Sea, with the cutting of large channels up to 100 m deep, possibly by outbursts of meltwater from the ice sheet. Ice flowed south down the Irish Sea to reach the Bristol Channel, and Welsh ice carved out the Severn lowland,

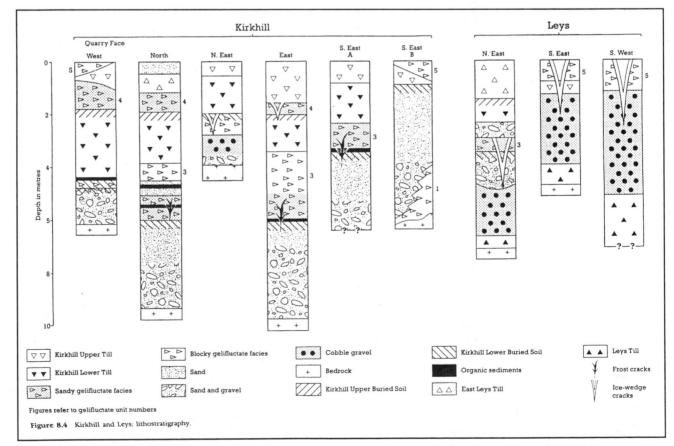

Figure 8.4 Kirkhill and Leys: lithostratigraphy.

Figure 6.3 The lithostratigraphy of the sediment sequences formerly exposed in various faces at Kirkhill Quarry and Leys Quarry, NE Scotland. (After Hall and Jarvis, 1993).

Figure 6.4 Kirkhill: the sequence of sediments in the SE face of the quarry in 1979. The podzolic Lower Buried Soil appears in the middle of the photo where a dark organic (Ah) horizon is underlain by the bleached (Ea) horizon. (Photo: E.R. Connell).

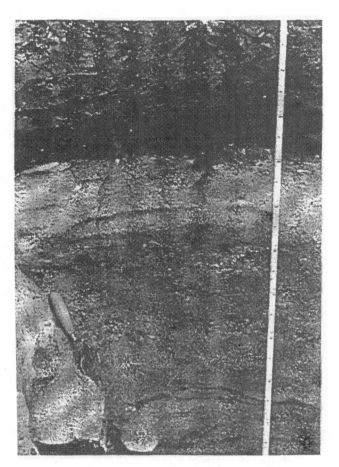

Figure 6.5 Kirkhill: detail of the Lower Buried Soil, showing the organic (Ah) horizon and the bleached (Ea) horizon. (Photo A.M. Hall).

beheading the ancestral source streams of the Thames. Ice moving down the North Sea basin, sourced initially from Norway but then subsequently from northern England and Scotland, excavated the Fen basin and reduced the chalk cuesta of Suffolk and Norfolk to a subdued ridge. Sediment volumes in the North Sea suggest that this was a time of intense glacial erosion in Scotland and it is likely that many major glacial troughs were significantly deepened, if not created at this time.

In Europe, the Elsterian was succeeded by the Saalian glacial phase, which included at least two distinct phases of ice advance. Glacial till and meltwater deposits from this period survive at several sites in NE Scotland and indicate that ice passed beyond the present coastline. Large subaqueous moraines were deposited in the outer Moray Firth, about 150 km east of Fraserburgh, beneath a floating ice sheet margin as the ice retreated northward (Andrews *et al.*, 1990). There is little doubt that ice covered northern England at this time but the status of the penultimate cold stage in central England, where it is termed the Wolstonian, has become uncertain, as there are strong reasons to regard the sediments in the type area around Coventry as Anglian in age.

The longest Quaternary sequence on land in Scotland comes from Kirkhill, near Fraserburgh. Here an old quarry revealed a stacked sequence of tills, periglacial deposits and interglacial sediments (Figures 6.3 and 6.4). Although dating evidence is limited, it appears that the Upper Buried Soil is of last interglacial age and that the oldest glacial sediments may be of Anglian age. Organic sediments associated with the podzolic Lower Buried Soil (Figure 6.5) include pollen

of pine, alder and even lime. The preservation of this remarkable sequence is testament to the limited erosive power of successive ice sheets in Buchan (Hall and Jarvis, 1993).

6.4 Late Quaternary

6.4.1 The last interglacial (130-117 ka)

An interglacial is a long period between cold stages when temperatures are as warm or warmer than today. The Late Quaternary begins with the last interglacial, termed the Ipswichian in England and the Eemian in NW Europe. This corresponds with Oxygen Isotope Stage 5e (130-117 ka) in the North Atlantic record.

First results from the GRIP Greenland ice core in 1993 indicated that the last interglacial climate was highly unstable, with major shifts in temperature over just a few decades. More recent analysis suggests that these abrupt changes may be partly an artifact created by shearing within the basal layers of the ice sheet. The idea, however, that past interglacial climates were as stable as the present Holocene interglacial has been fundamentally challenged.

There is no doubt, however, that the last interglacial included long periods of unusual warmth. Marine microfauna show that the warm waters of the North Atlantic Drift reached close to the coast of Greenland and that North Sea temperatures were perhaps 2°C warmer than at present. A wide range of exotic mammals existed in southern England, including hippopotamus, straight-tusked elephant, narrow-nosed rhinoceros and, more diminutively, the European pond tortoise. Broad leaf forests, with oak, elm,

Figure 6.6 Fugla Ness, Shetland. The interglacial peat occurs at the level of the spade and is overlain by periglacial slope deposits and by till. (Photo: A.M. Hall).

lime and hornbeam, were widespread in northern England.

At Fugla Ness, Shetland (Figure 6.6), a peat is preserved beneath till and periglacial slope deposits (Hall *et al.,* 1993). This peat contains small stumps of Scots Pine and pollen of plants now confined to the maritime heathlands of SW Ireland. The presence of these plants at what is an exposed, treeless site today points to a warm or less windy climatic phase. A Uranium-series date indicates that the peat belongs to the last interglacial. Unfortunately, there are no reliably dated sites from the climax of the last interglacial on the mainland of Scotland and so the nature of the vegetation at this time is uncertain. The decline of the last interglacial is recorded in organic muds and sands at Teindland, near Elgin (Figure 6.7). The earliest pollen of hazel and alder is replaced by pine and then heathland. Burning of the heathland, shown by the abundance of charcoal, led to an influx of sands that were then colonised by grasses. This sequence of vegetation change points to a cooling climate at the close of the interglacial (Hall *et al.,* 1995).

6.4.2 Early Devensian (117-74 ka)

In recent years it has become apparent that the climate of the last glacial stage, the Devensian of Britain and Weichselian of NW Europe, has been highly unstable. A total of 24 short periods of relative warming (interstadials) is recognised since the last interglacial in the Summit ice core from the Greenland ice sheet (see Chapter 5, Figure 5.10) (Dansgaard *et al.,* 1993). Changes in air temperatures in the ice core occurred in phase with changes in sea surface temperatures in the North Atlantic and with fluctuations in the extent of the major Northern Hemisphere ice sheets. Pulses of coarse sediment accumulation in North Atlantic cores from phases of accelerated ice-rafting appear to reflect the culmination of advances of the Laurentide ice sheet and the onset of rapid retreat. These Heinrich Events coincide with abrupt changes in sea surface temperatures and suggest that the North Atlantic Drift acts as an on-off switch for major glaciation around the North Atlantic (see Chapter 5).

Figure 6.7 The Buried Soil at Red Burn, Teindland, comprising a dark organic (Ah) horizon (at the level of the spade handle) and a bleached (Ea) horizon below. The soil dates from the end of the last interglacial and is overlain by periglacial and glacial deposits. (Photo: A.M. Hall).

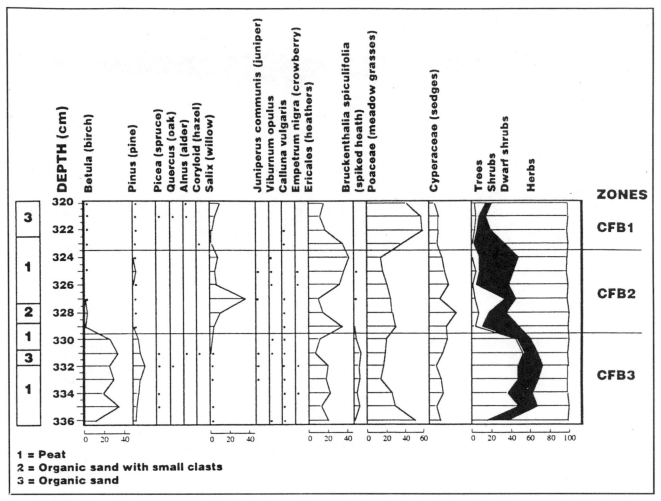

Figure 6.8 Pollen diagram from an Early Devensian interstadial peat at Camp Fauld, Peterhead, Buchan. (After Whittington *et al.,* 1993).

The Early Devensian includes two long and cool temperate interstadials, equivalent to the Brørup and Odderade stages in the Low Countries. Both saw the development of pine-birch forests, with stands of spruce and larch, across much of NW Europe. In north-east Scotland, birch or birch-pine woodland developed (Figure 6.8). Further north, on Shetland, buried peat at Sel Ayre (Figure 6.9) records the development of a rich heathland and grassland with few trees. These interstadials were characterized by more continental conditions than today, with summer temperatures close to those of the present but colder winters. This continentality may be a reflection of a weakened North Atlantic circulation and the reduced size of the North Sea.

6.4.3 Middle Devensian (74-24 ka)

Periglacial and glacial environments prevailed across much of NW Europe in this period. After 75 ka, the Scandinavian ice sheet expanded beyond the Norwegian coast. Over the next 60 ka, the ice front advanced and retreated several times (Figure 6.10) but most of the Scandinavian mountains probably retained an ice cover throughout this period (Mangerud, 1991). It is likely that equivalent fluctuations affected the Scottish ice sheet.

In north Germany, organic sediments from two later interstadials, the Oerel (58-54 ka) and Glinde (51-48 ka), record an open shrub tundra. In Scotland, there are few, if any, organic materials that appear to represent interstadials in the interval 75-40 ka. Dates for dripstones from the Assynt caves show phases of growth, implying water availability

and limestone solution and therefore climatic amelioration from glacial or permafrost conditions, at 60 ka and around 55 ka. These dates imply that this part of the NW Highlands was ice-free around these times (Lawson, 1995).

Important evidence of near-shore environments is provided by the marine shell beds found beneath till and above sea level around the Moray Firth and the Firth of Clyde. Many earlier workers suggested that these shell beds were *in situ,* based largely on the apparent lack of glacial disturbance, sub-horizontal attitude and the large size of the deposits. Others advocated glacial transport as large erratic masses. It is often difficult to resolve this key question, however, as these deposits are often poorly exposed. Recent exposures at Oldmill, Mintlaw (Figure 6.11), show that rafts of glaciomarine mud up to 100 m long may be glacially transported with very little disturbance to bedding. Nonetheless, the included high-boreal to low-arctic marine fauna indicate periods with cold, open water in the Moray Firth, Firth of Clyde and the Minch. Amino acid ratios for shells from these deposits suggest that two or more ice-free periods may have occurred in the present coastal zone during the Middle Devensian.

A major ice advance probably occurred between 75-60 ka and glacial and glaciomarine sediments that may date from this stage have been identified from the outer Moray Firth and the Hebridean shelf (Andrews *et al.,* 1990; Stoker *et al.,* 1993). On land, a total of four till units have been identified overlying the organic deposits at Teindland and at least the oldest of these is probably of Middle Devensian age.

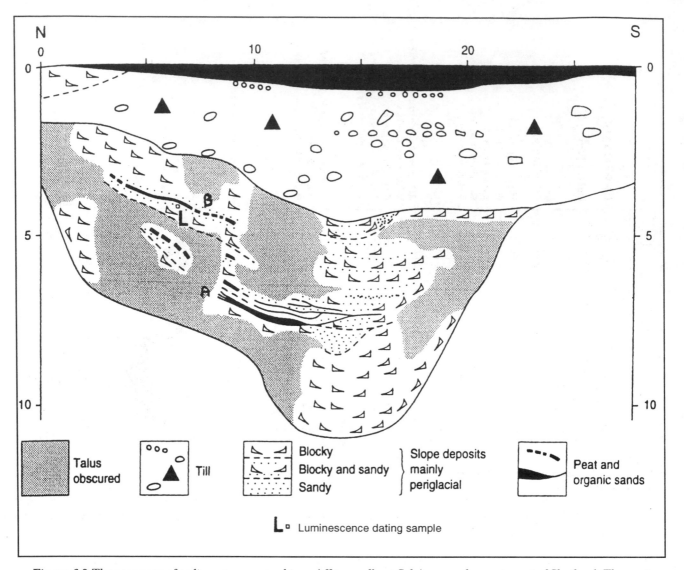

Figure 6.9 The sequence of sediments preserved in a cliff-top gully at Sel Ayre on the west coast of Shetland. The peat bed (A) and organic sands and gravels (A-B) lie between periglacial slope deposits and record an interstadial environment in which trees were absent and the vegetation largely comprised heath and grassland. Luminescence dating gave an age range of *c.* 105-98 ka for the upper part of the organic sands and gravels.

At least one other later major ice advance probably occurred between 50-30 ka. There is growing evidence of the presence of glacier ice in the lowlands around Glasgow in the period before about 30 ka. At Sourlie, Irvine, interstadial deposits that began to accumulate around 33 ka rest on unweathered lodgement till. At Bishopbriggs, gravels and sands include bones of woolly rhinoceros, one of which is radiocarbon dated to about 27 ka BP. These outwash deposits pass downwards into water-lain tills, indicating the proximity of glacier ice. Given the advance of Loch Lomond Stadial ice to the outskirts of Glasgow, any substantial build-up of ice in the Scottish Highlands prior to Oxygen Isotope Stage 2 would have reached the lowlands around the Firth of Clyde. Near Fraserburgh, sands from an ice-proximal glaciofluvial gravel fan have given luminescence ages of 45±4 ka and 37±4 ka, implying the presence of glacier ice at this part of the Moray Firth coast. This is consistent with the deposition of glaciomarine muds in the inner Moray Firth in the later part of the Middle Devensian.

An interstadial at around 30 ka is increasingly well documented, as elsewhere in northwest Europe. The type site is Sourlie, where organic-rich muds, resting on till, lie beneath two Late Devensian tills. The organic materials have given radiocarbon dates of 33-29 ka BP and provide evidence of an open, tundra vegetation on which large mammals, such as reindeer and woolly rhinoceros, grazed. Finds of mammoth bones in the last century from around the Glasgow area may also date from this interstadial. Reindeer bones from the Inchnadamph caves have given a range of radiocarbon dates from 31.5 to 22 ka BP. Radiocarbon dates on shells from rafts of marine mud also suggest that The Minch and the inner Firth of Clyde were free of glacier ice at this time.

The overall picture of the last interglacial-glacial cycle in Scotland is therefore one of rapidly fluctuating environments. After the unusual warmth of the last interglacial, the Early Devensian was characterised by stadial periods with widespread periglacial conditions and possible mountain glacierisation separated by two long, cool temperate phases in which birch-pine forests developed across much of Scotland. The Middle Devensian period was colder and there was extensive glaciation. A number of short, slightly warmer and perhaps drier phases brought ice retreat from peripheral areas. An important interstadial marks the boundary with the Late Devensian, the period of greatest expansion of the Scottish ice sheet in the last 125 ka.

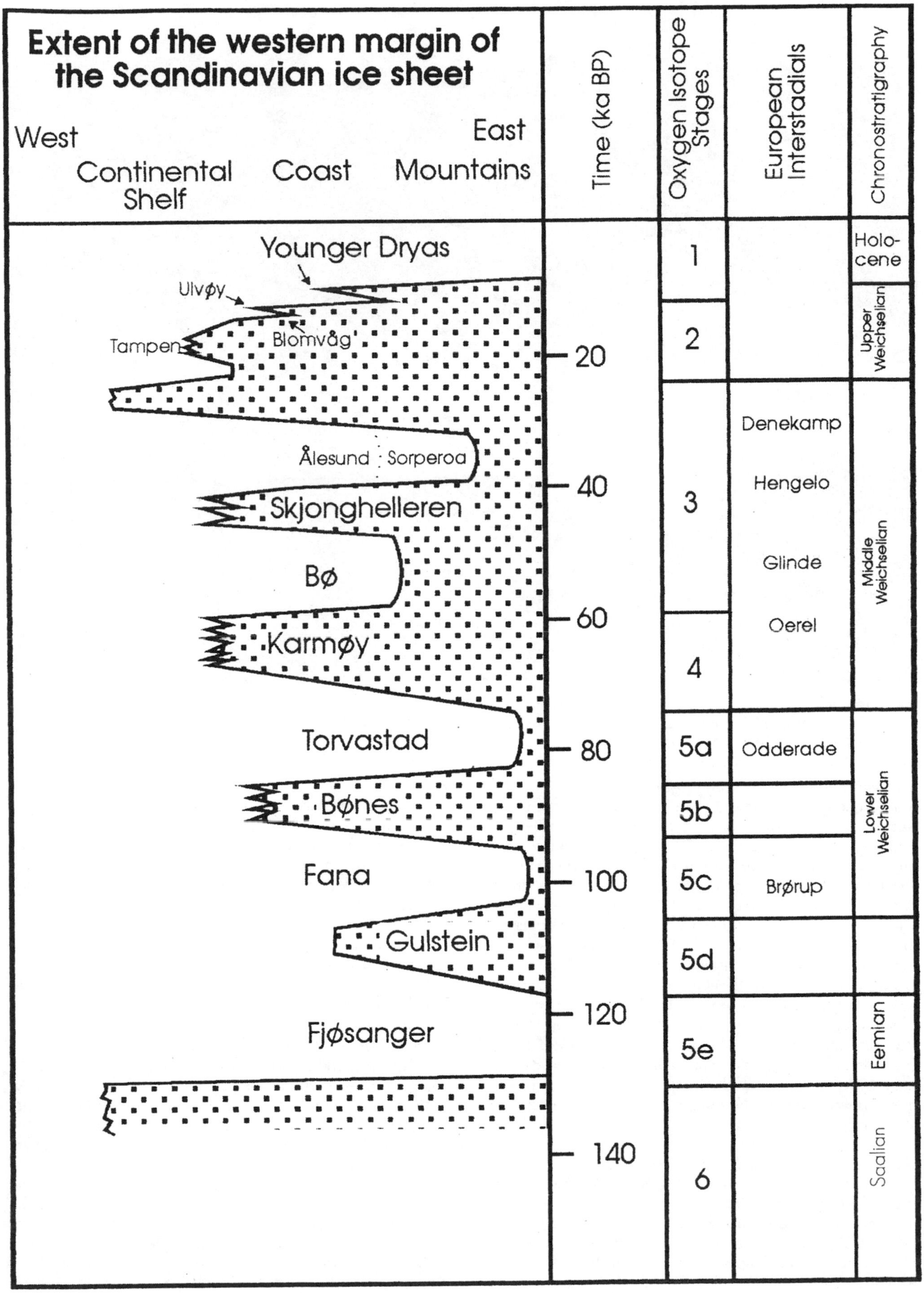

Figure 6.10 Fluctuations of the western margin of the Scandinavian ice sheet during the last interglacial-glacial cycle. (After Baumann *et al.*, 1995).

Figure 6.11 A small raft of Jurassic mudstone transported by ice from the Moray Firth to Oldmill, SE of Mintlaw, NE Scotland. The raft (above the hammer) rests on glaciofluvial gravels and, with the overlying sands, shows glaciotectonic deformation. (Photo: A.M. Hall).

6.5 Late Devensian ice sheet glaciation

The behaviour of the last ice sheet is of fundamental importance in understanding the Scottish landscape. Although many large features, like glacial troughs and corries, were already in existence, the Late Devensian ice sheet was a powerful agent of erosion, scouring bedrock surfaces and extensively removing earlier deposits (see Chapters 4 and 13). A wide variety of landforms of glacial and meltwater deposition was left in the areas outside the limits of the later, briefer and much more spatially restricted Loch Lomond Stadial glaciation (Chapter 8). The ice sheet was many hundreds of metres thick and led to regional isostatic depression of the crust. Rebound when the ice began to melt led to the formation of staircases of raised beaches in many coastal areas (Chapter 12). Yet, despite over 150 years of research (Chapter 1), a number of key questions concerning the timing and extent of the last ice sheet remain unresolved.

6.5.1 The build-up of the Late Devensian ice sheet

The timing of the first advance of the last ice sheet is only loosely constrained. Dates of 33-29 ka BP for organic deposits beneath till from Sourlie, Irvine, indicate that the Glasgow area was ice-free at this time (Jardine *et al.*, 1988). Conditions were cold, however, and it is probable that small ice caps existed in the western Highlands (see Chapter 5). The Greenland ice core record indicates that after about 29 ka the intensity and duration of cold phases increased and these stadials were only occasionally interrupted by brief

but rapid interstadial warming. This date probably marks an acceleration in the build-of of the last ice sheet.

The ice sheet had apparently reached the outer Moray Firth and the Hebridean shelf by about 22 ka BP (Peacock *et al.*, 1992; Sejrup *et al.*, 1994). This implies heavy snowfall and rapid build-up of ice. Price (1983) used an analogy with Loch Lomond Stadial glaciers to suggest that the front of the last ice sheet advanced at a rate of about 30 m per year, with vertical thickening of 0.3 m per year. This is remarkably rapid but the dates above indicate that these figures are slightly conservative.

6.5.2 When was the maximum of the last ice sheet?

Until recently it had become widely accepted that the last ice sheet reached its maximum extent at around 18 ka BP. A key locality is Holderness in eastern England where organic silts of this radiocarbon age are overlain by till. The organic materials accumulated under a severe tundra environment, before advance of an ice lobe down the North Sea coast. Yet the silts rest on an undulating till surface and the possibility that this older till was also of Late Devensian age was not widely considered. A rethink of the significance of the Holderness material was prompted by the dates cited above from the margins of the Scottish ice sheet. In particular, Sejrup *et al.*, (1994) provided radiocarbon dates on shells and foraminifera from the northern North Sea that seem to indicate that the last Scottish ice sheet advanced to its maximum position before 22 ka BP and then withdrew, only to advance again at around 18 ka BP. This two-stage model of the Late Devensian glaciation is not yet underpinned by a sufficient number of radiocarbon dates but seems to match the timing of temperature changes in the GRIP ice core (*cf.* Chapter 5) and of fluctuations in the extent of the Laurentide and Scandinavian ice sheets. The model is of great interest as it implies that the last Scottish ice sheet advanced and retreated on at least two occasions and may have left complex sequences of deposits and assemblages of landforms in peripheral areas.

6.5.3 What was the maximum extent of the last ice sheet?

For nearly a century, the view that the last ice sheet covered the whole of Scotland, including the major islands, went largely unchallenged. After 1950, however, evidence began to accumulate that peripheral parts of Scotland might have escaped glaciation by the last ice sheet. In central Buchan and, subsequently, in Caithness, it was noted that chemically weathered bedrock was widespread and that tills were absent from upper slopes, apparently soliflucted downslope. This evidence is insecure, as neither the presence of weathered rock nor the absence of till need imply an absence of glaciation. More convincing, however, was stratigraphical and chronological data that appeared to indicate that Late Devensian tills were absent from Buchan, Caithness, Orkney and NW Lewis. In Buchan, near-surface tills were known to pass below Late Devensian tills at the coast and could therefore pre-date this glaciation. Important supporting evidence came from Crossbrae, Turriff. Here till of western provenance was overlain by peat dated to 26.4 ka BP and 22.4 ka BP and by solifluction deposits, implying that this area was not covered by ice at the maximum of the last glaciation. In north-east Caithness and Orkney, shells from the latest tills gave amino acid ratios suggestive of a last interglacial age or older. The scarcity of ratios suggestive of a Middle Devensian age for the shells led to the claim that these tills were of Early Devensian age and that these areas were not glaciated in the Late Devensian. In north-west Lewis, the apparent absence of till from above the Galson Beach around Galson, whilst Late Devensian till covered this raised beach to the north and south, indicated that this stretch of coastline lay just outside the maximum limit of local ice on Lewis in the Late Devensian (Sutherland and Walker, 1984). The convergence of this evidence led to a fundamental reassessment of the extent of the Late Devensian ice sheet (Sutherland, 1984) (Figure 6.12). The idea of a relatively restricted ice sheet soon became widely accepted (Bowen *et al.,* 1986; Cameron *et al.,* 1987; Bowen, 1991).

Recent findings suggest, however, a complete cover of ice over Scotland at the maximum of the last glaciation, except, perhaps, for a few nunataks in peripheral mountain areas.

In Buchan, re-examination of the Crossbrae site indicates that the peat there belongs to the Early Devensian and that it is overlain by glaciofluvial gravel, as well as soliflucted till. The site therefore no longer provides evidence of the presence or absence of ice cover in this area in the Late Devensian. Other evidence does point strongly to glaciation of Buchan by the last ice sheet, including:

(i) the regionally integrated network of meltwater channels (Clapperton and Sugden, 1977), which is suggestive of Late Devensian glaciation;

(ii) the presence of moraines marking Late Devensian ice sheet limits at least 25 km east of the present North Sea coast, implying ice thickness over central Buchan of up to 500 m; and

(iii) the existence of glaciomarine silts at St. Fergus close to sea level and radiocarbon-dated to about 15.3 ka BP (Hall and Jarvis 1989). The low global sea levels at this date mean that these silts can only have been deposited whilst this area remained depressed from a recently removed ice cover of considerable thickness.

In Caithness and Orkney, a key question is the age of the shelly till or tills that occur in these areas. Although results from amino acid ratios suggest that many included shells are of Stage 5 age or older, it is clear that at some sites, especially around Dunbeath, the included shells are younger, probably Stage 4 or 3 in age (Bowen and Sykes, 1988). At least some shelly tills therefore date from the Late Devensian. Even tills that incorporate only older shells may be of Late Devensian age if the source material for the till was an old marine mud. The regional pattern of ice flow from SE to NW indicated by striated bedrock surfaces is consistent with the carry of material by ice out of the Moray Firth towards the north coast of Caithness and across Orkney in a single glacial event. Moreover, evidence of Late Devensian maximum ice limits well to the west of Orkney (Stoker *et al.,* 1993) implies a thick ice cover in Caithness and Orkney.

In NW Lewis, an ice-free area was identified on the basis of the lack of Late Devensian till overlying the Galson Beach around Galson (Peacock, 1984; Sutherland and Walker, 1984). Recently, thin diamictons overlying the Galson Beach in this area have been reinterpreted as glacial deposits. The small size of the ice-free area (<10 km^2) and the lack of ice-marginal features cast further doubt on its reality (Hall, 1995). Hence there is no longer firm evidence that this part of Lewis remained unglaciated in the Late Devensian. Only St. Kilda seems to represent an area not inundated by the last Scottish ice sheet (Sutherland *et al.,* 1984).

The evidence above indicates that the maximum limit of the Late Devensian ice sheet lay beyond the present coastline of Scotland. Members of the British Geological Survey and others have identified offshore drift limits and morainal topography that appear to relate to the maximum and early retreat stages of the last ice sheet (see Chapter 7). In the central North Sea, till of the Wee Bankie Formation (Stoker *et al.,* 1985) has been mapped on the sea bed for only a few tens of kilometres offshore and terminates eastwards in a zone of sea-bed ridges interpreted as end moraines (Figure 6.12). This Wee Bankie Moraine could mark the eastern limit of grounded ice in the Late Devensian (Thomson and Eden, 1977). Seismic surveys indicate that the Wee Bankie Formation passes eastwards into arctic and glaciomarine deposits (Stoker *et al.,* 1985). Dates from borehole 74/7 of 17.7 ka BP and 21.7 ka BP for lignitised wood from this Marr Bank Formation (Holmes, 1977) indicate a Late Devensian age. These formations can be traced northward into the outer Moray Firth, where tills extend east to the Bosies Bank Moraine, beyond which only glaciomarine deposits apparently occur (Hall and Bent, 1990).

The apparent lack of till east of the Wee Bankie Moraine and the Bosies Bank Moraine is perhaps the main reason why the maximum ice limit has been placed at these moraines. Recently, however, several writers have claimed that the Late Devensian ice sheet extended further east across the present bed of the North Sea. Wingfield (1989) has identified several generations of linear incisions on the seafloor that may have been formed by outbursts of meltwater from ice sheet margins. The youngest generation of these incisions was cut in the Weichselian and appears to imply that the Late Devensian ice sheet extended at least as far as the Median Line (Ehlers and Wingfield, 1991). The

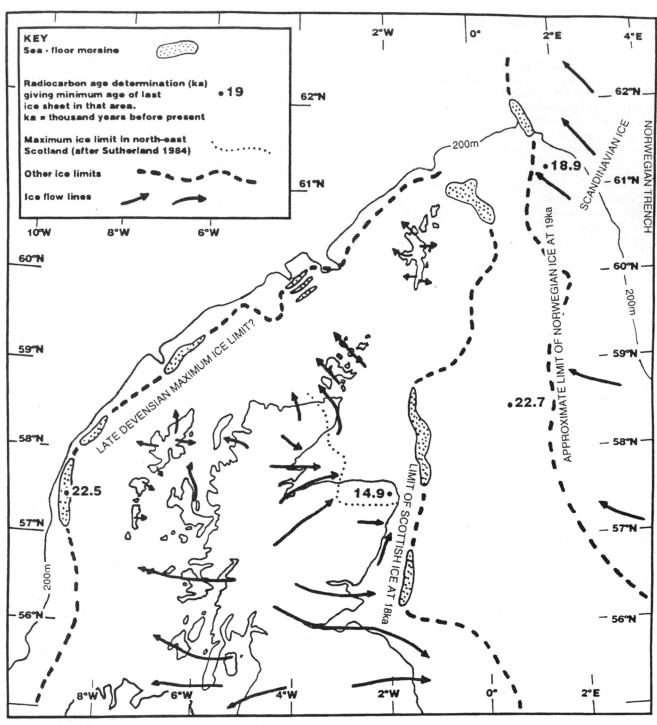

Figure 6.12 Limits of the Late Devensian ice sheet and directions of ice movement.

extension of the last Scottish ice sheet to the outer Moray Firth is also supported by the dates given by Sejrup *et al.* (1994) and by patterns of isostatic loading (Ekman, 1995).

6.5.4 *The vertical extent of the last ice sheet*

There has been a long debate over the whether the Late Devensian ice sheet rose above the level of the mountain summits in Scotland. It was widely believed for over a century that it covered all the mainland mountain tops. A few authors, however, argued for the existence of nunataks on the basis of the survival of high-level tors, the presence of kaolinite in mountain soils and the distribution of blockfields (Godard, 1965). These arguments are equivocal, as all these features may have survived beneath cold-based

ice masses (Sugden, 1968). In recent years, the debate has received new impetus from the identification of possible ice-free peripheral areas in Scotland (Sutherland, 1984) and from careful observation of the distribution and characteristics of mountain-top frost-weathered detritus. It is increasingly clear that on the mountains of Wester Ross (Ballantyne *et al.,* 1987; McCarroll *et al.,* 1995), Skye (Ballantyne, 1990) and Harris and south-east Lewis (Ballantyne and McCarrol, 1995) there is a sharp lower limit to blockfields and that mountain-top soils contain clay minerals, notably gibbsite, which are absent or poorly represented at lower levels (Ballantyne, 1994). This evidence is consistent with the view that the lower limit of these blockfields marks a glacial trimline at the maximum vertical extent of an ice sheet.

This is an intriguing possibility, with major implications for reconstruction of the vertical and lateral dimensions of the last Scottish ice sheet at its maximum. It seems unlikely, however, that the trimlines mark the maximum vertical elevation of the Late Devensian ice sheet. On northern Skye a trimline drops from 600 m to 450 m OD in 24 km (Ballantyne, 1994), a gradient and elevation that are difficult to reconcile with an apparent maximum ice sheet limit close to the islands of Sula Sgeir and Rona (Stoker *et al.*, 1993), nearly 200 km to the north. Similarly on Harris, the ice sheet profile extrapolated from trimlines terminates just 7-10 km west of the present coast, whereas the Late Devensian maximum limit appears to lie 75 km west of North Uist (Peacock *et al.*, 1992). These trimlines may relate instead to a readvance of the Late Devensian ice sheet, perhaps including the limit marked by the major end moraine on the floor of the Minch, east of the Eye Peninsula on Lewis. It has recently been proposed that similar trimlines in western Norway relate to a readvance of the Scandinavian ice sheet around 19 ka BP (Larsen *et al.*, 1995) and it was suggested above that the Scottish ice sheet also readvanced across the North Sea floor at around 18 ka BP.

6.5.5 Patterns of ice sheet flow

The basic pattern of flow of the last Scottish ice sheet on the mainland was known by the turn of the century (Geikie, 1901). The main centres of ice dispersal were the Western and North West Highlands, with an ice shed running south from Sutherland to the Rannoch basin and the Cowal Peninsula, and the Southern Uplands, where an ice shed extended from Merrick eastward to the Lowther Hills (Figure 6.12). Secondary ice centres developed over the eastern massifs of the Cairngorms, South-East Grampians and the Cheviots, as well as on the islands of Skye, Mull and Arran.

The main changes in the interpretation of lines of ice movement have been the recognition that the Outer Hebrides and Shetland were independent centres of ice accumulation (Price, 1983). Until 1970, it was widely held that ice from the Highlands had crossed the Outer Isles during the last glaciation. Evidence of ice movement towards the east coast of the islands led, however, to the identification of an ice centre or centres developed over, or to the west of, the island chain (von Weymarn, 1979). The concept that the Shetland Islands were glaciated by ice from Scandinavia (Peach and Horne, 1879) was largely unchallenged for more than a century. Again, however, evidence that the latest ice movement was towards the east coast of the islands led to the identification of an elongate ice dome centred over Shetland (*cf.* Birnie *et al.*, 1993).

Careful reconstruction has revealed fluctuating patterns of ice flow within the last Scottish ice sheet (Sutherland, 1984). At an early stage of the Late Devensian, ice from the Highlands was able to cross the Central Lowlands to the foot of the Southern Uplands and leave erratics and a lower till unit (Kirby, 1968). In western Ayrshire, this lower till contains shells derived from the Firth of Clyde. The increasing strength of the Southern Uplands ice centre then pushed back and diverted the Highland ice. An upper till with Southern Uplands erratics was deposited in south-central Scotland (Sutherland, 1993) and Highland ice was pushed westward to flow over Arran, Kintyre and Jura (Sutherland. 1984), against the grain of the terrain, and into Northern Ireland. In Buchan and Caithness, inland tills of possible Late Devensian age underlie tills derived from the Moray Firth (Hall and Bent, 1990). This stratigraphy is consistent with an initial expansion of ice from local centres

in the eastern Grampians and eastern Sutherland and subsequent exclusion of local ice from these areas after strengthening of the flow of the Moray Firth ice stream, sourced in the NW Highlands.

A puzzling feature of the pattern of flow of the last ice sheet is the manner in which ice spread out from the Moray Firth and Firth of Forth to flow north and south along the present coastline (Figure 6.12). One suggestion has been that Scottish ice was hemmed in by Scandinavian ice advancing across the bed of the North Sea. This may have happened at the maximum of the Late Devensian before 22 ka, but thereafter it appears that the two ice sheets were not in contact in the outer Moray Firth (Sejrup *et al.*, 1994). On Orkney it seems that even the final flow of ice was towards the Atlantic (Hall, 1996), and so some other mechanism must be sought. Sharp changes in the direction of ice flow are known to occur when ice sheets move from rigid to deformable beds, as the last Scottish ice sheet did when moving from the current land area on to the muddy floor of the North Sea. This effect, coupled with the tendency of ice sheets to spread out over shelf areas and to depress the land beneath them, thereby creating a channel for flow, may be sufficient to explain this general tendency towards ice sheet diffluence.

6.5.6 The timing and pattern of deglaciation

Deglaciation, the retreat phase, can be said to have begun after the last ice sheet reached its second maximum at around 18 ka BP. The ice margin lay at St. Fergus on the Buchan coast at around 15 ka BP but was apparently still to the west of the Outer Hebrides at this time. The initial cause of ice retreat was not rising temperature. Studies of shallow marine muds, the Errol Beds, deposited in the western North Sea between 16-13 ka BP show a high arctic fauna. Rather, it seems that the ice sheet was starved of precipitation, perhaps because the Polar Front had moved south of Scotland, or stable high pressure systems dominated the Scottish glacial climate. It is uncertain when, or indeed if, the whole of Scotland was free of glacier ice. It is likely, however, that only small glaciers can have survived the warmth of the Late-glacial Interstadial, which began around 13 ka BP, through to the short, sharp phase of rapid cooling which saw the final phase of glacier expansion in Scotland during the Loch Lomond Stadial from 11-10 ka BP.

Until recently, rather little attention has been given to the pattern of deglaciation. It is becoming increasingly clear that the last ice sheet remained active during its retreat phase, rather than downwasted *in situ*, and that a number of significant readvances occurred along the ice sheet margins (Chapter 5). Several extensive readvances were recognised in Scotland by earlier writers, notably the Aberdeen-Lammermuir Readvance and the Perth Readvance. Whilst these supposed readvances were often based on dubious morphological evidence and so are no longer recognised as representing regionally integrated ice limits (Sissons, 1976), there is little doubt that important ice-marginal features, including moraines, occur locally. Terminal moraines have also been traced for many kilometres in Wester Ross (Ballantyne, 1993), on the floor of the Minch off Lewis (Sutherland, 1984) and on Islay and Jura (Sutherland, 1993).

An important aim for future research will be to map moraine systems in an effort to trace the stages of ice retreat. Strath Spey is of especial interest, as this valley extends to one of the source areas of the last ice sheet. At the mouth of the Spey it has long been known that staged retreat of the Moray Firth ice lobe dammed up a series of large proglacial lakes (Sutherland, 1984), and a number of moraines and other ice-marginal features have been identified (Hall *et al.*, 1995). Various marginal positions have been proposed for the Strath Spey ice lobe as it retreated up-valley. Recent work in the Cairngorms (Brazier *et al.*, 1996) has reaffirmed the work of officers of the Geological Survey in the early part of this century who identified a series of marginal positions for the Strath Spey glacier on the northern flank of the Cairngorms. The highest of the moraines is above 800 m OD and must mark quite an early stage in deglaciation, when the Cairngorm summits were first appearing from beneath the ice sheet surface. In both the Lairig Ghru and Gleann Einich, ice readvance formed push moraines and dammed large lakes in the lower glens, producing fine sequences of terraces once the lakes drained.

The recession of the last ice sheet was accompanied by the release of large volumes of meltwater which produced extensive systems of meltwater channels, glaciofluvial deposits and outwash terraces in many parts of Scotland (see Chapters 8 and 13). In the estuaries and sea lochs of the east and west coasts, thick sequences of glaciomarine deposits accumulated in association with the receding glaciers (the Errol Beds and Clyde Beds) (Chapters 5 and 12). Radiocarbon dates suggest that by about 13 ka BP, the ice had disappeared from the lowlands and the from lower ground in the Highlands.

6.6 Conclusion

Recent years have seen major advances in our understanding of the sequence and timing of Quaternary events, arising from the discovery of new sites and the application of new analytical methods to both these and older classic sites. In addition, the availability of lithostratigraphic and biostratigraphic evidence from offshore (Chapter 7) has greatly augmented the terrestrial record of events and led to revised interpretations. Significant impetus for the reinterpretation of conventional ideas has also come from a new awareness of the complexity and detail of Quaternary climate change as revealed in the North Atlantic ocean core and Greenland ice core records. Nevertheless, our knowledge of pre-Late Devensian events and environmental changes, in particular, remains very incomplete due to the paucity of sites which have survived later erosion. Even our understanding of the limits and behaviour of the last ice sheet includes many uncertainties. There are many challenging questions to be addressed.

References

Andrews, I.J., Long, D., Richards, P.C., Thomson, A.R., Brown, S., Chesher, J.A., and McCormac, M. 1990. *United Kingdom Offshore Regional Report: the Geology of the Moray Firth*. HMSO for the British Geological Survey, London.

Ballantyne, C.K. 1990. The Late Quaternary glacial history of the Trotternish Escarpment, Isle of Skye, Scotland, and its implications for ice-sheet reconstruction. *Proceedings of the Geologists' Association*, 101, 171-186.

Ballantyne, C.K. 1993. Gairloch Moraine. In: Gordon, J.E. and Sutherland, D.G. (Eds), *Quaternary of Scotland*. Chapman and Hall, London, 103-106.

Ballantyne, C.K. 1994. Gibbsitic soils on former nunataks: implications for ice sheet reconstruction. *Journal of Quaternary Science*, 9, 73-80.

Ballantyne, C.K. and McCarroll, D. 1995. The vertical dimensions of Late Devensian glaciation on the mountains of Harris and southeast Lewis, Outer Hebrides, Scotland. *Journal of Quaternary Science*, 10, 211-224.

Ballantyne, C.K., Sutherland, D.G. and Reed, W.J. 1987. Introduction. In: Ballantyne, C.K. and Sutherland, D.G. (Eds), *Wester Ross: Field Guide*. Quaternary Research Association, Cambridge: 1-63.

Baumann, K-H., Lackschewitz, K.S., Mangerud, J., Spielhagen, R.F., Wolf-Welling, T.C.W., Henrich, R. and Kassens, H. 1995. Reflection of Scandinavian ice sheet fluctuations in Norwegian Sea sediments during the past 150,000 years. *Quaternary Research*, 43, 185-197.

Birnie, J., Gordon, J.E., Bennett, K.D. and Hall, A.M. (Eds). 1993. *The Quaternary of Shetland: Field Guide*. Quaternary Research Association, London.

Boulton, G.S., Peacock, J.D. and Sutherland, D.G. 1991. Quaternary. In: Craig, G.Y. *(Ed.), Geology of Scotland*. The Geological Society, London, 503-543.

Bowen, D.Q. 1991. Time and space in the glacial sediment systems of the British Isles. In: Ehlers, J., Gibbard, P.L. and Rose, J. (Eds), *Glacial Deposits in Great Britain and Ireland*. A.A. Balkema, Rotterdam, 3-12.

Bowen, D.Q., Rose, J., McCabe, A.M. and Sutherland, D.G. 1986. Correlation of Quaternary glaciations in England, Ireland, Scotland and Wales. *Quaternary Science Reviews*, 5, 299-340.

Bowen, D.Q. and Sykes, G.A. 1988. Correlation of marine events and glaciations on the north-east Atlantic margin. *Philosophical Transactions of the Royal Society of London*, B318, 619-635.

Brazier, V., Gordon, J.E., Kirkbride, M.P. and Sugden, D.E. 1996. The Late Devensian ice sheet and glaciers in the Cairngorm Mountains. In: Glasser, N.F. and Bennett, M.R. (Eds), *The Quaternary of the Cairngorms: Field Guide*. Quaternary Research Association, London, 28-53.

Cameron, T.D.J., Stoker, M.S. and Long, D. 1987. The history of Quaternary sedimentation in the UK sector of the North Sea. *Journal of the Geological Society*, 144, 43-58.

Clapperton, C.M. and Sugden, D.E. 1977. The Late Devensian glaciation of north-east Scotland. In: Gray, J.M. and Lowe, J.J. (Eds), *Studies in the Scottish Lateglacial Environment*. Pergamon Press, Oxford, 1-13.

Dansgaard, W., Johnsen, S.J., Clausen, H.B., Dahl-Jensen, D., Gundestrup, N.S., Hammer, C.U., Hvidberg, C.S., Steffensen, J.P., Sveinbjornsdottir, A.E., Jouzel, J. and Bond, G. 1993. Evidence for general instability of past climate from a 250-kyr ice-core record. *Nature*, 364, 218-220.

Duller, G.A.T., Wintle, A.G. and Hall, A.M. 1995. Luminescence dating and its application to key pre-Late Devensian sites in Scotland. *Quaternary Science Reviews*, 14, 495-519.

Ehlers, J. and Wingfield, R. 1991. The extension of the Late Weichselian/Late Devensian ice sheets in the North Sea Basin. *Journal of Quaternary Science*, 6, 313-326.

Ekman, S.R. 1995. Late Weichselian to early Holocene litho- and biostratigraphy in the Devil's Hole area, central North Sea, and its relation to glacial isostasy. *Journal of Quaternary Science*, 10, 343-353.

Gatliff, R.W., Richards, P.C., Smith, K., Graham, C.C., McCormac, M., Smith, N.J.P., Long, D., Cameron, T.D.J., Evans, D., Stevenson, A.G., Bulat, J. and Ritchie, J.D. 1994. *United Kingdom Offshore Regional Report: the Geology of the Central North Sea*. HMSO for the British Geological Survey, London.

Geikie, A. 1901. *The Scenery of Scotland Viewed in Connection with its Physical Geology*. 3rd ed. Macmillan, London.

Godard, A. 1965. *Recherches de Géomorphologie en Écosse du Nord-Ouest*. Masson et Cie, Paris.

Gordon, J.E. and Sutherland, D.G. (Eds). 1993. *Quaternary of Scotland*. Chapman and Hall, London.

Hall, A.M. 1995. Was all of Lewis glaciated in the Late Devensian? *Quaternary Newsletter,* **76,** 1-7.

Hall A.M. (Ed.) 1996. *The Quaternary of Orkney: Field Guide.* Quaternary Research Association, London.

Hall, A.M. and Bent, A.J.A. 1990. The limits of the last British ice sheet in northern Scotland and the adjacent shelf. *Quaternary Newsletter,* **61,** 2-12.

Hall, A.M. and Jarvis, J. 1989. A preliminary report on the Late Devensian glaciomarine deposits at St. Fergus, Grampian Region. *Quaternary Newsletter, 59,* 5-7.

Hall, A.M. and Jarvis, J. 1993. Kirkhill. In: Gordon, J.E. and Sutherland, D.G. (Eds), *Quaternary of Scotland.* Chapman & Hall, London, 225-230.

Hall, A.M., Whittington, G. and Gordon, J.E. 1993. Interglacial peat at Fugla Ness, Shetland. In: Birnie, J., Gordon, J.E., Bennett, K.D. and Hall, A.M. (Eds), *The Quaternary of Shetland: Field Guide.* Quaternary Research Association, London, 62-76.

Hall, A.M., Whittington, G., Duller, G.A.T. and Jarvis, J. 1995. Late Pleistocene environments in lower Strathspey, Scotland. *Transactions of the Royal Society of Edinburgh: Earth Sciences,* **85,** 253-273.

Holmes, R. 1977. Quaternary deposits of the central North Sea, 5. The Quaternary geology of the UK sector of the North Sea between 56° and 58°N. *Report of the Institute of Geological Sciences,* No. **77/14.**

Jardine, W.G., Dickson, J.H., Haughton, P.D.W., Harkness, D.D., Bowen, D.Q. and Sykes, G.A. 1988. A late Middle Devensian site at Sourlie, near Irvine, Strathclyde. *Scottish Journal of Geology,* **24,** 288-295.

Johnson, H., Richards, P.C., Long, D. and Graham, C.C. 1993. *United Kingdom Offshore Regional Report: the Geology of the Northern North Sea.* HMSO for the British Geological Survey, London.

Kirby, R.P. 1968. The ground moraines of Midlothian and East Lothian. *Scottish Journal of Geology,* **4,** 209-220.

Larsen, E., Sandven, R., Heyerdahl, H. and Hernes, S. 1995. Glacial geological implications of preconsolidation values in sub-till sediments at Skorgenes, western Norway. *Boreas,* **24,** 37-46.

Lawson, T.J. (Ed.) 1995. *The Quaternary of Assynt and Coigach: Field Guide.* Quaternary Research Association, Cambridge.

McCarroll, D., Ballantyne, C.K., Nesje, A. and Dahl, S-O. 1995. Nunataks of the last ice sheet in northwest Scotland. *Boreas,* **24,** 305-323.

Mangerud, J. 1991. The last interglacial/glacial cycle in northern Europe. In: Shane, L.C.K. and Cushing, E.J. (Eds), *Quaternary Landscapes.* Belhaven Press, London, 38-75.

Peacock, J.D. 1984. Quaternary geology of the Outer Hebrides. *Report of the British Geological Survey* **16(2).**

Peacock, J.D., Austin, W.E.N., Selby, I., Graham, D.K., Harland, R. and Wilkinson, I.P. 1992. Late Devensian and Flandrian palaeoenvironmental changes on the Scottish continental shelf west of the Outer Hebrides. *Journal of Quaternary Science,* **7,** 145-162.

Price, R.J. 1983. *Scotland's Environment during the Last 30,000 years.* Scottish Academic Press, Edinburgh.

Sejrup, H.P., Haflidason, H., Aarseth, I., King, E., Forsberg, C.F., Long, D. and Rokoengen, K. 1994. Late Weichsellan glaciation history of the northern North Sea. *Boreas,* **23,** 1-13.

Stoker, M. S., Hitchen, K. and Graham, C.C. 1993. *United Kingdom Offshore Regional Report: the Geology of the Hebrides and West Shetland Shelves, and Adjacent Deep-water Areas.* HMSO for the British Geological Survey, London.

Stoker, M. S., Long, D. and Fyfe, J.A. 1985. A revised Quaternary stratigraphy for the central North Sea. *Report of the British Geographical Survey,* No. **17** (2).

Sugden, D.E. 1968. The selectivity of glacial erosion in the Cairngorm Mountains, Scotland. *Transactions of the Institute of British Geographers,* **45,** 79-92.

Sutherland, D.G. 1984. The Quaternary deposits and landforms of Scotland and the neighbouring shelves: a review. *Quaternary Science Reviews,* **3,** 157-254.

Sutherland, D.G. 1993. Nith Bridge. In: Gordon, J.E. and Sutherland, D.G. (Eds), *Quaternary of Scotland.* Chapman & Hall, London, 541-542.

Sutherland, D. G. (1993). Inner Hebrides: Introduction. In: Gordon, J.E. and Sutherland, D.G. (Eds), *Quaternary of Scotland.* Chapman & Hall, London, 359-363.

Sutherland, D.G., Ballantyne, C.K. and Walker, M.J.C. 1984. Late Quaternary glaciation and environmental change on St. Kilda, Scotland, and their palaeoclimatic significance. *Boreas,* **13,** 261-272.

Sutherland, D.G. and Walker, M.J.C. 1984. A Late Devensian ice-free area and possible interglacial site on the Isle of Lewis, Scotland. *Nature,* **309,** 701-703.

Thomson, M.E. and Eden, R.A. 1977. Quaternary deposits of the central North Sea, 3. The Quaternary sequence in the west-central North Sea. *Report of the Institute of Geological Sciences,* No. **77/17.**

Whittington, G., Hall, A.M. and Jarvis, J. 1993. A pre-Late Devensian pollen site from Camp Fauld, Buchan, Grampian Region. *New Phytologist,* **125,** 867-874.

Wingfield, R.T.R. 1989. Glacial incisions indicating Middle and Upper Pleistocene ice limits off Britain. *Terra Nova,* **1,** 538-548.

7. Quaternary Stratigraphy: the Offshore Record

Richard Holmes

> The key themes covered in this chapter are:
>
> - offshore sedimentary processes and the stratigraphic record during glacial-interglacial cycles;
> - methods of stratigraphic research;
> - sequences of sediments in the North Sea and offshore to the north and west of Scotland;
> - the offshore record of major events during the Quaternary.

7.1 Introduction

With the fluctuations in global sea level that accompanied the rhythmic pattern of glaciation, the geography of Scotland changed dramatically during the Quaternary ice ages. Lowered sea levels, perhaps by as much as 140m, allowed the great ice sheets from Scandinavia and Scotland to expand periodically across the floor of what is now the North Sea and across the Hebridean continental shelf and the Shetland and Orkney continental shelves west of Scotland (Chapter 6). Major thicknesses of glacial, glaciomarine and non-glacial sediments accumulated in sedimentary basins on the continental shelves around Scotland, on the continental slope and in adjacent oceanic basins on the NE margins of the Atlantic. Therefore, not only does a major part of the geomorphological and sedimentary record of the former ice sheets lie offshore of Scotland, but also a significant part of the sedimentary history and record of environmental changes during the Quaternary is preserved there.

For ease of description, the stratigraphies described in this chapter are related to broad areas that overlap the major structural geological regions which may be used to divide the major Quaternary depositional centres offshore to the east and west of Scotland (Figure 7.1). East of Scotland, the main basins are in the central North Sea and the northern North Sea, stratigraphical correlation between these areas of the continental shelf being possible across the sediments that thin over the East Shetland Ridge (Johnson *et al.*, 1993). West of Scotland, the depositional centres are divided along the outer continental margins by the Wyville-Thomson Ridge, that separates the west Shetland and Orkney shelves and slopes, and the Faeroe-Shetland Channel from the Hebrides Shelf and Slope and Rockall Trough. South of the Wyville-Thomson Ridge, the depositional centres are divided along the outer continental margin by the Geikie Bulge separating the northern Hebrides Shelf and Slope from the southern Hebrides Shelf and Slope. The north and south inner shelves are divided by the Rubha Reidh Ridge extending across the Minch at approximately 58°N.

Three predominant controls that vary spatially and with time interact to affect the sediment distribution, thickness and facies (the sum of features which characterise a sediment deposited in a particular environment) of submarine Quaternary sediments preserved offshore: 1) climate; 2) the geometry of the sedimentary basins; and 3) proximity to the sediment source. Extreme climate changes from glacial to interglacial conditions influenced global-to-local fluctuations in sea level and changes in ice dynamics, hydrodynamics, sediment depositional rates, sediment

pathways and sediment facies. The geometry of the sedimentary basins, for example their water depths which control the maximum thickness of submarine sediments accommodated within them, may vary in the short-term with relative sea-level change and in the longer-term with structural controls on basin physiography, such as tectonic subsidence and the previous depositional history. The area of the basins and the rate and location of the sediment supply may also influence the potential for sediment preservation or export on the shelf at any particular time. Proximity to sediment source typically determines variation of sediment facies within the Quaternary, and particularly dramatic changes occur at the margins of ice sheets. As the timing of the changes to the meteorological and submarine environments also varies spatially, the lack of synchroneity poses challenges to correlation of lithological and biological events in the Quaternary. However, if the spatial and temporal variations associated with climate change are kept constant, then schematic sections summarizing the processes generating contrasting styles of stratigraphic record to the east and west of Scotland can be related to the geometry of the sedimentary basins and proximity to sediment sources (Figures 7.2 and 7.3).

Under the imposition of ice sheets during glaciations, the sections illustrate that the continental margin around Scotland has experienced unusually high rates of erosion locally linked to unusually high rates of sedimentation. Large amounts of fluvial and glacigenic sediment were deposited on the shelf and were also swept from the Scottish mainland across the shelf to be deposited on the slope. A map may then schematically show that the main sediment transport pathways, depositional centres and areas of sediment bypass also varied through time according to the positions of the ice sheets (Figure 7.4). As sea level rises during a glacial-interglacial transition, the overall direct sediment input to the outer shelf and slope decreases, so that during a full interglacial, sediment movement is dominated by submarine processes that rework surface sediments along different pathways to those during glaciations (Figure 7.5). Regionally, the rate of sediment erosion and deposition during interglacials is far less than during glaciations. The overall effect of the variables summarized above is for Quaternary sediments to be distributed around Scotland in discrete regional depositional centres, or depocentres (Figure 7.6), the thickness and stratigraphical ranges of the sediments being controlled to a large extent by the structural settings of the basins and their relationships to the sediment sources. How are these changes reflected in the evolution of the offshore Quaternary stratigraphy and what information does the stratigraphy provide about the sequence of glacial and interglacial events and the pattern of environmental changes during the Quaternary in Scotland? This chapter attempts to address these questions with reference to a summary of published research from interpretation of information derived from sediment samples and high-resolution seismic reflection profiles.

7.2 Methods of stratigraphic research

Research on the regional Quaternary stratigraphy of the continental shelves and slopes around Scotland has been undertaken by the British Geological Survey (BGS) on a

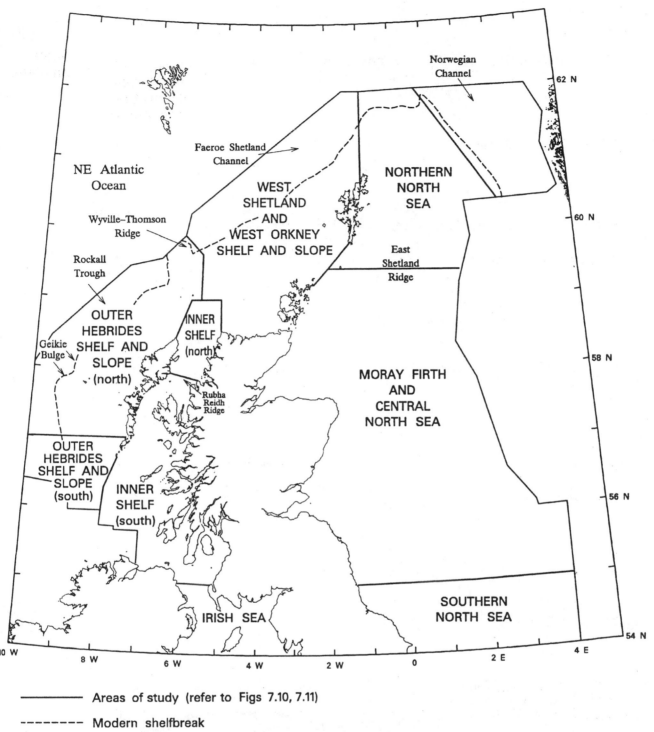

Figure 7.1 The geographical areas used to describe the offshore geology reflect the major structural geological regions. Note that geological boundaries commonly extend across the area boundaries shown.

systematic basis since approximately 1968. Following assessment of pre-existing land and marine data, the BGS research into the offshore Quaternary stratigraphy was by analyses of data acquired principally from ship-borne surveys (Figure 7.7). Interpretations of the seismic reflection data from such surveys are typically from profiles extending from seabed to several hundreds of metres or more below seabed (Figure 7.8). The seismic profiles comprising the regional surveys are generally spaced some 5-10 km apart, the initial interpretation of the data taking into account the recognition of seismic facies and boundaries separating them. Seismic facies are the reflector patterns seen on the profiles: their external morphology, reflection configuration, reflection continuity and reflector amplitudes. The patterns

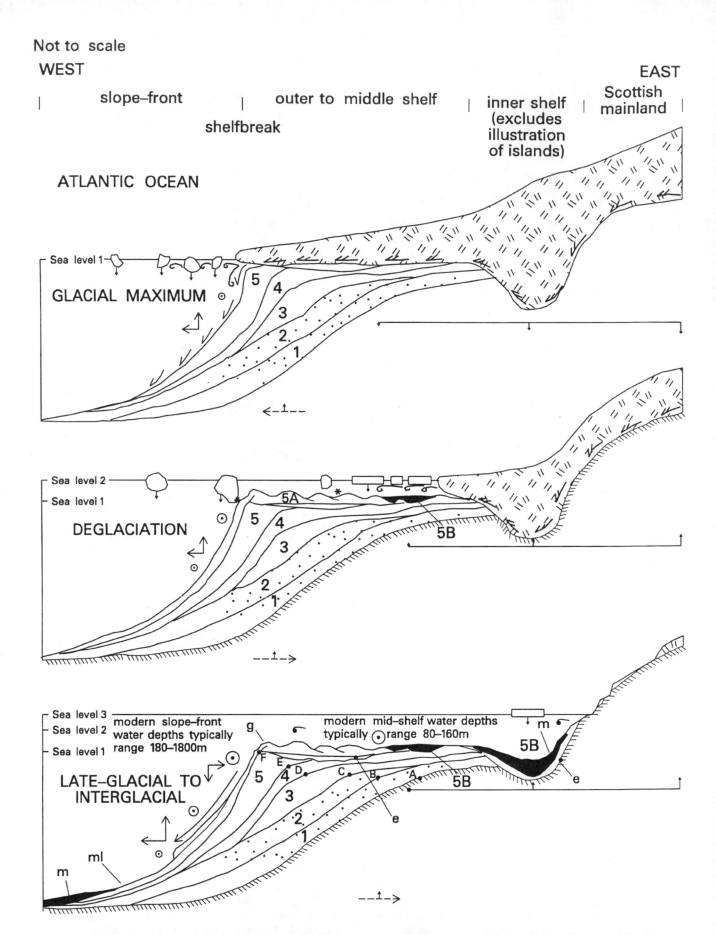

Figure 7.2 Schematic sections illustrating some of the processes affecting the stratigraphic record west of Scotland during a cycle from a maximum glaciation to an interglacial. The sections illustrate features associated with depocentres with high sediment input from cross-shelf transport (Figure 7.4). Different features are associated with areas of sediment bypass.

LEGEND

- Ice sheet
- Icebergs
- Sea ice
- circle diameters indicate relative strengths of north-flowing near-bottom currents
- pre Pliocene-Quaternary rock
- 1–2 sand-prone sediments, mainly Pliocene to early Quaternary, 'pre-dating regional shelf glaciation'
- 3–5 mud-prone sediments, early to late Quaternary, mainly deposited during shelf glacial cycles
- A–F stages of shelf build out: with long-term tectonic subsidence, the shelfedge may appear to migrate upwards as well as oceanwards
- 1–4 prograding units with records of previous glacial and interglacial events

GLACIAL MAXIMUM

- weight of ice depresses Earth's crust, particularly variable at mainland and nearshore sites, locally counteracts global sea-level fall
- crustal fore bulge generated seawards of ice-depressed crust locally accentuates then counteracts relative sea-level changes during global sea-level fall
- 5 prograding unit originating from current glacial cycle
- sub-ice truncation: re-working, erosion and transport of pre-existing sediments
- largescale over-deepened rock basin, many closed and some originating sub-ice, some fjord-like adjacent to mainland
- ice-rafted debris, maximum with onset of deglaciation and during ice surges
- sediment plumes
- sediment debris flows originate at the ice sheet margins and from shelfedge slumps
- slope-front builds upwards and outwards, shelf-edge extends oceanwards
- sections of pre-existing shelf sediments are variously preserved, parts dynamically reworked
- weak slope-parallel currents redistribute some sediments

DEGLACIATION

- loss of weight of ice leads to locally variable mainland and nearshore uplift, and interacts with global sea-level rise
- returning crustal forebulge locally counteracts then accentuates relative sea-level changes during global sea-level rise
- iceberg scour on slope and shelf, sea-ice scour on emergent shelf
- ice-rafted debris
- sediment plumes
- slope-front construction slows with retreat of ice mid-shelf landwards
- end moraines and other morainal banks typically mark stages of ice-sheet retreat, stillstand or re-advance
- 5B periglacial deltaic and glaciomarine sediments may locally top terrestrial and submarine moraines

LATE–GLACIAL to INTERGLACIAL

- loss of weight of ice leads to locally variable mainland and nearshore uplift and counteracts global sea-level rise
- raised beaches form at times when land rises faster than the eustatic sea-level: the highest (oldest) beach marks the inshore marine limit, older limits may not be preserved due to ice cover, at other times and locations the extent of coastal erosion /build-out varies locally
- g strong north-flowing slope and shelf currents assisted by wind-driven waves on the shelf erode seabed muds and sands leaving lithic gravel 'armour' at seabed, particularly at the shelf-slope margins and on shelf banks
- ml mudline generated on the slope-front divides sand-prone sediments from deeper-water mud-prone sediments
- m mud-prone sediments preserve correlative high-resolution palaeoceanographic records in middle and inner shelf basin backwaters and in the deep-water ocean basin
- biogenic debris forms important component of interglacial and interstadial seabed sand, gravel carbonate deposits form on banks, around islands and adjacent to land promontories swept by strong tidal currents and waves
- large periodic shelfedge and deeper slope-front failures form slides that partially destroy fans, the largest generating tsunami
- slope front regression at slide headwalls and sidewalls
- slope front and deep-water basin construction in the downslope areas of slides
- e repeat erosion at this level during the next severe glaciation extending to the shelfbreak will sweep much of unit 5 and other pre-existing shelf sediments over the shelfedge to form units 6 + on the slope front, less severe glaciations being associated with greater potential for preservation of pre-existing stratigraphic units on the shelf
- 5B late-glacial and younger marine-transgressive sediments fill hollows with muds typically deposited from suspension during periods of sea-ice cover and at other locations with low~energy environments

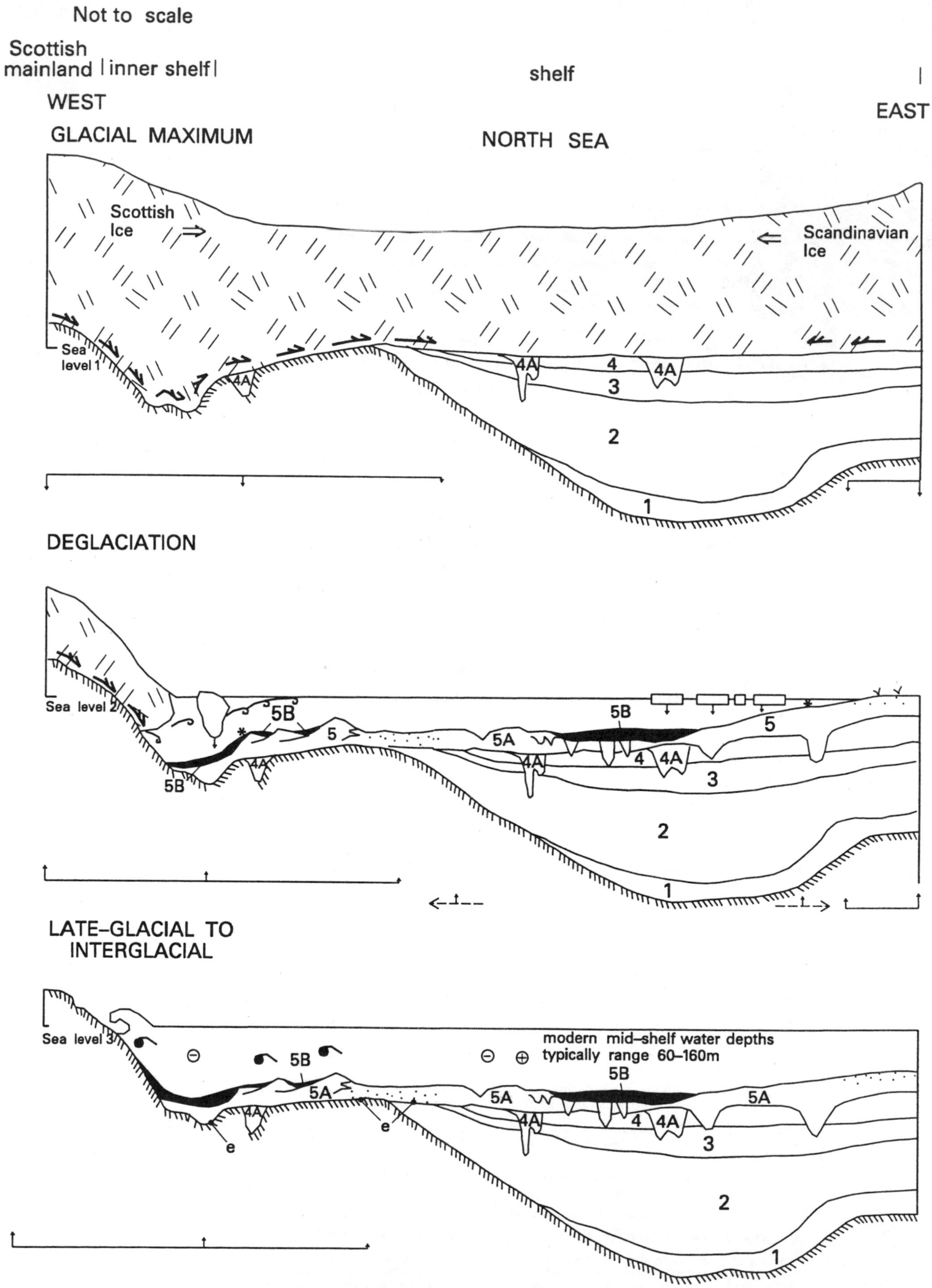

Figure 7.3 Schematic sections illustrating some of the processes affecting the stratigraphic record east of Scotland during a cycle from a maximum glaciation to an interglacial.

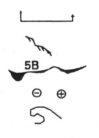
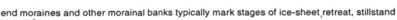
commonly vary with the environmental processes forming the features observed. An initial interpretation of seismic facies is typically based on published accounts, if any, of similar features and their overall geological setting. The positions of boreholes and other sample sites is then controlled by the need to investigate further the interpretations of seismic facies (Figure 7.9) and the significance of their boundaries. The seismic facies typically form units that are traceable along and between profiles and, on the basis of the assumption that the overlying mappable units are younger, a seismostratigraphic succession can be established by correlation of seismic marker horizons. After sampling, the interpretations of the origin and age of the seismostratigraphic succession may then be refined by research on lithology, including geotechnical testing, and palaeomagnetic, palaeontologic (biostratigraphic), aminostratigraphic studies and radiogenic isotopic dating on an area-by-area basis to provide a more secure stratigraphic framework (the choice of method used for best-estimates of sediment age depending on the type of deposit and its probable age (*e.g.* Smart & Frances, 1991)). The results from seismostratigraphic and onward sample research are then combined, and if sufficient information is available for recognition of regionally mappable units within a chronological framework, these units have been formally established by BGS as formations. Palaeogeographic

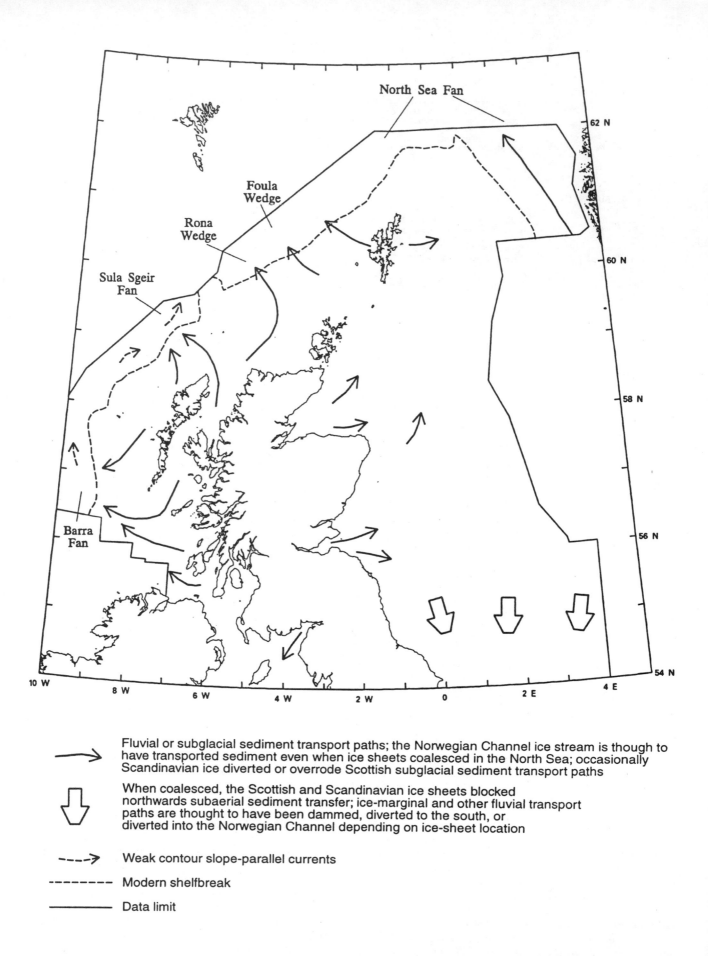

Fluvial or subglacial sediment transport paths; the Norwegian Channel ice stream is though to have transported sediment even when ice sheets coalesced in the North Sea; occasionally Scandinavian ice diverted or overrode Scottish subglacial sediment transport paths

When coalesced, the Scottish and Scandinavian ice sheets blocked northwards subaerial sediment transfer; ice-marginal and other fluvial transport paths are thought to have been dammed, diverted to the south, or diverted into the Norwegian Channel depending on ice-sheet location

Weak contour slope-parallel currents

Modern shelfbreak

Data limit

Figure 7.4 Model of major sediment pathways during maximum shelf glaciations based on evidence from sediment facies, distribution and geometry. (After Gibbard, 1988; Holmes and Stoker, 1990; Holmes *et al.*, 1993; Stoker *et al.*, 1993).

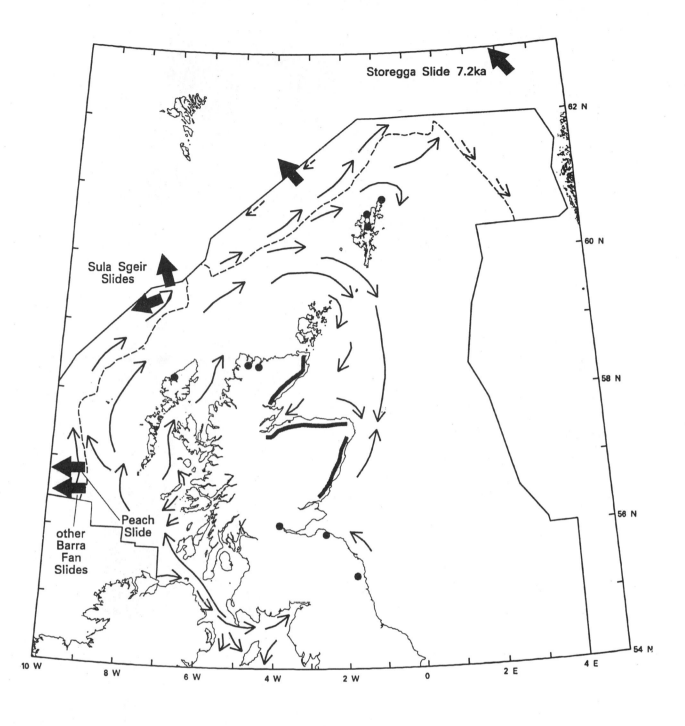

Storegga Slide 7.2ka

Sula Sgeir
Slides

Peach
Slide

other
Barra
Fan
Slides

62 N

60 N

58 N

56 N

54 N

10 W   8 W   6 W   4 W   2 W   0   2 E   4 E

⟶   Net sand transport pathways

--→   Net mud and sand transport pathways

7.2ka ▶   Slide: Storegga Slide dated from tsunami deposits on land

▶   Other slides, age uncertain but correlated on the basis of their
fresh appearance with possible late–glacial or interglacial events

▬▬   Tsunami deposits associated with Storegga Slide

●   Other possible sites of Storrega Slide tsunami deposits

Notes: many other slides exist but are buried; the larger slides (eg Storegga, Peach) have
a history of multiple failures, some predating Oxygen Isotope Stage 20

Figure 7.5 Model of major sediment pathways during interglacials based on sediment facies, distribution and geometry.
(After BGS, unpublished data (slides); Long *et al.,* 1989 (tsunami); Pantin, 1991 (seabed sediments).

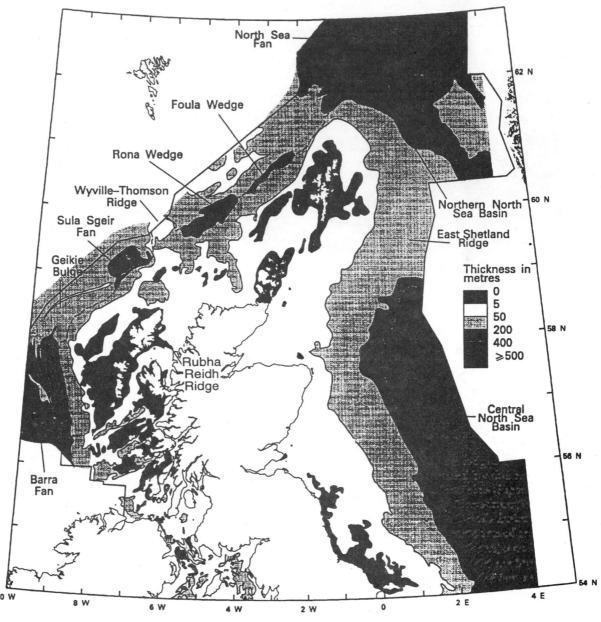

Figure 7.6 Distribution and structural setting of Pliocene-Quaternary depocentres.

reconstructions and regional predictions of lithological variation are then possible from interpretation of the data presented in formation maps. In this chapter the term 'sequence' is applied to a mappable Quaternary seismostratigraphic unit without sufficient chronostratigraphic information to establish it as a formation, sequences being mainly confined to areas west of Scotland (Figures 7.10 and 7.11). The term 'member' is applied to a named unit within a formation.

It should be noted that the nature of high-frequency Quaternary cyclicity entails that for age estimates great care must be taken to minimise the possibility of sample contamination from reworking of sediments. Age estimates from interpretations of relative, calibrated and numerical ages of assemblages of small biota such as foraminifers, dinoflagellate cysts, nannoplankton and pollen are particularly prone to error.

Compared to the North Sea, much less stratigraphic research has been completed for the offshore Quaternary deposits west of Scotland. Here, numerical age estimates

are generally not available for deposits pre-dating the Weichselian, so that correlation between the pre-Weichselian units and with the oxygen isotope stages is commonly unwarranted. For the most part, Quaternary sediments rest unconformably on older formations. However, west of Shetland, Pliocene (late Cenozoic) sediments on the outer shelf and the slope are commonly indistinguishable on the seismic reflection profiles from early Quaternary sediments. West of the Hebrides, Pliocene and early Quaternary sediments on the outer shelf and the slope are indivisible on the seismic reflection profiles and commonly rest on a regional Miocene unconformity (Evans, 1991; James, 1991). The thicknesses of Quaternary sediments estimated for areas west of the Hebrides, therefore, include some component of Pliocene sediments, although the few borehole data indicate that the Quaternary sediments predominate (Stoker *et al.*, 1994).

The terminology used in this paper follows the NW European chronostratigraphic classification (Figure 7.12) which is more complete for the early and middle Quaternary

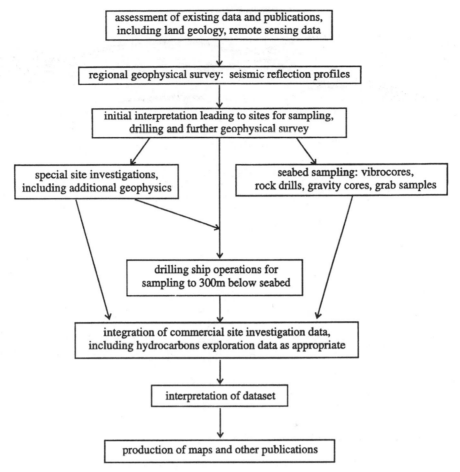

Figure 7.7 Outline methodology for offshore Quaternary investigations.

than the classification applied on land in Great Britain. The terms early, middle and late are used to divide the Quaternary in an informal sense, as defined in Figure 7.12, to accord with terminology in use for other chapters in this volume. The oxygen isotope record from deep-sea sediments appears to indicate that globally the most severe glaciations occurred during Isotope Stage 22 (Dorst) in the early Quaternary, and during Stages 16 (Cromerian), 12 (Elsterian), 10 and 6 (Saalian) and 2 (Late Weichselian) during the middle and late Quaternary (see Chapter 5, Figure 5.2b).

7.3 Early Quaternary (approximately 2.44 - 0.78 Ma)

The first appearance in the North Atlantic of ice-rafted debris at approximately 2.44 Ma (Shackleton *et al.,* 1984) may be considered to define the start of the Quaternary in northwest Europe. For the practical purposes of this report the Pliocene/Quaternary boundary is taken at approximately 2.44 Ma, correlative with the boundary of the Praetiglian with the Tiglian A and with the 'X' palaeomagnetic event within the Matuyama Reversed Polarity Chron (Figure 7.12).

The oxygen isotope record for the period 2.44-0.78 Ma indicates that relatively smaller global ice volumes occurred than in the middle and late Quaternary post-dating approximately 0.78 Ma (Chapter 5).

7.3.1 The 'pre-glacial' (approximately 2.44-1.2 Ma)

Although cold conditions were reported by King (1983) in studies of Pliocene sediments and Knudsen and Asbjornsdottir (1991) in studies of Praetiglian/Tiglian

sediments, in this chapter the term 'pre-glacial' is applied to the period pre-dating evidence for extensive glaciations on the continental shelf around Scotland.

The important formations are the Aberdeen Ground Formation and the Shackleton Formation in the North Sea, the Shackleton Formation and the Sinclair and Morrison sequences west of Shetland, and the Lower MacLeod sequence west of the Hebrides (Figures 7.10 and 7.11). The evidence from these units shows that the broad-scale picture was one where in the adjacent southern North Sea, the growth of early Quaternary deltas appears to have been largely unrelated to climate (Jeffery and Long, 1989), and where in the central North Sea, offshore from Scotland, contemporaneous pro-deltaic muds and sands accumulated (Stoker and Bent, 1985). West of Scotland the evidence is for oceanward build-out of the shelf, with deltaic and pro-deltaic sandy sediments on the fans; observations of ice-rafted debris in sandy sediments in fan and inter-fan areas are consistent with the periodic appearance of icebergs on the Atlantic margins (Stoker *et al.,* 1994).

North of approximately 56.5°N in the central North Sea the base of the Aberdeen Ground Formation, the oldest and thickest mapped Quaternary formation (Holmes, 1977; Stoker *et al.,* 1985), is defined on the seismic reflection profiles by an unconformity, the 'crenulate reflector' (Holmes, 1977). The Gauss-Matuyama palaeomagnetic boundary is locally interpreted to lie some 50 m below the crenulate reflector (BGS unpublished research), supporting a supposition for a late Pliocene to early Quaternary age for the reflector. North and west of 58°N01°E, the crenulate reflector observed from 3-D seismic reflection data consists of channels, some on average gradients of less than 0.5° and appearing to merge downslope with criss-crossed

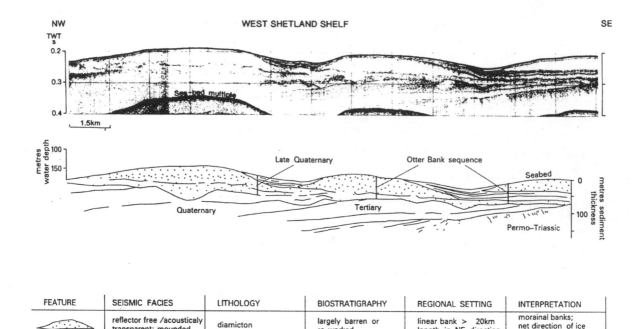

NW   WEST SHETLAND SHELF   SE

FEATURE	SEISMIC FACIES	LITHOLOGY	BIOSTRATIGRAPHY	REGIONAL SETTING	INTERPRETATION
	reflector free /acoustically transparent; mounded	diamicton	largely barren or re–worked	linear bank > 20km length in NE direction	morainal banks; net direction of ice retreat to SE
	well layered draped, onlapping, truncated	near seabed: mud–prone with dropstones	not known	in hollows, predate & postdate banks	rapidly deposited glaciomarine sediments

LEGEND

TWTs – two–way travel time seconds; seabed multiple – artifact of recording;
metres water depth – assumes velocity of sound in water 1500 metres/second
metres sediment thickness – assumes velocity of sound subseabed is 1800 metres/second
Location – see Figure 7.9

| vertical line indicates the extent of the interpretation shown

Figure 7.8 Interpreted seismic profile, West Shetland Shelf. Stratigraphy adapted after Holmes (1991) and Stoker and Holmes (1991).

furrows. Similar furrows are identified north and west of 56°N02°E, also in the Aberdeen Ground Formation but at a higher stratigraphic level (P. Andresen, written communication, 1997). On the basis of their geometry and gradient, the channels are tentatively identified with fluvial drainage, and the furrows with ice scour from grounded icebergs or sea-ice keels. The evidence for ice scour is consistent with deposition of the bulk of the Aberdeen Ground Formation under shallow marine conditions (Stoker and Bent, 1987) but appears to be at odds with pollen stratigraphy evidence from the European mainland for warm temperate conditions coeval with major northwards delta progradation originating from the continent, the sediments from this delta being largely confined to the North Sea south of 55°N (Cameron *et al.,* 1992). However, the observations of ice scour in the central North Sea accord with the occurrence of periodic ice-rafted debris on the Atlantic margins, and the evidence for fluvial channels is supportive of a theory that during the earliest Quaternary the sediments in the central North Sea were periodically subaerially exposed. The observations for shallow marine sediments in the North Sea are consistent with the 'layercake' appearance of the stratigraphic record observed in seismic profiles through the early Quaternary. Observations of shoreward attenuation of sediment thicknesses and occasional shorewards sub-aerial exposure accord with a theory that, overall in the North Sea, sedimentation has kept pace with tectonic subsidence (Figure 7.3).

Adjacent to Shetland in the North Sea, the base of the Shackleton Formation and the base of the Quaternary are identical and unconformable on Palaeogene and older sediments, but further east the Shackleton Formation extends without lithological break into the Pliocene (Skinner

et al., 1986). Investigations of the marine microfauna (foraminifers) and microflora (dinoflagellates) and magnetic polarity profiles in boreholes show that the sediments in this formation were deposited during the early Quaternary, although some are possibly older than approximately 2.4 Ma (Stoker *et al.,* 1983; Johnson *et al.,* 1993). Just to the south of the East Shetland Ridge, a regional acoustic reflector that divides lower sandy units in the Shackleton Formation from sandy clay above can be ascribed to marine erosion associated with reworking of pre-Quaternary sediments and possibly correlates with an early Quaternary mainland glaciation (Long *et al.,* 1988).

West of Shetland and south of approximately 62°N, sediments of the Morrison sequence are preserved under the modern continental shelf and slope and appear on the seismic reflection profiles as a finely-layered seismic facies. Comparison of this facies and its geological setting with those found in the modern environment indicate that the finely-layered facies was probably deposited as sediment drift from submarine currents on the slope. In contrast, south of approximately 61°N, the sediments of the Sinclair sequence appear to consist of deltaic and shore front sediments (Holmes, 1990, 1991). Although the tops of the mid-shelf and inner-shelf units are commonly truncated by subsequent ice sheet erosion during the early-to-late Quaternary, the stratal geometries of units under the outer shelf indicate their origin under environments with fluctuating sea levels, these observations being consistent with borehole evidence showing that parts of the Sinclair sequence comprise arctic, shelly, pebbly muds and deltaic to shallow marine sands (Unit 3 of Cockroft, 1987). West of the Hebrides, Pliocene and early Quaternary sediments comprising the lower parts (subsequence A) of the MacLeod sequence in the Sula Sgeir

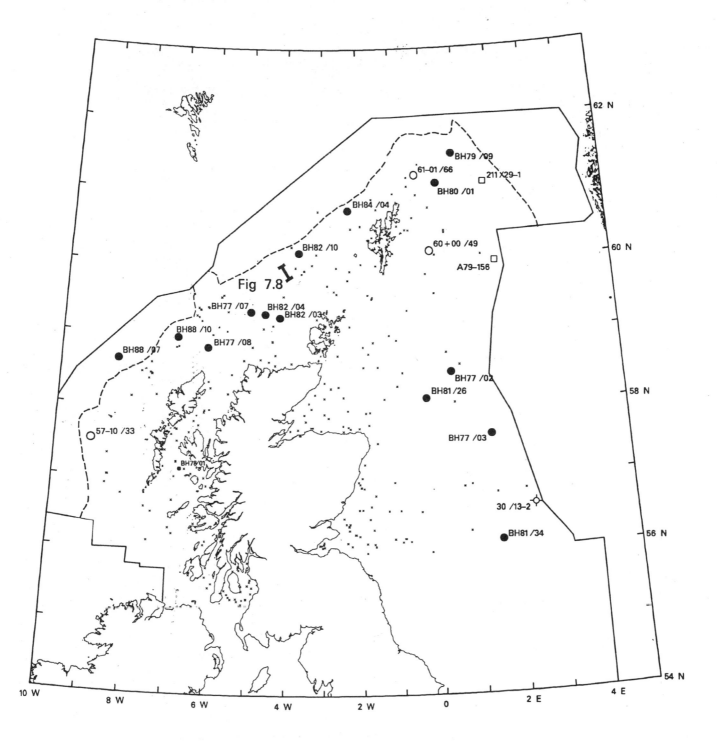

- ● BGS borehole referred to in text

- ⊙ BGS vibrocore referred to in text

- · Sites of other BGS boreholes

- ◇ Commercial well referred to in text

- □ Commercial soil boring referred to in text

- — Line of section, figure 7.8

Many other commercial wells, commercial soil borings and BGS vibrocore stations exist that have information on the stratigraphy of offshore Quaternary sediments, but to preserve clarity their positions are not illustrated. BGS borehole locations south of 55N are not shown

Figure 7.9 Locations of boreholes and samples referred to in the text.

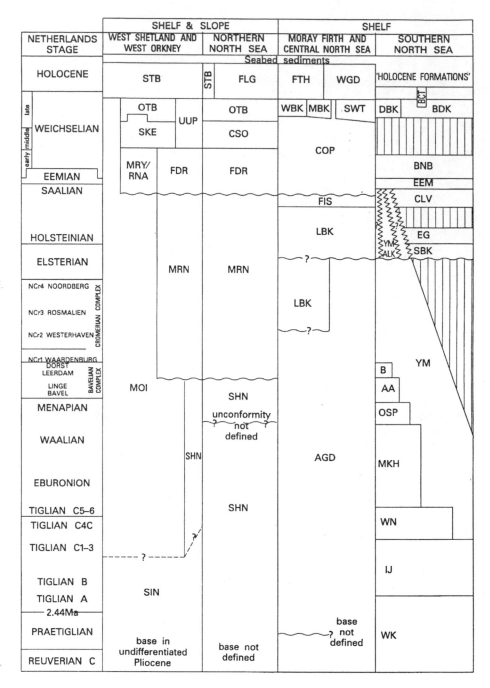

Adapted after Andrews et al, 1990; Johnson et al 1993; Gatliff et al, 1994; Funnell, 1995

For estimates of the age ranges of the Netherlands stages refer to Figure 7.12

Figure 7.10 Generalised offshore Quaternary stratigraphy for the North Sea and the continental margin north and west of Shetland.

Fan mainly consist of prograding units that are preserved on the fan slope-front (Stoker, 1991). To the south, prograding Pliocene to early Quaternary sandy deposits of the Lower MacLeod sequence form a wedge of sediments on the Barra Fan that spill over on to the slope front (Holmes *et al.,* in press). Between the Sula Sgeir and Barra Fans, sandy Pliocene and Early Quaternary sediments equated with the Lower MacLeod sequence are reported from the slope on the Geikie Bulge (Stoker *et al.,* 1994). Currently, the observations west of Scotland provide no information to allow correlation with early Quaternary cold periods, although in future it may be possible to relate the evidence for sea-level fluctuations with climate-driven, eustatic sea-level changes and with lithological changes. Overall the observations west of Scotland accord with a theory that the initiation of the fans and depocentres associated with the early spread of the Scottish shelf west into the NE Atlantic pre-dates regional shelf glaciation.

7.3.2 Early Quaternary glaciations (approximately 1.2-0.78 Ma)

The important formations are the Mariner Formation in the northern North Sea and the shelf and slope west of Shetland (Figure 7.10) and an un-named formation in the

Figure 7.10   Generalised offshore Quaternary stratigraphy, North Sea, Moray Firth and west Shetland and west Orkney shelf and slope

LEGEND

▯▯▯   Depositional hiatus, exist also outside the Southern North Sea, but are not shown due to insufficient stratigraphic resolution

〜   Regional unconformity

?   Precise age of boundary uncertain

Seismostratigraphical units: those underlined extend from the shelf to the slope

West Shetland and West Orkney shelves and slopes

FDR	Ferder Formation
MOI	Morrison sequence
MRN	Mariner Formation
MRY/RNA	Murray sequence, Rona sequence
OTB	Otter Bank sequence
SHN	Shackleton Formation
SIN	Sinclair sequence
SKE	Skerry sequence
STB	Stormy Bank sequence
UUP	Undifferentiated Upper Pleistocene

Northern North Sea shelf and slope

CSO	Cape Shore Formation
FDR	Ferder Formation
FLG	Flags Formation
MRN	Mariner Formation
OTB	Otter Bank Formation
SHN	Shackleton Formation
STB	Stormy Bank Formation

Central North Sea shelf

AGD	Aberdeen Ground Formation
COP	Coal Pit Formation
FIS	Fisher Formation
FTH	Forth Formation
LBK	Ling Bank Formation
MBK	Marr Bank Formation
SWT	Swatchway Formation
WBK	Wee Bankie Formation
WGD	Witch Ground Formation

Southern North Sea shelf

AA	Aurora Formation
B	Batavier Formation
BCT	Botney Cut Formation
BDK	Bolders Bank Formation
BNB	Brown Bank Formation
CLV	Cleaver Bank Formation
DBK	Dogger Bank Formation
EEM	Eem Formation
EG	Egmund Ground Formation
IJ	Ijmuiden Ground Formation
MKH	Markham's Hole Formation
OSP	Outer Silver Pit Formation
SBK	Swarte Bank Formation
WK	West Kapelle Ground Formation
WN	Winterton Shoal Formation
YM	Yarmouth Roads Formation
YM-ALK	Alkaid Member of Yarmouth Roads Formation

85

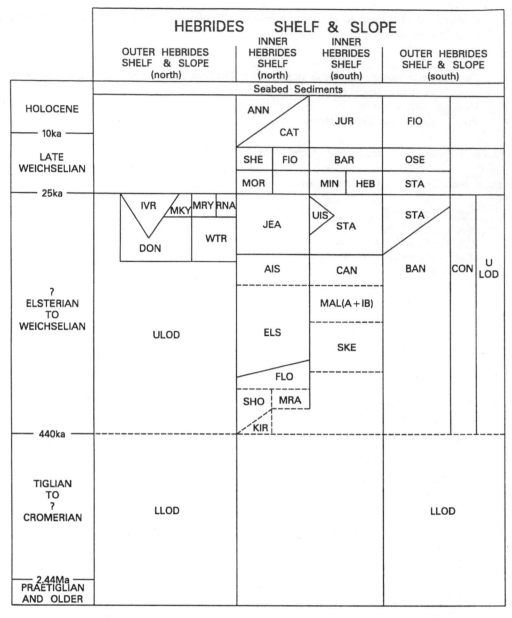

	HEBRIDES	SHELF & SLOPE		
OUTER HEBRIDES SHELF & SLOPE (north)	INNER HEBRIDES SHELF (north)	INNER HEBRIDES SHELF (south)	OUTER HEBRIDES SHELF & SLOPE (south)	
		Seabed Sediments		

Adapted after Fyfe et al, 1993; Stoker et al, 1993

Figure 7.11 Generalised offshore Quaternary stratigraphy for the continental margin north and west of mainland Scotland.

Norwegian sector of the Norwegian Channel. The broad-scale picture is for possibly at least two shelf glaciations pre-dating the Bavelian complex in the early Quaternary and extending into the northern North Sea.

At approximately 60°38'N in the Norwegian Channel the Cobb Mountain Event (1.19 Ma) within the Matuyama Reversed Polarity Chron (Figure 7.12) is identified immediately above a stratified diamicton (non-sorted sediments) interpreted as a till deposited during the 'Fedje Glaciation' (Sejrup *et al., 1995*). On the basis of the palaeomagnetic interpretation, the till is tentatively correlated with Oxygen Isotope Stage 36 (Figure 7.12). In the northern North Sea and west of Shetland the base of the Mariner Formation is regionally defined on seismic reflection profiles by an irregular glacigenic erosion surface which is locally overlain by an unsorted sediment (Johnson *et al., 1993*), possibly a till. In borehole BGS 78/09 a magnetic event mid-formation within the Matuyama Reversed Polarity Chron is correlated with the Jaramillo

Normal Polarity Subchron (0.99-1.07 Ma) (Stoker *et al., 1983*), the top of the subchron occurring just above the formation base (Skinner *et al., 1986*). These observations support correlation of the glacigenic event at the base of the Mariner Formation with Oxygen Isotope Stage 34 or 36. The possible implications are either for two early Quaternary glaciations preceding the Jaramillo Event, or, in the case of a single event, for an ice sheet extending from Scandinavia into the northern North Sea and on to shelf and slope areas west of Shetland, this last possibly during Oxygen Isotope Stage 36.

At approximately 58.5°N in the North Sea the 'crenulate reflector' is more than 150 m below a 10 m thick till in the Aberdeen Ground Formation (BGS unpublished information). In BGS borehole 81/26 this till occurs within the Matuyama Reversed Magnetic Polarity Chron, just above the Jaramillo Event (0.99-1.07 Ma), and on the basis of correlation of overlying foraminifers with the Leerdam interglacial (Oxygen Isotope Stage 25) (Figure 7.12), the till

Figure   7.11   Generalised offshore Quaternary stratigraphy, continental margin north and west of mainland Scotland

Seismostratigraphical units: those underlined extend from the shelf to the slope

Outer Hebrides Shelf (north)

DON	MacDonald sequence
IVR	MacIver sequence
LLOD	Lower MacLeod sequence
MKY	Mackay sequence
MRY	Murray sequence
RNA	Rona sequence
ULOD	Upper MacLeod sequence
WTR	Wyville-Thomson Ridge sequence

Inner Hebrides Shelf (north)

AIS	Aisla sequence
ANN	Annie sequence
CAT	Catriona sequence
ELS	Elspeth sequence
FIO	Fiona sequence
FLO	Flora sequence
JEA	Jean sequence
KIR	Kirsty sequence
MOR	Morag sequence
MRA	Moira sequence
SHE	Sheena sequence
SHO	Shona sequence

Inner Hebrides Shelf (south)

BAR	Barra Formation
CAN	Canna Formation
HEB	Hebrides Formation
JUR	Jura Formation
MAL (A+B)	Malin A and Malin B Formations
MIN	Minch Formation
SKE	Skerryvore Formation
STA	Stanton Formation
UIS	Uist Formation

Outer Hebrides Shelf (south)

BAN	Banks sequence
CAO	Caoilte sequence
COC	Conchar sequence
CON	Conan A and Conan B sequences
FIO	Fionn sequence
LLOD	Lower MacLeod sequence
OSE	Osean sequence
STA	Stanton Formation
ULOD	Upper MacLeod sequence

Not to scale

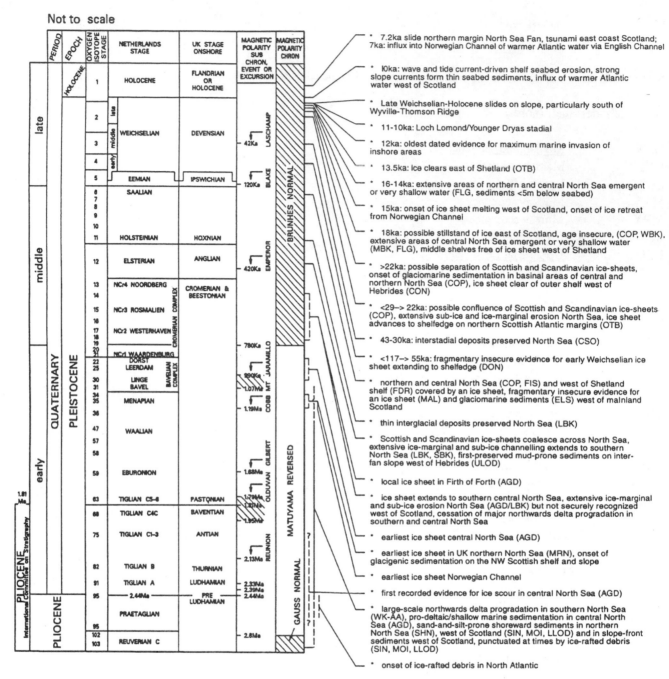

* 7.2ka slide northern margin North Sea Fan, tsunami east coast Scotland; 7ka: influx into Norwegian Channel of warmer Atlantic water via English Channel

* 10ka: wave and tide current-driven shelf seabed erosion, strong slope currents form thin seabed sediments, influx of warmer Atlantic water west of Scotland

* Late Weichselian-Holocene slides on slope, particularly south of Wyville-Thomson Ridge

* 11-10ka: Loch Lomond/Younger Dryas stadial

* 12ka: oldest dated evidence for maximum marine invasion of inshore areas

* 13.5ka: ice clears east of Shetland (OTB)

* 16-14ka: extensive areas of northern and central North Sea emergent or very shallow water (FLG, sediments <5m below seabed)

* 15ka: onset of ice sheet melting west of Scotland, onset of ice retreat from Norwegian Channel

* 18ka: possible stillstand of ice east of Scotland, age insecure, (COP, WBK), extensive areas of central North Sea emergent or very shallow water (MBK, FLG), middle shelves free of ice sheet west of Shetland

* >22ka: possible separation of Scottish and Scandinavian ice-sheets, onset of glaciomarine sedimentation in basinal areas of central and northern North Sea (COP), ice sheet clear of outer shelf west of Hebrides (CON)

* <29-> 22ka: possible confluence of Scottish and Scandinavian ice-sheets (COP), extensive sub-ice and ice-marginal erosion North Sea, ice sheet advances to shelfedge on northern Scottish Atlantic margins (OTB)

* 43-30ka: interstadial deposits preserved North Sea (CSO)

* <117-> 55ka: fragmentary insecure evidence for early Weichselian ice sheet extending to shelfedge (DON)

* northern and central North Sea (COP, FIS) and west of Shetland shelf (FDR) covered by an ice sheet, fragmentary insecure evidence for an ice sheet (MAL) and glaciomarine sediments (ELS) west of mainland Scotland

* thin interglacial deposits preserved North Sea (LBK)

* Scottish and Scandinavian ice-sheets coalesce across North Sea, extensive ice-marginal and sub-ice channelling extends to southern North Sea (LBK, SBK), first-preserved mud-prone sediments on inter-fan slope west of Hebrides (ULOD)

* local ice sheet in Firth of Forth (AGD)

* ice sheet extends to southern central North Sea, extensive ice-marginal and sub-ice erosion North Sea (AGD/LBK) but not securely recognized west of Scotland, cessation of major northwards delta progradation in southern and central North Sea

* earliest ice sheet central North Sea (AGD)

* earliest ice sheet in UK northern North Sea (MRN), onset of glacigenic sedimentation on the NW Scottish shelf and slope

* earliest ice sheet Norwegian Channel

* first recorded evidence for ice scour in central North Sea (AGD)

* large-scale northwards delta progradation in southern North Sea (WK-AA), pro-deltaic/shallow marine sedimentation in central North Sea (AGD), sand-and-silt-prone shoreward sediments in northern North Sea (SHN), west of Scotland (SIN, MOI, LLOD) and in slope-front sediments west of Scotland, punctuated at times by ice-rafted debris (SIN, MOI, LLOD)

* onset of ice-rafted debris in North Atlantic

Notes:

1. table showing correlation of Quaternary events with the Oxygen Isotope Stages, the Netherlands and UK Stages and palaeomagnetic polarity adapted after Funnell (1995). For references to the stratigraphical framework of events refer to the main text. There are vigorous ongoing controversies surrounding correlation between the Netherlands and UK stages and their correlation with the oxygen isotope stages.

2. ka = thousands of years; Ma = millions of years (all ages are approximate); for key to WGF, OTB etc refer to Figs 7.10, 7.11.

3. the complexity of events shown for the interval from the severe Late Weichselian glaciation to the Holocene may be analogous for the transition from severe glaciations to interglacials also in the early Quaternary period and the Cromerian, Elsterian and Saalian stages.

4. dashed correlation lines indicate uncertainty.

5. conventionally, oxygen isotope stages with even numbers generally refer to cold periods in the global glacial/interglacial cycle, those with odd numbers to warm periods. However, this does not always apply: thus stage 5 is broken down into 5a-5e, of which only 5e is a full interglacial. Not all the oxygen isotope stages are illustrated.

Figure 7.12 Summary of some of the major Quaternary events preserved in marine sediments around Scotland.

is thought to occur within the Bavelian complex (Sejrup *et al.*, 1987), this supposition being supported, although not conclusively proved, by the pollen assemblages (Ekman and Scourse, 1993). The implication from these observations is that glaciation may have covered parts of the northern North Sea within the period extending from approximately 0.78-0.99 Ma. The tentative biostratigraphic correlation of the overlying warm period with the Leerdam interglacial does not, however, rule out the possibility of correlation of invasion of the northern North Sea by ice during severe glaciation associated with the Dorst glaciation, Oxygen Stage 22 (Figure 7.12).

7.4 Middle Quaternary (approximately 0.78 Ma-130 ka)

7.4.1 'Late' Cromerian glaciation

The important formations are the Aberdeen Ground Formation and the Ling Bank Formation in the North Sea (Figure 7.10). The evidence from these formations shows that the broad-scale picture was one of major shelf glaciation associated with extensive channelling in the North Sea. There is also insecurely dated evidence for possible Cromerian and Elsterian ice sheets post-dating the Matuyama-Brunhes palaeomagnetic transition, possibly extending south of approximately 56°N.

The first evidence for Cromerian glaciation within the Brunhes Normal Polarity Chron is cited from tills near the top of the Aberdeen Ground Formation in the Forth Approaches and Moray Firth (Stoker and Bent, 1985; Bent, 1986). Further offshore a succession of isolated, anastomosing and occasionally stacked channels, some thought to originate as subglacial or ice-marginal tunnel valleys, truncates the top of the Aberdeen Ground Formation. These channels and their early infill with sediments of the Ling Bank Formation occur within the Brunhes Normal Polarity Chron and have been correlated on the basis of regional seismostratigraphical considerations with regional glaciation of the continental shelf during the Elsterian (Stoker *et al.*, 1985; Cameron *et al.*, 1987). Uranium-series dating from the top of the Aberdeen Ground Formation in BGS borehole 81/26 in the northern central North Sea, although yielding minimum ages, appears to be locally supportive of an Elsterian age for the channels (Sejrup *et al.*, 1987). However, several lines of evidence, including aminostratigraphy and boreal assemblages of foraminifers (Knudsen and Sejrup, 1993; Sejrup and Knudsen, 1993), pollen assemblages (Ansari, 1992) and the occurrence of the Arctic brackish-water ostracod, *Scottia brownia* (Penney, 1990), indicate a possible 'Late' Cromerian interglacial age for the base of the Ling Bank Formation at its type site in borehole 81/34. Arctic glaciomarine sediments that dominate the overlying deposits are correlated with the Elsterian on the basis of their aminostratigraphy (Sejrup and Knudsen, 1993), and the sediments near the top of the formation have been correlated with those in 'type' Holsteinian sections in Denmark and Germany (Knudsen and Sejrup, 1993). Therefore the previous supposition that the channelling truncating the top of the Aberdeen Ground Formation originated during the regional Elsterian glaciation appears now to be insecure east of Scotland. It is replaced by the possibilities, that some of the channelling is Late Cromerian in age, that channel fill may locally represent more than one glacial cycle and that in the Southern Central North Sea interruption of major deltic sediments originating to the south first occurred in the Cromerian (Figure 7.10 and Figure 7.12). The newer information also opens up the possibility that some of the channelling dividing the Aberdeen Ground Formation from the overlying Ling Bank Formation in the central North Sea could be related to severe Cromerian glaciation during Oxygen Isotope Stage 16.

7.4.2 Elsterian glaciation

The important formations are the Aberdeen Ground and Ling Bank formations in the North Sea (Figure 7.10), and the MacLeod sequence on the western shelf (Figure 7.11). The evidence from these units and from the contemporaneous Swarte Bank Formation in the southern North Sea (Figure 7.10) shows that the broad-scale picture was one of regional shelf glaciation with an ice sheet extending from Scandinavia to areas south of Scotland.

As indicated above, the preserved evidence for Elsterian glaciation in the type section in the central North Sea is equivocal, the identification of the channelling truncating the top of parts of the Aberdeen Ground Formation with an Elsterian glaciation previously being on the basis of general stratigraphic relationships (Stoker *et al.*, 1985). However, an extensive literature citing the sample and seismic evidence for regional Elsterian glaciation having extended from the north to approximately 53°N in the southern North Sea is summarized in Cameron *et al.* (1992), and to 51°N in the Irish Sea and adjacent land areas west of Britain, in Bowen *et al.* (1986) and Tappin *et al.* (1994). The wider regional picture therefore continues to support a supposition that the Scottish continental shelves were largely covered by an ice sheet during the Elsterian.

To the west, interpretation of calcareous nanoplankton assemblages within the lowermost Upper MacLeod sequence in BGS borehole 87/7,7A indicates that muddy Elsterian sediments are preserved on the slope on the Geikie Bulge, and are interpreted to be indicative of the first regional shelf glaciation in this area (Stoker *et al.*, 1994). This finding appears to support reconstructions based on the supposition that an Elsterian ice sheet eroded subglacial channels at the base of the Lower MacLeod sequence on the Hebridean shelf south of the Geikie Bulge (Holmes *et al.*, 1993; Stoker *et al.*, 1993). However, the current view from the North Sea indicates that such a supposition is insecure, one *caveat* being that the tunnel valleys at the base of the Lower MacLeod sequence could have originated under one of several inferred shelf ice sheets prior to the Elsterian. Another *caveat* to the supposition that Elsterian sediments record the first regional shelf glaciation is that the site of BGS borehole 88/7,7A is in an area of sediment bypass between the Sula Sgeir and Barra Fans, so that just as the evidence for Saalian glaciation appears not to have been preserved at this site (see below), the site environment may have prevented preservation of sedimentary evidence for pre-Elsterian glaciation.

7.4.3 Saalian glaciation

The important formations are the Fisher, Coal Pit and Ferder formations in the North Sea (Figure 7.10), and the Ferder and Malin Formations and the Elspeth sequence on the western shelf (Figures 7.10 and 7.11). The evidence from these formations shows that the broad-scale picture was one of an ice sheet extending into the central North Sea and to areas west of Shetland.

In the southern central North Sea, the base of the Fisher Formation, which succeeds the Ling Bank Formation (Figure 7.10), is identified with a marine transgression and has a thermoluminescence date of about 182 ka (Jensen and Knudsen, 1988). Although the thermoluminescence date is by itself insecure, other observations support correlation of the Fisher Formation deposits with events post-dating

Oxygen Isotope Stage 7. Arctic glaciomarine sediments of the Fisher Formation are thought to be contemporaneous with subglacial erosion north of approximately 58.6°N in the Inner Moray Firth (Bent, 1986) and with a till identified within the Fisher Formation (Sejrup et al., 1987). Infilling and extending beyond channels cut during the Saalian (Gatliff et al., 1993), the bulk of the overlying Coal Pit Formation was deposited in pulses of rapid glaciomarine sedimentation (Sejrup et al., 1987), separated in the northern and central North Sea by thin fragmentary evidence for marine deposition in warmer periods (Gatliff et al., 1994). Approximately 7.5 m above the base of the Coal Pit Formation, a reversed magnetic excursion in the Brunhes Normal Polarity Chron is attributed to the Blake Event (Stoker et al., 1985) and correlates with the transition between Oxygen Istope Stages 5e and 5d at approximately 120-117 ka (Tucholka et al., 1987), foraminiferal assemblages supporting correlation with the Ipswichian (Cameron et al., 1987). Therefore the glacial event represented by the Fisher Formation and in the glaciomarine sediments of the Coal Pit Formation can be attributed to the preceding Oxygen Isotope Stage 6, the extent of these deposits implying regional glaciation extending southwards in the central North Sea to approximately 56°N.

In the northern North Sea, basal sediments in the Ferder Formation fill deep glacigenic channels indicative of regional shelf glaciation at this time (Skinner et al., 1986). The Ferder Formation is seismostratigraphically extended to the shelf and slope west of Shetland to approximately 60°20'N (Stevenson, 1991; Holmes 1991), where it is identified with ice-proximal glaciomarine diamicton in borehole 84/04. These observations suggest the influence of an ice sheet extending from the northern North Sea to the western shelfbreak on the Atlantic margins. Assemblages of overlying foraminifers, indicative of ameliorating conditions, within the Ferder Formation are coeval with the Blake Event in borehole 80/1 (Stoker et al., 1983; Skinner et al., 1986), and similar assemblages in borehole 78/09 (Skinner and Gregory, 1983; Stoker et al., 1983; Skinner et al., 1986) are correlated with the Eemian-Weichselian transition between Oxygen Isotope Stages 5e and 5d at approximately 120-117 ka BP (Tucholka et al., 1987). These correlations imply that the lower glacial sediments in the Ferder Formation relate to the preceding Saalian cold stage (Oxygen Isotope Stage 6), and that regional shelf glaciation of the northern North Sea and west of Shetland occurred at this time.

On the Hebridean Shelf, pebbly, sandy muds and foraminifers at site 77/8 in the Elspeth sequence indicate deposition in glaciomarine conditions and form the uppermost of three sequences that form the bulk of the deposits in the west of the North Lewis Basin, the others being the MacIver and MacDonald sequences. Preliminary results from amino acid racemization analyses indicate that the Elspeth sequence is older than the MacIver sequence (see below) and possibly correlates with a pre-Weichselian glaciation, possibly the Saalian (Fyfe et al., 1993). The Malin Formation in the southern Inner Hebrides Shelf has been divided informally by Davies et al. (1984) into a diamicton of gravelly, sandy clays, Malin A, which exhibits a hummocky upper surface, indicative of an origin as a moraine, and the laterally equivalent Malin B sediments. Originating as a sub-glacial or ice-proximal deposit, the Malin Formation is speculatively correlated with glaciation during the Saalian and with Oxygen Isotope Stage 6. The age of the underlying Skerryvore Formation is unknown, but on the basis of its regional seismostratigraphical setting is tentatively ascribed to the middle Quaternary (Figure 7.11).

The sections of supposed Saalian Elspeth sequence and Malin Formations are disconnected and likely to be relict from formerly much more extensive Saalian sediments west of Scotland. The fragmentary nature of their preservation probably reflects their episodic subglacial erosion in the nearshore environments during subsequent Weichselian glaciations.

7.5 Late Quaternary (approximately 130 ka-present day)

Due to the bulk of the late Quaternary sediments being well preserved, they are finely resolved by seismic reflection survey techniques and many of the tops of the latest formations are buried at shallow depths under seabed sediments within an age range suitable for application of radiocarbon dating methods. These features commonly make the classification of sedimentary units easier, but the good state of preservation of late Quaternary sediments in many spatially disconnected basins combined with opportunities for detailed research has given rise to the definition of a plethora of formations. Only the major formations are considered here. Due to their good preservation, the geometries of late Quaternary sediment sequences can be used to model the likely form of those occurring during past maximum glaciations and the following deglaciation (Figure 7.2 and Figure 7.3).

7.5.1 Early Weichselian glaciation

The important deposits are the MacDonald and MacIver sequences and the Stanton Formation on the western shelf (Figure 7.11). The fragmentary evidence from these formations shows that the broad scale picture was one of likely glaciation on the shelf, possibly locally extending to the shelfbreak west of Scotland.

Shallow-water, glaciomarine pebbly muds in the MacIver sequence interdigitate with the top of the MacDonald sequence on the Hebrides Shelf. Amino acid racemization analyses from the MacIver sequence in borehole 88/10 (Stoker et al., 1993) suggest correlation with Saalian to Early Weichselian events. On the West Shetland Shelf, diamictons of the MacDonald sequence at sites 77/07, 82/4 and 82/3 are buried under the Otter Bank sequence of likely Late Weichselian age (see below), and a similar regional seismostratigraphical correlation with 88/7,7A appears to lend weight to an origin for the MacDonald sequence during the Early Weichselian (Stoker et al., 1993). Associated with the MacDonald sequence is a series of submarine end moraines (see Figure 6.3) (Stoker, 1988, 1990; Stewart and Stoker, 1990), supporting a model for an Early Weichselian ice sheet extending from the Hebrides Shelf and southern Shetland Shelf to the shelfbreak. The MacDonald sequence in the northern West Shetland Shelf appears to have been removed by erosion under the Otter Bank sequence (Holmes, 1991).

Acoustically well-layered, ice-distal glaciomarine silty pebbly clays of the Stanton Formation are more than 160 m thick and rest between 56°00'N to 58°00'N and 8°30'W to 6°40'W either on bedrock or on a widespread erosion surface across the top of the Malin Formation, and were at first tentatively correlated with the Saalian (Fyfe et al., 1993). In borehole 78/01, the foraminiferal assemblages indicate that a part of the Uist Member in the Stanton Formation was deposited in the severest cold conditions (D. Gregory, BGS unpublished data). The lack of seismic layering in the Uist Member originates from rapid deposition compared to the rest of the formation (Fyfe et al., 1993) and would suggest deposition close to a glacier margin. Amino acid racemization analysis of a shell from borehole 78/01B just below the base of the Uist Member (Fyfe *et al.*, 1993) gave a value intermediate between results from the MacIver sequence (possibly Early Weichselian) and the Elspeth Formation (possibly Saalian). On the basis of the aminostratigraphy and the regional seismostratigraphy, tentative correlation of the Stanton Formation at site 78/01B with Early Weichselian glaciation is now indicated, but is insecure. The offshore data thus provides fragmentary and insecure correlative evidence for extensive Early Weichselian ice sheet glaciation west of Scotland.

7.5.2 Late Weichselian glaciation

The important formations are the Coal Pit and Marr Bank Formations in the North Sea (Figure 7.10), and the Otter Bank sequence and Conan sequence on the western shelf (Figures 7.10 and 7.11). The evidence from these formations shows that the broad-scale picture at the Late Weichselian maximum was one of possible coalescing Scandinavian and Scottish ice sheets in the North Sea and an ice sheet locally extending to the shelfbreak west of Scotland.

A reversed magnetic polarity interval at the top of BGS borehole 77/3 in the Coal Pit Formation in the central North Sea is tentatively correlated with the Laschamp excursion (Stoker *et al.*, 1985) with a mean age of about 42 ka BP (Wurm, 1997) and is assigned to the Middle Weichselian Oxygen Isotope Stage 3 when the North Sea was free of glacier ice. The ages of the younger deposits in the Coal Pit Formation are constrained by AMS radiocarbon dates from glaciomarine sediments in BGS borehole 77/2 of approximately 22.6 ka BP, 20.9 ka BP and 19.7 ka BP, the implication being that although the central North Sea was cold during this period, it was free of grounded glacier ice. An AMS date of 42.3 ka BP, a maximum age, was obtained from mixed arctic benthic foraminifers in a reworked diamicton preserved under the glaciomarine sediments in BHS borehole 77/2. Possibly originating as a till, the diamicton is correlated with maximum glaciation of the central North Sea between approximately 29 ka BP and 22 ka BP in the Late Weichselian (Sejrup *et al.*, 1994). This interpretation hinges, however, on interpretation of the diamicton as a till, and although the Sejrup *et al.* (1994) data do not discriminate between reworking due to an origin under an ice sheet or under possible sea ice, the latest interpretation of the micromorphological evidence is that brittle shear observed at the base of the deformation layer is characteristic of a till (S. Carr, written communication, 1997). The eastern boundary of the 'Bosies Bank Moraine', part of the Coal Pit Formation (Bent, 1986), together with the eastern boundary of the Wee Bankie Formation, are also correlated with a Late Devensian ice limit at around 18 ka BP (Hall and Bent, 1990), an age supported by radiocarbon dates of approximately 17.7 ka BP and 21.7 ka BP (Holmes, 1977) from lignitised wood in the laterally-equivalent Marr Bank Formation. The implications from these observations are that offshore from eastern Scotland the maximum glaciation of the North Sea and the confluence of the southern Scandinavian and Scottish ice sheets may have pre-dated approximately 22 ka BP, and were possibly succeeded by a stillstand or re-advance of the Scottish ice sheet marked by the Wee Bankie and Bosies Bank moraines east of the present coast around 18 ka BP.

In the northern North Sea and West Shetland Shelf, a marine erosion surface defining the base of the Cape Shore Formation is correlated with deglaciation and climatic warming at the transition between Oxygen Isotope Stages 4 and 3 (Johnson *et al.*, 1993). In borehole 78/9 the foraminiferal assemblages associated with this climatic warming coincide with a magnetically reversed section tentatively correlated with the Laschamp excursion (Skinner *et al.*, 1986), with an estimated mean age of 42 ka BP (Wurm, 1997) within Oxygen Isotope Stage 3. Radiocarbon dates of 31.2 ka BP from shell fragments deposited in an arctic environment approximately 17.5 m below seabed in Brent Soil Boring I on the shelf in the northern North Sea (Figure 7.3) (Milling, 1975) and down-hole increasing AMS dates of 29.4 ka BP, 29.9 ka BP and 30.2 ka BP from shells in borehole A79-156 are associated with arctic foraminiferal assemblages (Rise and Rokoengen, 1984; Sejrup *et al.*, 1994) and are correlative with the closing events of Oxygen Isotope Stage 3. Identification of the Cape Shore Formation with Oxygen Isotope Stage 3 is therefore secure, this conclusion being significant for estimating the timing of regional glaciation in the northern North Sea and West Shetland Shelf associated with the overlying Otter Bank sequence.

Diamictons comprising the Otter Bank sequence east and west of Shetland locally originate as submarine moraines on the middle shelf (Figure 7.8) and possibly terrestrial or submarine till adjacent to Shetland. They are correlated on the basis of their regional seismostratigraphy in the northern North Sea with the Late Weichselian (Johnson *et al.*, 1993), Oxygen Isotope Stage 2. Diamictons comprising the Otter Bank sequence are correlated on the basis of their regional seismostratigraphy east of Shetland with the Tampen and Sperus Formations (Johnson *et al.*, 1993), deposited during Oxygen Istope Stage 2. Diamictons, commonly too thin or discontinuous to be resolved on the seismic reflection profiles, and therefore insecurely correlated with the Otter Bank sequence, are widespread on the seafloor adjacent to Shetland. Such diamicton in BGS vibrocore 60/+00/49, interpreted as a soft-sediment deformation till or a subaqueous glacigenic debris flow, yielded radiocarbon ages of approximately 13.2 ka BP and 13.7 ka BP, these ages possibly indicating a much later deglaciation around Shetland than on mainland Scotland (Peacock and Long, 1994). West of Shetland, mounded ridge and sheet-form diamictons of the Otter Bank sequence, in places more than 30 m thick, were deposited in front of a grounded glacier at borehole 82/10 (Unit I of Cockcroft, 1987) and are interpreted as submarine moraines. The diamictons locally extend over the shelf-edge to the upper slope where they were reworked by iceberg scour (Holmes, 1991). Shelly, gravelly sands resting on the Otter Bank unit indicate deposition in high-energy, shallow marine, glaciomarine and deltaic environments (Unit 0 of Cockcroft, 1987). These environments are thought to have originated during the shelf ice retreat but, as they are not easily resolved on the seismic reflection profiles, they are not mappable on a regional scale. In BGS vibrocore 61-01/66, a shell from glaciomarine sediment or a subglacial diamicton at the landward margin of the Otter Bank unit yielded a radiocarbon age of 18.2 ka BP, and another from overlying sandy muds, an age of 13.4 ka BP (Ross, 1996). The radiocarbon ages and seismostratigraphical correlation with the Cape Shore formation are currently thought to indicate further secure correlation of the Otter Bank unit with the Late Weichselian (Oxygen Isotope Stage 2).

Around the St Kilda Basin on the Outer Hebrides Shelf, the Caoilte sequence is contemporaneous with the sandy, pebbly muds that form the arcuate, ice-marginal, morainal banks of the Conan B sequence. Some 2.5 km wide and 10 m high above the seabed, the banks can be traced laterally into a more ice-distal environment where the pebbly muds of the sheet-like Conan A sequence are 10-60 m thick and only locally form seabed ridges, that are adjacent to, and parallel with, the shelfbreak. The Conan A and B sequences are both interpreted as glaciomarine deposits, the Conan B morainal banks possibly occurring where the ice-sheet covering the St Kilda Basin terminated (Selby, 1989). The Oisean, Caoilte and Conan sequences are correlated with Oxygen Isotope Stage 2, a radiocarbon date from a shallow core on the outer shelf in the Conan A sequence of approximately 22.5 ka BP supporting a hypothesis for contemporaneous glaciomarine sedimentation west of the morainal banks (Selby, 1989).

The observations from the northern North Sea appear to suggest that two episodes of ice sheet extension occurred in the Late Weichselian, the older possibly associated with confluence of the Scottish and Scandinavian ice sheets in the northern North Sea sometime between 29 and 22 ka BP, the younger with an ice sheet limit, possibly a readvance, at the landward margins of the North Sea at the Wee Bankie and Bosies Bank moraines possibly around 18 ka; these latter features have been identified in the literature with the offshore maximum extent of the ice (see Chapters 5 and 6). The possible readvance east of Scotland is insecurely correlated with the maximum extent of ice onshore in eastern England during the Dimlington Stadial. West of Shetland, BGS mapping appears to show that ice extended to the shelfbreak and beyond (Holmes, 1991; Stoker et al., 1993), and outer-to-mid-shelf ridges (Figure 7.8) are interpreted as still-stand submarine moraines formed as the ice on the northern shelf locally oscillated during net retreat to the east (Holmes, 1991; Stoker and Holmes, 1991). There is no substantive evidence as yet reported from this area for a re-advance, and Ross (1996) concluded that the pattern of ice recession initially reflected tidewater calving controlled by the rising relative sea level. The ice margin may then have grounded at around the current -100 m bathymetric contour and from there retreated terrestrially, the pattern of later deglaciation reflecting the complex variations in topography around the Shetland archipelago. The radiocarbon date of 22.5 ka BP from the glaciomarine deposits west of the Hebrides appears to be consistent with their correlation with a possible North Sea maximum glaciation pre-dating 18 ka BP.

7.5.3 Latest Weichselian deglaciation and marker events in the Holocene

The sediments and assemblages of foraminifers in two shallow marine cores from the Hebridean Shelf provide evidence for the timing of deglaciation and the changing environmental and climatic conditions during the Late-glacial (Peacock et al., 1992; Austin and Kroon, 1996). The onset of ice sheet melting west of Scotland is dated to about 15.2 ka BP, apparently before the onset of warming in the North Atlantic, and possibly related to rising sea-level. Radiocarbon dates from foraminifers indicate that the estimated onset of ice retreat from the Norwegian Channel was about 15 ka BP (Sejrup et al., 1995). In the Cape Shore Formation in the northern North Sea, overconsolidated sediments originating from desiccation are overlain by sediments thought to have been deposited from sea-ice transport. These observations suggest that the Viking Bank west of the Norwegian Channel was subaerially exposed between approximately 16-14 ka BP, much of the northern central North Sea and northern North Sea north of approximately 58°N also possibly being subaerially exposed or inundated by a very shallow sea at this time (Peacock, 1995). This hypothesis accords with a maximum age of approximately 14.1 ka BP for the onset of glaciomarine

sedimentation at the base of the Witch Ground Formation to the south (Sejrup et al., 1994) and also with the evidence for sea-ice scour at the base of the Witch Ground Formation (Stoker and Long, 1985).

Between 13.5-13 ka BP, the cold water on the Hebrides Shelf, previously associated with deposition in a low-energy environment sheltered from waves by sea-ice throughout much of the year, was replaced by warmer water, and a higher-energy environment with less sea-ice (Peacock et al., 1992). Radiocarbon dates from Portlandia arctica, a high arctic marine bivalve no longer found around Scotland, in BGS vibrocore 58+00/111 indicate that polar water and probably sea-ice were also in the central North Sea until at least 13.2-13.1 ka BP (Peacock and Harkness, 1990). Seawater warming and release of methane gas at seabed from the Witch Ground Formation occurred at approximately 13 ka BP (Long, 1992). There is also evidence for a return to extensive sea ice on the Hebrides Shelf during the Loch Lomond Stadial, approximately 11.0 ka to less than 10.2 ka BP, before rapid warming by some 8°C before 10 ka BP and establishment of high energy sedimentation from vigorous wave and current action typical of the onset of the Holocene. Abrupt changes in oxygen isotope values correlated with the flow of warmer Atlantic water into the Norwegian Channel are dated to just preceding approximately 7 ka BP (Lehman et al., 1991). Tsunami deposits on the east and north nearshore area of Scotland (see Chapter 12) are correlated with a submarine slide west of Norway (Dawson et al., 1988) and correlative with tsunami deposits on the west coast of Norway dated at approximately 7.2 ka BP (Bondevik et al., 1997). Large-scale slide failure, thought to be postglacial on account of its obliteration of ice-scour at the shelf-edge, as yet unrelated to tsunami, is also a feature of the slope west of the Hebrides (Holmes et al., in press).

The pattern of sea-level changes in the shoreward areas around Scotland during the Late-glacial and Holocene is summarised in Chapter 12.

7.6 Conclusions

The marine sediments around Scotland contain a much more temporal and spatially extensive record of Quaternary events than on land (Figure 7.12).

Ice-scour forms the first evidence for ice entering the North Sea at times near the start of the Quaternary (defined here at around 2.44 Ma), and ice-scour is one of the last Late-glacial erosion events to be recorded in the Late Weichselian. The intervening accumulation of more than 800 m thickness of shelf sediments within the North Sea basin during many Quaternary climatic cycles indicates that similar ice scour is likely to be a commonly-preserved feature of the Quaternary succession.

The earliest evidence for extensive ice-sheet glaciation in the northern North Sea appears to pre-date the Jaramillo Normal Polarity Subchron (1.07 Ma) in the early Quaternary, and if correlated with events post-dating the Cobb Mountain Normal Polarity Subchron (1.19 Ma), may be speculatively identified with Oxygen Isotope Stages 34 or 36. The evidence from the regional seismostratigraphy may indicate that the effects from this glaciation are also the first to interrupt 'pre-glacial' marine sedimentation on the northern slopes west of Shetland, and indicate some regional potential for shelf glaciation during the early Quaternary also affecting slope sediments west of the Hebrides.

Phases of regional ice cover in the northern North Sea are insecurely established in the early Quaternary: possibly two phases of glaciation occurred. During the middle and late Quaternary, they are more securely established, with regional glaciation extending across the central North Sea during the 'Late' Cromerian, the Elsterian, Saalian and Late Weichselian. West of Scotland there is insecure evidence for early Quaternary glaciation of the northern shelf, secure evidence for ice-distal sedimentation affecting the slope west of the Hebrides, this last probably associated with Elsterian shelf glaciation, and fragmentary, insecure evidence for Saalian and Early Weichselian shelf glaciation west of the Hebrides. Secure local evidence exists for regional glaciation extending to the shelfbreak during the Late Weichselian.

The schematic process model summarized for the shelf east of Scotland indicates a fundamentally different style of preservation for the stratigraphic record compared to that preserved west of Scotland. In the fan areas west of Scotland, sediments recording previous glacial/interglacial cycles have been periodically swept over the shelf-edge to the slope and have been subject to extensive reworking by gravitational sliding in the slope areas south of the Wyville-Thomson Ridge. In the North Sea to the east, the shelf sedimentary record is likely to be more complete, but possibly the most complete Quaternary Scottish climatic record is preserved in the deepest-water basins below the mudline on the NE Atlantic margins.

Acknowledgements

The work presented here is a personal, brief review from the British Geological Survey regional survey programme encompassing the shelves and slopes around Scotland in the BGS 1:1 000 000 and 1:250 000 Quaternary Regional Map Series and the Quaternary Chapters in the BGS United Kingdom Offshore Regional Report Series, and from review of the scientific literature. Because of the rapid developments since the publication of the BGS maps and reports, the majority before 1995, views expressed in this chapter do not necessarily reflect those of the BGS literature. The sincerest thanks are due to my colleagues, without whose research this work would have been impossible. Special thanks are due to Dave Long and Robin Wingfield who made many useful suggestions for improvements, and to Eileen Gillespie who drafted the figures. This paper is published with the permission of the Director of the British Geological Survey.

References

Ansari, M.H. 1992. Stratigraphy and palaeobotany of Middle Pleistocene interglacial deposits in the North Sea. Unpublished PhD thesis, University of North Wales.

Austin, W.E.N. and Kroon, D. 1996. Late glacial sedimentology, forminifera and stable isotope stratigraphy of the Hebrides continental shelf, northwest Scotland. In: Andrews, J.T., Austin, W.E.N., Bergsten, H. and Jennings, A.E. (Eds), *Late Quaternary Palaeoceanography of the North Atlantic Margins*. Geological Society, Special Publication 111, 187-213.

Bent, A. J. A. 1986. Aspects of Pleistocene glaciomarine sequences in the northern North Sea. Unpublished PhD thesis, University of Edinburgh.

Bondevik, S., Svendsen, J.I., Johnsen, G., Mangerud, J. and Kaland, P.E. 1997. The Storegga tsunami along the Norwegian coast, its age and runup. *Boreas*, 26, 29-53.

Bowen, D.Q., Rose, J., McCabe, A.M. and Sutherland, D.G. 1986. Correlation of Quaternary glaciations in England, Ireland, Scotland and Wales. *Quaternary Science Reviews*, 5, 299-340.

Cameron, T.D.J., Stoker, M.S. and Long, D. 1987. The history of Quaternary sedimentation in the UK sector of the North Sea Basin. *Journal of the Geological Society of London*, 144, 43-58.

Cameron, T.D.J., Crosby, A., Balson, P.S., Jeffery, D.H., Lott, G.K., Bulat, J. and Harrison, D.J. 1992. *United Kingdom Offshore Regional Report: the Geology of the Southern North Sea*. HMSO for the British Geological Survey, London.

Cockcroft, D.N. 1987. The Quaternary sediment of the Shetland Platform and adjacent continental shelf margin. Unpublished PhD thesis, University of Keele.

Davies, H.C., Dobson, M.R. and Whittington, R.J. 1984. A revised seismic stratigraphy for Quaternary deposits on the inner continental shelf west of Scotland between 55°30'N and 57°30'N. *Boreas*, 13, 49-66.

Dawson, A.G., Long, D. & Smith D.E. 1988. The Storegga Slides: evidence from eastern Scotland for a possible tsunami. *Marine Geology*, 82, 271-276.

Ekman, S.R. and Scourse, J.D. 1993. Early and middle Pleistocene pollen stratigraphy from the British Geological Survey borehole 81/26, Fladen Ground, central North Sea. *Review of Palaeobotany and Palynology*, 79, 285-295.

Evans, C.D.R. 1991. *St Kilda Sheet 57N°-0°W. Quaternary Geology*. 1:250 000 Map Series. British Geological Survey.

Funnell, B.M. 1995. Global sea-level and the (pen-)insularity of late Cenozoic Britain. In: Preece, R.C. (Ed.), *Island Britain: a Quaternary Perspective*. Geological Society, Special Publication 96, 3-13.

Fyfe, J.A., Long, D. and Evans, D. 1993. *United Kingdom Offshore Regional Report: the Geology of the Malin-Hebrides Sea Area*. HMSO for the British Geological Survey, London.

Gatliff, R.W., Richards, P.C., Smith, P.C., Graham, C.C., McCormac, M., Smith, N.J.P., Long, D., Cameron, T.D.J., Evans, D., Stevenson, A.G., Bulat, J. and Ritchie, J.D. 1994. *United Kingdom Offshore Regional Report: the Geology of the Central North Sea*. HMSO for the British Geological Survey, London.

Gibbard, P.L. 1988. The history of the great northwest European rivers during the last three million years. *Philosophical Transactions of the Royal Society of London*, 318B, 559-602.

Hall, A.M. and Bent, A.J.A. 1990. The limits of the last British ice sheet in northern Scotland and the adjacent shelf. *Quaternary Newsletter*, 61, 2-12.

Holmes, R. 1977. Quaternary deposits of the central North Sea, 5. The Quaternary geology of the UK sector of the North Sea between 56° and 58°N. *Report of the Institute of Geological Sciences*, No. 77/14.

Holmes, R. 1990. *Rona Sheet 59°N 06°W. Quaternary Geology*. 1:250 000 Map Series. British Geological Survey.

Holmes, R. 1991. *Foula Sheet 60°N 04°W. Quaternary Geology*. 1:250 000 Map Series. British Geological Survey.

Holmes, R. and Stoker, M.S. 1990. Pleistocene glaciomarine facies on the continental shelf and slope northwest of Scotland. *Abstract in 13th International Sedimentological Congress*, 230.

Holmes, R., Jeffery, D.H., Ruckley, N.A.R. and Wingfield, R.T.R. 1993. *Quaternary Sediments around the United Kingdom North Sheet*, 1:1 000 000. British Geological Survey, Edinburgh.

Holmes, R., Long, D. and Dodd, L.R. (in press) Large-scale debrites and submarine landslides on the Barra Fan, west of Britain. *Special Publication Geological Society, London*.

James, J.W.C. 1991. *Peach Sheet 56°N 10°W. Quaternary Geology*. 1:250 000 Map Series. British Geological Survey.

Jensen, K.A. and Knudsen, K.L. 1988. Quaternary foraminiferal stratigraphy in boring 81/29 from the central North Sea. *Boreas*, 17, 273-287.

Jeffery, D.H. and Long, D. 1989. Early Pleistocene sedimentation and geographic change in the UK sector of the North Sea. *Terra Abstracts, 1, 425.*

Johnson, H., Richards, P.C., Long, D. and Graham, C.C. 1993. *United Kingdom Offshore Regional Report: the Geology of the Northern North Sea.* HMSO for the British Geological Survey, London.

King, C. 1983. Caenozoic micropalaeontological biostratigraphy of the North Sea. *Report of the Institute of Geological Sciences,* No. **82/7.**

Knudsen, K.L. and Asbjornsdottir, L. 1991. Plio-Peistocene foraminiferal stratigraphy and correlation in the central North Sea. *Marine Geology,* **101,** 113-124.

Knudsen, K.L. and Sejrup, H.P. 1993. Pleistocene stratigraphy in the Devils Hole area, central North Sea: foraminiferal and amino-acid evidence. *Journal of Quaternary Science,* **8,** 1-14.

Lehman, S.J., Jones, G.A., Keigwin, L.D., Andersen, E.S., Butenko, G. and Ostmo, S.R. 1991. Initiation of Fennoscandian ice-sheet retreat during the last deglaciation. *Nature,* **349,** 513-516.

Long, D.L., Skinner, A.C. and Rise, L. 1988. *Halibut Bank Sheet 60°N 00°W. Quaternary Geology.* 1:250 000 Map Series. British Geological Survey.

Long, D.L., Smith, D.E. and Dawson, A.G. 1989. A Holocene tsunami deposit in eastern Scotland. *Journal of Quaternary Science,* **4,** 61-66.

Long, D.L. 1992. Devensian Late-glacial gas escape in the central North Sea. *Continental Shelf Research,* **12,** 1097-1110.

Milling, M.E. 1975. Geological appraisal of foundation conditions, northern North Sea. *Proceedings of Oceanology International, Brighton,* 310-319.

Pantin, H. 1991. The seabed sediments around the United Kingdom. *British Geological Survey Research Report,* **SB/90/01.**

Peacock, J.D. 1995. Late Devensian to early Holocene palaeoenvironmental changes in the Viking Bank area, northern North Sea. *Quaternary Science Reviews,* **14,** 1029-1042.

Peacock, J.D. and Harkness, D.D. 1990. Radiocarbon ages and the full-glacial to Holocene transition in seas adjacent to Scotland and southern Scandinavia: a review. *Transactions of the Royal Society of Edinburgh: Earth Sciences,* **81,** 385-396.

Peacock, J.D. and Long, D.L. 1994. Late Devensian glaciation and deglaciation of Shetland. *Quaternary Newsletter,* **74,** 16-21.

Peacock, J.D., Austin, W.E.N., Selby, I., Graham, D.K., Harland, R. and Wilkinson, I.P. 1992. Late Devensian and Flandrian palaeoenvironmental changes in the Scottish continental shelf west of the Outer Hebrides. *Journal of Quaternary Science,* **7,** 145-161.

Penney, D. . 1990. Quaternary ostracod chronology of the central North Sea: the record from BH 81/29. *Courier Forschunginstitut Senckenberg,* **123,** 97-109.

Rise, L. and Rokoengen, K. 1984. Surficial sediments in the Norwegian sector of the North Sea between 60°30'and 62°N. *Marine Geology,* **58,** 287-317.

Ross, H. 1996. Last glaciation of Shetland. Unpublished PhD thesis, University of St Andrews.

Sejrup, H.P. and Knudsen, K.L. 1993. Paleoenvironments and correlations of interglacial sediments in the North Sea. *Boreas,* **22,** 223-235.

Sejrup, H.P., Aarseth, I., Ellingsen, E., Reither, E., Jansen, E., Lovlie, R., Bent, A., Brigham-Grette, J., Larsen, E. and Stoker, M. 1987. Quaternary stratigraphy of the Fladen area, central North Sea: a multidisciplinary study. *Journal of Quaternary Science,* **2,** 35-58.

Sejrup, H. P., Haflidason, H., Aarseth, I., King, E., Forsberg, C. F., Long, D. and Rokoengen, K. 1994. Late Weichselian glaciation history of the northern North Sea. *Boreas,* **23,** 1-13.

Sejrup, H.P., Aarseth, I., Haflidason, H., Lovlie, R., Bratten, A., Tjostheim, G., Forsberg, C.F. and Ellingsen, K.L. 1995. Quaternary of the Norwegian Channel; paleoceanography and glaciation history. *Norsk Geologisk Tidsskrift,* **75,** 65-87.

Selby, I. 1989. Quaternary geology of the Hebridean continental margin. Unpublished PhD thesis, University of Nottingham.

Shackleton, N.J. and sixteeen others. 1984. Oxygen isotope calibration of the onset of ice rafting and history of glaciation in the North Atlantic region. *Nature,* **307,** 620-623.

Skinner, A. C., and Gregory, D.M. 1983. Quaternary stratigraphy in the northern North Sea. *Boreas,* **12,** 145-152.

Skinner, A.C., McElvenney, E., Ruckley, N., Rise, L. and Rokoengen, K. 1986. *Cormorant Sheet 61°N 00°. Quaternary Geology.* 1:250 000 Map Series. British Geological Survey.

Smart, P.L. and Frances, P.D. (Eds) 1991. *Quaternary Dating Methods - a User's Guide.* Quaternary Research Association Technical Guide No. 4. Quaternary Research Association, Cambridge.

Stevenson, A.S. 1991. *Miller Sheet 61°N 02°W. Quaternary Geology.* 1:250 000 Map Series. British Geological Survey.

Stewart, F.S. and Stoker, M.S. 1990. Problems associated with seismic facies analysis of diamicton-dominated, shelf glacigenic sequences. *Geo-Marine Letters,* **10,** 151-156.

Stoker, M.S. 1988. Pleistocene ice-proximal glaciomarine sediments in boreholes from the Hebrides shelf and Wyville-Thomson Ridge, NW UK continental shelf. *Scottish Journal of Geology,* **24,** 249-262.

Stoker, M.S. 1990. Glacially influenced sedimentation on the Hebridean slope, northwestern United Kingdom continental margin. *Geological Society Special Publication,* **53,** 349-362.

Stoker, M.S. 1991. *Sula Sgeir Sheet 59°N 08°W. Quaternary Geology.* 1:250 000 Map Series. British Geological Survey.

Stoker, M.S. and Bent, A.J.A. 1985. Middle Pleistocene glacial and glaciomarine sedimentation in the west central North Sea. *Boreas,* **14,** 325-332.

Stoker, M.S. and Bent, A.J.A. 1987. Lower Pleistocene deltaic and marine sediments in boreholes from the central North Sea. *Journal of Quaternary Science,* **2,** 87-96.

Stoker, M.S. and Holmes, R. 1991. Submarine end-moraines as indicators of Pleistocene ice limits off NW Britain. *Journal of the Geological Society of London,* **148,** 431-434.

Stoker, M.S. and Long, D. 1985. A relict ice-scoured erosion surface in the central North Sea. *Marine Geology,* **61,** 85-93.

Stoker, M.S., Long, D. and Fyfe, J.A. 1985. A revised Quaternary stratigraphy for the central North Sea. *Report of the British Geological Survey,* No. **17.**

Stoker M.S., Skinner, A.C., Fyfe, J.A., and Long, D. 1983. Palaeomagnetic evidence for early Pleistocene in the central and northern North Sea. *Nature,* **304,** 332-334.

Stoker, M.S., Hitchen, K. and Graham, C.C. 1993. *United Kingdom Offshore Regional Report: the Geology of the Hebrides and West Shetland shelves, and Adjacent Deepwater Areas.* HMSO for the British Geological Survey, London.

Stoker, M.S., Leslie, A.B., Scott, W.D., Briden, J.C., Hine, N.M., Harland, R., Wilkinson, I.P., Evans, D. and Ardus, D.A. 1994. A record of late Cenozoic stratigraphy, sedimentation and climate change from the Hebrides Slope, NE Atlantic Ocean. *Journal of the Geological Society, London,* **151,** 235-249.

Tappin, D.R., Chadwick, R.A., Jackson, A.A., Wingfield, R.T.R. and Smith, N.J.P. 1994. *United Kingdom Offshore Regional Report: the Geology of Cardigan Bay and Bristol Channel.* HMSO for the British Geological Survey, London.

Tucholka, P., Fontugne, M., Guichard, F. and Paterne, M. 1987. The Blake magnetic polarity episode in cores from the Mediterranean Sea. *Earth and Planetary Science Letters,* **86,** 320-326.

Wurm, H-U. 1997. A link between geomagnetic reversals and events and glaciations. *Earth and Planetary Science Letters,* **147,** 55-67.

8. Geomorphological Change in the Scottish Late-glacial

J. Murray Gray

The key themes covered in this chapter are:

• **patterns of deglaciation of the last ice sheet and the landforms produced;**
• **landscape changes during the Late-glacial Interstadial;**
• **geomorphological and landscape changes during the Loch Lomond Stadial.**

8.1 Introduction

A geomorphologist living through the Scottish Late-glacial (see Chapter 9 for definition) would have had a busy and exciting research career. The period was one of rapid fluctuations of climate and changing environments, encompassing the emergence of Scotland from the almost complete glacial cover of the last ice sheet into mild climatic conditions equivalent to those of today. There was then a gradual return to glacial harshness before the climate recovered again.

These climatic oscillations are summarised in Figure 8.1 and they had a profound effect on the geomorphological processes operating in Scotland (Figure 8.2) and hence on the character of the Scottish landscape (Walker *et al.*, 1994). Meltwater, released as the last Scottish ice sheet melted, eroded channels in the landscape and deposited sands and gravels in the form of kames, eskers and outwash trains. Once deglaciated, the landscape gradually became stabilised by vegetation, and soils started to develop. However, the return to a climate of glacial severity brought a new advance

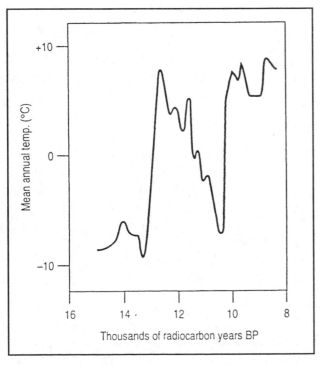

Figure 8.1 Reconstructed mean annual temperature for England, Wales and Southern Scotland based on beetle evidence. (Modified from Atkinson *et al.*, 1987).

Figure 8.2 Geomorphological processes in the Scottish Late-glacial. (Modified from Walker *et al.*, 1994).

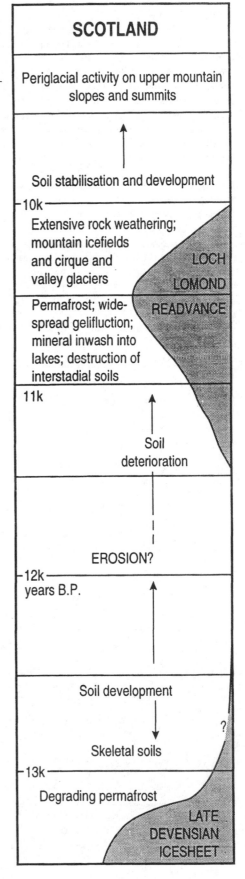

SCOTLAND

Periglacial activity on upper mountain slopes and summits

Soil stabilisation and development

— 10k —

Extensive rock weathering; mountain icefields and cirque and valley glaciers

LOCH LOMOND READVANCE

Permafrost; widespread gelifluction; mineral inwash into lakes; destruction of interstadial soils

11k

Soil deterioration

EROSION?

— 12k —
years B.P.

Soil development

Skeletal soils

— 13k —

Degrading permafrost

LATE DEVENSIAN ICESHEET

of glaciers to the highland areas, and elsewhere resulted in intense periglacial activity. This chapter offers a brief overview of these geomorphological changes.

8.2 Ice-sheet wastage

The Late-glacial began at "the apparently rapid thermal improvement that occurred between about 14,000 and 13,000 B.P." (Lowe and Gray, 1980). Scotland had been almost totally covered by ice during the maximum of the last ice sheet (Dimlington Stadial) about 18 ka BP. Only some marginal parts of the country and the higher mountain summits were free of ice at this time (Sutherland and Walker, 1984; Ballantyne, 1990; McCarroll et al., 1995). However, a steady waning of the ice sheet was accelerated by the rapid climatic warming at 14-13 ka BP, evident from terrestrial beetle assemblages and microfauna in ocean cores in the North Atlantic (Chapter 5). The conventional view is that this rapid warming was brought about by the retreat of polar waters from NW Europe and their replacement by the North Atlantic Drift (Ruddiman and McIntyre, 1973, 1981). However, other studies, indicating cold waters on the Norwegian coast and possibly even in the North Sea, suggest a more complex picture of water temperatures at this time.

Over the years, several authors have proposed readvances of the ice sheet during deglaciation but not all of these have survived modern scrutiny. Among those no longer accepted are the Perth and Aberdeen-Lammermuir readvances, but other proposed readvance stages in Wester Ross (Robinson and Ballantyne, 1979) and at Otter Ferry on Loch Fyne (Sutherland, 1984a) are more soundly based. In addition,

Merritt et al. (1995) have recently described evidence for minor readvances or stillstands of the ice sheet in the inner Moray Firth (e.g. at Ardersier and Alturlie) and have suggested that the field evidence elsewhere in eastern Scotland needs to be reassessed for evidence of readvances. They even imply that the Perth Readvance may be resurrected (see also Chapter 5).

Even when not readvancing, the ice-sheet margin in many places appears to have undergone active retreat during deglaciation rather than decaying in situ (Sutherland, 1984a). This can be demonstrated, for example, in Midlothian where the Highland and Southern Upland ice masses parted during deglaciation. Meltwater emerging from the latter formed outwash trains down the Esk Valley, which terminated in lakes dammed up by the northward retreating Highland ice in the Firth of Forth (Kirby, 1969).

The Southern Uplands ice appears to have continued to retreat in an orderly manner rather than breaking up into a series of smaller ice masses. This is indicated by several studies which have mapped the distribution of meltwater channels, eskers and related features (Figure 8.3) over the northern part of the Southern Uplands. These demonstrate a consistent and integrated drainage pattern from coast to coast with a general direction of meltwater flow towards the east-northeast (Sutherland, 1984a), mirroring the general slope of the ice-sheet surface. The features include the famous Carstairs 'Kames' and Carlops meltwater channel systems.

In the Dee valley, west of Aberdeen, Brown (1993) has recently attempted to reconstruct the character of ice decay

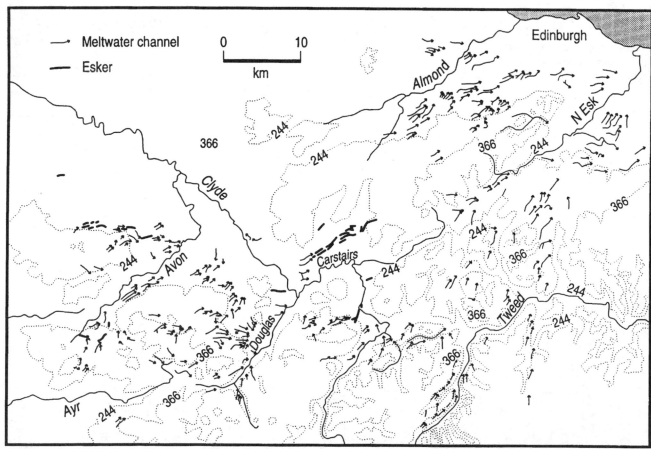

Figure 8.3 Distribution of meltwater channels and eskers in the northern Southern Uplands. (Reprinted from *Quaternary Science Reviews,* 3, D.G. Sutherland, 'The Quaternary deposits and landforms of Scotland and the neighbouring shelves: a review', 157-254, copyright (1984), with kind permission from Elsevier Science Ltd, The Boulevard, Longford Lane, Kidlington OX5 1GB, UK).

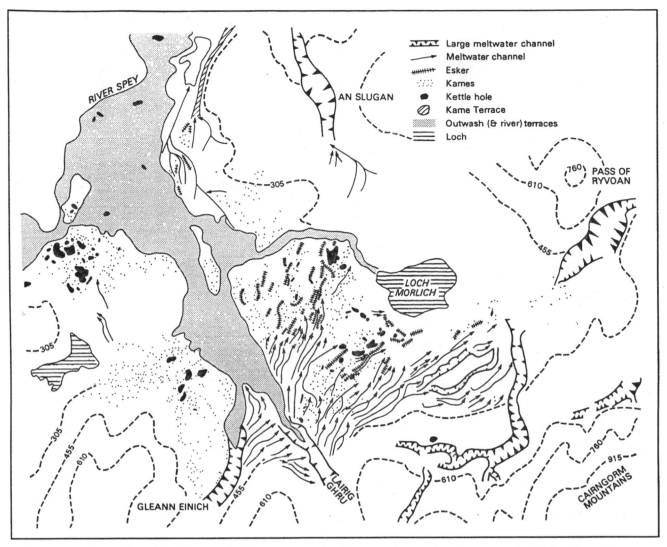

Figure 8.4 Glaciofluvial landforms of deglaciation in the Glenmore basin, near Aviemore. (Modified from Young, 1974).

from an integrated study of the depositional sequence and distribution of ice-contact, landform-sediment assemblages. He mapped a series of recessional stages of the ice front that were considered to be topographically controlled rather than related to climate, and he concluded that active retreat had occurred, but with a thin marginal zone of stagnant ice.

In several coastal areas there is an intimate relationship between deglaciation and sea-level change, also suggesting active ice retreat. This was accompanied by rapid drops in relative sea level that can be explained by rapid glacio-isostatic rebound of the land as it was released from its ice-sheet loading (see Chapter 12). Very good examples occur in some of the valleys between Oban and Lochgilphead (Gray and Sutherland, 1977). For example, in Glen Euchar, an upper series of outwash terrace fragments originates at *c.* 65 m OD at Lagganbeg and slopes downvalley at a gradient of *c.*6m/km to Kilninver where the terraces level off at 41 m OD for a distance of over 500 m. This is interpreted as indicating outwash deposition related to a relative sea level at 41 m, at which level a glaciomarine delta was formed. The ice front subsequently retreated to Loch Scammadale where a small group of kames, kettles, eskers and kame terraces is succeeded downvalley by outwash terraces that are clearly related to a level well below the upper terrace. It appears that while the ice front retreated 1.5 km, relative sea level fell by at least 12 m and probably by over 20 m.

The divergent downvalley long profiles of the outwash terraces result from meltwater flow during periods of rapid relative sea-level fall (Gray and Sutherland, 1977).

Active ice-sheet retreat is also indicated in the Forth estuary where the relationship between glaciofluvial features and raised shorelines indicates that the sea steadily encroached up-estuary as the ice front retreated. The most prominent shoreline produced during this time was the Main Perth Shoreline with a gradient of 0.43 m/km (Smith *et al.*, 1969).

However, not all areas indicate active retreat. For example, in the Glenmore basin Young (1974) demonstrated that the pattern of meltwater drainage changed direction as progressively lower cols became deglaciated and were utilised by escaping meltwaters. In the final stages, Strath Spey itself became ice free and outwash was deposited along the valley floor where small bodies of dead ice continued to decay (Figure 8.4).

A possible model of deglaciation would involve active retreat of an ice sheet in the early stages (18-14 ka BP) due to a decline in precipitation. On the other hand, the later stages of deglaciation may have been driven by the rapid rise in temperature between 14 and 13 ka BP, resulting in massive *in situ* stagnation of the ice sheet. Such a pattern is borne out by the climate record in North Atlantic sediment cores and Greenland ice cores (Chapter 5).

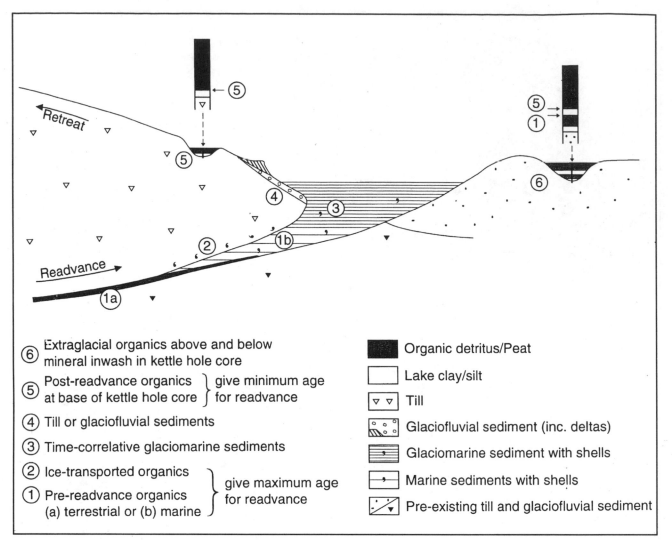

Figure 8.5 Types of dating evidence used to determine the timing of the Loch Lomond Stadial glaciation. See text for explanation

8.3 The Late-glacial Interstadial

It is still not certain that all ice melted in this climatic amelioration before the subsequent return of glaciers during the Loch Lomond Stadial, but given the temperatures reached during the Lateglacial Interstadial and the rate of retreat indicated at some sites, a complete deglaciation seems likely (but see Chapter 5). In any case the debate about whether some ice may have lingered on through the Lateglacial Interstadial is somewhat trivial, given the much more important questions related to the nature, rate and cause of ice-sheet decay, and the subsequent landscape modification that took place during the interstadial.

The retreat of the ice sheet inevitably left a very barren landscape behind that took time for vegetation to fully colonise. This landscape comprised glaciated bedrock, but also unconsolidated glacial and periglacial sediments that must have been very prone to reworking by surface processes including deflation by wind, rainsplash impact, rillwash, mudflow and biological disturbance. The net effect must have been significant slope modification and downslope movement of sediment. Very little research has been carried out on geomorphological processes in the Lateglacial Interstadial. Nonetheless it is clear that some of this reworked sediment found its way into lakes and ponds by way of slope or fluvial systems and settled out on to the lake floors. This early phase of slope instability is therefore represented in lake sediment cores by a basal layer of clay overlying the coarse sediments flooring the lake basins.

Eventually heath and grassland vegetation began to stabilise the slopes, and the lake floor sediments changed from being predominantly minerogenic to predominantly biogenic, comprising the organic detritus from the aquatic plants living in the lakes or aquatic and terrestrial plants growing in or around the lake margins (see Chapter 9). It is the radiocarbon dating of this detritus that has been used to indicate that much of Scotland was deglaciated by 13 ka BP, though the clear divorce between deglaciation and deposition of sufficient organic material to permit reliable dating is clear from the above description and was commented on by Gray and Lowe (1977) amongst others. The radiocarbon dates are therefore minimal for deglaciation.

Although maximum mean temperatures of around 14-16°C for July were probably reached at, or shortly after, 13 ka BP, the time lag involved in plant colonisation meant that the maximum vegetational development did not occur until after this time and did not reflect the extent of the warming. By the time tree birch did start to colonise favourable sites in southern Scotland, the climate had already begun to deteriorate towards the Loch Lomond Stadial. Disequilibria in environmental systems, such as that between climate and vegetation, are characteristic of the

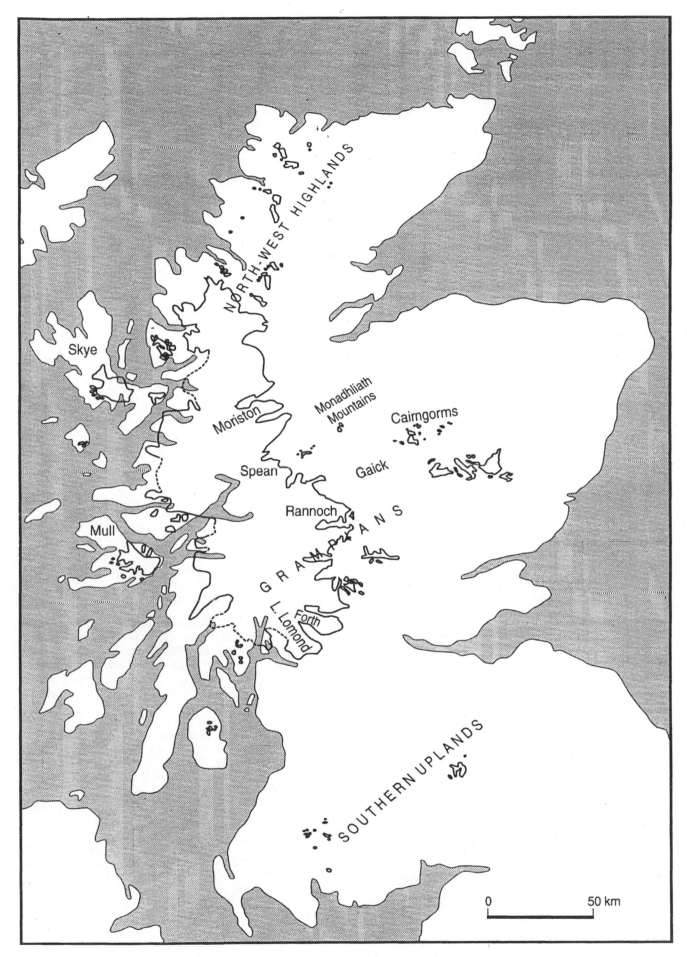

Figure 8.6 Glacier coverage during the Loch Lomond Stadial (from various sources).

99

Late-glacial and reflect the rapidly changing climate and the time required for the environment to adjust. Some systems are capable of adjusting more rapidly than others, one example being the rapid response of beetles compared with plants.

8.4 The Loch Lomond Stadial

The cooling trend that began shortly after 13 ka BP culminated in a short but intense period of cold climate known as the Loch Lomond Stadial. Its timing has been the subject of considerable debate, partly caused by errors and uncertainties in radiocarbon dating and partly by problems of defining where, on a continuum of change, to draw boundaries between geological periods. However, most authors would agree that the stadial lasted about 1,000 years, that glaciers reached their maximum extent between about 11 ka and 10.2 ka BP, but that there were probably many local variations in the way glaciers reacted to climatic changes.

Figure 8.5 illustrates the main types of dating evidence that have been used to establish the timing of the Loch Lomond Readvance. Organic material over-ridden or incorporated into the readvance till gives a maximum age for the readvance (1, 2), whereas organic sediments in the base of kettle holes on the surface of the readvance till give minimum ages (5). There is also the possibility of dating time-correlative glaciomarine sediments (3) or the glacial or glaciofluvial sediments themselves (4) using luminescence techniques, though little of this type of work has been carried out as yet. The arctic/alpine climate outside the glacial limits produced a corresponding vegetational deterioration that led to soil erosion and renewed minerogenic sediment input into the lochs and ponds of Scotland. Dating of the organic sediments above and below this minerogenic layer is a further means of establishing the age limits of the stadial climate (6).

There is general agreement that the explanation of this "dramatic conclusion to the Devensian" (Ballantyne and Harris, 1994) lies in the renewed southward migration of the oceanic polar front to the latitude of SW Ireland (Chapter 5). This was perhaps related to the influx of cold meltwater into the North Atlantic with the disintegration of the Scandinavian and North American ice sheets, though this is only one of the possible causes.

8.4.1 Glacier mapping

The maximum limits of the readvance were mainly mapped by Brian Sissons and research students between 1975 and 1985 and the general pattern of glacier coverage is clear (Figure 8.6), even if some details are still uncertain. A wide range of geomorphological evidence has been used to identify the areas covered by Loch Lomond Stadial glaciers (Figure 8.7) and to define the maximum extent of the glaciers (Gray and Coxon, 1991), including end and lateral moraines, maximum extent of hummocky moraines and boulder limits. To define the upper surfaces of glaciers, Thorp (1981, 1986) has mapped glacier trimlines running along the valley sides and separating smooth, ice-moulded bedrock below the trimline and severely periglaciated surfaces above it (Figure 8.8). The contrast in bog stratigraphies, identified by boring in infilled, former pond sites, is another type of evidence used to identify the extent of Loch Lomond Readvance glaciers, sites inside the limit having a more limited bog stratigraphy compared with those outside (see Figure 8.5).

By far the largest ice mass of the stadial glaciation was situated over the western Highlands (Figure 8.6) stretching 100 km from Loch Shiel in the west to Loch Rannoch in the

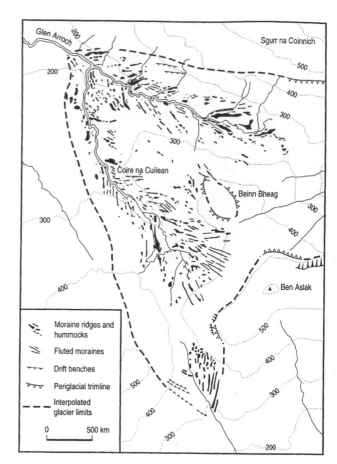

Figure 8.7 Loch Lomond Readvance landforms in Glen Aroch, Kyleakin Hills, Isle of Skye. (Reprinted from 'Glacier response to climatic change during the Loch Lomond Stadial and early Flandrian: geomorphological and palynological evidence from the Isle of Skye, Scotland' by Benn, D.I., Lowe, J.J. and Walker, M.J.C. from *Journal of Quaternary Science,* 7, 1992, 125-144. Copyright John Wiley & Sons Ltd. Reproduced with permission).

east and 175 km from Torridon in the north to Loch Lomond in the south, where Simpson (1933) recognised a large and distinct outlet glacier and used it to name the Loch Lomond Readvance. However, being a mountain ice cap there were numerous nunataks projecting through the ice, and Thorp's trimline mapping on over 60 of these in the central area around Rannoch Moor demonstrates that the icecap surface exceeded 700 m OD in places, while in the west several snouts descended to present sea-level. Ice thicknesses in excess of 400 m occurred in Rannoch Moor and the Great Glen. The icecap was markedly asymmetric with a large area over 600 m OD situated towards its eastern margin.

Over 200 other independent ice masses have been mapped in the Scottish Highlands and Inner Hebrides (Sutherland, 1984a). Three smaller ice caps have been identified in the Gaick area, on the plateau between Glen Clova, Glen Esk and Glen Muick and on the Isle of Mull. Most of the remainder were valley or corrie glaciers, with major groups identified in the north-west Highlands, Skye, the Cairngorms and south-east Grampians. Glaciers also developed on Harris, Rum and Arran. In the Southern Uplands, 11 glaciers have been mapped around Merrick and the Rhinns of Kells (Cornish, 1981), while others have been proposed around Broad Law, Green Lowther and The Cheviot.

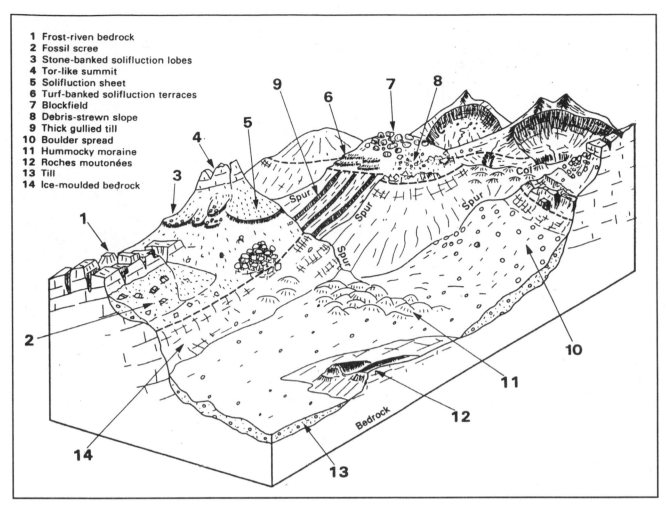

1 Frost-riven bedrock
2 Fossil scree
3 Stone-banked solifluction lobes
4 Tor-like summit
5 Solifluction sheet
6 Turf-banked solifluction terraces
7 Blockfield
8 Debris-strewn slope
9 Thick gullied till
10 Boulder spread
11 Hummocky moraine
12 Roches moutonées
13 Till
14 Ice-moulded bedrock

Figure 8.8 Evidence used by Thorp (1986) in delimiting stadial trimlines in the western Scottish Highlands. (Reprinted from 'A mountain icefield of Loch Lomond Stadial age, western Grampians, Scotland' by P.W. Thorp, from *Boreas,* 15, 1986, 83-97, by permission of Scandinavian University Press).

8.4.2 Palaeoclimate

Glaciers are an environmental response to climatic deterioration. Having established the three dimensional distribution of glaciers, attempts have been made to use them to reconstruct the palaeoclimate of the stadial (Sissons and Sutherland, 1976; Sissons, 1979; Sutherland, 1984b). Calculations demonstrate that the equilibrium lines (see Chapter 4) of the glaciers and ice caps described above rose from about 300 m on the Isle of Mull to over 1000 m in the Cairngorms, a trend that is mainly explained by the eastward decrease in precipitation. A lower accumulation means that glaciers can only survive where ablation is also lower, *i.e.* at higher altitudes where it is colder and less melting occurs. Sissons (1979) suggested that mean annual precipitation in the Cairngorms during the stadial may have been as low as 200-300 mm in places. The pattern of glaciers and equilibrium line altitudes also suggests that the main snow-bearing winds in the east came from south or south-easterly directions rather than as expected from the south-west. Sissons concluded that during the stadial, the main track of depressions was far to the south of that of the present day and lay across Britain, and that the major snowfalls were associated with southerly winds in advance of the warm fronts (Figure 8.9).

Other calculations from equilibrium line altitudes indicate that mean July temperatures were in the region of 6-7°C, indicating about a 10°C drop from the mean July temperatures of the Late-glacial Interstadial.

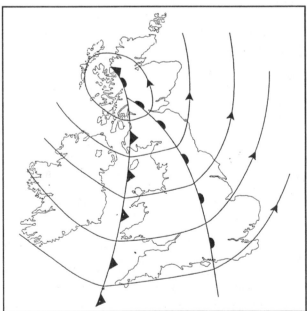

Figure 8.9 Suggested synoptic situation that would give stadial snowfall associated with southerly winds preceding warm fronts over Scotland. (Reprinted from J.M., Gray and P. Coxon, 1991, in Ehlers, J., Gibbard, P.L. & Rose, J. (Eds), *Glacial deposits in Great Britain and Ireland,* 1991, by permission of A.A. Balkema, P.O. Box 1675, Rotterdam, The Netherlands).

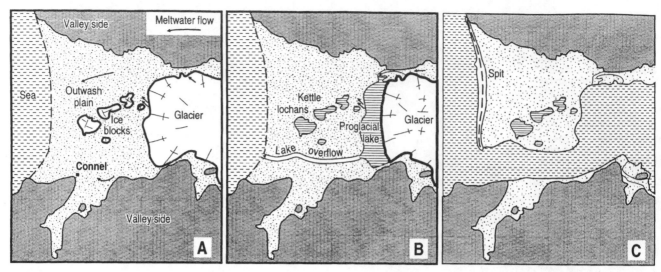

Figure 8.10 The evolution of the Loch Lomond glacier outwash plain and related features at Loch Etive, western Scotland. **A.** During the formation of the outwash plain. **B.** After partial retreat of the glacier when an ice-dammed lake formed in front of the glacier with kame terraces along its margins. **C.** At the time of the maximum postglacial sea level. (Reprinted from 'The kame terraces of lower Loch Etive' by J.M. Gray, from *Scottish Geographical Magazine,* 111, 1995, 113-118, by permission of the Royal Scottish Geographical Society.)

8.4.3 Deglaciation

The nature of deglaciation following the Loch Lomond Readvance maximum has been the subject of considerable interest over the last 15 years. Up until 1980 there was a general view that the Loch Lomond Readvance glaciers had stagnated *in situ* due to the rapid temperature rise at the end of the Loch Lomond Stadial. This view was based on the perception that, although some recessional moraines could be identified indicating initial active retreat, most of the moraines left behind were apparently chaotically-distributed, hummocky moraines, reflecting large-scale glacier disintegration.

This view was initially challenged by Eyles (1979, 1983) and has subsequently been developed by Bennett (Bennett and Glasser, 1991; Bennett and Boulton 1993a, 1993b) who has argued that a detailed pattern of active retreat can be detected from alignments within the hummocky landscapes. The evidence presented from the north-west Highlands and Cairngorms is certainly convincing, but it is not yet clear whether the pattern is universal and whether it applies for the entire deglacial period. On the Isle of Skye, for example, Benn *et al.* (1992) recognised an early deglacial stage of active retreat marked by stillstands and readvances, which they related to a decline in precipitation. However, this was followed by a period of uninterrupted retreat and rapid glacier stagnation in response to the sustained temperature rise of the early Holocene. If correct, the pattern of deglaciation of the Loch Lomond Stadial glaciers may have repeated that suggested above for the Late Devensian ice sheet.

On the west coast of Scotland the retreat positions of many tidewater glaciers were closely controlled by topographic 'pinning points' in the lochs where the fjord geometry changes significantly (Greene, 1992). In some cases the initial stages of deglaciation are marked by impressive outwash spreads and other glaciofluvial deposits. For example, at Connel north of Oban, the mouth of Loch Etive was formerly blocked by a 3 km wide outwash plain (Figure 8.10). The latter was at least partly fed by major meltwater rivers flowing along both sides of the Etive glacier, which deposited kame terraces. As the ice melted, lower kame terraces were formed and a proglacial lake overflowed across the outwash plain and began the downcutting that eventually

formed the narrow entrance to the modern Loch Etive (Gray, 1995).

The famous Parallel Roads of Glen Roy are lake shorelines associated with Loch Lomond Stadial glaciers advancing up the valleys north and east of Spean Bridge. A considerable amount of research on these shorelines and related features has elucidated the history of deglaciation and lake drainage (Sissons, 1981). The levels of the highest shorelines correspond with the levels of the lowest lake overflow routes at the heads of the glens. As deglaciation commenced, lower cols became ice-free and the lake levels dropped, thus producing lower lake shorelines. The later stages of deglaciation were apparently characterised by *jökulhlaups* (catastrophic floods) discharging northwards via Loch Ness. The lake shorelines are at least partly erosional, probably due to periglacial processes acting on the lake shore and cliff.

8.4.4 Coastal Evolution

Periglacial shore erosion has also been invoked to explain raised shore platforms on the sea coast, particularly the so-called Main Rock Platform in western Scotland (see also Chapter 12). This feature occurs a few metres above present sea level on the coastline between Ardnamurchan and the Firth of Clyde, with its best development in the Firth of Lorn area. Here the platforms are sometimes over 100 m wide with cliffs over 30 m high, and they are often developed in some sheltered locations and in some apparently very resistant rocks including basalt, quartzite, conglomerate and limestone. However, all these rocks are well jointed and would have been susceptible to frost action acting on the cliffs in conjunction with normal marine erosional processes. It has been argued, therefore, that the Main Rock Platform was formed by rapid cliff retreat under periglacial conditions during the Loch Lomond Stadial.

Several geomorphological arguments have been used to support this hypothesis. For example, the clear preservation of the platform on the sea loch coasts and headlands of western Scotland, where glacial erosion must have been intense, is indicative of formation since the last ice sheet. Its pattern of deformation and gradients (Figure 8.11) are in accord with a Late-glacial origin. Furthermore, rapid coastal erosion occurs on present day, high-latitude coasts and

102

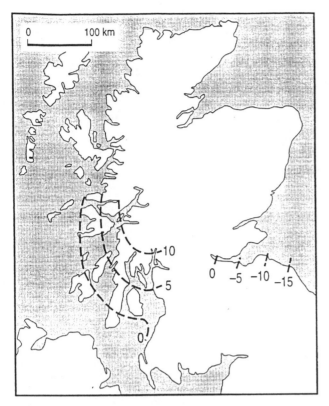

Figure 8.11 Isobases (in metres) for the Main Rock Platform/Main Lateglacial Shoreline in southern Scotland. Note that in eastern Scotland the shoreline has been traced as nearshore submarine platforms.

appears to have been effective on the Loch Lomond Stadial ice-dammed lakes at Glen Roy (Sissons, 1978).

These geomorphological arguments in support of a Loch Lomond Stadial age for the Main Rock Platform are fairly persuasive, but Uranium-series dating of cave stalactites on the Isle of Lismore in Loch Linnhe suggests that the origin may be more complex and that erosion during the stadial may simply have retrimmed pre-existing platforms (Gray and Ivanovich, 1988).

8.4.5 Other Processes

The periglacial conditions of the Loch Lomond Stadial must have had a significant effect on the whole landscape of Scotland outside the glacial limits (see also Chapter 14). There is evidence of widespread frost shattering of bedrock and accumulation of talus slopes. The landforms produced include protalus ramparts, where frost weathered material accumulated at the base of semi-permanent snow patches (*e.g.* Ballantyne and Kirkbride, 1984), and rock glaciers (*e.g.* Dawson, 1977). In addition, intense solifluction of soils took place, while runoff, slopewash, gulleying and alluvial fan formation were probably promoted by permafrost or seasonally frozen ground. Little work has been carried out on fluvial regimes in Scotland during the stadial, but evidence from England suggests that otherwise fairly quiescent rivers altered their regimes and greatly enhanced their capacities to erode and transport coarse sediments. This is characteristic of present day, high-latitude rivers.

8.5 Conclusions

It is clear, therefore, that the Scottish Late-glacial was a period of intense geomorphological change brought about by glacial and deglacial processes, periglaciation, slope processes, coastal evolution and changes in hydrology. Many of the changes produced in the Late-glacial are still very obvious in the landscape today, while others were more subtle but still left their mark on the sedimentary record of the period and testify to significant landscape modification.

References

Atkinson, T.C., Briffa, K.D. and Coope, G.R. 1987. Seasonal temperatures in Britain during the past 22,000 years, reconstructed using beetle remains. *Nature,* **325,** 587-592.

Ballantyne, C.K. 1990. The Late Quaternary glacial history of the Trotternish Escarpment, Isle of Skye, Scotland, and its implications for ice-sheet reconstruction. *Proceedings of the Geologists' Association,* **101,** 171-186.

Ballantyne, C.K. and Harris, C. 1994. *The Periglaciation of Great Britain.* Cambridge University Press, Cambridge.

Ballantyne, C.K. and Kirkbride, M.P. 1987. Rockfall activity in upland Britain during the Loch Lomond Stadial. *Geographical Journal,* **153,** 86-92.

Benn, D.I., Lowe, J.J. and Walker, M.J.C. 1992. Glacier response to climatic change during the Loch Lomond Stadial and early Flandrian: geomorphological and palynological evidence from the Isle of Skye, Scotland. *Journal of Quaternary Science,* **7,** 125-144.

Bennett, M.R. and Boulton, G.S. 1993a. Deglaciation of the Younger Dryas or Loch Lomond Stadial ice-field in the northern Highlands, Scotland. *Journal of Quaternary Science,* **8,** 133-145.

Bennett, M.R. and Boulton, G.S. 1993b. A reinterpretation of Scottish 'hummocky moraine' and its significance for the deglaciation of the' Scottish Highlands during the Younger Dryas or Loch Lomond Stadial. *Geological Magazine,* **130,** 301-318.

Bennett, M.R. and Glasser, N.F. 1991. The glacial landforms of Glen Geusachan, Cairngorms: a reinterpretation. *Scottish Geographical Magazine,* **107,** 116-123.

Brown, I.M. 1993. Pattern of deglaciation of the last (Late Devensian) Scottish ice sheet: evidence from ice-marginal deposits in the Dee valley, northeast Scotland. *Journal of Quaternary Science,* **8,** 235-250.

Cornish, R. 1981. Glaciers of the Loch Lomond Stadial in the western Southern Uplands of Scotland. *Proceedings of the Geologists' Association,* **92,** 105-114.

Dawson, A.G. 1977. A fossil lobate rock glacier in Jura. *Scottish Journal of Geology,* **13,** 37-42.

Eyles, N. 1979. Facies of supraglacial sedimentation on Icelandic and alpine temperate glaciers. *Canadian Journal of Earth Sciences,* **16,** 1341-1361.

Eyles, N. 1983. *Glacial Geology: an Introduction for Engineers and Earth Scientists.* Pergamon Press, Oxford.

Gray, J.M. 1995. The kame terraces of lower Loch Etive. *Scottish Geographical Magazine,* **111,** 113-118.

Gray, J.M. and Coxon, P. 1991. The Loch Lomond Stadial glaciation in Great Britain and Ireland. In: Ehlers, J., Gibbard, P.L. & Rose, J. (Eds), *Glacial Deposits in Great Britain and Ireland.* A.A. Balkema, Rotterdam, 89-105.

Gray, J.M. and Ivanovich, M. 1988. Age of the Main Rock Platform, western Scotland. *Palaeogeography, Palaeoecology, Palaeoclimatology,* **68,** 337-345.

Gray, J.M. and Lowe, J.J. 1977. The Scottish Lateglacial environment: a synthesis. In: Gray, J.M. and Lowe, J.J. (Eds), *Studies in the Scottish Lateglacial Environment.* Pergamon Press, Oxford, 163-181.

Gray, J.M. and Sutherland, D.G. 1977. The "Oban-Ford Moraine": a reappraisal. In: Gray, J.M. and Lowe, J.J. (Eds), *Studies in the Scottish Lateglacial Environment.* Pergamon Press, Oxford, 33-44.

Greene, D. 1992. Topography and former Scottish tidewater glaciers. *Scottish Geographical Magazine,* **108,** 164-171.

Kirby, R.P. 1969. Morphometric analysis of glaciofluvial terraces in the Esk Basin, Midlothian. *Transactions of the Institute of British Geographers,* **48,** 1-18.

Lowe, J.J. and Gray, J.M. 1980. *Studies in the Lateglacial of North-West Europe.* Pergamon Press, Oxford.

McCarroll, D., Ballantyne, C.K., Nesje, A. and Dahl, S.O. 1995. Nunataks of the last ice sheet in northwest Scotland. *Boreas,* **24,** 305-323.

Merritt, J.W., Auton, C.A. and Firth, C.R. 1995. Ice-proximal glaciomarine sedimentation and sea-level change in the Inverness area, Scotland: a review of the deglaciation of a major ice stream of the British Late Devensian ice sheet. *Quaternary Science Reviews,* **14,** 289-329.

Robinson, M. and Ballantyne, C.K. 1979. Evidence for a glacial readvance pre-dating the Loch Lomond Advance in Wester Ross. *Scottish Journal of Geology,* **15,** 271-277.

Ruddiman, W.F. and McIntyre, A. 1973. Time-transgressive deglacial retreat of polar waters from the North Atlantic. *Quaternary Research,* **3,** 117-130.

Ruddiman, W.F. and McIntyre, A. 1981. The mode and mechanism of the last deglaciation: oceanic evidence. *Quaternary Research,* **16,** 125-134.

Sissons, J.B. 1978. The parallel roads of Glen Roy and adjacent glens, Scotland. *Boreas,* **7,** 229-244.

Sissons, J.B. 1979. Palaeoclimatic inferences from former glaciers in Scotland and the Lake District. *Nature,* **278,** 518-521.

Sissons, J.B. 1981. Ice-dammed lakes in Glen Roy and vicinity: a summary. In: Neale, J. and Flenley, J. (Eds), *The Quaternary in Britain.* Pergamon Press, Oxford, 174-183.

Sissons, J.B. and Sutherland, D.G. 1976. Climatic inferences from former glaciers in the south-east Grampian Highlands, Scotland. *Journal of Glaciology,* **17,** 325-346.

Smith, D.E., Sissons, J.B. and Cullingford, R.A. 1969. Isobases for the Main Perth Raised Shoreline in south-east Scotland as determined by trend surface analysis. *Transactions of the Institute of British Geographers,* **46,** 45-52.

Sutherland, D.G. 1984a. The Quaternary deposits and landforms of Scotland and the neighbouring shelves: a review. *Quaternary Science Reviews,* **3,** 157-254.

Sutherland, D.G. 1984b. Modern glacier characteristics as basis for inferring former climates with particular reference to the Loch Lomond Stadial. *Quaternary Science Reviews,* **3,** 291-309.

Sutherland, D.G. and Walker, M.J.C. 1984. A Late Devensian ice-free area and possible interglacial site on the Isle of Lewis. *Nature,* **309,** 701-703.

Thorp, P.W. 1981. A trimline method for defining the upper limit of Loch Lomond Advance glaciers: examples from the Loch Leven and Glencoe areas. *Scottish Journal of Geology,* **17,** 49-64.

Thorp, P. W. 1986. A mountain icefield of Loch Lomond Stadial age, western Grampians, Scotland. *Boreas,* **15,** 83-97.

Walker, M.J.C., Bohncke, J.P., Coope, G.R., O'Connell, M., Usinger, H. and Verbruggen, C. 1994. The Devensian/Weichselian Late-glacial in northwest Europe (Ireland, Britain, north Belgium, The Netherlands, northwest Germany). *Journal of Quaternary Science,* **9,** 109-118.

Young, J.A.T. 1974. Ice wastage in Glenmore, upper Spey Valley, Inverness-shire. *Scottish Journal of Geology,* **10,** 147-158.

9. Vegetation and Climate in Scotland, 13,000 to 7000 Radiocarbon Years Ago

Michael J. C. Walker and J. John Lowe

> **The key themes covered in this chapter are:**
>
> * chronological definitions;
> * vegetation history;
> * climate reconstructions - types of evidence;
> * climate changes during the Late-glacial and early Holocene (post glacial);
> * environmental change in the wider North Atlantic context.

9.1 Introduction

The last thirty years have seen major advances in our understanding of environmental change during the Late Quaternary period. Data from deep-sea sediments and from cores taken from the polar ice sheets have provided new insights into the timing, frequency and intensity of glacial and interglacial episodes (Chapter 5). Superimposed upon these long-term global changes are climatic fluctuations over much shorter timescales, during which hemispherical changes in temperature and climatic régime appear to have occurred over time intervals measurable in hundreds of years or even less, and at rates which would have been considered totally unrealistic only a decade or so ago. These often dramatic short-term changes can be detected in a range of proxy climate records (the term 'proxy record' refers to any indirect measurement of climate), not only from marine and ice core data, but also from terrestrial sources.

The transition from the last cold stage (Devensian) to the present interglacial (Holocene), generally referred to as the 'Late-glacial period', is the most recent of these episodes of rapid climatic change. In this chapter, we discuss the legacy of these changes in the recent fossil record of Scotland, and outline the history of vegetation from the period following the wastage of the last great ice sheets through to the climatic optimum of the present interglacial. We show how the palaeobotanical evidence can be used in conjunction with other data to reconstruct the climatic history of this period, and we also attempt to set the Scottish record in the wider context of the North Atlantic region as a whole.

9.2 Chronology and climatic context

For many years, the chronology of the Late-glacial and Holocene periods has been based on radiocarbon (^{14}C) dating of organic materials (organic lake sediment, peat, wood, shell, bone etc). The radiocarbon evidence shows

Figure 9.1 Slochd Dubh, Isle of Skye. This large basin to the south of the Cuillin, which is over 100 m wide and almost 1 km in length, once contained a lake, but has subsequently been infilled with more than 10 m of lake muds and peats. The sediment record spans the time interval from the beginning of the Late-glacial to the mid-late part of the present (Holocene) interglacial. (Photo: M.J.C. Walker).

Figure 9.2 Pine stumps *(Pinus sylvestris)* of mid-Holocene age exposed in degrading blanket peat on Rannoch Moor. The surveying staff is 1.5 m in height. (Photo: M.J.C. Walker).

that the time period examined in this paper, *i.e.* from the beginning of the Late-glacial to the climatic optimum of the Holocene Interglacial, spans the interval from around 13,000 yrs before present (*c.* 13 ka BP) to 7000 years ago (7 ka BP). However, past variations in atmospheric ^{14}C production mean that radiocarbon years are not equivalent to calendar years, and hence radiocarbon dates need to be corrected for this effect. Calibration of the radiocarbon timescale can be achieved using a number of independent dating techniques, such as the Uranium-series (radiometric decay) method, dendrochronology (tree-ring dating), or the counting of annual layers in polar ice. These various calibrations indicate that radiocarbon years are approximately 750 years younger than calendrical years at *c.* 7 k ^{14}C yrs BP, and almost 2000 years younger at 13 k ^{14}C yrs BP (Stuiver and Long, 1993). Nevertheless, in view of the fact that the overwhelming number of dates from the Late-glacial and Holocene in Scotland have been obtained using the radiocarbon technique and hence most of the published literature refers to the radiocarbon timescale, it is more convenient for the purposes of this discussion to express ages of events in *radiocarbon years* before present.

The general model for climatic change during the Late-glacial and early Holocene is one of initially cold conditions which were terminated by an abrupt climatic amelioration at *c.* 13 ka BP; a thermal maximum between 13-12 ka BP; and a gradual decline in temperatures between 12 and 11 ka BP, this episode of more equable climate being referred to as the **Late-glacial** (or **Windermere**) **Interstadial.** Between 11 and *c.* 10 ka BP, conditions of arctic severity

returned to Scotland and, indeed, to much of the North Atlantic region. In Britain, this cold episode is termed the **Loch Lomond Stadial,** and in north-west Europe the **Younger Dryas Stadial.** At around, or shortly before, 10 ka BP climatic amelioration began once more, the rapid rise in temperatures marking the beginning of the present **(Holocene)** interglacial. The thermal maximum of this warm stage was achieved in Britain some time between *c.* 8-5 ka BP (Bell and Walker, 1992).

9.2 Vegetation history

9.2.1 *The nature of the evidence*

Most of the evidence for vegetation history in Scotland comes from lake sites, many of which have become infilled with lake (limnic) and terrestrial sediments (Figure 9.1), or from blanket peat profiles in the uplands. In some cases, peats and other organic materials (*e.g.* buried soils) are found beneath, or interbedded with, glacial, periglacial, fluvial or colluvial sediments. Samples can be obtained from these various depositional contexts, either by coring or by excavating open sections, and both macroscopic and microscopic plant remains recovered. The former range in size from minute fragments of plant tissue to pieces of wood (tree trunks, roots and branches) that can be measured in cubic metres (Figure 9.2), and include seeds, leaves, fruits, megaspores and cuticle fragments. Microscopic plant fossils consist of pollen (the male genetic propagules from flowering plants), spores (the reproductive material from lower plants) and diatoms, which are unicellular algae that live in a range

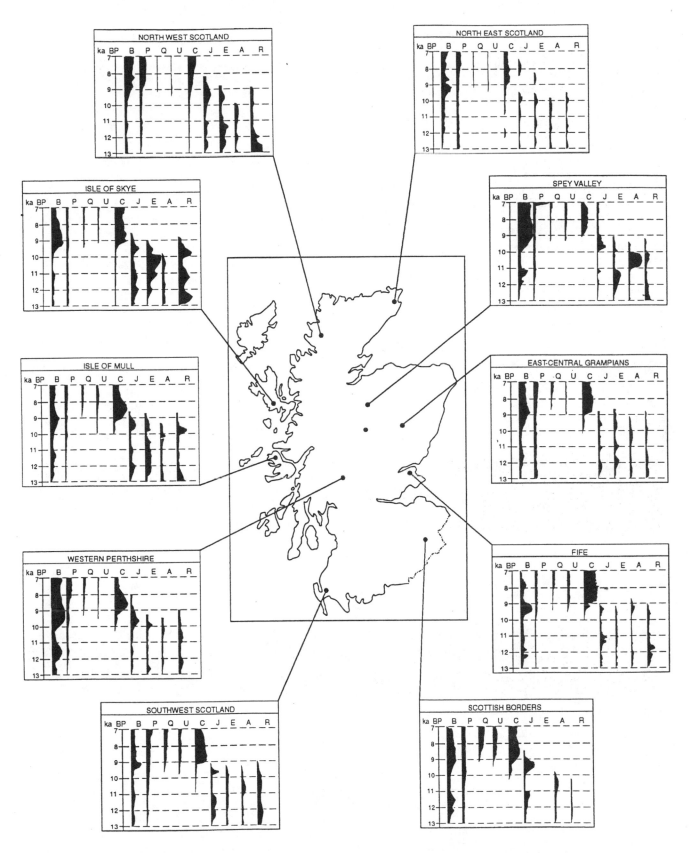

Figure 9.3 Pollen data for the period 13-7 ka BP from different areas of Scotland. These diagrams show the variations in abundance of different pollen taxa through time and therefore reflect regional changes in the former vegetation cover. B - *Betula* (birch); P *Pinus* (pine); Q - *Quercus* (oak); U - *Ulmus* (elm); C - *Corylus* (hazel); J - *Juniperus* (juniper); E - *Empetrum* (crowberry); A - *Artemisia* (mugwort); R - *Rumex* (sorrel). Northwest Scotland after Pennington *et al.* (1972); Northeast Scotland after Peglar (1979); Spey Valley after Walker (1975a), Birks (1970) and Birks & Mathewes (1978); East-Central Grampians after Walker (1975b), Huntley (1994); Fife after Whittington *et al.* (1991, 1996); Scottish Borders after Hibbert & Switsur (1976), Webb & Moore (1983); Southwest Scotland after Moar (1969); Western Perthshire after Lowe (1978, 1982); Isle of Mull after Lowe & Walker (1986a, 1986b); Isle of Skye after Birks & Williams (1983), Walker & Lowe (1990).

of aqueous habitats, but which occur widely in ponds and lakes. Where stratified sequences of sediment are found, analysis of consecutive levels through the profile enables the changing fossil composition (which represents changes in former vegetation) to be established through time, and this can be shown diagrammatically (Figure 9.3).

Pollen data provide evidence of past vegetation at a range of spatial scales (local, regional, extra-regional etc), whereas plant macrofossil and fossil diatom data are more site-specific, the former offering important insights into the nature and composition of plant communities growing in and around the site of deposition, while diatom records provide evidence of local habitat changes in lake ecosystems including, for example, variations in nutrient status, water transparency and salinity. Of the three lines of evidence, by far the most widely used in studies of vegetational history have been pollen and spores, and more than 200 pollen diagrams have now been published from different parts of Scotland for the time interval 13-7 ka BP (see Figure 9.3). However, the three approaches are not mutually exclusive, and in recent years there has been a trend towards multi-proxy (as opposed to single proxy) investigations, in which environmental reconstructions are based on data from all three palaeobotanical sources.

These lines of evidence can often be integrated with other forms of data to provide further insights into the patterns and processes of vegetational and landscape change. For example, physical and chemical properties of lake sediments can yield information on the timing and extent of erosion around the catchments, and also on the nature (trophic status etc) of the lake ecosystems. Of particular value are fossil insect remains, especially those of beetles (Coleoptera). Some beetles are obligate feeders and dwellers on specific host plants and their presence can therefore provide additional evidence of former vegetation composition. Certain beetle species, for instance, are associated with particular woodland habitats, and may indicate, *inter alia,* whether there were significant numbers of old or dead (decaying) trees. Water beetle remains might show whether the former lakes were choked with vegetation or were open water bodies, and so on. The ways in which all of these various proxy data sources can be employed to reconstruct past environments are considered in the following section.

9.2.2 The Late-glacial period

Following the wastage of the Late Devensian ice sheet, which reached its maximum around 20 ka BP (Chapters 5 and 6), newly deglaciated areas were colonised by an open-habitat herbaceous flora with arctic or alpine affinities. This included species of Poaceae (grasses), Cyperaceae (sedges), Caryophyllaceae (pink family), Chenopodiaceae (goosefoot family), Asteraceae (daisy family), *Artemisia* (mugworts), *Rumex* (sorrels) and *Saxifraga* (saxifrages), many of which are characteristic of bare or unstable soils. After the abrupt climatic amelioration at *c.* 13 ka BP, however, these pioneer plant communities were replaced by grassland and heathland, with isolated stands of wood and scrub, in which *Juniperus* (juniper), *Empetrum* (crowberry) and *Betula* (birch)

Figure 9.4 Core of Late-glacial lake sediments from an infilled kettle-hole basin at Tynaspirit, near Callander, Perthshire. The photograph shows, from left to right, light-coloured mineral sediments of early Late-glacial Interstadial age grading into darker organic sediments, this stratigraphic change reflecting stabilisation of the surrounding slopes, the cessation of mineral inwash, and the development of the basin ecosystem. This, in turn, reflects climatic amelioration. A return to colder conditions during the Loch Lomond Stadial, leading to the break-up of the vegetation cover and renewed mineral inwash, is marked by the lighter-coloured mineral sediment band to the right of the knife handle. The abrupt climatic improvement at the beginning of the Holocene Interglacial is reflected in the sharp boundary between mineral and organic sediment near the right-hand end of the core. (Photo: M.J.C. Walker).

were the principal components. The closing of the vegetation cover is evident not only in the palaeobotanical records, but also in the nature and composition of lake sediment sequences. These typically show a change from predominantly mineral to more organic sediments, reflecting the cessation of surface erosion and increasing soil maturity on slopes around the catchments, along with the development of richer lake basin ecosystems (Figure 9.4). The sediment profiles also show a fall in concentration of mobile bases (*e.g.* Na, K, Ca and Mg) as inwash of mineral detritus from around the lake catchments was reduced.

The Late-glacial Interstadial vegetation cover of Scotland varied quite markedly in response to a range of environmental influences, which included aspect, altitude, exposure, soil conditions and edaphic parameters, as well as competition and migration factors. In eastern Scotland, the central lowlands and the Scottish Borders, a closed grassland with *Juniperus* and *Salix* (willow) developed, with stands of tree birch in more sheltered localities after *c.* 12 ka BP. In the south-west and along the western seaboard, where more oceanic conditions prevailed, open grassland with *Juniperus, Empetrum, Erica* (heathers) and *Salix* was widespread, but birch, although present, was less well-represented than in the south and east. In northern Scotland, and in Orkney and Shetland, the Interstadial vegetation cover seems to have been one of dwarf-shrub heath, dominated by *Empetrum* with scattered *Juniperus,* and a similar pattern appears to have existed on the valley floors and lower slopes of the valleys of the Grampian and northern Highlands. On the higher slopes moss heaths and poor grassland communities were more characteristic, while wind-blasted montane heaths and arctic-alpine associations occupied sites on mountain summits and plateau surfaces. Although there are indications that scattered birch trees spread as far north as Skye and eastern Caithness, and that isolated stands of *Pinus sylvestris* (Scots pine) became established in parts of Aberdeenshire, the evidence suggests that the regional tree-line did not reach as far north as Scotland during the Late-glacial Interstadial.

The onset of the Loch Lomond Stadial at *c.* 11 ka BP is represented in lake sediment records by an increase in mineral sediment (Figure 9.4) and by higher concentrations of chemical bases, these lithological trends reflecting a marked increase in soil erosion around basin catchments following the break-up of the Interstadial vegetation cover in response to increasingly severe climatic conditions. The pollen and plant macrofossil records show that the *Empetrum-Erica* heathlands and grasslands with *Juniperus, Salix* and scattered tree birch that characterised the later part of the Interstadial were replaced once again by a tundra vegetation, with taxa indicative of bare and unstable soils, including species of *Artemisia, Rumex, Saxifraga, Thalictrum* (meadow rue), Asteraceae, Brassicaceae (cabbage family), Caryophyllaceae, Chenopodiaceae, and the clubmosses *Huperzia, Lycopodium* and *Selaginella*. The widespread occurrence of pollen and macrofossils of these various taxa in sediments of Loch Lomond Stadial age indicates that Interstadial soils must have been completely destroyed down to the lowest altitude. This, in turn, implies that almost all of the Scottish landscape would have supported a vegetation cover whose modern counterparts can be found today in high latitude regions of Fennoscandia, or in high arctic regions such as Greenland and Svalbard. However, many Stadial pollen spectra appear to have no clear modern analogues, and hence palaeoecological reconstructions of some of these cold-climate plant communities are far from straightforward.

In addition to providing evidence of vegetational changes at the regional scale, palaeobotanical data show how lake ecosystems themselves responded to the climatic fluctuations of the Late-glacial. Prior to the onset of Interstadial conditions, most lakes were barren habitats, with little by way of aquatic plant or diatom flora. Climatic amelioration was accompanied, however, by the expansion of both floating and rooted plant communities, with *Myriophyllum alterniflorum* (alternate water milfoil) and *M. spicatum* (spiked water milfoil) in more base-rich areas, *Nymphaea alba* (white water lily*), Nuphar lutea* (yellow water lily) and *Potamogeton* spp. (pondweeds), while more thermophilous (warmth-loving) diatom taxa also increased significantly. A similar expansion of aquatic flora is evident at the beginning of the Holocene. During the Loch Lomond Stadial, by contrast, aquatic plant communities contracted markedly, and lake basins in both uplands and lowland regions reverted to relatively sterile and impoverished conditions. Other aquatic organisms (*e.g.* diatoms and algae) also declined in abundance, populations being reduced both in terms of absolute numbers and in the frequencies of thermophilous elements.

9.2.3 The early/middle Holocene

The transition from the arctic climate conditions of the Loch Lomond Stadial to the much milder climate of the early Holocene is marked by the cessation of mineral inwash into lake basin sites, and by the beginning of a plant succession which culminated in deciduous woodland being established over large areas of lowland Scotland less than 2 ka later (Walker, 1984; Lowe, 1993). Early Holocene pollen records from most Scottish sites begin with a herbaceous phase in which Poaceae and *Rumex* are the dominant elements. This is followed by an episode in which shrubs, principally *Empetrum, Juniperus* and *Salix* are dominant, and then by the expansion of *Betula* (both *B. pubescens* and *B. verrucosa)* and *Corylus avellana* (hazel). Other pioneering tree species were *Sorbus aucuparia* (rowan)*, Populus tremula* (aspen) and *Salix* spp. Some measure of uncertainty surrounds the chronology of the Late-glacial/Holocene transition because of the problems involved with radiocarbon dating sediments from this time period (Lowe, 1991). However, using the conventional radiocarbon timescale, it appears that the transition from open grassland to *Empetrum* heaths and *Juniperus* scrub occurred in many areas before 10 ka BP, while tree birch expanded throughout southern and central Scotland shortly after 10 ka BP and had reached the far north of Scotland by 9 ka BP. Dates on the expansion of *Corylus* suggest that hazel had spread into southern Scotland by 9.3 ka BP, into the Isle of Skye by 8.8 ka BP and was established in the central Grampians by 8.7 ka BP. Early in the ninth millennium BP, therefore, most of the lowland areas of Scotland were blanketed by birch and hazel woodland, with stands of rowan, aspen and willow, and juniper scrub at higher elevations. Montane heath and grassland were, by now, confined to upper slopes and summit areas. In the far north, on Orkney and Shetland, and on the islands of the Outer Hebrides, the birch-hazel woodland would almost certainly have been more open and sporadic, woodland density being constrained by exposure to strong winds. However, earlier speculations that the offshore islands remained essentially treeless throughout the Holocene have been refuted by more recent pollen and, especially, plant macrofossil investigations, which indicate a considerable arboreal presence on the islands, particularly during the early and middle Holocene periods (Bennett, 1995).

In southern Scotland, in the central lowlands and in areas around the southern margins of the Grampians and along the western seaboard, the birch and hazel woodlands were invaded from *c.* 8.5 ka BP onwards by *Quercus* (oak), *Ulmus* (elm) and *Pinus sylvestris*. This mixed forest extended northwards into the valleys of the eastern Grampians and into Aberdeenshire, where pine appears to have been a more important woodland component. To the north of the Grampian Highland watershed, however, and extending northwards into the North-West Highlands, the mid-Holocene forests were dominated by birch and particularly by pine, *Pinus sylvestris* becoming established in increasing numbers from around 8 ka BP onwards. At its maximum between *c.* 7.5 and 5 ka BP, the great 'Caledonian Pine Forest' blanketed much of the Scottish Highlands (Bridge *et al.,* 1990), the tree-line attaining an elevation of almost 800 m on some of the more acid and well-drained soils of the Cairngorms. Further north in Caithness and Sutherland, mid-Holocene woodland was more sporadic, with copses of birch and hazel in sheltered localities and only scattered stands of Scots pine.

9.3 Climatic reconstructions

9.3.1 *The nature of the evidence*

Climatic reconstructions for the Late-glacial and early Holocene periods can be made on the basis of a number of different lines of evidence. Data from stratified contexts, including pollen, plant macrofossils, diatoms, lake sediment properties etc, can be used as a basis for qualitative inferences about past climates and, in particular, to demonstrate climatic **trends**, in other words cooling, warming, or a move towards drier or wetter conditions. More recently, however, attempts have been made to obtain quantitative estimates of former climatic conditions for the Late-glacial and Holocene periods, employing a number of different climatic proxies. Those which appear to offer the greatest potential in this respect are as follows:

- *Pollen evidence.* The traditional approach to climatic reconstruction based on pollen data has been to employ those taxa that have specific climatic requirements, either for survival or completion of their life cycle (*e.g.* minimum summer temperature thresholds required for seed germination; minimum winter temperature that can be tolerated etc). Such taxa may serve as **indicator species,** whose very presence permits inferences to be made about past climatic conditions (Moore *et al.,* 1991). A more sophisticated approach is to take entire pollen assemblages and to develop quantitative reconstructions of regional macroclimate using statistical manipulations involving transfer functions or other analogue methods. These involve the development of 'pollen-climate response surfaces',

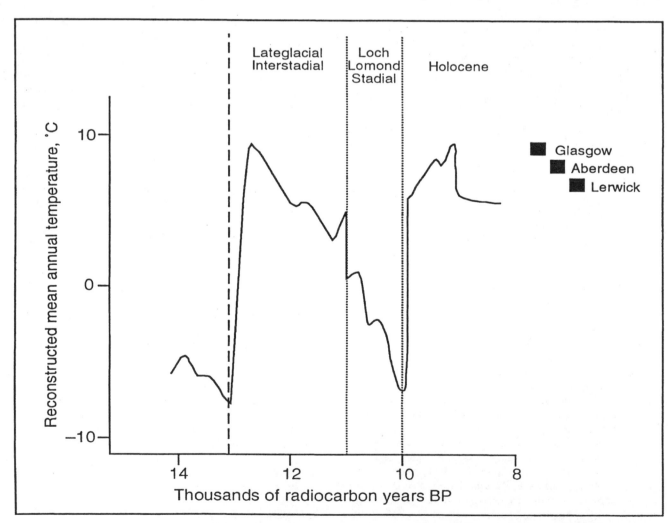

Figure 9.5 Reconstructed values for mean annual temperatures in England, Wales and southern Scotland based on coleopteran evidence (after Atkinson *et al.,* 1987). Also shown, for the purpose of comparison, are present-day mean annual temperatures at three stations in Scotland.

which define the statistical relationships between the composition of pollen assemblages in present-day surface samples and climatic variables at that locality. Multivariate statistical methods, involving ecological equations (transfer functions), are used to find close statistical relationships between these modern analogues and fossil pollen assemblages. The climatic values associated with the closest modern analogue then form the basis for estimating the climatic conditions that obtained when the fossil assemblage was formed (Webb *et al.,* 1993; Huntley, 1994).

- **Fossil insect evidence.** Fossil insects constitute one of the most valuable proxies for reconstructing past climates. So far, the most useful have proved to be the Coleoptera, for many members of this order are stenotopic (tolerating a narrow range of environmental conditions), with climate, particularly summer temperatures, being a major controlling variable at the regional scale. Certain contemporary species, whose thermal requirements are well known, can therefore be used as indicators of former climatic conditions, and quantitative temperature estimates, especially for the summer months, can be obtained. More recent work in this field has tended to concentrate on the whole fossil assemblage, rather than on individuals, and to establish the range of climates occupied at the present day by each beetle species represented in the fossil assemblage. The former climate indicated by the whole assemblage can then be taken to lie within the area of overlap of the climatic ranges of all of the species present. This is referred to as the Mutual Climatic Range method, and enables quantitative estimates to be obtained not only of past summer temperatures, but also of winter temperatures and of the annual temperature range (Atkinson *et al.,* 1987; Coope and Lemdahl, 1995; Figure 9.5). In addition to fossil beetles, inferences about past climates can also be made on the basis of other insect fossils, particularly the Chironomidae (midges) (Lowe and Walker, 1997).

- **Glacial evidence.** Glacial geomorphological evidence can be used as a basis for reconstructing the dimensions and morphological characteristics of former glaciers. Comparisons between reconstructed glaciers and their modern counterparts whose climate/glacier relationships have been determined by observation and measurement, enables quantified estimates to be obtained of former summer and winter temperatures, and of past precipitation régimes. This approach has been widely applied in the reconstruction of Loch Lomond Stadial climates in Scotland (Chapter 8).

- **Periglacial evidence.** Quantitative estimates of Loch Lomond Stadial climate have also been obtained using periglacial evidence, again employing contemporary features in present-day arctic and alpine environments and their climate/environment relationships as analogues. The distribution and occurrence of such relict periglacial features as protalus ramparts and rock glaciers in upland areas, and indicators of permafrost (*e.g.* ice wedge casts and tundra polygons) in lowland regions, provide a basis for reconstructions of former mean annual air temperatures (MAATs), and of precipitation régimes during the Loch Lomond Stadial (Ballantyne and Harris, 1994) (see also Chapter 14).

9.3.2 The Late-glacial period

Prior to the climatic amelioration at around 13 ka BP, Scotland appears to have experienced a climatic régime of arctic intensity, with mean July temperatures of, at most, 10°C, mean January temperatures in the range -20°C to -30°C, and mean annual air temperatures of perhaps -8°C to -12°C. These estimates are for lowland regions, and climatic conditions in the uplands would have been even more severe. Extreme aridity also seems to have been widespread, with annual precipitation totals no higher than perhaps 250 mm a^{-1}. Around 13 ka BP, however, a significant change in climate appears to have occurred, with a dramatic rise in summer temperature to *c.* 16-18°C in southern Scotland, and perhaps 15°C in the far north within a matter of decades (Atkinson *et al.,* 1987). A marked rise also occurred in winter temperatures so that, perhaps for the first time since the last interglacial some 110 ka previously, mean annual air temperatures in lowland Scotland exceeded 0°C.

By 12.5 ka, however, the thermal maximum of the Interstadial appears to have passed, and temperatures had begun to fall. Coleopteran evidence suggests a significant cooling in both summer and winter temperatures by *c.* 12 ka BP, with mean July temperatures in southern Scotland falling to 12-14°C. The second millenium of the Interstadial was characterised by a further decline in summer temperatures of *c.* 4°C, and an even greater drop in January values. There also appear to have been marked temperature fluctuations during this period, the earliest of which at around 11.8 ka BP saw mean January temperatures falling as low as -16 to -17°C in some upland areas, which would have been sufficient for periglacial activity to have resumed for 100-200 years (Huntley, 1994).

During the Loch Lomond Stadial, conditions of arctic severity returned once more to Scotland. Mean July temperatures at sea level fell to *c.* 7.0°C for the southwest Grampian region, and to 6°C in the eastern Grampian area and on Skye. Winter temperatures at sea level dropped to -20°C, and may have fallen to -25°C in some areas. Mean annual air temperatures in NE Scotland have been estimated at -7°C to -8°C, which would indicate that continuous permafrost extended throughout much of the northern and eastern parts of Scotland during the Stadial. Similar conditions would have prevailed at low levels throughout much of the rest of the country. At altitude, the climatic régime would have been even more severe, with mean July temperatures at 600 m below 5°C and at 1000 m of no more than 1-2°C. The comparable values for January may have been as low as -25°C and -30°C, or even lower.

A marked south-west to north-east precipitation gradient appears to have existed across the Scottish Highlands during the Stadial, with annual values around, or perhaps below, those of the present day in the SW Grampians (3000-4000 mm), ranging to 500-600 mm (25-30% of present values), or even less, in the Cairngorms. In central areas such as Strath Spey, markedly arid conditions appear to have obtained, with precipitation values in the range 200-300 mm a^{-1}. There are also indications that the earlier part of the Loch Lomond Stadial was significantly wetter than the later part, when a more arid climatic régime appears to have prevailed. It has been suggested that the mountain glaciers, which were nourished by heavy snowfall from southerly, south-westerly and south-easterly winds during the early Stadial, began to retreat under a markedly more arid climatic régime which became established during the final centuries of the Stadial, perhaps reflecting the brief re-establishment of high pressure over NW Europe. This would have resulted in a greater dominance of easterly winds, drier conditions and initially slow glacier retreat as a result of diminished snowfall (Ballantyne and Harris, 1994). Several different proxy sources (glacial geomorphological and periglacial evidence; pollen records; coleopteran data) tend to support such a scenario.

9.3.3 The early/middle Holocene

The climatic amelioration that occurred at the end of the Loch Lomond Stadial appears to have been just as dramatic as that marking the onset of the Late-glacial Interstadial some 3 ka previously, for the coleopteran records from various parts of Britain indicate a rise in temperature of between 1.7°C and 2.8°C per century (Atkinson *et al.*, 1987). The evidence suggests that by 9.8 ka BP, both summer and winter temperatures over much of southern Scotland were comparable with those of the present (15-17°C). In some insect and plant macrofossil records, there are indications of a short-lived decline in temperatures during the first millennium of the present interglacial, but by 9.0 ka BP, climate had ameliorated once more to give temperatures, especially during the summer months, a degree or so warmer than at the present day. These slightly warmer, and perhaps also drier conditions, lasted for the next two millennia.

9.4 The wider context: the Late-glacial and early Holocene in the North Atlantic region

Although it is generally accepted that the major influence on Quaternary climatic change is orbital forcing, *i.e.* changes in terrestrial receipt and distribution of solar radiation caused by variations in the earth's orbit and axis, these trends are modulated and amplified by a range of other factors. These include ocean circulation changes, variations in the production of deep ocean water, growth and decay of continental ice sheets, changes in atmospheric trace gas content, and fluctuations in the amount of radiant energy emitted by the sun. A number of these factors may have combined to produce the dramatic climatic changes experienced in Scotland and in other parts of the North Atlantic region during the transition from the last cold stage to the present interglacial.

In recent years, a considerable body of data has been assembled on the sequence and pattern of climatic change in the North Atlantic region for the period 14-9 ka BP (Lowe *et al.*, 1994; Walker, 1995), and a remarkable correspondence has begun to emerge between the climatic signals from terrestrial, marine and ice-core records (Figure 9.6). The data suggest that of the various causal factors listed above, changes in salinity, temperature and circulation of ocean waters were of particular importance in determining the pattern and course of climate change. Around 14 ka BP, much of the Atlantic north of 40°N latitude was covered by a cold meltwater layer fed by decaying glaciers and ice sheets on both the North American and European landmasses. Between 14 and 13 ka BP, the oceanic and atmospheric arctic and polar fronts swung northwestward around a pivot point to the east of Newfoundland. This allowed warm Atlantic waters to migrate rapidly north along the seaboard of western Europe, while the climatic amelioration that followed was further enhanced by heat released from the ocean surface as deep-water began to form in the North Atlantic. The consequence was the dramatic rise in temperatures that is manifest in the proxy records from Scotland and from elsewhere in the British Isles. This rapid warming trend is also reflected in microfossil records from the Norwegian Sea, and in the abrupt increase in snow accumulation and complementary decrease in dust deposition on the Greenland ice sheet (Figure 9.6). Around the coasts of western Scotland, sea-surface temperatures

were only 2-3°C below those of the present. Only in Scandinavia, where the waning ice sheet had a cooling effect on the peripheral landscape, is there no indication of climatic amelioration. Indeed, temperature differences between southern Scotland and western Norway may have been as much as 6-7°C at that time.

The progressive, almost step-wise decline in temperatures in Scotland during the course of the Late-glacial Interstadial, is also reflected in many of the proxy records from the North Atlantic region. In both the Greenland ice core profiles, and also in the marine records (Figure 9.6), there are indications of a gradual but progressive downturn in climate. The same trend is apparent in proxy records from western and southern Europe, although in Scandinavia the thermal maximum of the Interstadial was attained during the middle/ later part of the period as the cooling effects of the ice sheet were increasingly mitigated by the ameliorating influence of warmer waters around the northwest European coasts. Both the Greenland snow accumulation and marine microfossil records suggest a series of climatic oscillations of increasing amplitude as the Interstadial progressed. As noted above, there is evidence in Scotland for at least one major climatic fluctuation during the course of the Interstadial, and others have been detected in different proxy records from elsewhere in the British Isles and western Europe. The causes of these climatic oscillations remain unclear, but they may reflect pulses of meltwater into the North Atlantic from the decaying continental ice sheets, which chilled ocean surface waters and reduced temperatures on adjacent land areas.

During the Loch Lomond (or Younger Dryas) Stadial, the entire North Atlantic region experienced a return to conditions of arctic severity as the oceanic and atmospheric arctic and polar fronts swung southwards once more to a maximum southerly position off the coast of northern Portugal. Mountain glaciers, which had probably begun to form on the Scottish mountains during the later part of the preceding Interstadial, expanded dramatically (see Chapter 8) and the Scandinavian ice sheet also readvanced along the coast of western Norway. Beyond the ice sheets, permafrost existed as far south as the English Channel and over much of western and central Europe, while the tundra vegetation, so clearly represented in the Scottish palaeobotanical records, covered large areas of both upland and lowland northwest Europe. The very low temperatures inferred for Scotland find parallels elsewhere, for nowhere in northwest Europe do summer temperatures appear to have been much above 10°C, while winter temperatures as low as -20°C to -30°C seem to have been the norm. As in Scotland, there are indications that in many parts of Europe, the early part of the Younger Dryas (prior to 10.5 ka BP) was wetter, with a range of indicators (*e.g.* pollen, plant macrofossils, fluvial, lacustrine, glacial and periglacial evidence) pointing towards increasing aridity during the later part of the period.

The dramatic climatic improvement at the beginning of the present interglacial is again evident in all of the proxy data sources from around the North Atlantic, and once more reflects the rapid northward migration of polar and arctic waters from the central and eastern areas of the Atlantic basin. One of the most spectacular manifestations of this amelioration is found in the ice core records, where a rise in temperature of 7°C in no more than 50 years has been inferred (more than 1°C per decade!) and, moreover, the climate of the North Atlantic region as a whole changed to a milder and less stormy régime within the space of no more than 20 years! Equally dramatic is the evidence from the oceans, with isotopic and faunal data from off the coasts of northwest Scotland implying a summer bottom water warming of 8°C in less than 100 years at around 10 ka BP, while in the Greenland-Iceland-Norwegian Seas, microfossil evidence indicates that the Younger Dryas ended abruptly, with a rise in sea-surface temperatures of around 9°C within the space of half a century.

The various proxy records suggest that, throughout northwest Europe, temperatures comparable with those of today were established by 9.5-9.0 ka BP. The climatic improvement does not appear to have been unidirectional, however, for in many parts of Europe, and also in the marine and ice-core records (Figure 9.6) there are indications of at least one oscillation in climate during the first millennium of the present interglacial. As was noted above, a comparable oscillation, albeit short-lived, may have been experienced in Scotland. Thereafter, climatic warming became firmly established with the thermal maximum of the present interglacial being reached throughout much of Europe in the period 9-7 ka BP, when both summer and winter temperatures may have been as much as 2-3°C above those of the present day in many regions.

9.5 Conclusions

Proxy records from Scottish sites show, in considerable detail, the pattern of climate change during the Late-glacial and the early part of the present interglacial. The remarkable similarity between these data and those from ocean cores

and from the Greenland ice sheet, indicates that climatic changes were broadly synchronous across the entire northeast Atlantic province. This, in turn, suggests that the oceans, ice-sheets and atmosphere were functioning as a coupled system throughout the transition from the last cold stage to the present interglacial. Perhaps the most striking features to emerge from the climatic records are (a) the rapidity of warming at both 13 and 10 ka BP, when temperatures appear to have risen by several degrees celsius within the space of a single human lifetime, and (b) the marked fluctuations in temperature that occurred throughout the northeast Atlantic region during both the Late-glacial and early Holocene periods. Much still remains to be learned about the responses of terrestrial biota to such dramatic climatic changes, however, but Scotland, with its critical location on the Atlantic fringes of northwest Europe, and its rich and diverse palaeoenvironmental record, constitutes an ideal laboratory within which to explore these historical climate-biota relationships. Moreover, as many Scottish sites contain a high-resolution climate signal from the last glacial-interglacial transition, they form a data-base that is of vital importance to research programmes investigating the causal factors of climatic fluctuations at the end of the last cold stage. Hence Scotland seems destined to play a pivotal rôle in research on environmental change around the North Atlantic basin for some time to come.

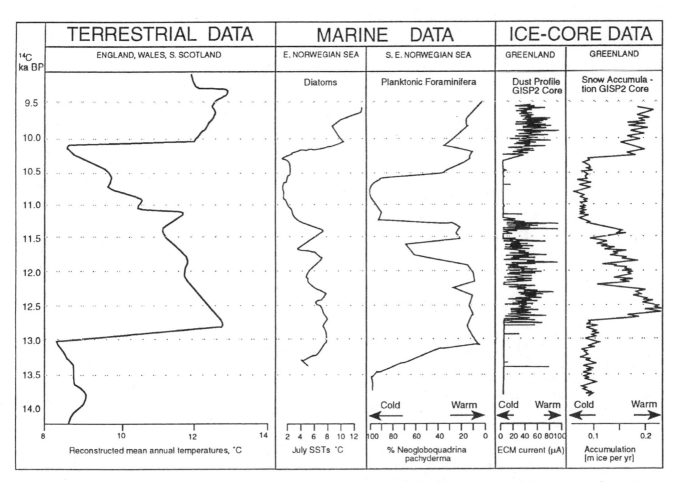

Figure 9.6 Climatic trends in the British Isles and adjacent regions of the North Atlantic, based on terrestrial, marine and ice core data. The terrestrial temperature curve is based on the fossil insect (coleopteran) record (Atkinson *et al*, 1987); the diatom-based sea-surface temperature (SST) record is from Koç Karpuz & Jansen (1992); the planktonic foraminiferal record, which also shows sea-surface temperature change, is from Lehman & Keigwin (1992); the dust profile and the snow accumulation records from the GISP2 ice core are from Taylor *et al*. (1993) and Alley *et al*. (1993), respectively.

References

Alley, R.B., Meese, D.A., Shuman, C.A., Gow, A.J., Taylor, K.C., Grootes, P.M., White, J.W.C., Ram, M., Waddington, E.D., Mayewski, P.A. and Zielinski, G.A. 1993. Abrupt increase in Greenland snow accumulation at the end of the Younger Dryas event. *Nature,* **361,** 527-529.

Atkinson, T.C., Briffa, K.D. and Coope, G.R. 1987. Seasonal temperatures in Britain during the past 22,000 years, reconstructed using beetle remains. *Nature,* **325,** 587-593.

Ballantyne, C.K. and Harris, C. 1994. *The Periglaciation of Great Britain.* Cambridge University Press, Cambridge.

Bell, M. and Walker, M.J.C. 1992. *Late Quaternary Environmental Change: Physical and Human Perspectives.* Longman, London.

Bennett, K.D. 1995. Insularity and the Quaternary tree and shrub flora of the British Isles. In: Preece, R.C. (Ed.), *Island Britain: a Quaternary Perspective.* Geological Society Special Publication, 96. The Geological Society, London, 173-180.

Birks, H.H. 1970. Studies in the vegetational history of Scotland. 1. A pollen diagram from Abernethy Forest, Inverness-shire. *Journal of Ecology,* **58,** 827-846.

Birks, H.H. and Mathewes R.W. 1978. Studies in the vegetational history of Scotland. V. Late Devensian and Early Flandrian pollen and macrofossil stratigraphy at Abernethy Forest, Invernesshire. *New Phytologist,* **80,** 455-484.

Birks, H.J.B. and Williams, W. 1983: Late-Quaternary vegetational history of the Inner Hebrides. *Proceedings of the Royal Society of Edinburgh,* **83B,** 269-292.

Bridge, M.C., Haggart, B.H and Lowe, J.J. 1990. The history and palaeoclimatic significance of subfossil remains of *Pinus sylvestris* in blanket peats from Scotland. *Journal of Ecology,* **78,** 77-99.

Coope, G.R. and Lemdahl, G. 1995. Regional differences in the Lateglacial climate of northern Europe based on coleopteran analysis. *Journal of Quaternary Science,* **10,** 391-395.

Hibbert, F.A. and Switsur, V.R. 1976. Radiocarbon dating of Flandrian pollen zones in Wales and northern England. *New Phytologist,* **77,** 793-807.

Huntley, B. 1994. Late Devensian and Holocene palaeoecology and palaeoenvironments of the Morrone Birchwoods, Aberdeenshire. *Journal of Quaternary Science,* **9,** 311-336.

Koç Karpuz, N. and Jansen, E. 1992. A high-resolution diatom record of the last deglaciation from the SE Norwegian Sea: documentation of rapid climatic changes. *Paleoceanography,* **7,** 499-520.

Lehman, S.J. and Keigwin, L.D. 1992. Sudden changes in North Atlantic circulation during the last deglaciation. *Nature,* **356,** 757-762.

Lowe, J.J. 1978. Radiocarbon-dated Lateglacial and Early Flandrian pollen profiles from the Teith Valley, Perthshire, Scotland. *Pollen et Spores,* **20,** 367-397.

Lowe, J.J. 1982. Three Flandrian pollen profiles from the Teith Valley, Perthshire, Scotland. 1. Vegetational history. *New Phytologist,* **90,** 355-370.

Lowe, J.J. 1991. Stratigraphic resolution and radiocarbon dating of Devensian Lateglacial sediments. In Lowe, J.J. (Ed.), *Radiocarbon Dating: Recent Applications and Future Potential.* Quaternary Proceedings, 1. Quaternary Research Association, Cambridge, 19-25.

Lowe, J.J. 1993. Isolating the climatic factors in early- and mid-Holocene palaeobotanical records from Scotland. In: Chambers, F.M. (Ed.), *Climatic Change and Human Impact on the Landscape.* Chapman & Hall, London, 67-82.

Lowe, J.J. and NASP Members 1995. Palaeoclimate of the North Atlantic seaboards during the last glacial/interglacial transition. *Quaternary International,* **28,** 51-62.

Lowe, J.J. and Walker, M.J.C. 1986a. Flandrian environmental history of the Isle of Mull Scotland. II. Pollen-analytical data from sites in western and northern Mull. *New Phytologist,* **103,** 417-436.

Lowe, J.J. and Walker, M.J.C. 1986b. Lateglacial and Early Flandrian environmental history of the Isle of Mull, Inner Hebrides, Scotland. *Transactions of the Royal Society of Edinburgh: Earth Sciences,* **77,** 1-20.

Lowe, J.J. and Walker, M.J.C. 1997. *Reconstructing Quaternary Environments.* 2nd edition. Addison-Wesley-Longman, London.

Lowe, J.J., Ammann, B., Birks, H.H., Björck, S., Coope, G.R., Cwynar, L.C., de Beaulieu, J.L., Mott, R.J., Peteet, D.M. and Walker, M.J.C. 1994. Climatic changes in areas adjacent to the North Atlantic during the Last Glacial-Interglacial Transition (14-9 ka BP): a contribution to IGCP-253. *Journal of Quaternary Science,* **9,** 185-198.

Moar, N.T. 1969. Late Weichselian and Flandrian pollen diagrams from southeast Scotland. *New Phytologist,* **68,** 433-467.

Peglar, S. 1979. A radiocarbon-dated pollen diagram from Loch of Winless, Caithness, North-east Scotland. *New Phytologist,* **82,** 245-263.

Pennington, W., Haworth, E.Y., Bonny, A.P. and Lishman, J.P. 1972. Lake sediments in northern Scotland. *Philosophical Transactions of the Royal Society, London,* B264, 191-294.

Stuiver M. and Long A. (Eds) 1993. Calibration 1993. *Radiocarbon,* **28.**

Taylor, K.C., Lamorey, G.W., Doyle, G.A., Alley, R.B., Grootes, P.M., Mayewski, P.A., White, J.W.C. and Barlow, L.K. 1993. The 'flickering switch' of late Pleistocene climate change. *Nature,* **361,** 432-436.

Tipping, R.M. 1991. Climatic changes in Scotland during the Devensian Late Glacial: the palynological record. In: Barton, N., Roberts, A.J. and Roe, D.A. (Eds), *The Late Glacial in North-west Europe: Human Adaptation and Environmental Change at the End of the Pleistocene.* Council for British Archaeology Research Report 77, 7-21.

Walker, M.J.C. 1975a. Late Glacial and Early Postglacial environmental history of the central Grampian Highlands. *Journal of Biogeography,* **2,** 265-284.

Walker, M.J.C. 1975b. Two Late Glacial pollen diagrams from the eastern Grampian Highlands of Scotland. *Pollen et Spores,* **17,** 67-92.

Walker, M.J.C. 1995. Climatic changes in Europe during the last glacial/interglacial transition. *Quaternary International,* **28,** 63-76.

Walker, M.J.C. and Lowe, J.J. 1990. Reconstructing the environmental history of the last glacial-interglacial transition: evidence from the Isle of Skye, Inner Hebrides, Scotland. *Quaternary Science Reviews,* **9,** 15-49.

Walker, M.J.C., Bohncke, S.J.P., Coope, G.R., O'Connell, M., Usinger, H. and Verbruggen, C. 1994. The Devensian/Weichselian Late-glacial in northwest Europe (Ireland, Britain, north Belgium, The Netherlands, northwest Germany). *Journal of Quaternary Science,* **9,** 109-118.

Webb, J.A. and Moore, P.D. 1983. The Late Devensian vegetational history of the Whitlaw Mosses, southeast Scotland. *New Phytologist,* **91,** 341-398.

Webb, T., III, Bartlein, P.J., Harrison, S.P. and Anderson, K.H. 1993. Vegetation, lake levels and climate in eastern North America for the past 18,000 years. In: Wright, H.E. Jnr, Kutzbach, J.E., Webb, T., III, Ruddiman, W.F., Street-Perrott, F.A. and Bartlein, P.J. (Eds), *Global Climates since the Last Glacial Maximum.* University of Minnesota Press, Minneapolis, 415-467.

Whittington, G., Edwards, K.J. and Caseldine, C.J. 1991. Late- and post-glacial pollen-analytical and environmental data from a near-coastal site in north-east Fife, Scotland. *Review of Palaeobotany and Palynology,* **68,** 65-85.

Whittington, G., Fallick, A.E. and Edwards, K.J. 1996. Stable oxygen isotope and pollen records from eastern Scotland and a consideration of Late-glacial and early Holocene climate change for Europe. *Journal of Quaternary Science,* **11,** 327-340.

Further reading

Ballantyne, C.K. and Harris, C. 1994. *The Periglaciation of Great Britain.* Cambridge University Press, Cambridge.

Bell, M. and Walker, M.J.C. 1992. *Late Quaternary Environmental Change: Physical and Human Perspectives.* Longman, London.

Jones, R.L. and Keen, D.H. 1993. *Pleistocene Environments in the British Isles.* Chapman & Hall, London.

Lowe, J.J. and Walker, M.J.C. 1997. *Reconstructing Quaternary Environments.* 2nd edition Addison-Wesley-Longman, London.

Moore, P.D., Webb, J.A. and Collinson, M.B. 1991. *Pollen Analysis.* 2nd edition. Blackwell, Oxford.

10. Geomorphological Change and Fluvial Landscape Evolution in Scotland During the Holocene

Lindsey J. McEwen

The key themes covered in this chapter are:

- the geomorphology of river channels;
- river channel adjustment;
- climate change and rivers;
- land-use changes and rivers;
- geomorphological impact of floods.

10.1 Introduction

The rapid climatic warming at the beginning of the Holocene (around 10 ka BP) was accompanied by major adjustments in geomorphological processes and slope stability following the intense activity during the preceding Loch Lomond Stadial (Chapter 8). The glacial legacy included large volumes of unconsolidated sediment on unstable mountain slopes and valley floors, which became available for reworking by a range of fluvial and slope processes. Although the establishment of soil and vegetation covers (Chapter 9), combined with the less extreme climate, gradually saw a reduction in the intensity of geomorphological processes, there have nevertheless been significant changes in the landscape during the Holocene. Such changes have arisen from climatic fluctuations, and more recently from the effects of human activity on the vegetation cover (Chapter 11). This chapter examines the changes produced in the landscape by Scottish rivers during the present interglacial, the Holocene. Changes on the mountain summits (periglacial processes) and at the coast are reviewed in Chapters 12 and 14, respectively.

Scottish river landforms are distinctive in both their character and diversity. A range of fluvial environments is represented, including upland and lowland systems (or a juxtaposition of both), headwater and mainstream systems and high- to low- energy systems (Werritty *et al.*, 1994; Werritty and McEwen, 1997). Diversity is enhanced by the distinct climatic gradient across Scotland, with the west characterised by higher precipitation, and eastern catchments by rain shadow effects. This review investigates the geomorphology of these rivers and their floodplains and their spatial and temporal development during the Holocene. It evaluates the evidence for river channel adjustment, the impact of changes in fluvial controls (through climate change, catchment land use change and the geomorphic impact of floods) and the methodologies used to understand how rivers respond to internal and external change. This research is placed, where appropriate, in the context of the development of fluvial research in the UK and globally and of the progression of ideas over time. Figure 10.1 indicates the location of sites referred to in the text.

10.2 River channels

River channel form (both cross-sectional geometry and planform) reflects the balance between discharge and sediment supply over different timespans. A river has a number of properties (**degrees of freedom**) which it can adjust in response to changes in discharge and sediment supply. These include slope, velocity, channel roughness, sediment transport, hydraulic geometry and channel pattern. A river can be envisaged as being in **quasi-equilibrium** if, over a period of years, the discharge regime is able to transport the available sediment. If ability to transport is exceeded or reduced relative to sediment supply, then a period of disequilibrium will occur, characterised by erosion or aggradation, respectively, of the sediment store. The history of the relative adjustment between discharge and sediment supply determines the relationship between the present channel, its corridor, the floodplain and the valley

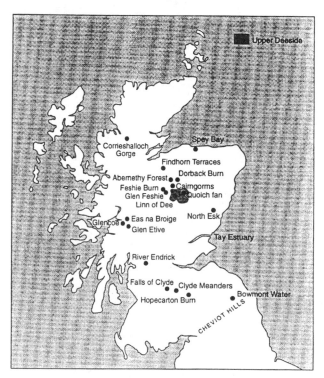

Figure 10.1 Location map of sites referred to in the text.

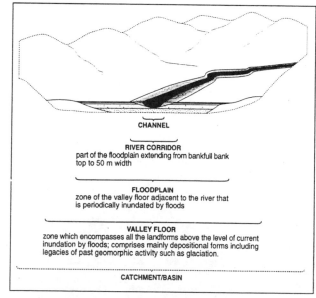

Figure 10.2 Zones of the valley floor within a river basin. (Modified from Newson, 1992b).

floor (Figure 10.2). Classically, river channels have been subdivided into braided and meandering channels. In early field-based work on rivers in the USA, Leopold and Wolman (1957) found that when bankfull discharge is plotted on a graph against channel slope, braided channels usually occur in reaches with higher slopes. This classification, however, requires modification for application to British rivers. Ferguson (1981), for example, identified four different river types in the UK - actively meandering, confined meandering, active low-sinuosity channels and inactive channels.

Scottish rivers broadly conform to Ferguson's classification. A model for a major Scottish river catchment comprises mountain, piedmont, lowland and estuarine zones, as depicted in Figure 10.3 and Table 10.1 (see Werritty *et al.,* 1994; Werritty and McEwen, 1997). Contemporary river types in Scotland range from highly confined bedrock gorges, such as Corrieshalloch Gorge (Wester Ross) (Figure 10.4) and Linn of Dee (Aberdeenshire), to different types of alluvial channels (Figure 10.5). An alluvial channel is potentially able to modify its boundary, reworking sediments which the river itself deposited at an earlier stage. Channel **planform**, or the configuration of a river channel when viewed from the air, can be envisaged as a continuum (Figure 10.6). In Scotland, at one extreme of this continuum there are the extensive divided gravel-bed reaches of Glen Feshie (Ferguson and Werritty, 1983) and the braided lower reaches of the River Spey, the closest to a proglacial sandur-type (outwash plain) environment in the United Kingdom (Lewin and Weir, 1977). At the other extreme, there are

Figure 10.4 Corrieshalloch Gorge, Wester Ross. (Photo: L.J. McEwen).

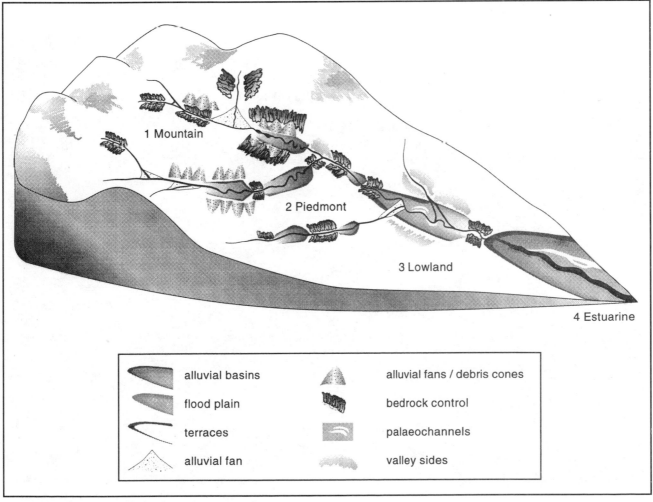

1 Mountain

2 Piedmont

3 Lowland

4 Estuarine

alluvial basins

flood plain

terraces

alluvial fan

alluvial fans / debris cones

bedrock control

palaeochannels

valley sides

Figure 10.3 A model of a Scottish river catchment.

117

Table 10.1 Characteristics of different zones within a model Scottish river catchment.

Zone	Channel types	Channel characteristics	Glacial legacy/ geomorphological setting	Activity rates	Human impacts	Example
1. Mountain	bedrock reach	steep, narrow, transportation zone for flushing through of sediment	meltwater gorge	very stable; conduit for sediment	minimal	Corrieshalloch Gorge
	mountain torrent	steep, coarse bedload	upper channel entrenched in glacigenic or fluvioglacial sediment; partial bedrock control again in upper reaches	episodic activity; binary system with high thresholds for sediment entrainment	minimal; local dredging possible after floods if river bridged.	Allt Mor, Cairngorms
	alluvial basin	gradual decrease in slope, sediment size and confinement above a local baselevel	glacially eroded valley with infill sediment	vary downstream with different thresholds for entrainment and channel change	minimal; local gravel extraction	Upper Strath Carron; Glen Derry
	fluvio-lacustrine delta	sediment fining down delta	former ribbon lake	episodic switching of channel	minimal; local gravel extraction	Glen Coe
2. Piedmont	wandering gravel-bed river	low sinuosity; coarse- grained; medium slope; bedload, active, incohesive banks	local partial confinement by fluvioglacial terraces	active; floods important as geomorphic agents; mobility depends on number of times per year when bed becomes mobile	gravel extraction; stabilisation of channel alignment	Dorback Burn, Abernethy Forest
	fluvio-lacustrine	fine-grained delta with spit and strathlochans	former ribbon lake	alignment relatively stable; deposition of sediment builds up deltas; loch acts as major regulator of flow and sediment trap	levees	River Balvag delta at head of Loch Lubnaig
3. Lowland	meandering	typically sand-bedded rather than gravel-bed; low slopes;	restricted to coastal fringe	highly stable	stability linked to engineering	Lower River Forth
	active meandering	sand-bedded; lack of confinement	lack of confinement; reworked sediment from upstream sources	active migration	primarily unengineered; local bank protection	River Clyde/Medwin meanders
	bedrock controlled	slot gorge	meltwater gorge	highly stable	HEP	Falls of Clyde near New Lanark
4. Estuarine	straight, wide channel	sand-bedded; tidal limit reached	links fluvial and coastal systems	stable alignment; bars shift	dredging	Tay estuary; Spey Bay

Note that the human impacts relate to the case-study examples.

Figure 10.5 River Glass, Strathglass; an alluvial channel actively reworking its floodplain. (Photo: L.J. McEwen).

highly tortuous meanders as evident on the River Clyde (Brazier *et al.,* 1993) and the River Endrick near Drymen (Bluck, 1971). Many Scottish channel planforms in mountain and piedmont reaches, however, display characteristics of both channel division and sinuosity and may be considered as active transitional forms - 'wandering gravel-bed rivers' as defined by Church (1983). An excellent large-scale example of a wandering gravel bed river occurs on the middle reaches of the River Feshie, while a well-documented instance of this channel type at a smaller scale is Dorback Burn, Abernethy Forest (Werritty, 1984). In addition, particularly in upland catchments, the same channel planform tends to persist for no more than a few channel widths (Ferguson, 1981). This is due to frequent spatial discontinuities in controls; for example, where the river is locally confined by terraces, or local base levels occur due to bedrock control. Thus it is rarely possible to characterise whole rivers in terms of a simple classification.

Scottish river channels are also highly variable in terms of their propensity to change over time. Bedrock gorges and partially confined bedrock channels are much more stable in alignment over short and intermediate timescales than alluvial channels. Bedrock gorges were cut principally by meltwater activity during at least one Devensian glaciation; process rates under present fluvial regimes are comparatively slow. These reaches now mainly act as conduits for the flushing through of sediment from upstream sources and are frequently located above alluvial fans or other zones of sediment accumulation. Alluvial sections, by contrast, can display very variable rates of change even within the same sediment zone in the same catchment over the same timescale. Propensity for adjustment depends on relative slope, entrainment thresholds, local sediment availability and degree of confinement (see Section 3.2). (Confinement is restriction on lateral channel migration which may arise from the presence of rock outcrops or terrace bluffs at the margin of a channel or floodplain). Floodplains owe their origin to the progressive migration or **avulsion** of these channels and the sequences of alluvial deposits created by these processes of channel shift (see Anderson *et al.,* 1996). (Avulsion is the excavation of a new channel, either within the river's present active area or in the floodplain). Different fluvial landforms within the same catchment (bar forms, channel planform, floodplains) therefore evolve over different timescales.

The importance of Scottish river variables (*e.g.* valley dimensions, channel morphology, discharge of water and sediment) and drainage basin variables (*e.g.* hillslope morphology, discharge of sediment and water from the system) also differ according to the timescale considered (see Schumm and Lichty, 1965). Rivers have 'historical hangovers' (Ferguson, 1981), possessing inherited features retained from past geomorphic regimes, which still exert varying degrees of control on present fluvial activity. Glacial legacy, particularly from the Late Devensian ice sheet glaciation (ending *c.* 13 ka BP) and the Loch Lomond Stadial (*c.* 11-10 ka BP), is important in terms of valley slope, confinement, size and quantity of sediment supply and the degree of coupling between colluvial (slope) and fluvial processes, particularly in mountain and piedmont zones. Landforms of glacigenic or glaciofluvial origin, or other palaeo-sediment assemblages, therefore condition the character and rates of present river activity. The concept of **'paraglaciation'** is useful - the role of glacial legacy in conditioning and modifying later non-glacial processes (Church and Ryder, 1972; Ballantyne and Benn, 1996).

This discussion of fluvial features also incorporates alluvial channels with higher slopes and smaller contributing areas

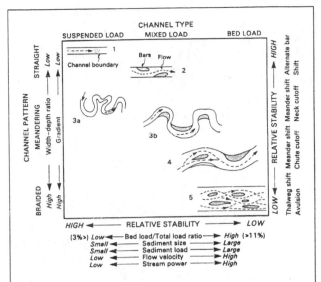

Pattern 1: Straight channel (bedload small proportion of total load; narrow channel; width to depth ratio < 10; intermediate slope)

Pattern 2: Channel relatively straight but the thalweg (or line of deepest part) of the straight channel may be sinuous

Pattern 3a: High sinuosity channel (bedload small proportion of total load; narrow channel; width to depth ratio < 10; low slope)

Pattern 3b: Mixed-load channel (width to depth ratio between 10-40; sinuosity between 1.3-2.0)

Pattern 4: Channel with some mid-channel bar development and multiple thalwegs (lines of deepest water; width to depth ratio >40; sinuosity low)

Pattern 5: Braided channel - greatest development of channels and bars (when ratio of bedload to total load is high)

Figure 10.6 A classification of river channel planforms based upon sediment load, cross-section and stability. (After Schumm, 1985).

and so includes alluvial fans (at upland and lowland valley confluences) and fluvially-modified debris cones (*e.g.* in Glen Etive and Glen Coe; see Brazier, 1987 for a classification and examples of different types of landforms). Sediment stored in alluvial fans (*e.g.* in the lower depositional reaches of tributaries) provides an important supply of material to mainstream channels; fans can also act as local base levels for the main streams and can lead to instabilities in the main stream (*e.g.* the River Feshie alluvial fan at the River Spey confluence; Figure 10.7).

10.3 River channel adjustment

Recent research into the dynamics of Scottish river channels and the evolution of floodplains and valley floors has focused on the nature and rate of river adjustment (in terms of sediment transport rates, hydraulic geometry and channel planform) at different spatial and temporal scales (1000, 40-300 and 1-10 year timespans). Adjustment can occur if there is a change in the balance between discharge and sediment supply (Figure 10.8). The nature, direction and scale of that change depends on the position of the channel with respect to process thresholds which need to be exceeded before particular types of adjustment can occur (Figure 10.9; see also Newson, 1992a). The methodology for studying river channel adjustment varies with the landforms (valley floor, floodplain or channel) and timescale involved. Table 10.2 outlines some of the main techniques used, with a brief assessment of their main strengths and limitations. Assessment is limited mainly to techniques which have been used to investigate Scottish rivers.

10.3.1 River adjustment over 1000s of years

Understanding of longer-term river evolution can be developed by studying different valley floor and floodplain

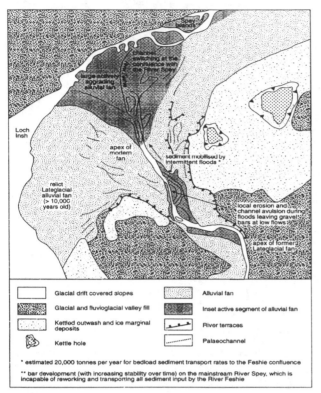

Figure 10.7 River Feshie alluvial fan. The build-up of sediment from the River Feshie acts to constrict the valley floor downstream of Loch Insh. This in turn exacerbates local flooding on the River Spey. (Modified from Brazier and Werritty, 1994).

features, such as terraces, alluvial fans accumulated at tributary confluences and palaeochannel networks. The sediment supply and the discharge regime at the time of formation (and during subsequent adjustment) are reflected in landform scale, surficial topography and stratigraphy. Former river levels, as indicated by terraces, can be classified as fill (formed by valley floor aggradation and subsequent channel incision), fill-cut (created by lateral stream erosion into recently deposited alluvium) and strath (where rock is cut, reflecting pauses in downcutting through bedrock). All can be either paired or unpaired (see Leopold and Miller, 1954; Bull, 1991). Many Scottish terraces reflect temporal changes in the balance between capacity for fluvial transport and sediment supply and so indicate phases of aggradation or fill, followed by periods of erosional downcutting, both of which have modified postglacial valley floors. If organic horizons or palaeosols are present, then radiocarbon dating of periods of stability of the landform surface between aggradational phases may be possible (see Roberts, 1989).

Since the Loch Lomond Stadial, Scottish rivers have adjusted to reduced glacial or periglacial sediment supply, depending on the location of the catchment considered (Ballantyne and Harris, 1994). The beginning of the Holocene was a period of high river activity and rapid fluvial change in Europe (Starkel, 1995). Stratigraphic evidence from Scottish loch sediments indicates high sediment availability and sediment supply immediately after deglaciation. In addition, there was an increased incidence of slope failures during the early Holocene, a legacy of accumulated stresses following deglaciation (Ballantyne, 1986, 1991b). At this time, an increased coupling of slopes and channels led to higher rates of sediment supply into river channels. This activity slowed down during the mid- to late- Holocene (Sutherland and Gordon, 1993), due to

postglacial reduction in sediment supply and stabilisation of slopes by the development of the vegetation cover.

Terraces

The scale of discharge decline during the Late-glacial and early Holocene in NE Scotland has been reconstructed by Maizels (1983) in a study of outwash features, river terraces and palaeochannels at four main levels in the dissected North Esk/West Water palaeosandur (Figure 10.10). The upper two outwash terraces (T1 & T2) have braided palaeochannels that are deeper and wider than those on the lower terraces (T3 & T4) which are shallower, narrower and more sinuous in planform. These differences reflect rapid Late-glacial and early Holocene adjustment in discharge and sediment supply (Maizels and Aitken, 1991). Although the palaeodischarges during and following Late Devensian deglaciation have been estimated at up to 50 times that of the present average discharge, there are no dates with which to establish a chronology for the changes.

Research to date has primarily focused on reconstructing the chronology and environments associated with the higher Late-glacial terraces in Scotland. Holocene terraces (their stratigraphy, chronology and implications for environmental reconstruction) have generally received scant attention, and further investigation is required to establish any regional synchronism in their patterns. A few studies have attempted to reconstruct the history of Holocene valley alluviation in Scotland, but at key sites with well preserved landform assemblages and primarily in individual catchments. Some larger valleys, such as Glen Feshie or the Findhorn catchment in the north-east Highlands, have well developed terrace sequences of both Late-glacial and Holocene age. In the case of the terraces in Glen Feshie, the chronology of river adjustment (and associated discharge decline) has been reconstructed using soil-stratigraphic dating methods (Robertson-Rintoul, 1986; Werritty and McEwen, 1993). Up to five terraces are present - the uppermost terrace represents pitted (or kettled) outwash, dating from *c.* 13 ka BP and

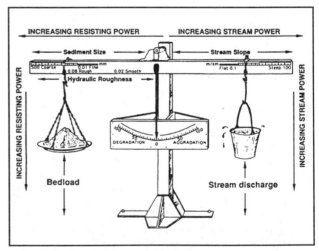

Figure 10.8 Schematic balance between modes of aggradation and degradation (or erosion) in streams. Interactions among different variables (including slope, sediment size and availability, discharge) determine whether a river system is in equilibrium or whether it departs significantly from an equilibrium state in time and space (originally from notes of E.W. Lane; reprinted from *Geomorphic Responses to Climate Change* by William B. Bull Copyright © 1991 by Oxford University Press, Inc. Used by permission of Oxford University Press, Inc.).

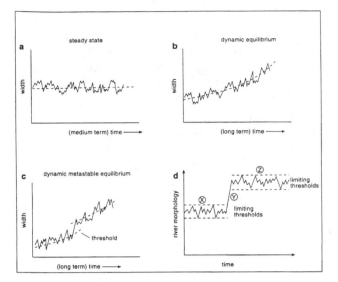

Figure 10.9 Schematic illustrations of different types of equilibrium in a river system. (After Richards, 1981; Werritty and Brazier, 1994).

A. A steady state system in which river channel activity fluctuates around a stable average condition due to the operation of negative feedback loops (*e.g.* in the maintenance of channel width as a meandering channel migrates across its floodplain).

B. A system in dynamic equilibrium in which river channel activity fluctuates around an average condition, which is itself trending over time. This trend may relate to changes in the input of discharge or sediment due to climate or landuse changes (*e.g.* a river channel becoming more divided due to an increase in floods competent to rework floodplain sediment sources).

C. A system in dynamic equilibrium in which river channel activity fluctuates around an average condition, which is itself trending over time and which is also subject to step-like discontinuities (or threshold effects). The result is periods of stability interspersed with abrupt changes of forms (*e.g.* when episodic floods alter the channel pattern in a stream with coarse channel-bed sediment, which normal flows are unable to rework).

D. Schematic illustration showing the distinction between robust and sensitive behaviour, the two types of geomorphic threshold and stable and unstable behaviour. X and Z denote **robust** behaviour, with the river repeatedly crossing intrinsic thresholds, but the overall response is stable within limiting thresholds, as negative feedback regulates change. Landforms retain stable identity as they form and reform. Y denotes **sensitive** behaviour in response to externally imposed change; the river moves across an extrinsic threshold to a new process regime. Landforms in the original regime X are destroyed and replaced by new landforms created in regime Z.

deposited during ice-sheet deglaciation. Three low-level terraces have been dated to 10 ka BP, 3.6 ka BP and 1 ka BP (located 5 m, 3 m and 1.5 m, respectively, above present river level). Reconstructions of palaeodischarges indicate the 3.6 ka BP and 1 ka BP channels carried discharges 100-120% and 8-34%, respectively, greater than the average for the present River Feshie (Robertson-Rintoul, 1986). In addition, there is also local evidence for a fifth (late 19th century) terrace. The River Findhorn at Ballachrochin

provides an example of another exceptional terrace sequence where locally up to 13 terrace levels have been identified (Auton, 1990). Of these, only the lowest five terraces are fluvial or glaciofluvial in origin. Although the massive, higher deposits of the middle and upper terraces have been researched in detail, the lower terraces have yet to be investigated: they will potentially allow insight into Holocene fluvial development and associated changes in discharge and sediment supply in the Findhorn valley (McEwen and Werritty, 1993). In the Southern Uplands, Tipping (1992) investigated the nature, timing and synchronism of coarse river gravel aggradations in the upland valleys of the Cheviot Hills. He found two phases of enhanced prehistoric geomorphic activity post-dating 4400 cal BP and concluded that larger portions of the floodplains were active than at present and that they frequently possessed braided or divided channels. More work is required to establish the regional extent of these patterns in the Southern Uplands.

Alluvial fans

Research into alluvial fan development (and associated periods of aggradation and incision) can provide information about changing patterns of discharge and sediment supply and the degree of coupling of slope and river systems. Research designs vary from site-specific assessments of individual landforms to attempts to reconstruct regional patterns of fan adjustment. Many alluvial fans are relict, as

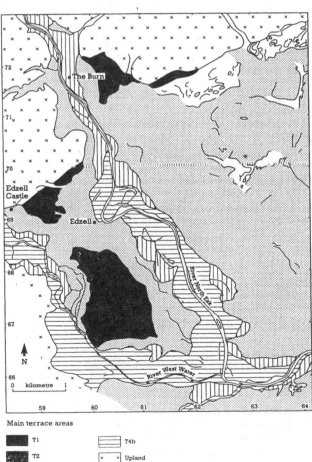

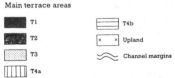

Figure 10.10 Terraces (T_1-T_4) of the River North Esk and West Water in the Edzell area. (After Maizels, 1983; reprinted from Gordon and McEwen, 1993).

a legacy of past sediment accumulation, and are primarily sites of erosion or reworking under the present process regime. Tipping and Halliday's (1994) work on the Hopecarton alluvial fan on the upper River Tweed, where deposition commenced in the 11th century AD, represents the former scenario. Here, sediment accumulation was interpreted as a local event, not being accompanied by any parallel changes on the mainstream River Tweed. A more regional approach to understanding the development of alluvial fans in the Grampian Highlands is provided by Brazier (1987). Such reconstructions usefully integrate information from different sources - geomorphological, sedimentological, palynological, archaeological and radiocarbon dating evidence - but also demonstrate some of the problems of cross-correlating local proxy data from different sources, using chronologies which lack enough accuracy. There is a need to investigate whether there is contemporaneous adjustment if a single change in controls (*e.g.* climate, landuse or a major flood) acts on catchments within a region. This work on the Holocene development of Scottish alluvial fans parallels related studies elsewhere in the UK (*e.g.* Harvey and Renwick, 1987, in the Bowland Fells, North-west England).

10.3.2 River adjustment over 40-300 years

To understand present channel form, it is necessary to understand the whole range of river channel response (Hickin, 1983). In addition, changes which have occurred over historical timescales cumulatively can provide insight into how rivers have developed throughout the Holocene. Several studies in the late 1980s and 1990s have reconstructed channel planform adjustment over the past 40-300 years, using historical sources such as estate plans, maps and aerial photographs (Table 10.2). These provide an important contrast to the longer timescales of environmental reconstruction (Section 10.3.1) and shorter monitoring timescales of years or decades (Section 10.3.3). Such historical sources, used discriminatingly in conjunction with field-based palaeochannel evidence, allow insight into the lateral response of rivers as a consequence of historical changes in discharge and or sediment supply (*e.g.* McEwen, 1989 on the River Dee, Aberdeenshire). As part of this approach, **synchronic analysis** involves comparison of the structure and function of landforms of different ages (for example, focusing on abandoned channels of different ages resulting from lateral channel migration across a floodplain) and provides 'slices' of information through time (at times of map or aerial photograph coverage). However, it is difficult to make inferences about cross-sectional adjustment (*e.g.* degree of entrenchment) from such sources, as well as the rates of change over time.

Studies of historical channel change have also evolved, from site-specific investigations to more regional assessments of river activity. For example, Brazier *et al.* (1993) reconstructed channel alignments over the past 150 years at the confluence between the River Clyde and the Medwin Water, Lanarkshire (Figure 10.11). The progression of meander bends and cut-offs indicated high rates of activity and floodplain development (with evidence of former point bars, meander scrolls and palaeochannel infills, channel cut-offs and oxbow lakes). In a contrasting upland environment, McEwen (1994) investigated spatial variations in the nature and rate of channel adjustment on the River Coe above Loch Achtriochtan, as it alters progressively downstream from a mountain torrent through a wandering gravel-bed river to a deltaic fluvio-lacustrine environment over only 2 km. While useful as investigations into the controls on

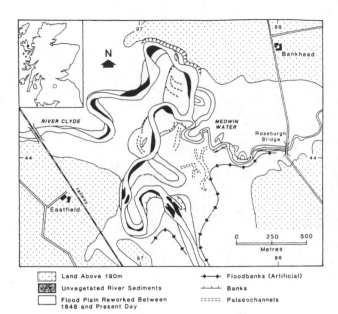

Figure 10.11 Map of the confluence of the River Clyde with the Medwin water. The present-day (April 1991) channel is shown along with the floodplain sediments and landforms worked by the rivers since 1848. Other former river channels (palaeochannels) are now partly infilled but can still be identified on the floodplain surface. (Reprinted from 'The Clyde-Medwin meanders' by V. Brazier, M. Kirkbride and A. Werritty from *Scottish Geographical Magazine*, 109, 1993, 45-49, by permission of the Royal Scottish Geographical Society.)

channel form and its adjustment, these studies also raise wider questions about the regional extent of the patterns observed and whether they also occur in similar locations elsewhere or in different basins. Other studies have therefore investigated variations in channel adjustment at the catchment scale using evidence from old published maps and palaeochannels (*e.g.* the upper River Dee, Aberdeenshire; McEwen, 1989). McEwen's (1989) results show increased channel division and floodplain reworking in some reaches of upland catchments in the late-19th century, whereas other reaches in the same catchments have remained relatively stable over the same period. In some basins, distinct alluvial zones can be identified (sometimes within a distinctly stepped long profile, indicating a sequence of local base levels) where the highest rates of channel change have taken place. These are best developed in eastern catchments (*e.g.* the River Clunie in the Dee catchment, Aberdeenshire). Although rates of fluvial activity generally slowed down in the mid- to late- Holocene, there is evidence to support a recent reactivation, with large proportions of the valley floors in some catchments reworked over the last 200-300 years. For example, Lewin and Weir (1977) found that post-1880, the lower River Spey had reworked approximately 50% of its available valley floor. In the Southern Uplands, Tipping (1994) identified two major Holocene terrace levels and four less significant surfaces on the valley floor of the Bowmont Water, Cheviot Hills. Evidence from cartographic, radiocarbon and palynological dating suggests that the later terraces formed within the last 250 years. One major terrace fill was found to have aggraded during the 18th century, with incision dated approximately to the end of the 18th century. This 'cut' has been correlated with channel trenching at other sites in the region and again provides evidence that a high

Table 10.2 Methodologies used to investigate river channel adjustment over different timescales.

1. Longer timescales (1000 years)

Approach: palaeoenvironmental reconstruction	Landforms: terraces, alluvial fans, palaeochannels (isolated or in networks)	Spatial scale: predominantly local or regional (within catchment)

Methodology for investigation:	Purpose:	Limitation:
• levelling/surveying/geomorphological mapping	to assess location, relative height and spatial relationship between different terrace levels and palaeochannel networks	interpretation can be problematic if geomorphological mapping is based solely on aerial photograph sources; terraces can be formed by both erosion and deposition; parallel field-based investigation is important
• stratigraphic and sedimentological analysis (identifying exposures; logging and mapping of sedimentary architecture in 2D/3D; logging key event horizons)	to identify geomorphic agent(s) responsible for deposition and subsequent reworking of sedimentary deposits	difficulties in reconstructing the regional and local history of sediment deposition from partial evidence
• coring of lake sediments (varves indicate one year's sediment accumulation)	to establish relative sedimentation rates over time	problems in cross-correlating information from different lake cores
• dating techniques (radiocarbon (^{14}C) dating; pollen analysis; archaeological evidence; see Roberts, 1989)	to date the absolute or relative age of valley floor and floodplain deposits, using buried organic layers including palaeosols (fossil or buried soils)	problems in cross-correlating local dating sources; dating reliability increased by using a number of dating techniques together
• palaeodischarge estimates (from palaeochannel evidence)	to establish the relative scale of river discharge at different times in the Late-glacial and Holocene	establishing the potential scale of errors in estimates

2. Intermediate timescales (40-300 years)

Approach: historical reconstruction	Landforms: channel planform (reconstruction of the nature of planform and the rate of change)	Spatial scale: case-study (reach) and regional (catchment)

Methodology for investigation:	Purpose:	Limitation:
• field reconnaissance and geomorphological mapping (e.g. of palaeochannel networks)	to establish the relationship between the present channel and its corridor/floodplain; to establish the evidence for past channel adjustment	may be difficult to establish the spatial ordering of landforms without aerial pohotographs to assist interpretation
• overlay of map and aerial photograph evidence (most sophisticated method - use of Geographical Information Systems)	to reconstruct the nature of channel planform and rate of change (identify past channel alignments and areas of floodplain reworking)	stage dependency of channel pattern; resolution of maps; lack of information about cross-sectional adjustment; important to complement with field reconnaissance of palaeochannel evidence
• use of contemporary historical sources/ documentary-based evidence (e.g. estate plans/ records; journals; see Hooke and Kain, 1982)	to identify the timing of channel changes and/or artificial alterations to channel or catchment	sporadic in occurrence; evidence should be corroborated (where possible) with other sources
• dating techniques radiocarbon dating (^{14}C)	to date the absolute or relative age of to deposits (e.g. in stratigraphic analysis of palaeochannel fills or exposures of floodplain deposits eroded by the present river channel)	^{14}C inapplicable for samples younger than c. 150 years
• incremental dating methods (e.g. dendrochronology - tree-ring dating; lichenometry - establishing a lichen size-age curve for *Rhizocarpon geographicum*)	to date the absolute or relative age of floodplain surfaces or flood deposits	establishing a reliable size/age relationship for lichenometry

3. Short timescales (1-10 years)

Approach: monitoring	Landforms: channel planform; hydraulic geometry	Spatial scale: normally reach level

Methodology for investigation:	Purpose:	Limitation:
• use of Vigil or monitoring network; fixed points for repeat mapping and cross-sectional surveys (see Emmett and Hadley, 1968)	to monitor short-term changes in channel planform and/or hydraulic geometry	not known how representative current patterns of adjustment are of long-term trends; active rivers rework floodplain evidence
• erosion pin networks; automated assessment of bank erosion possible (sensor linked to logger)	to monitor types and rates of bank erosion	technique can cause bank instability and preferential erosion; spatial extrapolation of results
• use of sediment (bedload) traps	to assess sediment characteristics and supply; to establish rates of sediment transport in relation to discharge	need several years of monitoring to identify annual variation and trends

proportion of the valley floor of the Bowmont Water has been reworked over the past 250 years. While recent reworking of large proportions of valley floors is interesting in terms of geomorphic activity, it does, however, mean a lack of preservation of earlier Holocene landforms for investigation.

The local degree of coupling between river and slope processes can also change over historical time. For example, three debris cones have accumulated in Glen Feshie since c. 2 ka BP, primarily through reworking of upslope glacial and periglacial sediment sources (Brazier and Ballantyne, 1989). However, the bulk of the cones developed since the 15th century, with their episodic development linked to the lateral migration and basal erosion of the River Feshie. At present, local undermining of these debris flows by the river is allowing direct sediment input but this has varied in the past.

10.3.3 Recent river adjustment

Monitoring of adjustment in channel form can provide insight into the nature and scale of recent channel changes and the sensitivity of the present system to change. Werritty (1984) used the Vigil network approach, with fixed survey points for repeat survey (see Table 10.2), to investigate cross-sectional as well as planform change from 1978-1981 on Dorback Burn, a typical small-scale wandering gravel-bed river in Abernethy Forest. A similar approach was used by Werritty and Ferguson (1980) to study channel adjustment over an eleven-year period on the middle River Feshie, an exceptional example of a wandering gravel-bed river. Some reaches of wandering gravel-bed rivers (e.g. in Glen Feshie or the lower River Spey) have a history of rapid channel shift or avulsion and have some of the highest documented rates of floodplain migration in the UK. For example, the middle Feshie widened by 136% from 1977 to 1981, with bank erosion locally exceeding 10 m a^{-1} (Ferguson and Werritty, 1983). The problem with short-term monitoring, however, is that the record of channel-forming events may be atypical and thus can lead to erroneous extrapolation of recent channel activity to longer-term trends. Both the work on Dorback Burn and the River Feshie used historical sources to place recent channel changes in a longer-term context. Short-term monitoring accompanied by use of historical sources can also inform the development of management strategies, for example Riddell and Fuller's (1995) geomorphological assessment of the lower River Spey. Here, c. 20,000 to 25,000 m^3 of the 30,000 m^3 of coarse- and fine- grained sediments estimated to have accumulated at the coast during the 22 month study period were supplied by the river.

10.4 Controls on fluvial change

Evidence to date indicates that different types of Scottish river channel have displayed different propensities for change over different timescales during the Holocene. When trying to explain these spatial and temporal variations, there are a number of competing multiple working hypotheses. Potential explanations for channel changes include adjustment triggered by climate changes or fluctuations, landuse changes and the impact of quasi-random extreme flood events. The difficulty of untangling cause from effect is substantial, because temporal correlation does not imply causality. This is most evident when explaining channel changes over longer timescales (see Ballantyne, 1991b) where there is a lagged response of vegetation changes to climatic shifts. For example, at a catchment level, changes to the nature or extent of tree-cover can lead to changes in the runoff regime; at a floodplain level, alterations to vegetation can increase or decrease channel stability. Additional problems with an empirical approach to studying and predicting channel changes occur though 'indeterminacy' and 'equifinality'. 'Indeterminacy' exists where stream channels respond to change in different ways; 'equifinality' occurs where the same channel form can result from more than one process. An example of 'indeterminacy' is where similar discharges lead to different sorts of response in the same channel at different times; channel response will depend on how close the channel is to thresholds for change and this may alter, for example, depending on the past sequence of floods. An illustration of 'equifinality' is where the same channel change could have been triggered by a climatic event or a land use change because the effects of both on discharge regime may in some instances be similar.

Changes in fluvial controls can also take place at a hierarchy of scales - at national, regional and local levels. For example, climate changes can be envisaged as producing effects at national or regional scales, whereas land use changes can be anticipated to have catchment-level impacts. Even with more recent anthropogenic changes, river system responses may not be immediate but lagged over a period of years or decades. In addition, it is difficult to predict quantitatively the nature or the scale of any change. However, Schumm (1969) has established some functional qualitative relationships, which can inform geomorphic assessments of potential anthropogenic impacts.

Recent research has also investigated the relative **sensitivity** or **robustness** of the present fluvial landscape and landforms in the United Kingdom to externally induced change - whether by climatic or human triggers (e.g. Downs and Gregory, 1993). Models of stable and unstable channel behaviour have been developed (Werritty and Brazier, 1991; Figure 10.9D). Establishing the sensitivity of a river to change over different timespans can inform strategies for effective conservation-sensitive management (so reinforcing the links between pure and applied research).

The following sections examine the relative importance of climate and land use changes and quasi-random extreme floods in explaining fluvial adjustment in Scottish river systems over short, intermediate and long timespans. Although these timespans are considered separately, the same catchment will frequently respond to different sorts of climate and land use changes over different timespans and it is important to determine the relative importance of these alterations on the discharge and sediment supply to rivers (Section 10.4.3). Starkel (1995) summarises the dramatic changes in the nature of Polish rivers in the transitional phase of the early Holocene in terms of both discharge and sediment supply. This was followed by relative channel stability during the middle Holocene and rapid adjustment of rivers over the past 200-300 years. Broadly, a similar pattern seems to have occurred in Scotland, but the detail is currently lacking.

10.4.1 Climate change

Climatic fluctuations are now known to have occurred during the Holocene, but the associated history of fluvial adjustments is not well known (see Sutherland and Gordon, 1993). Since alluvial valley floors are one of the most sensitive environments to both large-scale and subtle shifts in hydroclimate, they potentially contain in their landforms and sediments a valuable proxy record of such fluctuations. However, the relationship between hydro-meteorological conditions, river flows and geomorphic response is complex.

Flood hydrology in a catchment will depend not only on the flood-causing factors (the magnitude, intensity, seasonality and duration of precipitation and antecedent conditions) but also on flood intensifying conditions (at basin, network and channel scales; see Ward, 1981; Newson, 1994). For example, an increase in long-duration winter rainfall may have different effects on large lowland catchments, compared with small upland catchments where the flashiness of runoff response is much higher. Relatively small changes in climatic controls can potentially lead to large changes in flood characteristics.

The period back to the 18th century is particularly interesting as it incorporates the latter stages of the Little Ice Age cold period (Lamb, 1995). The Little Ice Age involved several short cold periods (*e.g.* 1880s-1900s), which were synchronous on the hemispheric or global scale (see Bradley and Jones, 1992). By establishing the characteristics of high rates of fluvial geomorphic response triggered by the climatic deterioration of the Little Ice Age (drop in mean temperature *c.* 1°C) and its subsequent warming, these periods can be used as analogues for understanding the potential changes associated with present climate warming (Section 10.3.3; Newson and Lewin, 1991). Periods such as the latter stages of the 19th century were characterised by a higher than average frequency of moderate floods (evident in the River Dee, Spey and Tweed catchments) and this has been associated with increased propensity for channel division in some upland catchments (Section 10.3.2; River Dee; McEwen, 1989).

Increased patterns of flood frequency in the late 19th century are also reported from catchments in Northern England (*e.g.* Wear; Archer, 1987; Macklin, *et al.,* 1992). For example, Rumsby and Macklin (1994) examined the timing, nature and magnitude of river response in upland, piedmont and lowland reaches of the Tyne to high frequency changes in climate and flood regime since AD 1700 and found alternating periods of incision and stability. Further afield, Probst (1989) found discharges in excess of the long-term average for periods in the latter half of the 19th century for selected North European rivers. Synchronism in channel adjustment (*e.g.* erosive phases or accelerated fluvial activity during the Little Ice Age) has been identified across different catchments not only in Scotland, but also in Europe and globally (Brakenridge, 1980).

Predictions suggest that the hydrological impact of recent climate changes will be greatest in north and west Britain (see Newson and Lewin, 1991). Research on hydrological changes (post-1970) in Scotland has identified shifts in mean annual river flow and patterns of discharge extremes, most defined in catchments in the west and north-west (see Smith and Bennett, 1994; Anderson and Black, 1993). Winter runoff from some of Scotland's major rivers (Clyde, Tay and Ness) has been increasing in recent years, particularly in the north-west. These changes in discharge patterns have been linked to changes in the incidence of synoptic weather types (Grew and Werritty, 1995). Accompanying the shifts in mean values of discharge is an increased flow variability and a move to a 'flood rich' period with more extreme winter floods. This is evident on the Rivers Tay (1990, 1993), Clyde (1994; Bennett, 1995) and Ness (1989) in recent years. It raises questions as to whether there has been a significant regional geomorphic response to these hydrological changes, and, in particular, whether different types of river system are more susceptible to change. Rivers in north and west Scotland, which are high energy and amongst the least managed in the UK, potentially allow assessment of the response of 'natural' channels to these climatic shifts. Most research on geomorphic activity over the last 300 years has,

however, been in eastern catchments. Analysis of hydrological change and fluvial adjustment in western catchments is hampered by sparse historical records and the short length and limited density of hydrometric coverage. (Hydrometric coverage refers to both precipitation and discharge records). Thus further research is required to unravel the complexity and timescale of channel response to climate changes, not only in Scotland but also more generally in the UK. Newson and Lewin (1991), in assessing the hydrological and geomorphic impacts of recent climate change, anticipate considerable and widespread changes in patterns and rates of both river sediment transport and floodplain deposition in much of upland and lowland Britain.

10.4.2 Land use changes

Scottish catchments have undergone a number of changes in vegetation cover and land use during the Holocene; some climatically induced, others of anthropogenic origin. Despite the fact that many remote Scottish catchments might be considered the most 'natural' in the United Kingdom, few catchments lack any human alteration. Changes can be subdivided into: (1) those which are principally indirect and affect catchment processes, and hence potentially runoff response and sediment supply; and (2) those which involve direct alteration to the channel.

Indirect changes include deforestation, which has been widespread and can be anticipated to have had effects on sediment supply and floodplain stability. For example, local fluvial aggradation in the Cheviot Hills after 4.4 ka BP has been explained by woodland clearance for farming in a period of 'intensive and upland settlement' (Tipping, 1992); climatic controls were not considered causal because there was little evidence for the periods of geomorphic activity coinciding with evidence for climatic perturbations (either globally or locally). Native Caledonian pine forests *(Pinus sylvestris)* in the Scottish Highlands were depleted in the 18th, 19th and 20th centuries (Steven and Carlisle, 1959) and this may explain local temporal changes in floodplain stability. However, care is required in making the assumption that regional changes, which appear synchronous, are caused by the same land use change, and one has to be wary of 'chicken and egg' arguments in explaining evidence for change, given the resolution of the chronology for geomorphic activity and climate change over longer timescales.

Impacts of afforestation can also have significant effects on mean discharges, flood frequency and sediment supply, through both forestry practice and changes in the vegetation cover. Early work by Law (1956) at Stocks Reservoir, Lancashire, confirmed that forests use more water than rough moorland, and subsequent investigation, notably at the Institute of Hydrology experimental catchment at Plynlimon, has examined the scale of the effects. Impacts on flood magnitude and frequency depend on the percentage area affected and its location within the catchment (*e.g.* Acreman, 1985). Forestry can also have large impacts on sediment yield; data from the Institute of Hydrology experimental catchment at Balquidder, Central Highlands, indicates that afforestation (with associated ditching) can increase yields in small catchments by 121%, and clear felling by 595%, over former levels of sediment yield (Johnson, 1993). The effects of such changes on sediment budgets, specifically in Scottish catchments, have yet to be systematically investigated. Land use changes can also influence sediment supply to rivers by altering the nature and rate of processes active on slopes. Brazier *et al.*

(1988) linked anthropogenic activity (burning natural vegetation) with fluvial reworking and erosion of a relict debris cone in Glen Etive.

Direct channel/floodplain changes include channelisation or extraction of gravel resources. The scale and persistence of the activity will determine the nature and scale of local and/or downstream impacts on river morphology. Reconstruction of past channel forms can provide insight into channel response to structural protection. For example, an analysis of documentary and map sources for the River Tay indicates that the channel was an unstable, multi-channeled, wandering gravel-bed river in the 18th and 19th centuries. However, embankments for flood protection have now confined the channel to narrower single channel reaches, characterised by limited channel migration (Gilvear and Winterbottom, 1992; Gilvear, 1993). The lower Spey, too, has undergone a reduction in its degree of braiding in the 20th century, possibly due to bank protection works and afforestation of floodplain areas (Lewin and Weir, 1977). It is now recognised as both possible and desirable to manage rivers in a manner that is sensitive to conservation, allowing natural development of the channel within tolerable boundaries.

10.4.3 Interaction of climate and land use

Macklin and Lewin (1993) describe the British Holocene fluvial record as an alluvial sequence that has been 'climatically driven' but 'culturally blurred'. It is possible that climate and land use changes may be mutually reinforcing or self-cancelling. It is recognised that land use changes can increase the susceptibility of the river system to climate changes; for example, grazing pressure may reduce floodplain stability and increase vulnerability to change during periods of increased flood frequency. Thus, Macklin and Lewin (1993) suggest that the propensity towards more active braided rivers in the 18th and 19th centuries was due to an increase in flood magnitude and frequency, combined with increased sediment supply caused by climatic fluctuations and land use changes. It is important to note, however, that while the historical period allows some insights into the relative strength of the climatic and cultural signals in the UK, this largely predates the increasingly direct influence of human culture and the power of structural constraints on rivers to restrict natural geomorphic responses to climate (Newson and Lewin, 1991). Research by Macklin et al. (1992) in the Tyne basin in Northern England provides a good example of the sort of chronological work that still needs to be done in most Scottish basins. 'It is concluded that anthropogenic activity and climatic change need not be considered as competing hypotheses for explaining the timing and the pattern of Holocene alluviation and river erosion. River response to environmental change should instead be viewed in terms of a continuum between these two factors, which, in particular circumstances and at certain times, can each control water and sediment yields and the alluvial record of a drainage basin' (Macklin, et al., 1992, p. 123).

10.4.4 Geomorphic impact of floods

Channel response to floods of different magnitudes and frequencies has been investigated across a range of environments including Scotland. Geomorphic impact can be defined in terms of sediment transport, immediate landforming capacity and the persistence of landforms - the ability of landforms to survive the return period of the formative event (see Wolman and Gerson, 1978). Early work by Wolman and Miller (1960) in the United States supported the dominance of more moderate events in terms of sediment transport in large basins with low slopes, small sediment sizes and limited vegetative cover. This model, however, requires some modification when applied to high energy upland environments, including Scotland. A number of Scottish case studies have looked at the immediate channel-forming impact and persistence of flood-induced landforms both within channel and floodplain (Table 10.3). Perhaps the most catastrophic flood in historic records was the August 1829 flood, a long duration regional event caused by summer frontal rainfall, which caused major geomorphic disruption and significant channel changes in rivers in NE Scotland (Lauder, 1830). For example, the Quoich alluvial fan in the upper Dee catchment underwent rapid adjustment in a few hours, with the whole fan surface reworked. Palaeochannels from this event are still evident on the present fan surface and this one event has been more significant in the development of the fan than any flows since. If climatic changes are to lead to an increase in more extreme regional floods, then it is important to establish their longer-term impact and their role in transporting pulses of sediment downstream from upstream sediment stores.

There is a growing amount of evidence to support the high geomorphic impact of localised convective storms in small catchments with coarse sediment sizes and high entrainment thresholds (e.g. Acreman, 1983, 1991; McEwen and Werritty, 1988). Cumulatively their impact can be significant in high energy mountain systems, where channels can be considered as having two modes of activity: under normal flows which are incompetent to transport a high percentage of the available coarse sediment load (derived from reworked glacigenic or glaciofluvial deposits), and under flood conditions which are competent to transport sediment and carry out geomorphic work. It is important that more recent flood-generated sediment transport is placed in a longer-term Holocene context; for example, Ballantyne (1991a) indicates that current rates of sediment transport by mountain streams (e.g. Ardessie Burn; c. 9.3 t km^{-2} a^{-1}) are not exceptional when placed in this context. Evidence also indicates that post-flood entrenchment in recent flood deposits can in some circumstances lead to very rapid local development of terrace-type features over periods of months (see Acreman (1991) on the Hermitage Water, Roxburghshire). This confirms that interpretation of lower terrace levels on floodplains requires care. Research on the geomorphic impact of recent and historic floods in reworking both channels and floodplains needs to be more systematic, so that models of response can be developed for different environmental settings. Such immediate post-flood assessment is also essential to determine the persistence or degree of degradation of landforms over longer timescales and is important in informing channel management (see Petts, 1985).

More recent research indicates the importance of understanding thresholds for change and the magnitude and frequency of formative flood events. A good example is work on the wandering gravel-bed planforms of the River Feshie, where Werritty and Ferguson (1980) observed cyclical planform changes. Here, extreme events trigger a chaotic, divided channel pattern, whereas more moderate events rework sediment and rationalise the system to a more sinuous and less divided pattern. In upland catchments, channel form may relate not only to the magnitude and frequency of channel forming events, but also to those which trigger slope activity. The channel's ability to rework sediment inputs from adjacent slopes (particularly coarse-grained deposits of glacigenic or glaciofluvial origin) will be critical. For example, Acreman's (1991) report of the flood

Table 10.3   Some examples of case studies of the geomorphic impact of floods in Scotland.

Location	River	Date	Catchment area (km²)	Discharge m³s⁻¹	Estimated return period	Sources used	Geomorphic impact	Reference
Wester Ross	Ardessie Burn	September 1981	13.5	65.0	100 years	post flood reconstruction	distruption of alluvial fan surface	Acreman, 1983
Cairngorms	Alt Mor, tributary of the River Druie	August 1978	16.4	66-81	50 years	aerial photographs sediment size/ trash marks	variable impact	McEwen and Werritty, 1988
Roxburghshire	Hermitage Water	July 1983	36.9	170	c. 150 years	field evidence	peat slides on several hillsides; extensive erosion of river banks	Acreman, 1991
Central Highlands	River Tay	February 1990	3210	1747	70 years	maps, aerial photographs, surveying of eroded channels	5 m erosion on the outside of a meander bend over 300 m length	Gilvear and Harrison, 1991

of 25 July 1983 on Hermitage Water, Roxburgh, cites the importance of slope activity and peat slides in providing very high but spatially localised sediment inputs to upland river systems. McEwen and Werritty (1988) also emphasise that different events may have different impacts on slopes and rivers depending on their relative stability thresholds and the inter-arrival times of major storms. Although low-magnitude, high-intensity convective storms may be relatively rare over a single catchment, their geomorphic importance is increased when considering their cumulative work done in the Scottish uplands.

10.5 Conclusions

Although research into the development of Scottish rivers during the Holocene has started to establish a framework for understanding river response over different timescales, there are still a large number of gaps which require investigation. In particular, two areas may be highlighted.

1. The Holocene alluvial record in Scotland requires a more systematic analysis to establish the sensitivity of different fluvial systems (mountain, piedmont, lowland) to external changes. While interesting results (and fine-tuning of the research questions) have developed out of case-studies, a more regional approach is now required. In particular, this requires a spatial extension of the main focus from the Cairngorms and Southern Uplands to other catchments and regions in the east and west of Scotland.

2. To gain insight into the development of a drainage basin, a number of geomorphological, environmental and cultural elements need to be reconstructed and linked. There are major problems in unravelling the relative importance of climatic versus land use effects - both may exert impacts in the same catchment but over different spatial and temporal scales. Additional uncertainties occur in temporal correlation of fluvial adjustment with local or regional changes in discharge or sediment supply within and between catchments, the timing of which may also be imprecise. Linking cause to effect is additionally problematic when there may be lagged responses to the same external change.

In conclusion, the Holocene in Scotland has been a dynamic period in terms of climatic shifts and there is still a need to establish the relative scale of fluvial geomorphic response to these changes, particularly over longer timescales in the early- to mid-Holocene. The resurgence of fluvial activity over the last 200-300 years has been accounted for in some areas through climatic deterioration due to the Little Ice Age. It also has been explained through changed hydrological and sedimentological inputs due to land use changes, such as increased grazing pressure in upland areas. More work is therefore required on identifying the *causes* of fluvial change, as well as focusing on timing or geomorphic effects, if progress is to be made in understanding fluvial adjustment throughout the Holocene.

References

Acreman, M.C. 1983. The significance of the flood of September 1981 on the Ardessie Burn, Wester Ross. *Scottish Geographical Magazine*, **100**, 37-49.

Acreman, M. C. 1985. Effects of afforestation on the flood hydrology of the upper Ettrick valley. *Scottish Forestry*, **39**, 89-99.

Acreman, M. C. 1991. The flood of July 25th 1983 on the Hermitage Water, Roxburghshire. *Scottish Geographical Magazine*, **107**, 170-178.

Anderson, J. and Black, A. 1993. Tay flooding: Act of God or climate change. *Circulation: The Newsletter of the British Hydrological Society*, **38**, 1-4.

Anderson, M.G., Walling, D.E. and Bates, P.D. 1996. (Eds) *Floodplain Processes*. Wiley, Chichester.

Archer, D. 1987. Improvement in flood estimates using historical information on the River Wear at Durham. *Proceedings of the National Hydrology Symposium, Hull*. British Hydrological Society, Wallingford, 5.1-5.9.

Auton, C. A. 1990. The middle Findhorn valley. In: Auton, C. A., Firth, C.R. and Merritt, J.W. (Eds), *Beauly to Nairn: Field Guide*. Quaternary Research Association, Cambridge, 74-96.

Ballantyne, C.K. 1986. Landslides and slope failures in Scotland: a review. *Scottish Geographical Magazine*, **102**, 134-150.

Ballantyne, C.K. 1991a. Late Holocene erosion in upland Britain: climatic deterioration or human influence. *The Holocene*, **1**, 81-85.

Ballantyne, C.K. 1991b. Holocene geomorphic activity in the Scottish Highlands. *Scottish Geographical Magazine,* **107**, 84-98.

Ballantyne, C.K. and Benn, D.I. 1996. Paraglacial slope adjustment during recent deglaciation and its implications for slope evolution in formerly glaciated environments. In: Anderson, M.G. and Brooks, S.M. (Eds), *Advances in Hillslope Processes.* Vol. 2. Wiley, Chichester, 1173-1195.

Ballantyne, C.K. and Harris, C. 1994. *The Periglaciation of Great Britain.* Cambridge University Press, Cambridge.

Bennett, T. 1995. Flooding in Strathclyde. *Circulation: Newsletter of the British Hydrological Society,* **45**, 1-2.

Bluck, B. J. 1971. Sedimentation on the meandering River Endrick, Scotland. *Scottish Journal of Geology,* **7**, 93-138.

Brakenridge, G. R. 1980. Widespread episodes of stream erosion during the Holocene and their climatic causes. *Nature,* **283**, 655-656.

Bradley, R.S. and Jones, P.D. 1992. Climate since A.D. 1500: introduction. In: Bradley, R.S. and Jones, P.D. (Eds), *Climate Since A.D. 1500.* Routledge, London, 1-16.

Brazier, V. 1987. Late Quaternary alluvial fans, debris cones and talus cones in the Grampian Highlands. Unpublished PhD thesis, University of St. Andrews.

Brazier, V. and Ballantyne, C.K. 1989. Late Holocene debris cone evolution in Glen Feshie, western Cairngorm Mountains, Scotland. *Transactions of the Royal Society of Edinburgh: Earth Sciences,* **80**, 17-24.

Brazier, V., Whittington, G.W. and Ballantyne, C.K. 1988. Holocene debris cone evolution in Glen Etive, western Grampian Highlands, Scotland. *Earth Surface Processes and Landforms,* **13**, 525-531.

Brazier, V., Kirkbride, M. and Werritty, A. 1993. The Clyde-Medwin meanders. *Scottish Geographical Magazine,* **109**, 45-49.

Brazier, V. and Werritty, A. 1994. Conservation management of dynamic rivers: the case of the River Feshie, Scotland. In: O'Halloran, D., Green, C., Harley, M., Stanley, M. and Knill, J. (Eds), *Geological and Landscape Conservation.* Geological Society, London, 147-152.

Brookes, A. 1991. Geomorphology/geology. In: Gardiner, J. L. (Ed.), *A Manual for the Holistic Appraisal of Rivers.* Wiley, Chichester, 57-66.

Bull, W.B. 1991. *Geomorphic Responses to Climatic Change.* Oxford University Press, New York.

Church, M. 1983. Pattern of instability in a wandering gravel-bed channel. In: Collinson, J.D. and Lewin, J. (Eds), *Modern and Ancient Fluvial Systems. International Association of Sedimentologists, Special Publication,* **6**. Blackwell, London, 169-180.

Church, M. and Ryder, J.M. 1972. Paraglacial sedimentation: a consideration of fluvial processes conditioned by glaciation. *Bulletin of the Geological Society of America,* **83**, 3059-3072.

Downs, P.W. and Gregory, K.J. 1993. The sensitivity of river channels in the landscape system. In: Thomas, D.S.G. and Allison, R.J. (Eds), *Landscape Sensitivity.* Wiley, Chichester, 15-88.

Emmett, W.W. and Hadley, R.F. 1968. The Vigil network: preservation and access of data. *U.S. Geological Survey Circular,* **460-C**.

Ferguson, R.I. 1981. Channel form and channel changes. In: Lewin, J. (Ed.), *British Rivers.* Allen and Unwin, London, 90-125.

Ferguson, R.I. and Werritty, A. 1983. Bar development and channel changes in the gravelly River Feshie Scotland. In: Collinson, J.D. and Lewin, J. (Eds), *Modern and Ancient Fluvial Systems. International Association of Sedimentologists, Special Publication,* **6**. Blackwell, London, 181-193.

Gilvear, D. 1993. River management and conservation issues on formerly braided river systems: the case of the River Tay, Scotland. In: Best, J.L. and Bristow, C.S. (Eds), *Braided Rivers. Geological Society Special Publication,* **75**, 231-240.

Gilvear, D.J. and Harrison, D.J. 1991. Channel change and the significance of floodplain stratigraphy: 1990 flood event, lower River Tay, Scotland. *Earth Surface Processes and Landforms,* **16**, 753-761.

Gilvear, D.J. and Winterbottom, S.J. 1992. Channel change and flood events since 1783 on the regulated River Tay, Scotland: implications for flood hazard management. *Regulated Rivers: Research and Management,* **7**, 247-260.

Gordon, J.E. and McEwen, L.J. 1993. North Esk and West water glaciofluvial landforms. In: Gordon, J.E. and Sutherland, D.G. (Eds), *The Quaternary of Scotland.* Chapman & Hall, London, 499-502.

Grew, H. and Werritty, A. 1995. Changes in flood frequency in Scotland 1964-1992. *Proceedings of BHS 5th National Hydrology Symposium, Edinburgh.* British Hydrological Society, Wallingford, 3.1-3.9.

Harvey, A. M. and Renwick, W. H. 1987. Holocene alluvial fan and terrace formation in the Bowland Fells, Northwest England. *Earth Surface Processes and Landforms,* **12**, 249-257.

Hickin, E.J. 1983. River channel changes: retrospect and prospect. In: Collinson, J.D. and Lewin, J. (Eds), *Modern and Ancient Fluvial Systems. International Association of Sedimentologists, Special Publication,* **6**. Blackwell, London, 61-83.

Hooke, J.M. and Kain, R.J.P. 1982. *Historical Change in the Physical Environment: a Guide to Sources and Techniques.* Butterworths, London.

Johnson, R.C. 1993. Effects of forestry on suspended solids and bedload yields in the Balquidder catchments. *Journal of Hydrology,* **145**, 403-417.

Lamb, H.H. 1995. *Climate, History and the Modern World.* Routledge, London.

Lauder, T.D. 1830. *An Account of the Great Floods of August, 1829 in the Province of Moray and adjoining District.* Adam Black, Edinburgh.

Leopold, L.B. and Miller, J.P. 1954. A post-glacial chronology for some alluvial valleys in Wyoming. *U.S. Geological Survey Water-Supply Paper,* **1261**.

Leopold, L.B. and Wolman, M.G. 1957. River channel patterns - braided, meandering and straight. *Professional Paper. United States Geological Survey,* **282B**.

Lewin, J. and Weir, M.J.C. 1977. Morphology and recent history of the lower River Spey. *Scottish Geographical Magazine,* **93**, 45-51.

McEwen, L. J. 1989. River channel changes in response to flooding in the upper River Dee catchment, Aberdeenshire, over the last 200 years. In: Carling, P. and Beven, K. (Eds), *Floods: Hydrological, Sedimentological and Geomorphological Implications.* Wiley, Chichester, 219-238.

McEwen, L.J. 1994. Channel planform adjustment and stream power variations on the middle River Coe, Western Grampian Highlands, Scotland. *Catena,* **21**, 357-374.

McEwen, L.J. and Werritty, A. 1988. The hydrology and long-term geomorphic significance of a flash flood in the Cairngorm Mountains, Scotland. *Catena,* **15**, 361-377.

McEwen, L.J. and Werritty, A. 1993. Findhorn terraces. In: Gordon, J.E. and Sutherland, D.G. (Eds), *The Quaternary of Scotland.* Chapman & Hall, London, 187-189.

Macklin, M.G. and Lewin, J. 1993. Holocene alluviation in Britain. In: Douglas, I. and Hagedorn, J. (Eds), *Geomorphology and Geoecology. Fluvial Geomorphology. Zeitschrift für Geomorphologie,* Suppl. Bd, **88,** 109-122.

Macklin, M.G., Passmore, D.G. and Rumsby, B.T. 1992. Climatic and cultural signals in Holocene alluvial sequences: the Tyne basin, northern England. In: Needham, S. and Macklin, M.G. (Eds), *Alluvial Archaeology in Britain.* Oxbow Monograph 27. Oxbow Books, Oxford, 123-139.

Maizels, J.K. 1983. Proglacial channel systems: change and thresholds for change over long, intermediate and short timescales. In: Collinson, J.D. and Lewin, J. (Eds), *Modern and Ancient Fluvial Systems. International Association of Sedimentologists, Special Publication,* 6. Blackwell, London, 251-266.

Maizels, J.K. and Aitken, J.F. 1991. Palaeohydrological change during deglaciation in upland Britain: a case-study from northeast Scotland. In: Starkel, L., Gregory, K.J. and Thornes, J.B. (Eds), *Temperate Palaeohydrology.* Wiley, Chichester, 105-145.

Newson, M. 1992a. Geomorphic thresholds in gravel-bed rivers. In: Billi, P., Hey, R.D., Thorne, C.R. and Tacconi, P. (Eds), *Dynamics of Gravel-bed Rivers.* Wiley, Chichester, 3-20.

Newson, M. 1992b. *Land, Water and Development.* Routledge, London.

Newson, M. 1994. *Hydrology and the River Environment.* Oxford University Press, Oxford.

Newson, M. and Lewin, J. 1991. Climatic change, river flow extremes and fluvial erosion- scenarios for England and Wales. *Progress in Physical Geography,* **15,** 1-17.

Petts, G.E. 1995. Changing river channels: the geographical tradition. In: Gurnell, A. and Petts, G.E. (Eds) *Changing River Channels.* Wiley, Chichester, 1-23.

Probst, J-L. 1989. Hydroclimatic fluctuations of some European Rivers since 1800. In: Petts, G.E. (Ed.), *Historical Change of Large Alluvial Channels: Western Europe.* Wiley, Chichester, 41-55.

Richards, K. 1982. *Rivers. Form and Process in Alluvial Channels.* Methuen, London.

Riddell, K.J. and Fuller, T.W. 1995. The Spey Bay geomorphological study. *Earth Surface Processes and Landforms,* **20,** 671-686.

Robertson-Rintoul, M.S.E. 1986. A quantitative soil-stratigraphic approach to the correlation and dating of post-glacial terraces in Glen Feshie, Western Cairngorms. *Earth Surface Processes and Landforms,* **11,** 605-617.

Roberts, N. 1989. *The Holocene: an Environmental History.* Blackwells, Oxford.

Rumsby, B.T. and Macklin, M.G. 1994. Channel and floodplain responses to recent abrupt climate change: the Tyne Basin, Northern England. *Earth Surface Processes and Landforms,* **19,** 499-516.

Schumm, S.A. 1969. River metamorphosis. *Journal of Hydraulics Division, Proceedings of the American Society of Civil Engineers,* **95,** 255-273.

Schumm, S.A. 1985. Patterns of alluvial rivers. *Annual Review of Earth and Planetary Sciences,* **13,** 5-27.

Schumm, S.A. and Lichty, R.W. 1965. Time, space and causality in geomorphology. *American Journal of Science,* **263,** 110-119.

Smith, K. and Bennett, A.M. 1994. Recently increased river discharge in Scotland: effects of flow hydrology and some implications for water management. *Applied Geography,* **14,** 123-133.

Starkel, L. 1995. Changes of river channels in Europe during the Holocene. In: Gurnell, A. and Petts, G. (Eds), *Changing River Channels.* Wiley, Chichester, 27-42.

Steven, H.M. and Carlisle, A. 1959. *The Native Pinewoods of Scotland.* Oliver and Boyd, Edinburgh.

Sutherland, D.G. and Gordon, J.E. 1993. The Quaternary in Scotland. In: Gordon, J.E. and Sutherland, D.G. (Eds), *Quaternary of Scotland.* Chapman Hall, London, 11-45.

Tipping, R. (1992). The determination of cause in the generation of major prehistoric valley fills in the Cheviot Hills, Anglo-Scottish border. In: Needham, S. and Macklin, M.G. (Eds), *Alluvial Archaeology in Britain.* Oxbow Monograph 27. Oxbow Books, Oxford, 111- 121.

Tipping, R. 1994. Flood chronology and valley floor evolution of the upper Bowmont valley, Borders Region, Scotland. *Earth Surface Processes and Landforms,* **19,** 641-657.

Tipping, R. and Halliday, S.P. 1994. The age of alluvial fan deposition at a site in the Southern Uplands of Scotland. *Earth Surface Processes and Landforms,* **19,** 333-348.

Werritty, A. 1984. Stream response to flash floods in upland Scotland. In: Burt, T.P. and Walling, D.E. (Eds), *Catchment Experiments in Fluvial Geomorphology.* Geobooks, Norwich, 537-562.

Werritty, A. and Brazier, V. 1994. Geomorphic sensitivity and the conservation of fluvial SSSIs. In: Stevens, C., Green, C.P., Gordon, J.E. and Macklin, M.G. (Eds), *Conserving Our Landscape: Evolving Landforms and Ice-age Heritage.* English Nature, Peterborough.

Werritty, A. and Ferguson, R.I. 1980. Pattern changes in a Scottish braided river over 1, 30 and 200 years. In: Cullingford, R.A., Davidson, D.A. and Lewin, J. (Eds), *Timescales in Geomorphology.* Wiley, Chichester, 53-68.

Werritty, A. and McEwen, L.J. 1993. Glen Feshie. In: Gordon, J.E. and Sutherland, D.G. (Eds), *Quaternary of Scotland.* Chapman & Hall, London, 298-303.

Werritty, A. and McEwen, L.J. (1997). Fluvial geomorphology of Scotland. In: Gregory, K.J. (Ed.), *Fluvial Geomorphology of Great Britain.* Chapman & Hall, London.

Werritty, A., Brazier, V., Gordon, J.E. and McManus, J. 1994. Geomorphology. In: Maitland, P.S., Boon, P.J. and McLusky, D.S. (Eds), *The Freshwaters of Scotland. A Resource of International Significance.* Wiley, Chichester, 65-88.

Wolman, M.G. and Miller, J.P. 1960. Magnitude and frequency of forces in geomorphic processes. *Journal of Geology,* **68,** 54-74.

Wolman, M.G. and Gerson, R. 1978. Relative scales of time and effectiveness of climate in watershed geomorphology. *Earth Surface Processes,* **3,** 189-208.

General reading

Newson, M. (1994). *Hydrology and the River Environment.* Oxford University Press, Oxford.

Newson, M. and Lewin, J. 1991. Climatic change, river flow extremes and fluvial erosion- scenarios for England and Wales. *Progress in Physical Geography,* **15,** 1-17.

Werritty, A. and McEwen, L.J. (1997). Fluvial geomorphology of Scotland. In: Gregory, K.J. (Ed.), *Fluvial Geomorphology of Great Britain.* Chapman & Hall, London.

Werritty, A., Brazier, V., Gordon, J.E. and McManus, J. 1994. Geomorphology. In: Maitland, P.S., Boon, P. J. and McLusky, D.S. (Eds), *The Freshwaters of Scotland. A Resource of International Significance.* Wiley, Chichester, 65-88.

11. Human Activity and Landscape Change During the Holocene

Kevin J. Edwards and Graeme Whittington

The key themes covered in this chapter are:

- climate change during the Holocene (post-glacial);
- landscape changes during the Mesolithic period;
- landscape changes associated with the development of a farming economy;
- landscape changes during the early Historic period.

11.1 Introduction

The major change to the landscape of Scotland, after the retreat of the Loch Lomond Stadial (Younger Dryas) glaciers, was the establishment of a forest cover. Changes to this were made by human interference which, in general terms, increased over time. Evidence of these changes comes mainly from pollen analysis which has been carried out at sites throughout the mainland and the islands. Pollen analysis (palynology) involves the study of subfossil pollen and spores which are preserved in peat, lake sediments and acid soils (Moore *et al.,* 1991). A cubic centimetre of deposit could contain a million pollen grains and the identification of a representative sample of these enables the reconstruction of past vegetation and associated environments. Such work has often led to the modification of previous views about landscape change and has also been responsible for the development of new explanations and debates (*cf.* Tipping, 1994; Edwards and Whittington, 1997). Contrary to previous interpretations, it is now appreciated, for example, that many parts of the Western and Northern Isles were wooded throughout the first five millennia of the current interglacial (the Holocene) (Figure 11.1); that

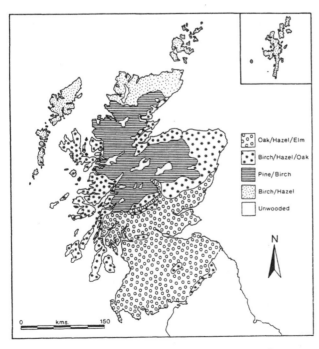

Figure 11.1 Woodland in Scotland *c.* 5 ka. (After Tipping 1994, with changes).

interference with woodland may have occurred prior to the time of the first agricultural expression *c.* 5 ka BP; and that the spread of blanket peat was not simply a response to a climatic downturn *c.* 2.5 ka BP.

11.2 The Holocene climate

With the end of the Younger Dryas (Loch Lomond Stadial) period *c.*10 ka BP, a major change in climatic conditions was initiated. Temperatures rose significantly, although not without temporary downward fluctuations (Whittington *et al.,* 1996), so that by about 7-5 ka BP the climate in Scotland would have been about 1-3°C warmer than it is today. There is debate as to overall climatic trends from that period onwards, although temperatures seem to have experienced a downward trend; it is probable, however, that three warmer periods lasting several centuries occurred between 3.1-2.8 ka BP, during the Roman period and again from 1.1-0.6 ka BP. It is possible that any fluctuations may have been local rather than global in nature and therefore difficult to identify. There has been, and still remains, considerable support for the onset of a cooler and wetter period c. 2.5 ka BP but as yet there is no unequivocal evidence for this being a phenomenon which operated over the whole of the country. A major problem in deciphering the characteristics of the climate lies in the nature of the evidence used which can be strongly influenced by human interference in the landscape. This is exemplified in the following section which discusses the nature of the development of peat growth.

11.3 The Mesolithic period

The Mesolithic period in Scotland probably spanned the period *c.* 10-5 ka BP, with local expansion beyond that date in certain localities but doubtless an earlier termination in others. The first possible interference with the established Holocene woodland cover could have been achieved by Mesolithic hunter-gatherers. There are many suggestions as to the way in which that might have occurred. It is noticeable that in many pollen diagrams the pollen of hazel *(Corylus avellana)* gains prominence by about 9 ka BP (Figure 11.2). Claims have been made that this results from the coppicing or burning of hazel shrubs in attempts to increase the production of nuts, which would have been an important food resource, and to promote the growth of timber for domestic purposes and other uses associated with hunting - both activities would enhance flowering and pollen production (*cf.* Smith, 1970). Recent research on this topic suggests that any human intereference with hazel growth was not of great consequence but that a climatic cause was more likely (Huntley, 1993); small amounts of fossil charcoal in those sections of pollen profiles covering the maxima in hazel do not lend support to the notion that *Corylus* was part of a fire climax community (Edwards, 1990). There is a similar situation concerning alder *(Alnus glutinosa).* It shows a sudden expansion in the pollen diagrams, usually after 7 ka BP, and frequently this is accompanied by a rise in the representation of charcoal fragments. This possibly involved an interference, through burning, with the tree cover, leading to soil erosion, increased runoff and waterlogging of valley bottoms, which gave rise to conditions favouring the spread of alder. A direct anthropogenic connection remains elusive, however, although alder was spreading at a time when Mesolithic peoples were present over much of Scotland.

The rises to sustained high levels of hazel and alder pollen in the fossil records are macro-scale events evident in many pollen diagrams. In an effort to reveal changes at the local scale, modern investigations have involved extremely time-consuming high resolution analysis. This has been repaid by the discovery of minor fluctuations in the pollen profiles. These temporary reductions in the tree cover could represent the removal of woodland for the construction of shelters or for fuel. There are other ways in which the temporary and minor fluctuations in the tree cover of this period could have been brought about. A major feature of the economy would have been hunting and there are suggestions that the Mesolithic people created clearings so as to attract deer to areas where good opportunities for browsing occurred. A counter argument to human interference having caused such clearances can be found in natural phenomena which affect all woodlands, such as disease, fires from lightning strikes and windthrow; even the browsing activities of deer alone by preventing tree regeneration could, over a long time period, have created clearings. There are, however, sites on Shetland, South Uist, Rum and Islay which suggest that human interference with woodland did occur at this time. On Rum, the evidence comes from peat overlying a raised beach adjacent to Scotland's oldest known Mesolithic site at Farm Fields, Kinloch, at the head of Loch Scresort, and dating back to *c.* 8590 BP (Wickham-Jones, 1990). The palaeoenvironmental data, extending back to 7.8 ka BP, indicate that the landscape disturbances associated with hunter-gatherer activities also led to soil erosion and the deposition of minerogenic materials on the accumulating peat surface. Of particular interest is the lack of archaeological evidence for a human presence in the Outer Hebrides and Shetland during the Mesolithic period. It has been proposed that rising sea levels, the shoreward movement of machair sands and cloaking blanket peat all hide archaeological evidence for early occupation (Edwards, 1996). If this is so, then palynology provides the means to reveal landscape impacts where artefactual evidence is lacking (Whittington and Edwards, 1994).

The Mesolithic landscape, for much of its duration, should probably be viewed as a well-wooded one for most of Scotland. As is indicated in Figure 11.1, which depicts a proposed distribution of woodland at the tail end of the Mesolithic (*c.* 5 ka BP), the southern half of the country was dominated by oak *(Quercus)*-hazel-elm *(Ulmus)* woods. Pine *(Pinus)* and birch *(Betula)* would have been constituents of woodland in the highland areas of the north, whereas west coast and north-east coastal areas would have favoured the growth of birch-hazel-oak communities. Even the Western and Northern Isles (together with Sutherland and Caithness), traditionally cast as largely unwooded (McVean and Ratcliffe, 1964; Bennett, 1989) are now envisaged as having been far from barren. Pollen data point to a substantial tree cover for many sites where birch and hazel communities were common (Edwards, 1996) and macrofossil evidence, largely limited to the species growing on peat bogs (Figure 11.3; Fossitt, 1996), shows the widespread occurrence of pine, birch and willow *(Salix)*. Exceptions to this are to be found and Reineval on South Uist (Figure 11.4) is one of these. It shows a sporadic presence of mainly deciduous

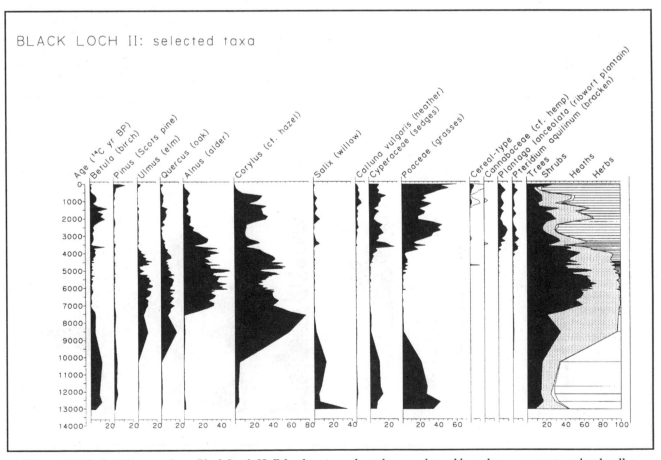

Figure 11.2 Pollen diagram from Black Loch II, Fife, showing selected taxa only and based on a percentage land pollen count. Note x5 exaggeration on the curves for cereal-type and Cannabaceae.

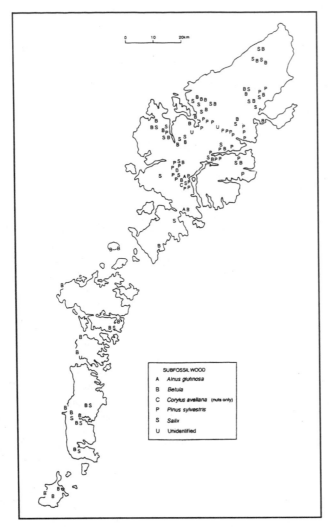

Figure 11.3 Wood macrofossil remains from the Western Isles. (Based on the compilation of Fossit 1996, with additions).

trees through the first half of the Holocene, but also the overwhelming occurrence of heathland taxa as blanket peat spread in the area from *c.* 4-5 ka BP.

In many places the vegetational landscape of the Mesolithic period was probably not an unbroken vista of trees. Open areas would have been common along river courses and on the higher slopes of mountains and, of course, as detailed above, where natural or artificial causes acted to create clearings. Such useful areas are likely to have been exploited both by human and animal populations.

11.4 The development of a farming economy

The beginning of major woodland clearance has always focused on the period around 5 ka BP which witnessed in Scotland, as across north-west Europe, the event known as the elm *(Ulmus)* decline. It is now known that this decline was not an isolated event in the history of the Scottish woodland but that marked falls in elm pollen did recur at later dates. There is, however, debate not only as to the cause of the earliest decline, but also about its significance as a marker for the introduction of farming to the landscape. The decline in elm pollen (see Figure 11.2) has been laid at the door of several factors. A popular cause, heightened by very recent experience, is found in Dutch elm disease which is a fungal pathogen spread by insect infestation of the elm trees. A further explanation is found in a climatic change which may have led to temperatures which prevented the tree from flowering as profusely; however, there is no good evidence for that. A third explanation, which also could involve the spread of disease, results from the observation that most pollen diagrams at the time of the elm decline show an increase in grasses (Poaceae), a sudden rise in ribwort plantain *(Plantago lanceolata),* a feature of ground disturbance, and a widespread occurrence of weed and cereal pollen. Collectively, this evidence is traditionally associated with the initiation and development of farming. It is suggested that elms preferred good soils. Such soils would have been attractive to the early farmers, leading to elm clearance. The opening of the forest would also have

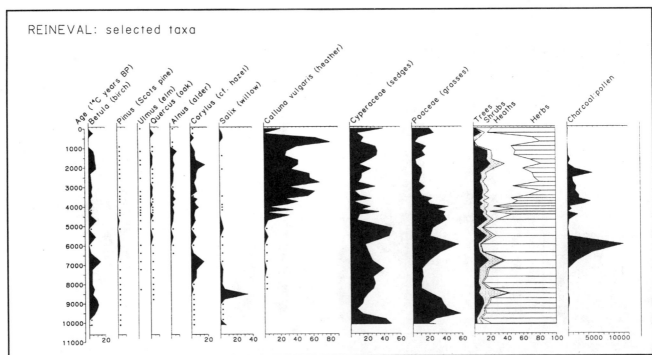

Figure 11.4 Pollen and charcoal diagram from Reineval, South Uist, showing selected taxa only and based on a percentage land pollen count; • signifies < 2%.

132

encouraged the spread of the disease-carrying beetles. That explanation is feasible but it does raise another issue, that of whether the first farming did occur at the time of the elm decline.

At an increasing number of sites, including Rhoin Farm, Kintyre, and Moorlands, Arran, pollen analyses have shown the existence of cereal-type pollen grains from a time previous to the elm decline. Caution must be observed in that such pollen taxa can include the wild, non-cultivated grasses. If, however, the pollen from some of these sites is derived from cereals, then it raises the possibility that arable farming had become established at an earlier date than hitherto considered, perhaps by about 5.8 ka BP, and that it had been adopted by the pre-Neolithic population, or that in-migration of farmers had been an earlier event than has been generally accepted on the basis of dated monuments (Edwards and Whittington, 1997).

Regardless of the exact time of the introduction of farming, it is clear that it had an increasing effect on the woodland cover and hence the appearance of the landscape. Pollen diagrams show that there were alternations of phases of woodland clearance and regeneration. These have been explained by the *landnam* ('land take' in Old Norse) concept whereby cultivators employed a system of shifting cultivation to allow for the recovery of impoverished levels of soil nutrients following upon many years of cereal growing. While there is little doubt that the landscape did show a mosaic of woodland and farmed clearances, it may well be that the *landnam* explanation for this cloaks the reality of the situation. The recovery of the woodland may not indicate the total abandonment and exploitation of such areas. It could be that a forest farming economy existed in which woodland resources were exploited by means of coppicing and the utilisation of leaves from some deciduous tree species for use as cattle fodder, at a time when sown grasses for pasture was an unknown husbandry method. Leaf foddering, in which the leaves and twigs of elm and birch especially were fed to animals, was a common practice until recent times in Norway and is known historically, for instance, from England and Switzerland.

The continuing process of woodland removal and crop cultivation inevitably fostered soil erosion. This is demonstrated by increased inputs of minerogenic material, rich in elements such as sodium, potassium and magnesium, to loch sediments, as at Black Loch in Fife (Whittington *et al.,* 1991); sharp rises in rates of bulk sedimentation, as at Braeroddach Loch, Aberdeenshire (Edwards and Rowntree, 1980); and colluvial deposits, as on the steep hillslopes above Kinloch, Rum (Hirons and Edwards, 1990).

From about 4 ka BP, the forest cover came under sustained attack. Pollen diagrams from all over the country attest to the fact that there must have been a growing human population which led to an ever increasing demand for agricultural land. The representation of the pollen of grasses, cereals and the weeds of cultivation increases at the same time as the tree cover diminishes. Over most of the mainland, the mosaic pattern of woodland cover and farming landscapes did continue, albeit on a reduced scale, well into the later Bronze and Iron ages. In certain areas, especially the Outer Hebrides, Orkney and Shetland, changes to the landscape were more drastic. In these areas, which appear to have been more marginal for tree growth, the depredations of the Neolithic farmers appear to have reduced the landscape to the condition which obtains today. It is possible that these western and northern areas also experienced a wetter and stormier climate which led to increased soil erosion and the widespread initiation or extension of peat growth.

On the mainland, in its western and upland areas in particular, there is extensive evidence of prehistoric settlement and landuse where today there are only peaty heath and mires. The initiation of the peat and its development is still not clearly understood. There is debate as to whether it was a purely natural phenomenon, occurring due to a stronger influence of oceanic tendencies in the climate or whether it was due to human activities. Continued use of the plough does induce compaction in soils, producing what is known as a plough sole. The development of this feature can impede soil drainage and, if cultivation had also decreased the availability of soil nutrients required by many plants, the result may well have been colonisation of the now wetter ground by plants, especially *Sphagnum,* that thrived in mire conditions. The lack of aeration of the ground and its continuing wetness would have prevented the complete decay of plant remains, leading to the initiation of peat and its continued development. Thus large areas of the country went under peat and the landscape in such areas became dominated by wet heathland. Some areas of Scotland became dominated by blanket bog; for example, in Shetland, it provides an almost continuous cover over Yell, the western part of Unst and central and western Mainland. The most extreme example of its development lies in the Flow Country of Sutherland and Caithness - an area of about 400,000 ha of mainly blanket mires (Lindsay *et al.,* 1988). Charman (1992) examined the basal peats from four sites at the Cross Lochs and was unable to demonstrate that any single factor was responsible for the peat formation. The presence of charred remains persuaded him that anthropogenic burning had removed much of the birch woodland cover at least as early as 7.5 ka BP. Subsequent waterlogging may have been a response to the forest clearance or may have been associated with a widespread increase in climatic wetness. Pine woodland, as shown by pine stumps frequently stratified with the blanket peat, was present on a peat surface between 4.5 ka BP and about 3.5 ka BP, after which it declined sharply. Once again, a variety of possible explanations has been advanced to explain this vegetational change, including climatic alteration, podzolization and acid rain deposition (Gear and Huntley, 1991; Blackford *et al.,* 1992; Charman, 1994).

Although there is a widely-held belief that the spread of peat is a relatively recent phenomenon, with inception associated with a downturn in climate at around 2.5 ka BP, radiocarbon dating of the basal layers of blanket peat indicates that its growth is a feature which extends back to at least 9.5 ka BP (Tipping, 1995). The initiation and subsequent stages of development, however, are extremely complex, as is shown by a study on the Monadliath plateau where the Allt na Feithe Sheilich burn has exposed a section through blanket peat (Birks, 1993).

The fact that peat spread may have accelerated during the last few millennia could encourage the assumption that human influences, following the intensification of agriculture, were prominent in originating a peatland cover. Given the possibilities of climatic and natural soil deterioration during this time, separating natural and human causes becomes virtually impossible and a multi-causal explanation may be apposite (Moore, 1993).

11.5 The early Historic period

Pollen diagrams, especially from the eastern parts of the country where a more continental type of climate occurs, show that the decimation of the woodland continued, so that trees would have become more and more restricted to those areas where agriculture was not an attractive option or to which access was difficult. Some pollen diagrams, however, reveal an interesting feature which seems to point not only to the halting of tree removal but to a regeneration of the woodland. At some stage during the latter period of the Roman presence in Britain, pollen evidence suggests that the settled, farming life of eastern Scotland was badly disrupted. Tree and shrub cover increased, cereal pollen disappears from the record and the weeds of cultivation go into a great decline. This was not due to a worsening climate as the Roman period was one of considerable warmth. During the fourth century AD there was increased unrest among the native peoples and it is possible that this reached such a pitch that the Romans mounted a punitive campaign which led to the destruction of habitation and the cessation of farming. This is a feature which needs further research but there can be no doubt that the landscape of Scotland probably north from Fife into Aberdeenshire would have had a very different character from that which had been developing over many previous centuries (Whittington and Edwards, 1993). In contrast to that situation in eastern Scotland, sites located on either side of Hadrian's Wall suggest that woodland clearance preceding the Roman period was maintained during the occupation, supporting, at least, the idea of an economic accommodation between Roman and native.

From the sixth century AD the landscape, even in these eastern areas, showed further changes in the vegetation as farming dominated the countryside. The pollen diagrams show an increase in the importance of arable crops in the east as compared with the west; although the pollen of grass is dominant in all areas, that of the weeds of cultivation and cereals is more prominent in the east. Until the advent of the potato and turnip as field crops, features which lie outside the scope of this chapter, the most striking and surprising addition to the vegetation cover would have been hemp *(Cannabis sativa)*. From about AD 1000 and for some three to four hundred years, it would have been a cultivated crop, used for the production of canvas and ropes (Whittington and Edwards, 1990), a feature which would have given common ground to the Scottish landscape with the rest of northern Europe.

11.6 Conclusion

As the foregoing has shown, and a perusal of journals concerned with publishing articles on the nature of past environments would endorse, recent years have seen a considerable volume of research into, and re-evaluation of, Scotland's landscape during the Holocene. Certain aspects of this have been highlighted here and many of them are in need of further concentrated and directed investigation. The nature, and especially the areal distribution, of any Mesolithic impact on the landscape and the relationship of people with that culture to the new lifestyle introduced by the Neolithic farmers are still poorly understood. The exploitation of fossil charcoal is a major revelation in recent studies of landscape development but its true significance is still rather obscure. The upland areas of the country, now given over to moorland or planted with conifers, reveal widespread traces of former settlement and agricultural activity. Why abandonment of these areas occurred is not clear. It may well be that an increase in rainfall and a lowering of temperatures were the main causes, in combination with agriculturally-induced soil deterioration. Volcanic activity, with associated acid fallout, as much as supposed climatic impact, has also been advanced as having an effect on marginal settlement in these upland areas. Until palaeoenvironmental research focuses more directly upon

climatic change rather than drawing conclusions about it from evidence garnered for other reasons, little progress in this important area will be made. This chapter has shown that there is now a better understanding than previously of Holocene landscapes but much of it relates to restricted areas of the country or is based on inadequate evidence.

References

Bennett, K.D. 1989. A provisional map of forest types for the British Isles 5000 years ago. *Journal of Quaternary Science,* **4,** 141-144.

Birks, H.J.B. 1993. Allt na Feithe Sheilich. In: Gordon, J.E. and Sutherland, D.G. (Eds), *Quaternary of Scotland.* Chapman & Hall, London, 289-292.

Blackford, J.J., Edwards, K.J., Dugmore, A.J., Cook, A.J. and Buckland, P.C. 1992. Icelandic volcanic ash and the mid-Holocene Scots pine *(Pinus sylvestris)* pollen decline in northern Scotland. *The Holocene,* **2,** 260-265.

Charman, D.J. 1992. Blanket mire formation at the Cross Lochs, Sutherland, northern Scotland. *Boreas,* **21,** 53-72.

Charman, D.J. 1994. Late-glacial and Holocene vegetation history of the Flow Country, northern Scotland. *New Phytologist,* **127,** 155-168.

Edwards, K.J. 1990. Fire and the Scottish Mesolithic. In: Vermeersch, P.M. and Van Peer, P. (Eds), *Contributions to the Mesolithic in Europe.* Leuven University Press, Leuven, 71-79.

Edwards, K.J. 1996. A Mesolithic of the Western and Northern Isles of Scotland? Evidence from pollen and charcoal. In: Pollard, T. and Morrison, A. (Eds), *The Early Prehistory of Scotland.* Edinburgh University Press, Edinburgh, 23-38.

Edwards, K.J. and Rowntree, K.M. 1980. Radiocarbon and palaeoenvironmental evidence for changing rates of erosion at a Flandrian stage site in Scotland. In: Cullingford, R.A., Davidson, D.A. and Lewin, J. (Eds), *Timescales in Geomorphology.* Wiley, Chichester, 207-223.

Edwards, K.J. and Whittington, G. 1997. Vegetation change. In: Edwards, K.J. and Ralston, I.B.M. (Eds), *Scotland: Environment and Archaeology, 8000BC-AD1000.* Wiley, Chichester, 63-82.

Fossitt, J.A. 1996. Late Quaternary vegetation history of the Western Isles of Scotland. *New Phytologist,* **132,** 171-196.

Gear, A.J. and Huntley, B. 1991. Rapid changes in the range limits of Scots pine 4000 years ago. *Science,* **241,** 544-547.

Hirons, K.R. and Edwards, K.J. 1990. Pollen and related studies at Kinloch, Isle of Rhum, Scotland, with particular reference to possible early human impacts on vegetation. *New Phytologist,* **116,** 715-727.

Huntley, B. 1993. Rapid early-Holocene migration and high abundance of hazel *(Corylus avellana* L.): alternative hypotheses. In: Chambers, F.M. (Ed.), *Climate Change and Human Impact on the Landscape.* Chapman & Hall, London, 205-215.

Lindsay, R.A., Charman, D.J., Everingham, F., O'Reilly, R., Palmer, M., Rowell, T.A. and Stroud, D.A. 1988. *The Flow Country: the Peatlands of Caithness and Sutherland.* Nature Conservancy Council, Peterborough.

McVean, D.N. and Ratcliffe, D.A. 1962. *Plant Communities of the Scottish Highlands.* HMSO, London.

Moore, P.D. 1993. The origin of blanket mire, revisited. In: Chambers, F.M. (Ed.), *Climate Change and Human Impact on the Landscape.* Chapman & Hall, London, 217-224.

Moore, P.D., Webb, J.A. and Collinson, M.E. 1991. *An Illustrated Guide to Pollen Analysis.* 2nd ed. Blackwell Scientific, Oxford.

Smith, A.G. 1970. The influence of Mesolithic and Neolithic man on British vegetation. In: Walker, D. and West, R.G. (Eds), *Studies in the Vegetational History of the British Isles.* Cambridge University Press, Cambridge, 81-96.

Thompson, D.B.A., Hester, A.J. and Usher, M.B. (Eds) 1995. *Heaths and Moorland: Cultural Landscapes.* HMSO, Edinburgh.

Tipping, R. 1994. The form and fate of Scotland's woodlands. *Proceedings of the Society of Antiquaries of Scotland,* **124,** 1-54.

Tipping, R. 1995. Holocene landscape change at Carn Dubh, near Pitlochry, Perthshire, Scotland. *Journal of Quaternary Science,* **10**, 59-75.

Whittington, G. and Edwards, K.J. 1990. The cultivation and utilisation of hemp in Scotland. *Scottish Geographical Magazine,* **106,** 167-173.

Whittington G. and Edwards, K.J. 1993. *Ubi solitudinem faciunt pacem appelant;* the Romans in Scotland, a palaeoenvironmental contribution. *Britannia,* **24,** 13-25.

Whittington, G. and Edwards, K.J. 1994. Palynology as a predictive tool in archaeology. *Proceedings of the Society of Antiquaries of Scotland,* **124,** 155-171.

Whittington, G., Edwards, K.J. and Cundill, P.R. 1991. Late- and post-glacial vegetational change at Black Loch, Fife, eastern Scotland - a multiple core approach. *New Phytologist,* **118,** 147-166.

Whittington G., Fallick A.E. and Edwards K.J. 1996. Stable oxygen isotope and pollen records from eastern Scotland and a consideration of Late-glacial and early Holocene climate change for Europe. *Journal of Quaternary Science,* **11,** 327-340.

Wickham-Jones, C.R. 1990. *Rhum: Mesolithic and Later Sites at Kinloch. Excavations 1984-1986.* Society of Antiquaries of Scotland, Monograph Series No. 7. Edinburgh.

Smout, T.C. (Ed.) 1993. *Scotland Since Prehistory: Natural Change and Human Impact.* Scottish Cultural Press, Aberdeen.
A mixture of general and more detailed accounts of some of the environmental, prehistoric and historic features of the Scottish landscape.

Further Reading :

Bell, M. and Walker, M.J.C. 1992. *Late Quaternary Environmental Change: Physical and Human Perspectives.* Longman, London.
A good basic text on the environmental and human background to landscape change, with an extensive bibliography; strong on British examples.

Birks, H.H., Birks, H.J.B., Kaland, P.E. and Moe, D. (Eds) 1988. *The Cultural Landscape - Past, Present and Future.* Cambridge University Press, Cambridge.
A research level book which is particularly strong on the use of palynology and anthropogenic contexts, with particular reference to Britain and Scandinavia.

Chambers, F.M. (Ed.) 1993. *Climate Change and Human Impact on the Landscape.* Chapman & Hall, London.
Research level contributions, very much concerned with human-environment interactions and with climate change; strong on British examples.

Edwards, K.J. and Ralston, I.B.M. (Eds) 1997. *Scotland: Environment and Archaeology, 8000BC - AD1000.* Wiley, Chichester.
A comprehensive overview of environmental change in Scotland and a consideration of the archaeological record from the Mesolithic to the early Norse periods.

12. Sea-level Change in Scotland During the Devensian and Holocene

David E. Smith

The key themes covered in this chapter are:

- review of Scottish sea-level studies;
- sea-level changes before the Late Devensian;
- sea-level changes during the Late Devensian;
- Holocene (post-glacial) sea-level changes;
- patterns of coastal evolution

12.1 Introduction

The coastline of Scotland is one of the most varied of any comparable areas in the world. From the great cliffed coastlines of the north to the extensive estuarine areas of the east and south, most types of coastal setting are represented. The main feature of the coastal outline in general is the contrast between the deeply indented fiordland coast of the west and the more regular, open coast

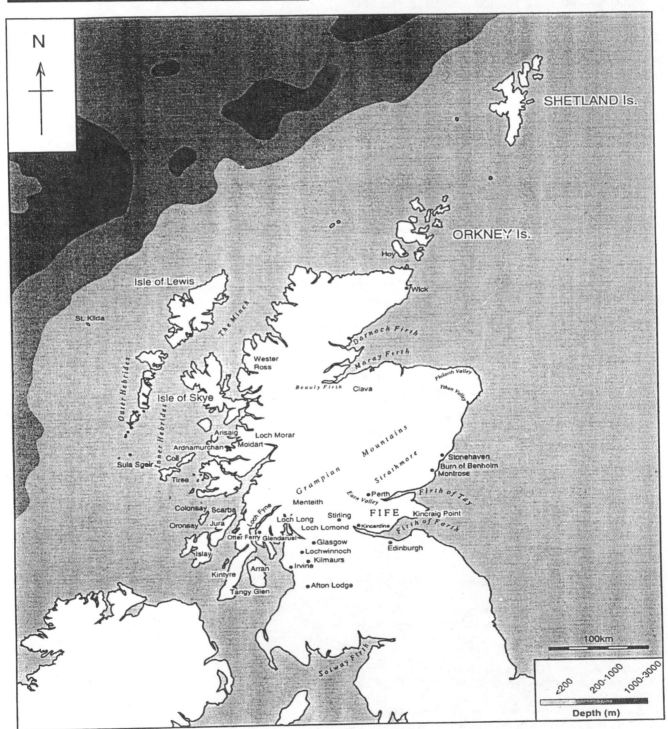

Figure 12.1 The setting of Scotland on the continental shelf and places mentioned in the text.

of the east. This contrast is essentially a product of both the underlying geology (see Chapter 1) and the development of the drainage pattern, modified by repeated glaciation during the Quaternary.

The local detail of the present coastline is, however, the product of sea-level change and associated coastal processes. Surrounded by the shallow waters of the continental shelf off north-west Europe (Figure 12.1), the Scottish coastline has radically changed its position in response to ice sheet growth and decay and associated sea-level changes. An often hostile wind and wave climate regime to the north and west, combined with frequent storm surges in the North Sea to the east, has also ensured that coastal geomorphic processes have been very active, especially on exposed coastlines.

This chapter examines the role of sea-level change which, together with coastal processes, has been largely responsible for the present coastal landscape. It begins with an outline of the concepts, terminology and methodology associated with studies of sea-level change in Scotland, followed by a brief review of the last episodes of glaciation, which had a profound effect on the present form of the coast. The evidence for sea-level change, both during and following glaciation, is then considered. The chapter concludes with some remarks on the effects of sea-level change on coastal evolution.

12.2 Scottish sea-level studies

Scotland has long been a focus of studies of sea-level change, and a number of fundamental concepts in sea-level research were established here. Thus, writing in Edinburgh in 1841, Maclaren (1842) was apparently the first to articulate the concept that the growth and decay of ice sheets would affect global sea levels (**glacio-eustasy**), whilst from field work in eastern Scotland, Jamieson (1865) was the first to outline the concept that glacier growth and decay might cause crustal depression and uplift (**glacio-isostasy**). Later, from studies on the west coast, Wright (1934) first put forward the view that shorelines in a glacio-isostatically uplifted area would be time-transgressive (*i.e.* their age would vary along their length, being oldest towards the centre of uplift where they would have emerged first) (his 'isokinetic theory'). More recently, from work in south-east Scotland, Sissons developed a now widely used methodology for the study of former sea levels in glacio-isostatically affected areas, which has contributed greatly to the present understanding of Scottish sea-level change (*e.g.* Sissons *et al.*, 1966).

Modern studies of sea-level change in Scotland have employed a wide range of techniques, and have involved increasingly detailed investigations both onshore and offshore on the continental shelf. On land, studies now commonly combine both morphological work (*i.e.* based upon studies of landforms) and stratigraphical work (*i.e.* based upon studies of sediments). Morphological studies commonly involve detailed field mapping and survey, both of former shore features and deposits and of related features (*e.g.* river terraces and glacier limits). Altitudes of former shore features are determined from Ordnance Survey Newlyn Datum bench marks and compared to modern analogues. Analysis of the results of the mapping and survey of former shore features normally involves the determination of former shorelines, defined here as comparable former levels of the sea surface at the coast. Shoreline gradients are determined from shoreline altitudes plotted along the most steeply sloping direction (normally towards the area of greatest land uplift), the altitudinal trends defined by linear regression analysis. Patterns of land uplift

indicated by the altitudes of particular shorelines are commonly shown by isobase maps (maps showing lines of equal uplift), increasingly described statistically with the use of trend surface analysis (polynomial regression analysis). Stratigraphical studies now involve detailed descriptions of the sediments (lithostratigraphy), often supported by particle size and geochemical studies as well as analysis of the macrofossil or microfossil content (biostratigraphy). Macrofossil remains include those of both plants and molluscs; microfossil remains include pollen, diatoms, ostracods, foraminifera dinoflagellate cysts and even chironomids (midges). Several stratigraphical studies have involved the technique of investigating isolation basins, relatively small enclosed basins in rock or glacial deposits which were temporarily flooded by rising or falling sea levels and in which marine deposits may therefore be preserved. The records of these basins may be of great value in determining former sea levels.

Beyond the present coastline, detailed morphological and stratigraphical studies on the continental shelf offshore are increasingly providing valuable evidence for former sea levels. In particular, microfossil and geochemical studies of marine sediments from boreholes off both Atlantic and North Sea coasts are providing information on changing sea water salinity, temperature and depth both during and following the last glaciation (see Chapter 7).

Complementing both morphological and stratigraphical work onshore and offshore, absolute dating has been widely undertaken and, in particular, radiocarbon dates now provide a chronological framework for several former Scottish sea levels. In the summary account here, all altitudes are expressed in metres above Ordnance Datum Newlyn, and all dates quoted are in radiocarbon years before present (BP).

Fundamental to an understanding of sea-level change and coastal response in Scotland is the nature of the complex interplay between movements of the land (mainly due to glacio-isostasy) and movements of the surrounding sea surface (mainly due to glacio-eustasy). Thus in reality, sea-level changes in Scotland are **relative** sea-level changes and are highly specific to the Scottish coastline.

12.3 Scottish sea levels and coastal changes in context

Scottish coastal landforms today are to a large extent the product of processes during the Late Quaternary (defined here as the last 125 ka including the last interglacial, last glacial (the Devensian) and present interglacial (the Holocene)). However, by far the majority of the features were formed during the Devensian (mainly the Late Devensian, the period from the *c.* 26-10 ka BP) and Holocene. Many graphs of changes in sea-surface levels have been produced for the Late Devensian and Holocene, and three of these are shown in Figure 12.2. It may be assumed that sea-surface levels around Scotland at this time changed generally in the same timescale and by broadly similar amounts.

The glacio-isostatic component of Scottish sea level change is probably largely attributable to the growth and decay during the Late Devensian of the main ice sheet and possibly of the smaller ice masses during the Loch Lomond Readvance. The main ice sheet is believed to have reached its maximum around 18-22 ka BP, and covered much, if not all, of Scotland (see Chapter 6). Shetland is believed to have had its own ice cap (*e.g.* Flinn, 1978; Peacock and Long, 1994). Ice thickness at the maximum of the main ice sheet is largely unknown, although some of the highest hills on the mainland, Skye and the Outer Hebrides may have stood

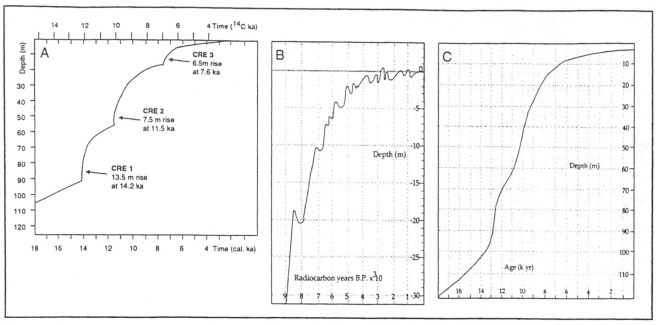

Figure 12.2 Late Devensian and Holocene sea-surface changes according to Blanchon and Shaw (1996) [A], Mörner (1971) [B] and Fairbanks (1989) [C].

out as nunataks (*e.g.* Ballantyne, 1990; Dahl *et al.* 1996). It may be reasonable to assume that the maximum ice surface altitude may not have exceeded *c.* 1500 m and that with the amplitudes of the deepest valleys beneath the ice sometimes approaching 1000 m, the ice may have locally been relatively thin, even near to the centre of the ice sheet. The margins of the main Scottish ice sheet were surrounded by extensive areas of dry land across the adjacent continental shelf (Sejrup *et al.*, 1994); in the east the ice formed a major moraine system, the Wee Bankie Moraine (*e.g.* Thompson and Eden, 1977). As the ice ultimately retreated, stillstands or readvances may have occurred (see Chapters 5 and 6). In Wester Ross, a prominent moraine, the Wester Ross moraine (Robinson and Ballantyne, 1979), probably marks a readvance of the ice sheet there. In the Moray Firth, evidence of a readvance is present at Ardersier, near Inverness (Merritt *et al.*, 1995), whilst near Stirling, Perth and in Strathmore, the ice margin is believed to have stabilised for a time (the Perth stage) (*e.g.* Sissons, 1963). It is difficult to tell whether these limits reflected broader regional or global changes in climate affecting the ice sheet, local meterological effects or the influence of topographic controls and ice sheet dynamics.

By about 13 ka BP, most if not all of the ice sheet had disappeared and an interstadial period of warmer conditions ensued. However, subsequent deterioration in climate resulted in a regrowth of glaciers, the Loch Lomond Readvance, which lasted until about 10 ka BP. The limits of the Loch Lomond Readvance are generally well defined (Chapter 8). It is thought likely that soon after 10 ka BP no glacial ice remained in Scotland. It is not known whether the Loch Lomond Readvance resulted in further glacio-isostatic crustal depression, although it has been suggested that it did (Sutherland, 1981b; Firth, 1984). It seems likely that the land uplift still continuing in Scotland (see Section 12.5.2) is glacio-isostatic in origin.

12.4   Sea-level changes

12.4.1 *Sea levels before the Late Devensian*

Offshore evidence. Beyond the present-day coastline of Scotland, the sea floor contains evidence of former sea levels lower than at present. Off the west coast, Sutherland

(1984b, 1987) described pre-Late Devensian rock platforms at -120 m off St Kilda and -155 m and - 125 m off Sula Sgeir (the -125 m feature may be partly of Late Devensian age). Off the east coast, in the North Sea, evidence has been described for phases of marine erosion (*e.g.* Holmes, 1977) although interpretations differ (see Sissons, 1981). Wingfield (in Plag *et al.*, 1996) has emphasised the erosional potential of lower sea levels, implying that evidence for associated features may be widespread across the continental shelf around Scotland. At a number of locations, glaciomarine deposits (laid down beneath, or in association with, glacier ice terminating in the sea, for example as ice shelves) of pre-Late Devensian age indicate episodes of marine activity across the continental shelf (see Chapter 7), but these have not been linked with particular sea levels.

Onshore evidence. Both stratigraphical and morphological evidence for sea levels higher than present before the Late Devensian has been described from a number of locations around Scotland. Stratigraphical evidence consists either of marine deposits laid down in a range of former coastal environments, overlain by till, or of glaciomarine sediments. Marine deposits overlain by till have been described from the island of Hoy, in the Orkney archipelago, Clava, near Inverness, from the valley of the Burn of Benholm, near Montrose, from Afton Lodge and Kilmaurs in Ayrshire, Tangy Glen in Kintyre and in southern Arran (*e.g.* Gordon and Sutherland, 1993). Many of these deposits occur at levels well above visible raised shore features and Sutherland (1981a) suggests that such high-level marine deposits might have accumulated early in the Devensian, as a Scottish ice sheet extended into high sea surface levels. Such high levels might have occurred because the Scottish ice sheet developed rather earlier than the major ice sheets elsewhere (*i.e.* before sea surface levels had fallen significantly), combined with the fact that isostatic depression of the land was taking place in Scotland as the ice developed. This theory encounters two problems: first, some of the marine deposits occur at altitudes above 200 m, which would require both a very high sea level prior to ice sheet growth and isostatic depression of the crust normally associated with a Scottish ice sheet at its greatest extent; and second, at least some of the marine deposits may in reality have been transported to their present location as frozen monoliths by glacial action. The latter explanation has been advanced for the Clava deposit (Merritt, 1992). Resolution of the argument must await further study of the deposits involved, including absolute dating, although some support for Sutherland's hypothesis has been provided by Benn and Dawson (1987) who describe ice-proximal glaciomarine deposits up to 70m on Islay, assigning them to an age earlier than the Late Devensian (A.G. Dawson, pers. comm.).

Morphological evidence for sea levels higher than present before the Late Devensian comes almost exclusively from the west coast of mainland Scotland, and largely consists of elements of the coastal rock platform sequence first studied by Wright (1911) and more recently investigated by McCann (1968), Gray (1978), Sissons (1981, 1982), Dawson (1980a, 1980b, 1994) and others. Evidence for a surface cut prior to the last glaciation in Tiree and Coll, analogous with the Norwegian strandflat, has been described by Dawson (1994). Since the surface slopes downwards to the west, it is concluded that it was developed during an episode or episodes of glaciation in Scotland, and subsequently uplifted glacio-isostatically. Dawson (1980b) has also described an intertidal rock platform on Jura, Islay, Colonsay and Oronsay at altitudes of between 0 and 2 m, which he termed the Low Rock Platform. He suggested that the feature is interglacial in age, because it shows evidence of having been glaciated (and thus must have been formed before the last ice occupied the area), and its altitude shows no regional gradient, thus indicating that it must have been formed when little or no ice occupied Scotland. At higher altitudes, it seems likely that the Main Rock Platform and High Rock Platform (discussed below) are in part composite features, elements of them having been produced before the Late Devensian (*e.g.* Sissons, 1981; Dawson, 1984).

Amongst the few depositional features which may have formed before the Late Devensian is a raised beach along a 7 km stretch of coastline in north-west Lewis (Sutherland and Walker, 1984). This overlies a peat with an interglacial pollen spectrum, although the age of the raised beach is unknown.

12.4.2 Late Devensian sea levels

Most features and deposits related to sea-level change along the Scottish coastline date from the Late Devensian and Holocene. The Late Devensian was a time of enhanced erosional and depositional processes in Scotland, which left evidence for changing sea levels around the Scottish coast. The pattern of sea-level change during the Late Devensian probably began with low sea levels on the continental shelf well beyond the maximum limit of the ice sheet, then as the ice receded, rising sea levels advanced across the shelf to invade the margins of the present land area which was still recovering from its ice load. Evidence for sea-level change at this time can thus be found in both offshore and onshore locations.

Offshore evidence. To the west of Scotland, sea floor sediments record the invasion of marine waters across the continental shelf as the Late Devensian ice sheet disintegrated, although no shorelines have so far been identified. For example, from a study of two cores from south of St Kilda, in areas where the sea bed today lies at c. - 150 m, Peacock *et al.* (1992) concluded that by 13 ka BP, water depths there had attained -40 m, a view supported by Lambeck (1995). From further study of these cores and others in the same area, Austin and Kroon (1996) maintained that the area had already been occupied by cold, low salinity

water by c. 15.2 ka BP but that by c. 13 ka BP the seas there had become much warmer. These and other studies west of the Outer Hebrides and in The Minch and the Sea of the Hebrides document a rapid break-up of ice and invasion by the sea from about 22 ka BP to about 13 ka BP.

In the North Sea, invasions of the sea, following the recession of the Scandinavian and Scottish ice sheets (Sejrup *et al.*, 1994), are recorded in several boreholes. Thus, from an examination of cores from the Viking Bank, east of Shetland, Peacock (1995) concluded that before 15.5 ka BP sea levels may have been below -140 m, whilst between 15.5 ka BP and 13.6 ka BP, sea levels lay at more than -100 m to -110 m. By, or shortly after, 12 ka BP, sea levels had risen to between -80 m and -100 m. A surface of marine planation between -60 m and -100 m, possibly related to the Late Devensian glacial maximum, has been reported from offshore beneath the North Sea, to the west of the Wee Bankie Moraine (Holmes, 1977). West of the Wee Bankie Moraine, the St Abbs Beds (Thompson and Eden, 1977), probably glaciomarine sediments, record the invasion of the sea to within the former Late Devensian ice limit.

Onshore evidence. Onshore, evidence for Late Devensian sea levels consists of both areas of sediments, normally without any apparent morphology, and terraces, the latter both erosional and depositional. This evidence is particularly well displayed on the east and west coasts of the Scottish mainland.

The east coast

On the east coast, some of the earlier marine deposits from this period may include the 'red clays' of north-east Scotland, first studied by Jamieson (1874). These deposits can be seen to rest upon glaciofluvial deposits apparently produced during ice decay, and thus may post-date, or be contemporary with, the retreat of the ice sheet in the area. Their marine origin is supported by the presence of marine fossils within the deposits, and, occurring up to at least 70 m, 'the red clays' may relate to an early invasion of the sea as the ice sheet decayed. However, the fossils are not *in situ* and the deposits are complex. Their age is uncertain. Alternative origins are possible and further study is awaited. Further south in eastern Scotland, near Montrose and around the Firths of Tay and Forth, a distinctive deposit of reddish clays, silts and sands known as the Errol Beds (Peacock, 1975) occurs widely up to 40 m. These glaciomarine deposits contain a mid- to high-arctic fauna and are believed to have accumulated in the same rising sea levels as the St Abbs Beds offshore. Glaciomarine silts near St Fergus, in north east Scotland, dated at 15,320 ± 200 BP (Hall and Jarvis, 1989) may be a local equivalent of the Errol Beds (Boulton *et al.*, 1991). Given the spatial extent of Errol Beds, it seems likely that they vary greatly in age, being related to different ice limits in different areas and probably to the different shorelines in the shoreline sequences described below. This view is implied in the age range normally assigned to them, of between 18 ka and 13 ka BP (*e.g.* Boulton *et al.*, 1991).

Arguably the earliest unequivocal evidence of shorelines indicating sea levels associated with ice-sheet decay on the east coast can be found further south, between Stonehaven and the Firth of Forth. Here, at least eight raised shorelines have been identified by Cullingford and Smith (1980) sloping eastwards along the valleys and estuaries of the coastal margins of this area (Figure 12.3D). These shorelines are marked by generally narrow (less than 100 m wide) terraces of sand and gravel occurring up to 40 m, occasionally with shell fragments, often eastward

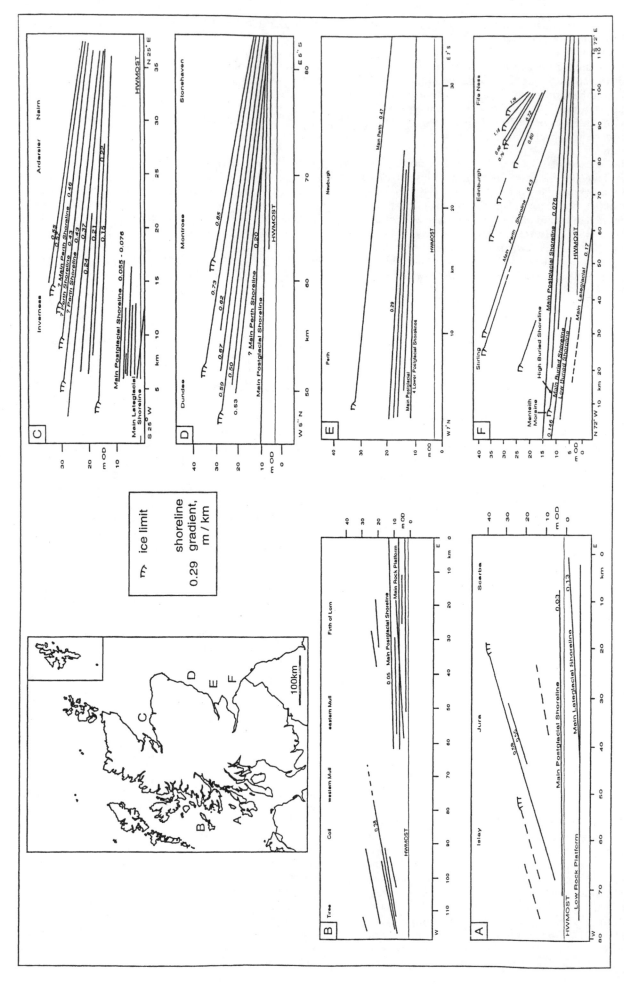

Figure 12.3 Shoreline diagram for six Scottish coastal areas. **A.** Jura, Scarba and Islay (after Dawson, 1984); **B.** Tiree and Coll (after Dawson, 1994) and Mull (after Gray, 1974); **C.** the inner Moray Firth, (after Firth, 1989 and Firth and Haggart, 1989); **D.** Dundee to Stonehaven (after Cullingford and Smith, 1980); **E.** the Firth of Tay (after Cullingford. 1977); **F.** the Firth of Forth (after Smith, 1965 and Sissons et al., 1966).

Figure 12.4 Late Devensian raised shoreline terraces at Kincraig Point, Fife. The shorelines are erosional features cut into volcanic agglomerate. (Photo: C.J. MacFadyen).

continuations of glacial outwash terraces which rise up to the west. Each shoreline slopes less steeply eastward than the one above and penetrates further westward, indicating a broadly continuous pattern of ice retreat. The higher terraces of the well known sequence at Kincraig Point, in Fife, belong to this time (Figure 12.4).

In the south of this area, the later retreat of the ice margin is recorded along the inland reaches of the Forth and Tay estuaries. Here, the most prominent shore features are the terraces associated with shorelines related to former ice limits near Stirling and Perth (*e.g.* Sissons *et al.,* 1966). Along the shores of both the Firth of Forth and Firth of Tay, these shorelines slope down towards the east, the higher shorelines sloping more steeply than those below them. In the Forth (Figure 12.3F), the highest shoreline can be traced as far west as Kincardine, where it merges with an outwash terrace formed close to an ice limit. Below this shoreline, a second continues westwards towards Stirling, where it too ends in outwash, and below this a third shoreline also terminates at Stirling. It is estimated that whilst ice occupied the Forth Valley west of Stirling, the relative level of the sea at Stirling fell from 38 m (the altitude of the second of the three shorelines) to 20 m (the altitude of the lowest), a fall in the marine limit of 18 m as the land recovered from ice loading. In the Tay, several shorelines are recognised (Figure 12.3E) but the highest is particularly prominent, merging with outwash terraces in the lower Earn valley at 33 m. Beyond the westward limit of these prominent shorelines in the Forth and Tay valleys, lower shorelines probably related to this period occur, but the outwash-related limits referred to above are taken as evidence of significant pauses in the retreat of the ice. They may not, however, be climatically related since they occur at significant constrictions in both valleys, where the retreating ice margin may have been

pinned for a time. After this research was undertaken, discoveries of foraminifera (indicating marine conditions) were made in deposits occurring as high, or even higher, than the highest shoreline in both valleys, and lying west of the westward limit of the highest shoreline, questioning the view that substantial drops in the marine limit may have occurred (Browne *et al.,* 1981). However the foraminifera concerned are sparse and there is no supporting evidence that the deposits in which they occur are *in situ,* or are even of Late Devensian age. With the absence of corroborating evidence, this discovery is considered of doubtful value at the present time (Smith and Cullingford, 1982).

In the Moray Firth, Merritt *et al.* (1995) have identified a complex pattern of ice decay and shoreline change following the maximum of the Late Devensian, which in general terms is similar to that in south-east Scotland. Here, deglaciation involved several phases of rapid ice retreat to pinning points as calving took place in a rising sea level. Each phase of retreat was followed by stillstands or minor advances of the ice stream. As the ice initially withdrew, glaciomarine sediments accumulated up to at least 40 m in the Ardersier-Inverness area. Subsequently, relative sea level fell and the ice readvanced to form a moraine at Ardersier, but later relative sea level rose and reached 46 m at Inverness. The subsequent fall saw 10 shorelines forming (Figure 12.3C), the third highest of which has been correlated with the Main Perth Shoreline in south-east Scotland (Firth, 1989).

In south-east Scotland, the sequence of falling sea levels through the Late Devensian is continued in the development of a widespread buried surface, known in the Forth estuary as the Buried Gravel Layer (Sissons, 1969). This feature, which reaches up to 2 m and slopes eastward at 0.14 m/km there (Figure 12.3F) is buried beneath later sediments but is believed to represent a significant period of marine erosion,

Figure 12.5 The High Rock Platform on the northern coast of Islay. The lower Main Rock Platform is also clearly developed. (Photo: J.E. Gordon).

perhaps during the Loch Lomond Readvance (Sissons, 1969, 1974b). A similar feature has been found in the Tay estuary (Cullingford, 1977).

The west coast

On the west coast, some of the most distinctive raised marine features are the high-level rock platforms which occur widely in the Inner Hebrides at altitudes of between 18 m and 51 m (Figure 12.5). However, these are regarded as composite features and, although some may have been occupied and even extended during the Late Devensian, most, if not all, owe their origin at least in part to processes associated with earlier sea levels.

Dawson (1984) provides a valuable review of relative sea levels associated with ice sheet deglaciation on the west coast. He remarks that the shorelines which have been identified slope upwards towards the former ice sheet centre and therefore downwards in general terms towards the west. No shorelines from this period are identified from the Outer Hebrides, perhaps because that area was occupied by ice at the Late Devensian maximum and may have maintained a separate ice cap for a time as calving in The Minch disrupted the continuity of the ice sheet while sea levels rose (Sissons, 1980).

Shorelines formed during ice sheet deglaciation on the west coast are, like those on the east coast, represented by terraces of sand and gravel, often fragmentary, their distribution determined by the vagaries of sediment supply and coastal configuration. Some of the earliest are found on Islay and Jura. On Islay, the earliest shoreline terminates eastward at the Central Islay Moraine, where a fall in the marine limit of *c.* 12 m occurs, whilst on Jura a slightly later

shoreline is found at a lower altitude. Both these shorelines appear to relate to a Late Devensian ice sheet which reached a limit across these two islands. The gradients of these shorelines are similar to those of the highest shoreline in East Fife (Dawson 1982) (Figure 12.3A).

After the lower shoreline of this period on Jura had been reached, falling relative sea levels are recorded in a spectacular array of largely unvegetated beach ridges along the west coasts of Islay and Jura (Figure 12.6). In Jura, at one location a sequence of 55 such ridges occurs, the highest at *c.* 36 m and the lowest at 16 m. In this sequence, a large shingle ridge, the Colonsay Ridge at 19-20 m, may mark a prolonged halt in the falling sea level or possibly a Late Devensian transgression (Dawson, 1982).

To the north-west, Sissons and Dawson (1979) have described sea levels associated with the Wester Ross Readvance of the ice sheet. This limit is recorded by a clear end moraine, unlike ice limits of this time variously identified in the Moray Firth and in south-east Scotland. The shoreline associated with this limit has a gradient of 0.33-0.39 m/km and reaches a height of 24 m; it has been suggested that this might equate to the Main Perth Shoreline in south-east Scotland. Further south, the marine limit reaches 27 m in Moidart and 41 m in Ardnamurchan. In the south-west Highlands at least seven Late Devensian shorelines associated with ice sheet retreat have been identified by Sutherland (1981b), the most prominent of them being correlated with the Main Perth Shoreline. In these areas, drops in the marine limit have been identified at former ice margins at Otter Ferry (16 m), Glendaruel (22 m), Loch Long (26 m), Loch Morar (11 m), and Arisaig (23 m). They may be due to ice sheet readvance, but they may equally reflect stabilisation of the retreating ice margin as it became

Figure 12.6 Late Devensian shingle beach ridges, Jura. (Photo: D.E. Smith).

pinned at valley constrictions or rock bars. A summary shoreline diagram for the area between Tiree, Coll and Mull is given in Figure 12.3B.

For the Clyde estuary a clear pattern of Late Devensian sea-level change has yet to emerge. The topography of the area, with a major valley (the Clyde) draining towards the possible ice sheet centre and a major gap (the Lochwinnoch gap) lying between the Clyde valley and the Ayrshire coast, may have introduced complications into the pattern of deglaciation. Incursion of the sea into the area as deglaciation proceeded is uncertain, some authors believing that the sea invaded the area through the Lochwinnoch gap, others maintaining that flooding proceeded along the Clyde estuary. The highest Late Devensian raised shorelines appear to reach 25-26 m in the Glasgow area and *c.* 24 m at Irvine, south of the Lochwinnoch gap. These features lie well below

ice-dammed lake deposits which reach *c.* 90 m east of Glasgow. This is the main area of the Clyde Beds (Peacock, 1981), greyish-brown clayey silts and sands which occur up to 35 m around the Clyde estuary, and at several locations in Kintyre and Argyll. These deposits, like the Errol Beds, do not normally form topographic features. They probably began forming before 13 ka BP as rising sea levels invaded the land and had probably ceased to accumulate after *c.* 12 ka BP. They contain diverse faunas of a broadly arctic to boreal habitat, and are probably associated with a range of sea levels. The environment indicated is thus complex, but generally the Clyde Beds are thought to reflect a milder climate than the Errol Beds (*e.g.* Sutherland, 1984a).

As with the east coast, relatively few absolute dates are available for the shoreline sequences identified on the west coast. However, recently Shennan *et al.* (1994, 1995) have

Figure 12.7 Carselands of the Main Postglacial Shoreline in the Forth valley, near Stirling. (Photo: D.E. Smith).

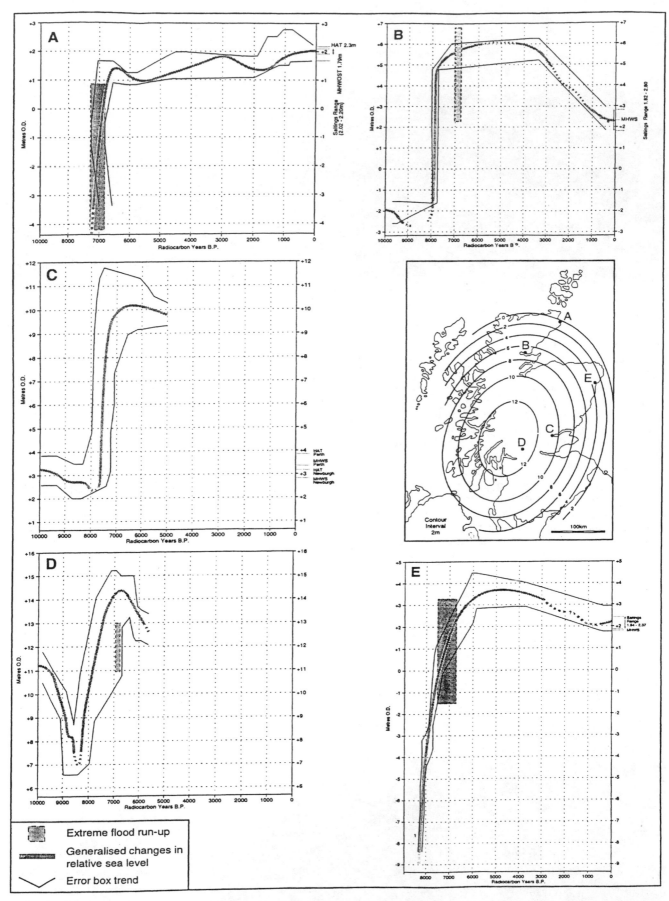

Figure 12.8 Graphs of Holocene relative sea level change. **A.** Wick (after Dawson and Smith, 1997); **B.** the Dornoch Firth (after Smith *et al.,* 1992); **C.** the Earn-Tay confluence (after Cullingford *et al.,* 1980 and Smith *et al.,* 1985b); **D.** the Forth valley (after Robinson, 1993); **E.** the Ythan estuary (after Smith *et al.,* in press). For an explanation of the construction of the graphs, see Dawson and Smith (1997). Isobase map for the Main Postglacial Shoreline after Firth *et al.* (1993).

144

Figure 12.9 Section showing the Storegga tsunami deposit (the lighter layer above the blade of the spade) at Maryton, near Montrose. (Photo: R.E. Cullingford).

dated the fall of the sea level towards the end of the Late Devensian at a number of locations using isolation basin deposits. They identified an apparently continuous fall in sea level in that area between *c.* 12 - 10 ka BP.

Over large areas of the west coast and adjacent Inner Hebridean islands a well developed rock platform is found at lower altitudes than the high-level rock platform fragments, but above the intertidal Low Rock Platform. This has been called the Main Rock Platform (Gray, 1974). It reaches an altitude of *c.* 10-11 m in the Oban area, declining westward, south-westward and southward at up to 0.16 m/km (see Chapter 8). Its formation has been attributed to wave action assisted by freeze-thaw during the Loch Lomond Stadial (Sissons, 1974b; Dawson, 1980). Sissons (1974b) equated this feature with the Buried Gravel Layer on the east coast, and named it the Main Lateglacial Shoreline.

12.4.3 Holocene sea levels

It is not known how far, or even whether, sea levels fell after they had reached the Main Lateglacial Shoreline, but the subsequent record of sea-level change at the end of the Loch Lomond Stadial and through the succeeding Holocene is one of extensive sediment accumulation in rising sea levels. The most complete record comes from the western Forth valley and was largely determined by Sissons and co-workers (*e.g.* Sissons *et al.,* 1966). In this area, the earliest events involve the accumulation of estuarine sediments across outwash associated with the Loch Lomond

Readvance limit there, the Menteith Moraine. A 'High Buried Beach', lying up to 13 m, occurs down-valley from the moraine and across some higher outwash deposits. Based upon its distribution and relationship to underlying deposits, Sissons maintained that it formed after sea levels rose across the outwash and whilst ice still remained at the moraine. Below this feature, a 'Main Buried Beach', occurring up to 11 m on lower outwash deposits and within the moraine, represents a fall in sea levels from the High Buried Beach after ice had retreated from the moraine and consequent flooding of areas within the moraine. A still lower feature, the 'Low Buried Beach', occurring up to 8 m, records the continued fall of sea level. As sea levels fell during this episode, peat began to accumulate widely across the buried beach surfaces revealed. Radiocarbon dating, supported by microfossil analyses, places the withdrawal of the sea from the Main and Low buried beaches at *c.* 9.3-9.6 ka BP and 8.8 ka BP, respectively (*e.g.* Robinson, 1993). After a continued fall in sea level to levels as yet unknown, a relatively rapid rise ensued, carrying levels to *c.* 15 m at the head of the valley, during which time the estuarine sediments of the carselands (Figure 12.7) accumulated across the underlying peat. At two locations peat accumulation persisted as islands of peat developed (Sissons and Smith, 1965), and along the valley sides peat accumulation also kept pace with the rising sea levels. Subsequently, sea level fell probably in stages (Smith, 1968) to reveal the carselands as areas of former estuarine mudflats and allow the widespread accumulation of surface peat, the clearance of which during the eighteenth and nineteenth centuries to reveal the present carseland landscape is well documented.

The sequence of events identified in the western Forth valley has been implicitly used as a model for studies of Holocene sea-level changes in other areas of Scotland. Thus on the east coast, elements of the sequence described above are claimed to have been identified in East Fife and the Tay valley (*e.g.* Morrison *et al.,* 1981), the Montrose Basin (Smith and Cullingford, 1985), the Ythan valley (Smith *et al.,* 1983), the Philorth valley (Smith *et al.,* 1982), the Beauly Firth (Haggart, 1987) the inner Moray Firth (Firth, 1989) and the Dornoch Firth (Smith *et al.,* 1992).

Local equivalents of the Main Buried Beach have been reported from the Beauly Firth (Haggart, 1986) and the Dornoch Firth (Smith *et al.,* 1992), and both the Main and Low buried beaches have been reported from the Tay estuary (Cullingford *et al.,* 1980). Evidence for local equivalents of the highest Holocene raised shoreline in the Forth valley have been reported from East Fife, where it reaches 7 m, and the Tay valley (11 m) (Morrison *et al.,* 1981), the Montrose Basin (7 m) (Smith and Cullingford, 1985), the Ythan Estuary (4 m) (Smith *et al.,* 1983), the Philorth valley (1.5 m) (Smith *et al.,* 1982), the inner Moray Firth (10 m) (Firth and Haggart, 1989), the Wick River valley (1.5 m) (Dawson and Smith, 1997), the Loch Long-Loch Fyne area (*c.* 12 m) (Sutherland 1981b), Islay, Jura and Scarba (5 m) (Dawson, 1983), the Solway Firth (*c.* 9m) (Jardine, 1975, 1980) and a number of other areas. In addition, one or more lower shorelines below the highest Holocene raised shoreline have been reported from the Tay estuary, the Montrose Basin, the Ythan estuary, the inner Moray Firth, the Dornoch Firth, the Loch Long-Loch Fyne area and the Solway Firth in the studies cited above. Interestingly, no equivalents of the buried beach sequence have been claimed for the west coast (Dawson, 1984), and from detailed studies of several isolation basins on the west coast, Shennan *et al.* (1993) failed to find any evidence for an early Holocene marine transgression. They therefore questioned whether such an event took place. Plainly, the

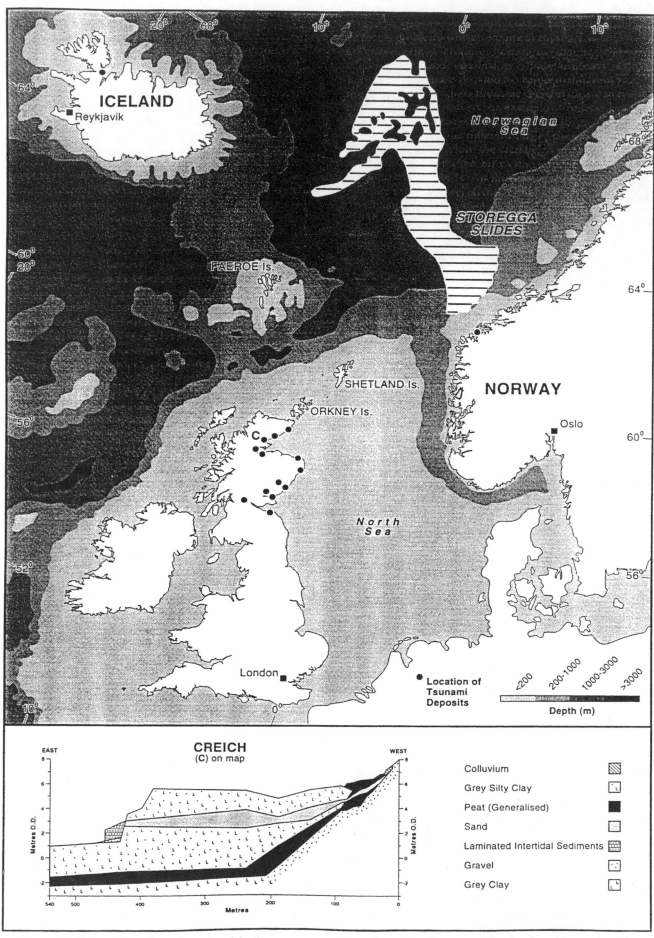

Figure 12.10 Locations where deposits of the Storegga tsunami have been found in eastern Scotland, and its stratigraphy at a typical site.

observations of Shennan *et al.* are at variance with those of Sissons *et al.* (1966) at the head of the Forth valley, where the sedimentological evidence of the silty fine sands of the High and Main buried beaches resting upon glacial outwash is cited as evidence there of an early Holocene transgression. Thus either the sea level record for the west coast at the time of the buried beaches is different to that of the east coast, or else the observations of Shennan *et al.* or of those who have worked in the western Forth valley are incorrect. Clearly, more research needs to be undertaken to solve this interesting problem.

There is no disagreement on the transgression which followed the accumulation of peat on the buried beach surfaces. This event is known as the Main Postglacial Transgression (Sissons, 1974a), and the shoreline reached at its culmination, the Main Postglacial Shoreline (Sissons *et al.*, 1966). A number of graphs of sea level change during the Holocene in Scotland document the evidence (Figure 12.8). The transgression was probably under way by *c.* 8.5 ka BP and had ended by *c.* 6 ka BP. Smith *et al.* (1983) maintained that the culmination occurred increasingly later in sites where the Main Postglacial Shoreline is lower (towards the periphery of the uplifted area), thus supporting the 'isokinetic theory' of Wright (1934) that such shorelines should be time-transgressive.

Recent work has provided information on sea-level change in Scotland since the culmination of the Main Postglacial Transgression. This is illustrated in a comparison of the graphs in Figure 12.8. In the areas most strongly uplifted, such as the Forth and Tay (D, C, Figure 12.8), the culmination is followed by a distinct fall and the record is unavailable for more recent times than *c.* 5ka BP. In areas less strongly uplifted, such as the Ythan and Dornoch Firth (E, B, Figure 12.8), more recent dates suggest that sea levels stood at the maximum for longer, possibly to as late as *c.* 4 ka BP, before falling, and in areas nearer the edge of the uplifted area, such as Wick (A, Figure 12.8) several fluctuations are present. Such progressive changes reflect the registration of minor sea level fluctuations in areas where glacio-isostatic uplift is less strong. They also indicate that large areas of the carselands were probably occupied by the sea long after the culmination of the transgression had occurred, an observation supported by the presence of several levels in the large carseland areas. It is also interesting to note that in areas where glacio-isostatic uplift was relatively slight, later fluctuations reached higher levels than those attained at the culmination, as for example at Wick (see above, Figure 12.8).

As the Main Postglacial Transgression took place, a number of locations along the east coast were inundated by a high energy flood. At sites in sheltered or estuarine areas a thin (up to *c.* 70 cm) layer of silty sand occurs within the estuarine silty clays, normally those which form the carselands (Figure 12.9). The layer is persistent over large areas and can be seen within valley side peat. Its stratigraphical context and distribution are shown in Figure 12.10. Radiocarbon dates for peat directly below and above the layer cluster around 7 ka B.P. The state of preservation of the microfossils indicates turbulent water, and the particle size profile consistently fines upwards, often in several sequences. Originally thought to have been accumulated following a storm surge (Smith *et al.,* 1985a), the deposits have recently been interpreted as having been laid down following a tsunami generated by one of the world's largest submarine slides on the continental slope off south-west Norway (*e.g.* Dawson *et al.,* 1988). Corroborating evidence has recently been found along the Norwegian coast (*e.g.* Bondevik, 1996) and Icelandic coast (Hansom and Briggs,

1991), whilst studies of contemporary tsunami deposits support the present interpretation for the Scottish sites (Shi, 1995).

12.4.4 *Patterns of crustal uplift*

Both observational and theoretical studies have been undertaken to determine the pattern of crustal uplift indicated by the morphological and stratigraphical evidence summarised above. Taking into account the general pattern of ice cover over Scotland during the last glaciation and with the benefit of studies elsewhere, it is assumed that shorelines reached and subsequently uplifted during the Late Devensian and Holocene reflect a broad dome-like pattern of uplift, the centre located over the southern Grampians where ice is thought to have been thickest. Maps showing the possible general pattern of uplift were produced by a number of early writers, but the first map based upon measured altitudes was that of Sissons (1967) for uplift following the Main Postglacial Shoreline. Sissons' map, however, was only based upon isobases interpolated by eye. Trend surface analysis was subsequently employed to describe the distribution of altitudes for particular shorelines. Thus, isobases for the Main Perth Shoreline were produced by Smith *et al.* (1969), and for the Main Lateglacial Shoreline by Gray (1978). More recently, isobases for the Main Postglacial Shoreline were produced for eastern Scotland by Cullingford *et al.* (1991) and for Scotland as a whole by Firth *et al.* (1993) (Figure 12.8). Some authors have claimed that comparisons of isobase maps for different shorelines may indicate changes in the centre of uplift or in the pattern of uplift between shorelines (*e.g.* Gray, 1983). However, such conclusions are probably premature because it now seems likely that the isobase maps so far produced are in need of further refinement. Thus, from isolation basin studies, Shennan *et al.* (1993) identified discrepancies of up to 4 m between Sissons' (1983) predicted altitudes for the Main Postglacial Shoreline in parts of western Scotland and the observed altitude of the marine limit associated with the shoreline. In the context of these results, theoretical studies of crustal uplift for Scotland have been undertaken by Lambeck (*e.g.* 1993), based upon possible ice extent and thickness, water loading on the nearby continental shelf and characteristics of the sub-crust, and are largely driven by geophysical considerations, although they are modified by reported shoreline altitudes. Lambeck produced isobase maps for uplift for successive periods following the start of deglaciation. Such maps provide a good general indication of uplift, but lack the detail given by those based entirely upon measured altitudes.

The broad patterns of crustal movement from which the raised shorelines around Scottish coasts were produced are thus becoming known, although much detail remains to be determined, whatever method is being used. Thus the role of non-uniform uplift, in which the crust moves in sections bounded by fault lines, is not known. Observations by Sissons (1972) in the Forth valley demonstrate that this may be a locally important feature of the uplift pattern.

12.5 Coastal evolution

The events of the Late Quaternary are the latest act in the story of the evolution of the coastline of Scotland. The fluctuating growth and decay of the glaciers and ice sheets of the Devensian glaciation was accompanied by the transport of large quantities of sediment towards and beyond the present coastline, there to be reworked during changing relative sea levels. Beyond the coast, the sea surface, having attained levels during the last interglacial equal to, or perhaps higher than, present levels, and having fallen to at least 140 m below present during the Devensian, subsequently rose

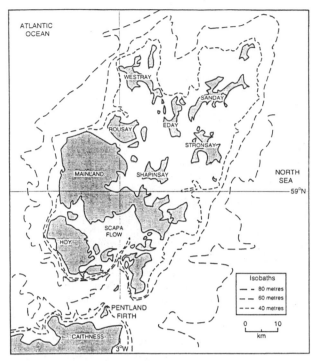

Figure 12.11 Orkney, showing offshore bathymetry in metres.

rapidly towards the present, and is in fact still rising today. These events have had a profound effect upon the evolution of the present coastline.

12.5.1 Devensian coastal change

Pre-Late Devensian coastal deposits are scarce and landforms equivocal, and the present coastal landscape of Scotland owes much to the Late Devensian glaciation and the associated changes in land and sea levels. As the main Late Devensian ice sheet decayed, and surrounding sea-surface levels rose, differential glacio-isostatic uplift carried areas near the former ice centre above the rising sea surface but allowed more peripheral areas to be flooded. Thus, extensive coastal progradation (extension) occurred along the east coast from the Dornoch Firth to Dunbar, and along the west coast from Skye to the Solway Firth, whilst the north of Scotland, the Outer Hebrides and the Northern Isles suffered widespread inundation and coastline retreat (*e.g.* Ritchie, 1966). In addition, the accumulation of glacial and glaciofluvial sediments nearer to the centre of the decaying ice sheet, especially following the Perth Stage in central Scotland (Sissons, 1963), enabled the coastline to be further extended, and provided sediments to be reworked into terraces marking the many raised shorelines of this time. It is possible that many of the shoreline terraces formed during the Late Devensian accumulated over very short periods of time, and were virtually synchronous, rather than time-transgressive, because of the rapid supply of sediment.

Notwithstanding the importance of coastal depositional activity during the Late Devensian, erosional activity may have been significant even in areas experiencing relative sea-level fall. Thus, on the west coast, shore erosion accelerated by frost action during both the Dimlington Stadial and the Loch Lomond Stadial may have had a significant effect on coastal retreat, whilst elsewhere, and particularly in areas being flooded (notably along the north coast), erosion of the newly-deposited glacial and glaciofluvial sediments may have been marked. Overall, the Late Devensian was probably a time of rapid coastal change.

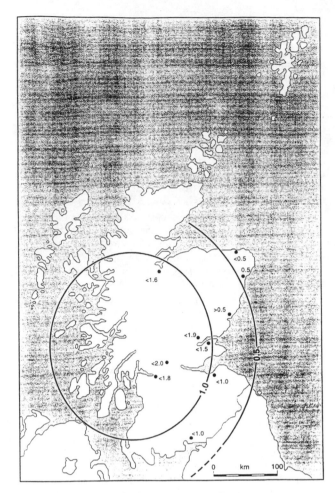

Figure 12.12 Estimated current rates of crustal movement in Scotland in mm/yr. (After Shennan, 1989).

12.5.2 Holocene coastal change

The further evolution of the Scottish coastline during the Holocene reflected the interaction between glacio-isostasy, sea surface change and the supply of sediment to the coast. In areas where a relative uplift of the land continued (nearer to the centre of glacio-isostatic uplift) and where sediments were abundantly available, widespread coastal progradation occurred. Such coastal extension is most notable in the carselands, where perhaps 1,000 km^2 have been added to the Scottish coastline since *c.* 6 ka BP, but it is also evident in the formation of a range of raised coastal depositional features, including the raised spits and forelands along the Moray Firth coast (Ogilvie, 1923; Firth *et al.,* 1995).

In many coastal areas where sediments are abundant, widespread dune areas, including the machair of NW Scotland and the Hebrides, developed during the Holocene (Mather and Ritchie, 1977; Ritchie, 1979). The origins of the sediments are varied, but many were originally derived from Late Devensian glacial and glaciofluvial deposits or from Late Devensian marine deposits previously exposed during lower sea levels at the start of the Holocene.

In areas peripheral to the centre of glacio-isostatic uplift, inundation continued during the Holocene. Extensive drowned landscapes developed, most notably in parts of the Outer Hebrides (*e.g.* Ritchie, 1966, 1985) and in the Northern Isles. Orkney probably consisted of only one island less than 10 ka ago since, even allowing for possible isostatic effects, it seems likely that sea levels there lay somewhere near the 40 m isobath at that time (Figure 12.11).

At present, the sea surface around Scotland is probably rising by c. 1.5 mm per year. Tide gauge records imply that against this sea surface, the land may be rising by about 2 mm per year near the centre of glacio-isostatic uplift, but that the sea surface is rising against the land in peripheral areas (see Figure 12.12). It seems likely that if the sea surface rise continues in the foreseeable future, increasing areas of the Scottish coastline will experience a rise in relative sea levels as the area of glacio-isostatic uplift contracts. However, future coastal change may not involve coastal recession everywhere, since the abundant sediments delivered to the coast during deglaciation may yet be further reworked to mitigate this problem.

12.6 Conclusion

The form of the present coastline of Scotland is the result of a complex interplay of geological factors and geomorphological processes. In particular, the effects of glaciation and changes in the relative levels of the land and sea during the Quaternary have added significantly to the diversity of coastal forms. Erosional processes associated with sea-level change and different climatic conditions have produced distinctive rock platforms along the west coast, and may well have accelerated the development of the spectacular cliff scenery in many areas. The reworking of sediments made available to the coastal zone during deglaciation has resulted in distinctive depositional features. Thus, the widespread estuarine deposits forming the carselands of eastern Scotland reflect extensive coastal progradation, and the raised beaches, raised estuarine terraces and related outwash landforms form prominent features especially on the east coast and at the head of many of the sea lochs in the west. Sea-level change, resulting in both positive and negative movements of the coastal margin, has therefore had a varied effect along Scotland's coastline, and the latest stage in coastal evolution is a complex and fascinating one.

Acknowledgements

Thanks are due to Dr A G Dawson, Mrs S Dawson, Dr C R Firth and Dr J E Gordon for their helpful comments. David Berry drew the illustrations and Michelle Walton typed the manuscript.

References

Austin, W.E.N. and Kroon, D. 1996. Late glacial sedimentology, forminifera and stable isotope stratigraphy of the Hebridean continental shelf, northwest Scotland. In: Andrews, J. T., Austin, W. E. N., Bergsten, H. and Jennings, A. E. (Eds), *Late Quaternary, Palaeoceanography of the North Atlantic Margins*. Geological Society of London, Special Publication, No. 111, 187-213.

Ballantyne, C.K. 1990. The Late Quaternary glacial history of the Trotternish escarpment, Isle of Skye, Scotland, and its implications for ice-sheet reconstruction. *Proceedings of the Geologists' Association,* 101, 171-186.

Benn, D.I. and Dawson, A.G. 1987. A Devensian glaciomarine sequence in western Islay, Inner Hebrides. *Scottish Journal of Geology,* 23, 175-187.

Blanchon, P. and Shaw, J. 1995. Reef drowning during the last deglaciation: evidence for catastrophic sea-level rise and ice-sheet collapse. *Geology,* 23, 4-8.

Bondevik, S. 1996. The Storegga tsunami deposits in western Norway and postglacial sea-level changes on Svalbard. Dr Scient. thesis, University of Bergen.

Boulton, G.S., Peacock, J.D. and Sutherland, D.G. 1991. Quaternary. In: Craig, G.Y. (Ed.), *Geology of Scotland*. The Geological Society, London, 503-543.

Bowen, D.Q., Rose, J., McCabe, A.M. and Sutherland, D.G. 1986. Correlation of Quaternary glaciations in England, Ireland, Scotland and Wales. *Quaternary Science Reviews,* 5, 299-340.

Browne, M.A.E., Armstrong, M., Paterson, I.B. and Aitken, A.M.N. 1981. New evidence for Late Devensian marine limits in east-central Scotland. *Quaternary Newsletter,* 34, 8-15.

Cullingford, R.A. 1977. Lateglacial raised shorelines and deglaciation in the Tay-Earn area. In: Gray, J.M. and Lowe, J.J. (Eds), *Studies in the Scottish Lateglacial Environment*. Pergamon Press, Oxford, 15-32.

Cullingford, R.A. and Smith, D.E. 1980. Late Devensian raised shorelines in Angus and Kincardineshire, Scotland. *Boreas,* 9, 21-38.

Cullingford, R.A., Caseldine, C.J. and Gotts, P.E. 1980. Early Flandrian land and sea-level changes in Lower Strathearn. *Nature,* 284, 159-161.

Cullingford, R.A., Smith, D.E. and Firth, C.A. 1991. The altitude and age of the Main Postglacial Shoreline in eastern Scotland. *Quaternary International,* 9, 39-52.

Dahl, S-O., Ballantyne, C.K., McCarroll, D. and Nesje, A. 1996. Maximum altitude of Devensian glaciation on the Isle of Skye. *Scottish Journal of Geology,* 32, 109-115.

Dawson, A.G. 1980a. Shore erosion by frost: an example from the Scottish Lateglacial. In: Lowe, J.J., Gray, J. M. and Robinson, J. E. (Eds), *Studies in the Lateglacial of North-West Europe*. Pergamon Press, Oxford, 45-53.

Dawson, A.G. 1980b. The Low Rock Platform in Western Scotland. *Proceedings of the Geologists' Association,* 91, 339-344.

Dawson, A.G. 1982. Lateglacial sea-level changes and ice limits in Islay, Jura and Scarba, Scottish Inner Hebrides. *Scottish Journal of Geology,* 18, 253-265.

Dawson, A.G. 1983. *Islay and Jura, Scottish Hebrides: Field Guide*. Quaternary Research Association, Cambridge.

Dawson, A.G. 1984. Quaternary sea-level changes in western Scotland. *Quaternary Science Reviews,* 3, 345-368.

Dawson, A.G. 1994. Strandflat development and Quaternary shorelines on Tiree and Coll, Scottish Hebrides. *Journal of Quaternary Science,* 9, 349-356.

Dawson, A.G., Long, D. and Smith, D.E. 1988. The Storegga Slides: evidence from eastern Scotland for a possible tsunami. *Marine Geology,* 82, 271-276.

Dawson, S. and Smith, D.E. 1997. Holocene relative sea level changes on the margin of a glacio-isostatically uplifted area: an example from northern Caithness, Scotland. *The Holocene,* 7, 59-77.

Fairbanks, R.G. 1989. A 17,000-year glacio-eustatic sea level record: influence of glacial melting rates on the Younger Dryas event and deep-ocean circulation. *Nature,* 342, 637-642.

Firth, C.R. 1984. Isostatic depression during the Loch Lomond Stadial: preliminary evidence from the Great Glen, northern Scotland. *Quaternary Newsletter,* 48, 1-9.

Firth, C.R. 1989. Late Devensian raised shorelines and ice limits in the Inner Moray Firth area, northern Scotland. *Boreas,* 18, 5-23.

Firth, C.R. and Haggart, B.A. 1989. Loch Lomond Stadial and Flandrian shorelines in the inner Moray Firth area, Scotland. *Journal of Quaternary Science,* 4, 37-50.

Firth, C.R., Smith, D.E. and Cullingford, R.A. 1993. Late Devensian and Holocene glacio-isostatic uplift patterns in Scotland. *Quaternary Proceedings,* 3, 1-14.

Firth, C.R., Smith, D.E., Hansom, J.D., and Pearson, S.G. 1995. Holocene spit development on a regressive shoreline, Dornoch Firth, Scotland. *Marine Geology*, 124, 207-214.

Flinn, D. 1978. The most recent glaciation of the Orkney-Shetland Channel and adjacent regions. *Scottish Journal of Geology*, 14, 109-123.

Gordon, J.E. and Sutherland, D.G (Eds.) 1993. *Quaternary of Scotland*. Chapman & Hall, London.

Gray, J.M. 1974. Lateglacial and postglacial shorelines in western Scotland. *Boreas*, 3, 129-138.

Gray, J.M. 1978. Low-level shore platforms in the south-west Scottish Highlands: altitude age and correlation. *Transactions of the Institute of British Geographers*, NS, 3, 151-164.

Gray, J.M. 1983. The measurement of shoreline altitudes in areas affected by glacioisostasy, with particular reference to Scotland. In: Smith, D.E. and Dawson, A.G. (Eds), *Shorelines and Isostasy*. Academic Press, London, 97-128.

Haggart, B.A. 1986. Relative sea-level changes in the Beauly Firth, Scotland. *Boreas*, 15, 191-207.

Haggart, B.A. 1987. Relative sea-level changes in the Moray Firth area, Scotland. In: Tooley, M.J. and Shennan, I. (Eds), *Sea Level Changes*. Blackwell, Oxford, 67-108.

Hall, A.M. and Jarvis, J. 1989. A preliminary report on the Late Devensian glaciomarine deposits at St Fergus, Grampian Region. *Quaternary Newsletter*, 59, 5-7.

Hall, A.M. and Bent, A.J.A. 1990. The limits of the last British ice sheet in northern Scotland and the adjacent shelf. *Quaternary Newsletter*, 6, 2-12.

Hansom, J.D. and Briggs, D.J. 1991. Sea-level changes in Vestfirdir, northwest Iceland. In: Maizels, J.K. and Caseldine, C.J. (Eds), *Environmental Change In Iceland: Past and Present*. Kluwer Academic Publishers, Dordrecht, 79-92.

Holmes, R. 1977. Quaternary deposits of the Central North Sea. 5. The Quaternary geology of the UK sector of the North Sea between 56° and 58° N. *Report of the Institute of Geological Sciences*, No. 77/14.

Jamieson, T.F. 1865. On the history of the last geological changes in Scotland. *Quarterly Journal of the Geological Society of London*, 21, 161-203.

Jamieson, T.F. 1874. On the last stage of the glacial period in north Britain. *Quarterly Journal of the Geological Society of London*, 30, 317-337.

Jardine, W.G. 1975. Chronology of Holocene marine transgression and regression in south-western Scotland. *Boreas*, 4, 173-196.

Jardine, W.G. 1980. Holocene raised coastal sediments and former shorelines of Dumfriesshire and eastern Galloway. *Transactions of the Dumfriesshire and Galloway Natural History and Antiquarian Society*, 3rd series, 55, 1-59.

Lambeck, K. 1993. Glacial rebound of the British Isles - II. A high-resolution, high-precision model. *Geophysical Journal International*, 115, 960-990.

Lambeck, K. 1995. Glacial isostasy and water depths in the Late Devensian and Holocene on the Scottish shelf west of the Outer Hebrides. *Journal of Quaternary Science*, 10, 83-86.

McCann, S.B. 1968. Raised shore platforms in the western Isles of Scotland. In: Bowen, E.G., Carter, H. and Taylor, J.A. (Eds), *Geography at Aberystwyth*. University of Wales Press, Cardiff, 22-34.

Maclaren, C. 1842. The glacial theory of Professor Agassiz of Neuchatel. *American Journal of Science and Arts*, 42, 346-365.

Mather, A.S., and Ritchie, W. 1977. *The Beaches of the Highlands and Islands of Scotland*. Countryside Commission for Scotland, Perth.

Merritt, J.W. 1992. The high-level, marine shell-bearing deposits of Clava, Inverness-shire and their origins as glacial rafts. *Quaternary Science Reviews*, 11, 759-779.

Merritt, J.W., Auton, C.A. and Firth, C.R. 1995. Ice-proximal glaciomarine sedimentation and sea-level change in the Inverness area, Scotland: a review of the deglaciation of a major ice stream of the British Late Devensian ice sheet. *Quaternary Science Reviews*, 14, 289-329.

Morrison, J., Smith, D.E., Cullingford, R.A. and Jones, R.L. 1981. The culmination of the Main Postglacial Transgression in the Firth of Tay area, Scotland. *Proceedings of the Geologists' Association*, 92, 197-209.

Mörner, N.A. 1971. The Holocene eustatic sea level problem. *Geologie en Mijnbouw*, 50, 699-702.

Ogilvie, A.G. 1923. The physiography of the Moray Firth coast. *Transactions of the Royal Society of Edinburgh*, 53, 377-404.

Peacock, J.D. 1975. Scottish late- and post-glacial marine deposits In: Gemmell, A.M.D. (Ed.), *Quaternary Studies in the North-East Scotland*. Department of Geography, University of Aberdeen, Aberdeen, 45-48.

Peacock, J.D. 1981. Scottish late-glacial marine deposits and their environmental significance. In: Neale, J. and Flenley, J. (Eds), *The Quaternary in Britain*. Pergamon Press, Oxford, 222-236.

Peacock, J. D. 1995. Late Devensian to Early Holocene palaeoenvironmental changes in the Viking Bank Area, Northern North Sea. *Quaternary Science Reviews*, 14, 1029-1042.

Peacock, J.D. and Long, D. 1994. Late-Devensian glaciation and deglaciation of Shetland. *Quaternary Newsletter*, 74, 16-21.

Peacock, J.D., Austin, W.E.N., Selby, I., Graham, D.K., Harland, R. and Wilkinson, I.P. 1992. Late Devensian and Flandrian palaeoenvironmental changes in the Scottish continental shelf west of the Outer Hebrides. *Journal of Quaternary Science*, 7, 145-161.

Plag, H.P. *et al.* (12 authors) 1996. Late Quaternary relative sea-level changes and the role of glaciation upon continental shelves. *Terra Nova*, 8, 213-222.

Ritchie, W. 1966. The post-glacial rise in sea-level and coastal changes in the Uists. *Transactions of the Institute of British Geographers*, 39, 79-86.

Ritchie, W. 1979. Machair development and chronology of the Uists and adjacent islands. *Proceedings of the Royal Society of Edinburgh*, B77, 107-122.

Ritchie, W. 1985. Inter-tidal and sub-tidal organic deposits and sea-level changes in the Uists, Outer Hebrides. *Scottish Journal of Geology*, 21, 161-176.

Robinson, M. 1993. Microfossil analyses and radiocarbon dating of depositional sequences related to Holocene sea-level change in the Forth valley, Scotland. *Transactions of the Royal Society of Edinburgh: Earth Sciences*, 84, 1-60.

Robinson, M. and Ballantyne, C.K. 1979. Evidence for a glacial readvance pre-dating the Loch Lomond Advance in Wester Ross. *Scottish Journal of Geology*, 15, 271-277.

Sejrup, H.P., Haflidason, H., Aarseth, I., King, E., Forsberg, C.F., Long, D. and Rokoengen, K. 1994. Late Weichselian glaciation history of the northern North Sea. *Boreas*, 23, 1-13.

Shennan, I. 1989. Holocene crustal movements and sea-level changes in Great Britain. *Journal of Quaternary Science*, 4, 77-89.

Shennan, I., Innes, J.B., Long, A. and Zong, Y. 1993. Late Devensian and Holocene relative sea level changes at Rumach, near Arisaig, northwest Scotland. Norsk Geologisk Tidsskrift, **73**, 161-174.

Shennan, I., Innes, J.B., Long, A. and Zong, Y. 1994. Late Devensian and Holocene relative sea level changes at Loch nan Eala, near Arisaig, northwest Scotland. *Journal of Quaternary Science*, **9**, 261-283.

Shennan, I., Innes, J.B., Long, A.J. and Zong, Y. 1995. Late Devensian and Holocene relative sea-level changes in north-western Scotland: new data to test existing models. *Quaternary International*, **26**, 97-123.

Shi, S. 1995. *Observational and theoretical aspects of tsunami sedimentation.* Unpublished PhD thesis, Coventry University.

Sissons, J.B. 1963. The Perth Readvance in central Scotland. *Scottish Geographical Magazine*, **79**, 151-163.

Sissons, J.B. 1967. *The Evolution of Scotland's Scenery.* Oliver and Boyd, London.

Sissons, J.B. 1969. Drift stratigraphy and buried morphological features in the Grangemouth- Falkirk-Airth area, central Scotland. *Transactions of the Institute of British Geographers*, **48**, 19-50.

Sissons, J.B. 1972. Dislocation and non-uniform uplift of raised shorelines in the western part of the Forth valley. *Transactions of the Institute of British Geographers*, **55**, 145-159.

Sissons, J.B. 1974a. The Quaternary in Scotland: a review. *Scottish Journal of Geology*, **10**, 34-37.

Sissons, J.B. 1974b. Lateglacial marine erosion in Scotland. *Boreas*, **3**, 41-48.

Sissons, J.B. 1980. The glaciation of the Outer Hebrides. *Scottish Journal of Geology*, **16**, 81-84.

Sissons, J.B. 1981. The last Scottish ice sheet: facts and speculative discussion. *Boreas*, **10**, 1-17.

Sissons, J.B. 1982. The so-called high 'interglacial' rock shoreline of western Scotland. *Transactions of the Institute of British Geographers*, NS, **7**, 205-216.

Sissons, J.B. 1983. Shorelines and isostasy in Scotland. In: Smith, D.E., and Dawson, A.G. (Eds), *Shorelines and Isostasy.* Academic Press, London, 209-225.

Sissons, J.B. and Dawson, A.G. 1979. Former sea levels and ice limits in part of Wester Ross, North-west Scotland. *Proceedings of the Geologists Association*, **92**, 115-124.

Sissons, J.B. and Smith, D.E. 1965. Peat bogs in a postglacial sea and a buried raised beach in the western part of the Carse of Stirling. *Scottish Journal of Geology*, **1**, 247-255.

Sissons, J.B., Cullingford, R.A. and Smith, D.E. 1966. Late-glacial and post-glacial shorelines in south-east Scotland. *Transactions of the Institute of British Geographers*, **39**, 9-18.

Smith, D.E. 1965. Late and post-glacial changes of shoreline on the northern side of the Forth valley and estuary. Unpublished PhD thesis, University of Edinburgh.

Smith, D.E. 1968. Post-glacial displaced shorelines in the surface of the carse clay on the north bank of the river Forth, in Scotland. *Zeitschrift für Geomorphologie*, **12**, 388-408.

Smith, D.E. and Cullingford, R.A. 1982. New evidence for Late Devensian marine limits in east-central Scotland - a reply. *Quaternary Newsletter*, **35**, 12-14.

Smith, D. E. and Cullingford, R.A. 1985. Flandrian relative sea level changes in the Montrose Basin area. *Scottish Geographical Magazine*, **101**, 92-104.

Smith, D.E., Cullingford, R.A. and Brooks, C.L. 1983. Flandrian relative sea level changes in the Ythan valley, north east Scotland. *Earth Surface Processes and Landforms*, **8**, 423-438.

Smith, D.E., Cullingford, R.A. and Seymour, W.P. 1982. Flandrian relative sea-level changes in the Philorth valley, north-east Scotland. *Transactions of the Institute of British Geographers*, NS, **7**, 321-336.

Smith, D.E., Cullingford, R.A. and Haggart, B.A. 1985a. A major coastal flood during the Holocene in eastern Scotland. *Eiszeitälter und Gegenwart*, **35**, 104-118.

Smith, D.E., Dawson, A.G., Cullingford, R.A. and Harkness, D.D. 1985b. The stratigraphy of Flandrian relative sea level changes at a site in Tayside, Scotland. *Earth Surface Processes and Landforms*, **10**, 17-25.

Smith, D.E., Firth, C.R., Robinson, M., Brooks, C.L. and Collins, P.E. (in press). Holocene relative sea level changes in the Ythan estuary, north-east Scotland. *Transactions of the Royal Society of Edinburgh: Earth Sciences.*

Smith, D.E., Firth, C.R., Turbayne, S.C. and Brooks, C.L. 1992. Holocene relative sea-level changes and shoreline displacement in the Dornoch Firth area, Scotland. *Proceedings of the Geologists' Association*, **103**, 237-257.

Smith, D.E., Sissons, J.B. and Cullingford, R.A. 1969. Isobases for the Main Perth raised shoreline in south east Scotland, as determined by trend-surface analysis. *Transactions of the Institute of British Geographers*, **46**, 45-52.

Sutherland, D.G. 1981a. The high-level marine shell beds of Scotland and the build-up of the last Scottish ice sheet. *Boreas*, **10**, 247-254.

Sutherland, D.G. 1981b. The raised shorelines and deglaciation of the Loch Long/Loch Fyne area, western Scotland. Unpublished PhD thesis, University of Edinburgh.

Sutherland, D.G. 1984a. The Quaternary deposits and landforms of Scotland and the neighbouring shelves: a review. *Quaternary Science Reviews*, **3**, 157-254.

Sutherland, D.G. 1984b. The submerged rock platforms of the St Kilda archipelago, western Scotland. *Marine Geology*, **58**, 435-442.

Sutherland, D.G. 1987. Submerged rock platforms on the continental shelf west of Sula Sgeir. *Scottish Journal of Geology*, **23**, 251-260.

Sutherland, D.G. and Walker, M.J.C. 1984. A Late Devensian ice-free area and possible interglacial site on the Isle of Lewis, Scotland. *Nature*, **309**, 701-703.

Thompson, M.E, and Eden, R.A. 1977. Quaternary deposits of the central North Sea. 3. The Quaternary sequence in the west-central North Sea. *Report of the Institute of Geological Sciences*, No. 77/12.

Wright, W.B. 1911. On a pre-glacial shoreline in the western isles of Scotland. *Geological Magazine*, **48**, 97-109.

Wright, W.B. 1934. The isokinetic theory of glacially controlled shorelines. *Comptes Rendus du Congres International de Geographie, Varsovie*, Section II, 534-553.

13. Glacial Landforms and Sediments in Scotland

Douglas I. Benn

> **The key themes covered in this chapter are:**
>
> - the age of glacial landforms;
> - erosional landforms;
> - glacial deposits - subglacial, ice-marginal, proglacial, lacustrine and marine.

13.1 Introduction

The action of glaciers during the last two million years has profoundly influenced the landscape of Scotland, particularly in the more western and mountainous parts of the country. Glacial erosion has produced 'textbook' examples of corries, troughs and overdeepened rock basin lochs, while deposition of eroded material has formed fields of drumlins, end moraines, eskers, broad areas of 'kame and kettle' topography and many other landform types. This wealth of spectacular glacial landforms and sediments caught the attention of geologists over 150 years ago, and was used by Louis Agassiz as crucial support for his theory that the Earth had endured extensive glaciations in the past (Chapter 1). Today, the glacial record provides important evidence for past climate change and landscape evolution, and forms a vivid and accessible educational resource.

13.2 The age of glacial landforms in Scotland

Study of microfossils found in cores of sediment recovered from the ocean floors has shown that the Earth's climate has undergone numerous major swings between cold and warm periods since the beginning of the Quaternary period approximately two million years ago (Chapter 5). The cold (glacial) periods last approximately 100 ka, whereas the warmer intervals (interglacials) last only 10 ka or so. It is thought that the present warm period is an interglacial between the last glaciation, which ended some 10 ka ago, and a future glacial period. Scotland has probably been glaciated during many of the Quaternary cold periods, including episodes of ice sheet expansion, when most of the country was engulfed in ice, and periods of more restricted glaciation, when glacier tongues occupied upland glens and corries, fed by mountain snows (see Chapter 5). The geological record for glaciation in Scotland, however, is very incomplete, because each glacier advance swept away and destroyed the deposits left by earlier events. In consequence, only the most recent glacial event, the Late Devensian glaciation, is known in any detail (see Chapter 6). Like other glaciations, the Devensian is subdivided into cold episodes or stades separated by warmer interstades (Figure 13.1). The most recent ice sheet formed during the Dimlington Stade of 26 ka to 13 ka BP, when ice advanced beyond the present coastline in most parts of the country (Sutherland, 1984; Hall and Bent, 1990; Sutherland and Gordon, 1993; Chapters 6 and 7). After the glacial maximum, the ice retreated but deglaciation was interrupted on several occasions by readvances, the best known of which is the Wester Ross Readvance, marked by end moraines along the coastal fringe between Applecross and Loch Broom (Robinson and Ballantyne, 1979). There is evidence of ice-sheet stillstands or readvances along much of the west coast (Benn, 1997), and in many other parts of the country.

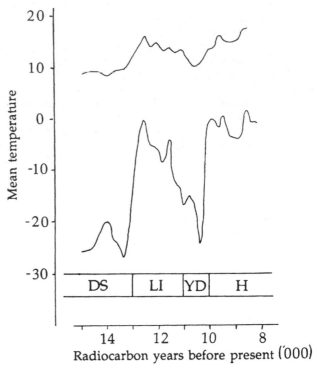

Figure 13.1 Reconstructed temperature curves for the Late Devensian and Holocene in lowland Britain, based on fossil beetle remains. The upper and lower curves show mean summer and winter temperatures, respectively. DS: Dimlington Stade; LI: Late-glacial Interstade; YD: Younger Dryas Stade; H: Holocene. (After Atkinson *et al.,* 1987).

The significance of such readvances is still unclear, although they may be local responses to the rapid climatic and oceanographic changes which are known to have characterized the end of the last glaciation in many parts of the world (Benn, 1997; Chapter 5). Warmer conditions returned to Scotland during the Late-glacial Interstade between 13 ka and 11 ka BP. Glaciers may have survived in Highland enclaves during this time, although firm evidence is lacking. The climate turned cold again during the Loch Lomond (or Younger Dryas) Stade of 11 ka to 10 ka BP, when glaciers expanded once more in the Scottish Highlands, parts of the Southern Uplands, and on the Hebridean islands of Arran, Mull, Rum, Skye and Harris (Sissons, 1967; Sutherland, 1984; Gray and Coxon, 1991; Chapter 8). The return to warm conditions and the final disappearance of glacier ice marked the beginning of the present interglacial, the Holocene.

Most glacial deposits and depositional landforms in Scotland were formed either during the Dimlington Stade or the Loch Lomond Stade, and only fragmentary deposits record older glaciations (*e.g.* Hall and Connell, 1991; Chapter 6). In contrast, erosional landforms such as troughs and corries record the cumulative effects of many successive glacial cycles, each glaciation inheriting and adding to the work of its predecessors. Although it is sometimes assumed that large-scale erosional forms reflect maximum ice sheet conditions, it is more likely that most glacial erosion took

Figure 13.2 Loch Leven viewed from the Mamore mountains. This sea loch occupies a deep glacial trough cut by westward-flowing ice. The southern (left) side of the trough is bounded by the mountains of Glen Coe. (Photo: D.I. Benn).

place under more restricted ice cover. Porter (1989) has argued that, throughout most of the Quaternary, the northern hemisphere ice sheets were about half of their maximum size, and that such 'average' conditions should be reflected in the large-scale features of the landscape. This certainly seems to be the case in parts of Scotland, where the distribution of troughs appears to reflect dispersal of ice from local centres. There is some evidence that erosional forms of different ages are superimposed in some areas. For example, in parts of the Cairngorms, corrie forms are nested one inside the other, suggesting distinct periods of erosion (Sugden, 1969).

13.3 Erosional Landforms

Erosional landforms can be divided into large-scale forms, including corries, troughs and ice-scoured terrain, and small- to medium- scale forms, such as *roches moutonnées* and sculpted rock surfaces (p-forms). Corries are among the most distinctive erosional landforms in Scotland, their scalloped forms lending much to the character of many mountain ranges. Typically, corries consist of a semi-circular headwall fringed by cliffs and an ice-smoothed floor, which may contain a rock basin lying behind a well-defined lip. Well-formed examples are Corrie Fee above Glen Clova in the Grampians, Coire an Lochain in Glen Coe, and Coire Lagan on Skye. During their occupation by glaciers, corries increase in size by a combination of **headwall retreat** as frost-shattered rock falls from cliffs overlooking the glacier and **downcutting** as the glacier erodes its bed by abrasion and quarrying (Haynes, 1968; Gordon, 1977). Corries are widely believed to be eroded by small glaciers that do not

extend far beyond the corrie lip, and corrie altitudes have been used in some studies to infer former glacier distributions and snowlines. However, a recent study in Scandinavia has shown that corries can be eroded below the upper reaches of large valley glaciers, and may therefore give a very misleading impression of former glacier extent (Richardson and Holmlund, 1996).

Most corries in Scotland face the quarter between north and east (Sissons, 1967), suggesting that throughout the Quaternary glaciers were nourished by south-westerly snow-bearing winds and accumulated in sheltered and shady lee-side locations. Glacier accumulation by south-westerly snow-bearing winds is also suggested by variations in corrie density across Scotland. In the Western Highlands, mountain watersheds have commonly been reduced to narrow arêtes by the growth of adjacent corries, indicating vigorous erosion by highly active glaciers. Conversely, in eastern ranges such as the Cairngorms, corries are typically separated by broad plateau surfaces indicating less intensive glaciation throughout the Quaternary.

Glacial troughs (sometimes, but not always accurately, called U-shaped valleys) are a characteristic feature of many parts of the Highlands, particularly in the west where flooded trough floors form the many fjord-like sea-lochs that indent the coast (Figure 13.2). Troughs typically have a parabolic cross profile, although the lower slopes are often masked by scree or other deposits. Classic examples include the Lairig Ghru in the Cairngorms and Glen Clova in the Grampians. Downvalley variations in the amount of erosion have, in some cases, resulted in overdeepened basins contained within rock bars, such as at Loch Coruisk on Skye and Loch Etive near Oban. The deepest rock basin in Scotland is at Loch Morar, the deepest point of which is more than 300 m lower than the rock bar at its seaward end. Overdeepening of trunk valleys is also responsible for forming **truncated spurs**, such as the Three Sisters of Glen Coe, and **hanging valleys** such as that above the Steall Waterfall in Glen Nevis.

The presence of troughs reflects the focusing of glacier erosion along narrow zones aligned parallel to glacier flow, resulting from concentrated ice flow in these areas. Glaciers tend to flow fastest where the ice is thick, so flow is commonly concentrated along the lines of pre-existing valleys. Because subglacial erosion is generally most effective below rapidly sliding, warm-based ice (Chapter 4), existing valleys tend to be deepened, which in turn leads to more efficient focusing of ice flow. Thus, a positive feedback is established between the land surface and patterns of ice flow, which favours the development of deep troughs between relatively lightly eroded areas. David Sugden coined the term 'landscapes of selective linear erosion' for areas affected by this process (Sugden, 1968; Sugden and John, 1976). In the Eastern Highlands, troughs such as upper Glen Dee and Glen Muick are isolated and separated by plateaux, suggesting that in this area successive ice sheets were drained by only a few ice streams. By contrast, in the west of Scotland there is a high density of troughs, forming an interconnected system of deep valleys linked by glacial breaches cut across pre-existing watersheds (Haynes, 1977, 1983). The high density of troughs in the west probably reflects much greater ice discharges than in the east, as a consequence of heavier snowfall during glacial periods. A model of trough erosion by ice streams and valley glaciers has been developed by Harbor (1992), which emphasises the importance of periods of glacial erosion interspersed with periods of subaerial weathering.

Some lowland areas of Scotland have suffered extensive glacial erosion or 'areal scouring' (Sugden and John, 1976; Gordon, 1981). This type of erosion forms **cnoc-and-lochan topography** named after the many knolls and water-filled, scoured hollows that characterise this irregular, rocky landscape. The position of scoured hollows is strongly controlled by rock structure, particularly the location of faults, joints and other weaknesses. Landscapes of areal scouring are formed in areas of unconfined ice flow, where the ice slides rapidly over a well-lubricated bed, and are particularly extensive on the ancient Lewisian gneiss rocks of northwest Scotland and the Outer Hebrides (Rea and Evans, 1996).

In some areas, the upper limit of glacial erosion is very sharp and forms a **trimline** crossing hillslopes and spurs (Thorp, 1981; Ballantyne, 1989; Benn *et al.*, 1992). Trimlines can be thought of as tidemarks which mark the limits of former glaciers, and are particularly clear on the massive, resistant gabbro rocks of the Cuillin Hills of Skye. Some trimlines delimit Loch Lomond Readvance glaciers, whereas others record the upper limit of the Late Devensian ice sheet (Ballantyne and McCarroll, 1995; Chapter 14).

It is also worth drawing attention to parts of the Scottish landscape where little or no glacial erosion has occurred. In some areas, particularly in North-east Scotland, ancient pre-glacial landscape elements survive, such as deeply weathered rock, tors, and Tertiary-age gravels on remnant plateau surfaces (Chapter 3). The presence of such features in areas that have probably been glaciated on more than one occasion suggests that some special circumstances have rendered subglacial erosion ineffective in these areas. The most likely explanation is that glacier ice in these areas was thin, inactive and frozen to its bed (Hall, 1986; Hall and Sugden, 1987). In the absence of active, sliding ice, no significant erosion could occur (see Chapter 4).

Small- to medium- scale glacial erosional landforms are well preserved in many areas of Scotland. Many corrie and trough floors contain *roches moutonnées,* which are asymmetrical bedrock humps with smoothed up-glacier faces and steep, angular down-glacier faces. The name comes from their supposed resemblance to the tight curls of old-style wigs, which were held in place with mutton fat. The shape of *roches moutonnées* results from bedrock abrasion on the up-glacier side, where rock fragments held in the base of the ice are brought into contact with the bed by glacier flow, and plucking on the down-glacier side (Figure 13.3). Plucking is encouraged by structural weaknesses in the bedrock (Rea and Whalley, 1996) and by the presence of low-pressure zones in the lee of humps, where the ice becomes separated from the bed and a water-filled cavity forms. Rock fragments are most likely to flake off during rapid falls in the water pressure in the cavity, when the pressure difference between the hump and the cavity is very large (Iverson, 1991; Hallet, 1996). Rapid water pressure fluctuations are thought to be characteristic of the beds of many valley glaciers due to daily variations in the amount of meltwater reaching the bed from the surface. Many *roches moutonnées* in Scotland are only a few metres high, but some, such as those between Ballater and Braemar in Glen Dee described by Sugden *et al.* (1992), are over 100 m high. Clear, easily accessible examples of *roches moutonnées* can be seen beside the A95 south of Grantown-on-Spey. Perhaps the finest, however, occupy the floor of the Coruisk trough and the corries of the Cuillin Hills of Skye (Benn, 1991a).

Plastically-sculpted forms, or p-forms, are sinuous grooves and hollows on polished bedrock surfaces, and can be up to 1m deep, 3m wide and 20 m long. Their origin is controversial, with some researchers attributing them to erosion by rapidly moving ice or till at the glacier bed, and others to the action of subglacial meltwater streams (Dahl, 1965; Gray, 1993). P-form sites on the islands of Mull and Islay have been documented by Gray (1981, 1984, 1993). Large channels indisputably cut by subglacial meltwaters occur in many parts of Scotland, particularly the Grampian Highlands and parts of the Southern Uplands (Chapter 8). Such meltwater channels mark the former position of conduits beneath the ice, fed by water melted from the glacier bed or from surface meltwater that reached the bed after pouring down crevasses or vertical channels called moulins. Water beneath glaciers is often under high pressure, and as a result can flow uphill as well as down. Subglacial channels, therefore, can have up-and-down long profiles or can begin abruptly on cols on ridges, characteristics that are never associated with normal subaerial stream channels. Spectacular subglacial meltwater channels can be seen at the Slochd on the A9 south of Inverness, at the Ryvoan Pass to the west of Loch Morlich by Aviemore, and near Carlops, 20 km SW of Edinburgh (Gordon and Sutherland, 1993). Meltwater channels formed at or near lateral ice margins are cut across many upland slopes and are well developed on the northern flanks of the Cairngorms (Gordon, 1993a).

13.4 Glacial Deposits

The sediment eroded by glaciers and their associated meltwaters is redeposited in many different environments, resulting in a wide range of deposits and landforms. We can broadly subdivide glacial deposits into (1) subglacial forms, deposited beneath the ice; (2) ice-marginal forms, deposited at the edge of the ice; (3) proglacial forms, deposited by

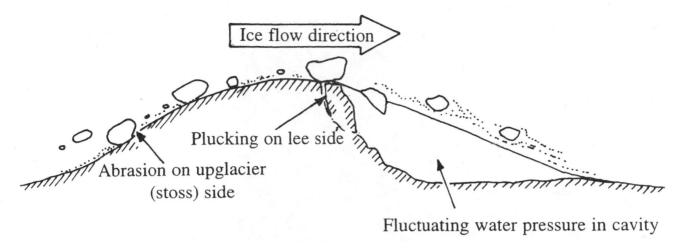

Ice flow direction

Plucking on lee side

Abrasion on upglacier
(stoss) side

Fluctuating water pressure in cavity

Figure 13.3 The formation of a *roche moutonnée* by abrasion of the up-glacier face and plucking in a lee-side cavity.

rivers beyond the margin of the glacier; and (4) lacustrine and marine forms, deposited in lakes and the sea.

13.4.1 Subglacial sediments and landforms

Sediments deposited or remoulded at the base of glacier ice are widespread in many parts of Scotland, particularly in the broad straths of the central belt and the eastern coastal lowlands. Subglacial sediments also occur on the floors of some Highland glens and corries, although they have a patchy distribution and are often buried beneath other glacial or postglacial deposits. There have been few detailed studies of subglacial deposits in the Scottish lowlands, and the origin of many deposits is not known with certainty. However, it is likely that many of the subglacial sediments and landforms originated by the remoulding of weak sedimentary rocks or pre-existing soft sediments, such as marine and lake muds. When a glacier is underlain by saturated soft sediment, the sediment can be much weaker than the ice and deform more easily under stress. This means that the glacier moves by riding along on a layer of deforming sediment, in addition to sliding and creeping of the ice (Figure 13.4; see also Chapter 4). This mechanism is now known to be important below some modern glaciers

(Boulton, 1979; Benn, 1995; Iverson *et al.,* 1995; Benn and Evans, 1996), and is thought to be the main process of glacier flow below some Antarctic ice streams (Alley *et al.,* 1986). Recent work in England and Wales indicates that deforming beds were widespread around the margins of the last British ice sheet (Hart *et al.,* 1990; Hart and Boulton, 1991), and it is probable that major ice streams draining the Scottish ice sheet (such as those in Strathclyde, the Forth and Tay valleys, and the Moray Firth) were also underlain by deforming sediment. The characteristics of subglacial deposits in the Scottish lowlands support their interpretation as **deformation tills**, or tills formed by the deformation of pre-existing sediment. The most common type of deposit is a structureless, fine-grained till with a high silt and clay content, containing polished and striated stones. Detailed descriptions of such tills from the southern end of Loch Lomond have been provided by Benn and Evans (1996), who pointed out their close similarity to modern deformation tills from Iceland. At Loch Lomond, the tills are underlain by sheared and dislocated sands, gravels and clays, providing strong supporting evidence for subglacial deformation (Figures 13.5a and 13.5b). Another example of deformation till from Achnasheen, west of Inverness, has been described by Benn (1996).

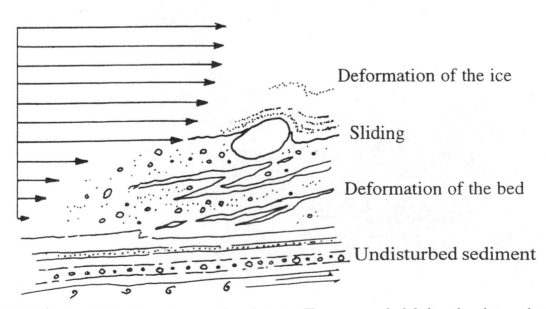

Deformation of the ice

Sliding

Deformation of the bed

Undisturbed sediment

Figure 13.4 Deformation of soft sediment by overriding glacier ice. The arrows on the left show the relative velocities of different layers of the ice-bed system: the upper layers of the ice ride along on the deforming lower layers.

Figure 13.5 A. Deformation till. **B.** Subglacially deformed sediment. Lenses of sand and gravel are enveloped in highly stretched layers of clay, Drymen **C.** Platy subglacial till, Isle of Skye. (Photos: D.I. Benn).

156

In some cases, extremely large blocks of pre-existing rocks and sediments occur within subglacial deposits. An outstanding example is the Leavad erratic in Caithness, which consists of a huge 'raft' of Cretaceous sandstone almost 900 m long, 550 m wide and 8 m thick (Sissons, 1967; Gordon, 1993b). Other, smaller rafts have been recognised near Clava, south of Inverness (Merritt, 1993). Such rafts may be sheared along beneath the ice in a frozen state, or are possibly transported as coherent masses within unfrozen deforming till.

Subglacial deposits in many parts of the Scottish lowlands are associated with **drumlins**. These are streamlined, oval- or spindle- shaped hills with their long axes aligned parallel to glacier flow, and which commonly occur in groups or swarms. The area to the north of Glasgow, and much of the city itself, is underlain by an impressive drumlin swarm recording former ice flow towards the east (Rose and Letzer, 1977; Menzies, 1981, 1996; Rose, 1987). Drumlins rarely occur within the limits of the Loch Lomond Readvance, but an exception is around the southern end of Loch Lomond, where ice spilled out into the Central Lowlands (Rose, 1981, 1987; Gordon, 1993c). The composition of Scottish drumlins is very varied. Some are rock cored, whereas others are cored by bedded sands or gravels or consist entirely of till. Rock- and sediment-cored drumlins are commonly mantled by a layer of subglacial till. Many theories have been proposed to account for the origin of drumlins. The theory which is most widely accepted today is that drumlins represent rigid or stiff regions of the glacier bed, round which soft sediments were deformed (Boulton, 1987). According to this view, drumlins are relict streamlined 'cores' left behind as mobile till was dragged across the landscape by the overriding ice (Figure 13.6). While this explains many of the characteristics of Scottish drumlins, such as the presence of a rock or sediment core and a mantle of till, more detailed field evidence is required to test the theory in Scotland.

Subglacial deposits in upland Scotland tend to be different in character to those in the Lowlands. The most common type of deposit is an extremely compact, stony till resembling concrete. Some tills are structureless, but occasionally many display horizontal fractures which may be fault planes or shear surfaces (Figure 13.5c; Benn, 1992a, 1993). These tills probably originated by a combination of **lodgement** (plastering of debris on to the bed from a sliding, melting glacier sole) and a limited amount of subglacial deformation. They are very similar to modern tills in the Norwegian mountains described by Benn (1994). The differences between the Highland tills and those in the Lowlands probably reflect the more rigid beds and better subglacial drainage beneath the steep Highland glaciers, compared with the weak, poorly drained beds of the Lowland parts of the ice sheet (Benn and Evans, 1996). Deformation tills similar to those in the Lowlands do occur in the Highlands, but only where glaciers advanced into lakes or shallow seas underlain by soft, deformable muds (Benn, 1996).

Drumlin-like landforms known as fluted moraines are found in many Highland glens and corries (Sissons, 1967; Benn, 1992a; Bennett, 1995). These are long, narrow ridges of sediment aligned parallel to glacier flow, up to a few metres wide and high and up to hundreds of metres long. They may occur singly or in groups, and are usually composed entirely of compact till, which is sometimes sheared. As for drumlins, there are several theories for their origin, but the most likely is that they represent till deposited or deformed into subglacial cavities on the lee (downglacier) side of obstacles on the bed, such as *roches moutonnées* or

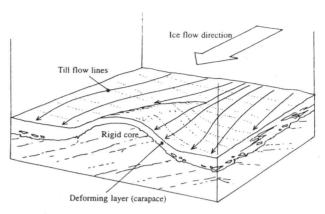

Figure 13.6 The formation of a drumlin by deformation of soft sediment around a rigid core.

large boulders (Figure 13.7). Modern examples have been described by Boulton (1976), Gordon *et al.* (1992), Benn (1994), Benn and Evans (1996) and Eklund and Hart (1996).

13.4.2 Ice-marginal deposits

The best known examples of ice-marginal landforms are **lateral** and **frontal moraines**, which are accumulations of sediment marking the position of former glacier margins. They can form by several processes, including (1) squeezing of soft till from under the margin; (2) dumping of debris from the glacier surface; (3) pushing of loose, surface material during forward movement of the ice; and (4) thrusting of large masses of weak rock or sediment. Squeeze moraines tend to be small, short-lived features that rarely survive long after glacier retreat, but moraines formed by the other three processes are well represented in Scotland. In many Highland corries, well-preserved moraines mark the maximum extent of glaciers during the Loch Lomond Stade. The internal composition of some of these moraines shows that many were formed by a combination of dumping and ice push. Natural and man-made cuttings typically expose crudely bedded debris flow deposits (sometimes known as flow tills), consisting of debris that has flowed off the ice, and sand and gravel deposits, laid down by meltwater streams. In many places, these sediments have been churned up, folded or fractured by forward movement of the ice either during or after deposition (Figure 13.8; Benn, 1992a; Bennett and Boulton, 1993). Some large Highland moraines have fans and terraces of outwash sloping down on their downvalley sides, indicating that they were partly built up by meltwater streams flowing from the ice. Impressive examples can be seen near the southern end of Strath Vaich, near the A835 Inverness to Ullapool road, and at the western end of Strath Carron, Ross-shire. Other Highland moraines are composed entirely of large boulders heaped up into ridges and mounds. One of the finest examples of this type is the end moraine in Coir' a' Ghrunnda on the Isle of Skye, which was one of the first moraines to be recognised in the British Isles, only six years after the introduction of the glacial theory to Scotland (Forbes, 1846). Other more accessible bouldery moraines may be seen in Coire an t-Sneachda and Coire an Lochain, two corries within easy reach of the Cairngorm car park near Aviemore. The boulders in these moraines probably fell on to the glacier surface from the corrie walls, and were then transported to the glacier margin. In other cases, moraines also contain sediment eroded from the glacier beds (Benn, 1992a; 1993).

Thrust moraines generally form where glaciers advance over soft sediments, such as marine sands and muds, which are detached in large blocks and thrust up in front of the

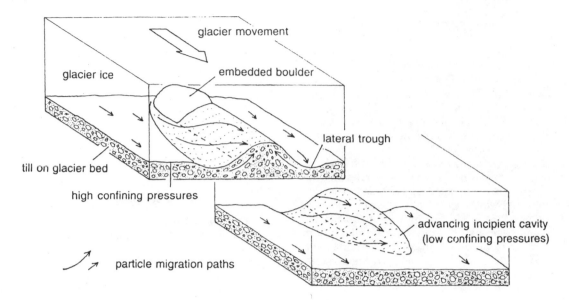

Figure 13.7 The formation of subglacial fluted moraines by the deformation of saturated till into the low pressure zone in the lee of an obstruction on the bed. (Reprinted from 'Fluted moraine formation and till genesis below a temperate glacier: Slettmarkbreen, Jotunheimen, Norway' by D.I. Benn, from *Sedimentology*, 41, 1994, 279-292, by permission of Blackwell Science Ltd).

ice. Impressive thrust moraines, composed of shell-bearing clay beds, encircle the east end of the Lake of Menteith and mark the limit of the Loch Lomond Readvance in this area (Gray and Brooks, 1972). Other examples around Loch Don on the Isle of Mull have been described by Benn and Evans (1993; Figure 13.9).

The floors of many Highland glens are choked by irregular ice-marginal deposits commonly known as 'hummocky moraine'. Until recently, such moraines were believed to be ice-stagnation deposits formed during the final wastage of Scotland's last glaciers (Sissons, 1967). However, they are now known to consist mainly of closely-spaced push and dump moraines, deposited during repeated minor readvances of dynamically active glaciers (Bennett and Glasser, 1991; Benn, 1992a, 1993, 1997; Bennett and Boulton, 1993; Bennett, 1994). Clear examples can be seen in Coire nan Ceud Cnoc (the Valley of a Hundred Hills) near Glen Torridon, and in Glen Arroch on Skye. In these cases, the 'hummocky' appearance of the moraines is misleading, as clear linear patterns become apparent with careful mapping (Figure 13.10). Some hummocky moraine, however, is genuinely chaotic, with no linear pattern, and may have been deposited by limited stagnation of dirty ice at glacier snouts. Other examples consist of ridges of till aligned parallel to glacier flow, together with randomly oriented mounds, and appear to be drumlins or large fluted moraines with a superficial covering of ice-marginal deposits. The classic occurrence of this type is in Glen Sligachan on the Isle of Skye (Benn, 1992a).

Medial moraines are another kind of moraine aligned parallel to glacier flow. On active glaciers, medial moraines are concentrations of debris along glacier flowlines, formed downvalley of glacier confluences or persistent debris sources such as gullies. They are let down on to the ground surface as ridges or lines of erratics when the glacier melts. Medial moraines are rare in Scotland, but clear examples can be seen below the south ridge of Blaven, Isle of Skye, to the south-east of Ben Alligin in Torridon, and on the western side of the Paps of Jura. The Jura moraine is known as Sgriob na Caillich (the Witch's Slide), and consists of angular quartzite blocks transported by westward movement of the last ice sheet (Dawson, 1979).

The large amounts of water produced when ice sheets and glaciers melt means that many landforms produced during ice retreat are composed almost entirely of water-sorted sediment such as sand and gravel. Melting glacier ice is commonly drained by rivers flowing beneath, through, or over the ice, and consequently the glacier margin can become buried by glaciofluvial deposits. When the ice melts, subsidence of the deposits results in a moundy, irregular landscape known as **kame and kettle topography**, the precise form of which reflects the former distribution of buried ice. In cases where large amounts of ice were buried, the surface is commonly highly irregular, consisting of numerous mounds and fragmentary ridges. In contrast, where small amounts of ice were buried below large quantities of glaciofluvial sediment, the landscape more typically consists of a plain pockmarked by isolated kettle holes. Modern examples in Iceland and Alaska have been described by Price (1969) and Gustavson and Boothroyd (1987). Kame and kettle topography is very widespread in Scotland, especially around the lowland fringes where it was formed during wastage of the Dimlington Stade ice sheet. Fine examples may be observed in the upper Clyde valley, northern Fife, the Angus glens, and the Moray lowlands. Good exposures are commonly available due to the value of these deposits as sand and gravel resources, and quarry managers are generally willing to allow interested parties to visit exposures, provided proper safety procedures are observed. Features to look for are well-bedded, sorted sediments recording fluctuating flow conditions, and faults and collapse structures resulting from the melt of buried ice blocks. Kame and kettle topography is sometimes associated with eskers, which are narrow, winding ridges of sand and gravel. Eskers represent the infill of former meltwater tunnels in or below the ice, and can display the same 'up-and-down' long profile as erosional meltwater channels. Classic examples of eskers include those at Carstairs, near Lanark (Gordon, 1993d), and at Kildrummie, west of Nairn (Auton, 1992) (although eskers, these landforms were confusingly called 'kames' when they were originally named).

13.4.3 Proglacial sediments and landforms

The influence of glaciers on the landscape commonly extends far beyond the ice margin itself. Meltstreams transport large volumes of sediment which are deposited in

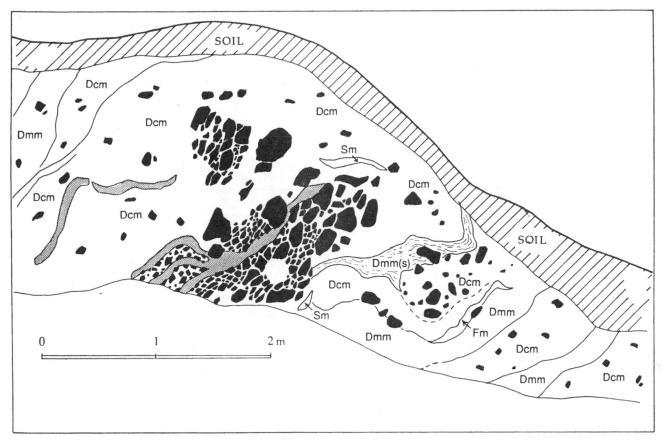

Figure 13.8 Exposure though a lateral moraine in Glen Arroch, Isle of Skye (K in Figure 13. 10). The folding and tilting of the layers is due to ice push. Dcm: massive, clast-supported diamicton (till). Dmm: massive, matrix-supported diamicton (till). Dmm(s): massive, matrix-supported diamicton (till) with shearing. Sm: massive sand. Fm: massive silts. Large clasts are shaded black. The stippled areas comprise sheared silts. (Reprinted from *Quaternary Science Reviews,* 11, D.I. Benn, 'The genesis and significance of 'hummocky moraine': evidence from the Isle of Skye, Scotland', 781-789, copyright (1992), with kind permission from Elsevier Science Ltd, The Boulevard, Langford Lane, Kidlington, OX5 1BG, UK).

Figure 13.9 Thrust moraine on the eastern side of Loch Don, Isle of Mull. (Photo: D.I. Benn).

159

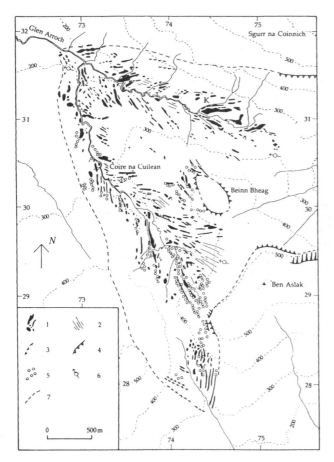

Figure 13.10 The distribution of lateral and frontal moraines in Glen Arroch, Isle of Skye. The chevron pattern of the moraines records successive positions of the glacier margins as they retreated at the end of the Loch Lomond Stade. 1. Moraine ridges and mounds; 2. Fluted moraines; 3. Drift benches; 4. Periglacial trimline; 5. Glacially transported boulders; 6. Striae; 7. Interpolated glacier limits. (Reprinted from 'Glacier response to climatic change during the Loch Lomond Stadial and early Flandrian: geomorphological and palynological evidence from the Isle of Skye, Scotland' by Benn, D.I., Lowe, J.J. and Walker, M.J.C. from *Journal of Quaternary Science*, 7, 1992, 125-144. Copyright John Wiley & Sons Ltd. Reproduced with permission).

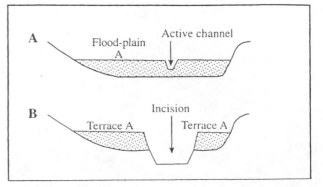

Figure 13.11 The formation of river terraces by incision of a floodplain.

Norwegian mountains, where conditions are probably rather similar to those in Scotland during the retreat of the last valley glaciers (Ballantyne and Benn, 1994, 1996). This work suggests that much of the sediment that blankets slopes in Scotland is of paraglacial origin.

13.4.4 Lacustrine and marine sediments and landforms

Many modern glaciers terminate in lakes or the sea, and large quantities of sediment are transported into standing water bodies by meltstreams. In consequence, lacustrine and marine sediments form an important class of glacial deposits which contains a wealth of information on former glacier behaviour and palaeoenvironmental conditions.

Moraines deposited by glaciers that end in deep water are distinctively different from other end moraines. Unlike the tongue-shaped snouts of glaciers that end on land, water-terminating glaciers usually have straight or slightly concave margins because icebergs break off from the glacier front along the line of transverse crevasses, in a process known as **calving**. As a result, moraines deposited beneath a calving ice edge commonly trend straight across valley, like those deposited in the former ice-dammed lakes at Glen Doe (Sissons, 1977) and Achnasheen (Figure 13.12; Sissons, 1982; Benn, 1989, 1992b; 1996). The moraines form by a variety of processes including ice-push, squeezing of soft till from underneath the glacier and/or the build-up of dumped and water-sorted sediment beneath the ice edge. Benn (1996) has described the internal composition of a lacustrine moraine at Achnasheen, which shows how different processes can act in combination (Figure 13.13). The east side of the moraine was deposited beneath the glacier and consists of deformation till and folded sands, showing that the glacier had a weak, saturated bed. On the west side of the moraine, which lay beneath the lake, are beds deposited by meltwater that poured out of tunnels beneath the ice, mixed with beds of flowed till. This internal structure is reflected in the cross-profile of the moraine, which has a gentle eastern slope where it was over-ridden by the ice, and a steeper western slope where sediment built out at a stable angle beneath the lake.

Deltas are flat-topped or gently sloping masses of sediment built out into lakes or the sea by rivers. They are not exclusively glacial features, but many fossil deltas in Scotland are of glacial origin, reflecting the large amount of sediment that was dumped into standing water by glacial meltstreams. Most glacial deltas in Scotland are 'Gilbert-type' deltas, named after the pioneering geologist G.K. Gilbert who first described examples from the American West in 1888. The upper surfaces of many Scottish deltas are the extensions of outwash plains built outwards into lakes

outwash plains far downvalley. After the disappearance of the ice, the supply of sediment to outwash plains is severely reduced, with the result that the postglacial rivers cut down into the glaciofluvial sediment (Chapter 11). Such incision means that outwash plains are reduced to **terraces** along the valley sides, perched high above the modern river channel (Figure 13.11). Glaciofluvial terraces are found in many Scottish glens, and in some cases form flights of several terraces one above the other. The oldest (highest) terraces in some glens show evidence for deposition in contact with glacier ice, in the form of kettle holes or kame mounds. Good examples can be viewed in Gleann Einich and Glen Feshie in the Cairngorms.

Glacial sediments are also subject to reworking on slopes after deglaciation, particularly in the decades immediately following disappearance of the ice when slopes are unvegetated (Chapter 10). Such reworking is known as **paraglacial sedimentation**, because it is conditioned by the former presence of glaciers. Studies of modern paraglacial sedimentation have been conducted in the

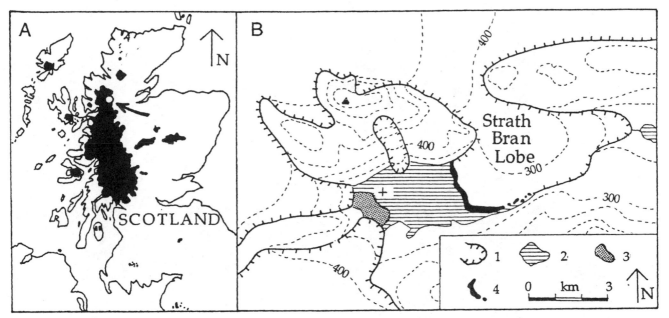

Figure 13.12 A. Glacier limits for the Loch Lomond Stade in Scotland, and the location of Achnasheen. **B.** Reconstruction of the Achnasheen lake and associated glacier limits. 1. Glacier margins; 2. Lake; 3. Delta terraces; 4. Moraine. (Reprinted from 'Subglacial and subaqueous processes near a glacier grounding line: sedimentological evidence from a former ice-dammed lake, Achnasheen, Scotland' by D.I. Benn, from *Boreas,* 25, 1996, 23-36, by permission of Scandinavian University Press.)

or the sea. Sediment deposited on the surface forms beds of sand and gravel known as topsets. However, much of the sediment load is carried beyond the delta surface and cascades down the delta front forming a series of inclined sheets of sand and gravel called foresets (Figure 13.14). The finest material (sand and silt) is carried farther out across the lake or sea floor in undercurrents of dirty water to be deposited as laminated bottomsets. With each new influx of sediment, deltas prograde outwards, burying earlier beds with new topsets, foresets and bottomsets. In Scotland, glacial deltas are often exposed high and dry due to the drainage of ice-dammed or moraine-dammed lakes or the emergence of the coast above glacial sea levels by isostatic

rebound. Excellent examples of lake deltas can be seen at Achnasheen west of Inverness (Benn, 1989, 1992b), and near Leuchars in Fife, and impressive raised coastal deltas occur north of Kyleakin and at Braes on Skye (Benn, 1991b).

Fine-grained sediments carried out into glacial lakes are deposited as laminated silts and clays. The alternating silt and clay layers reflect fluctuations in the sediment supply to the lake, which may occur on a daily or seasonal basis or due to changes in the weather. Laminated sediments deposited during an annual cycle are termed **varves,**

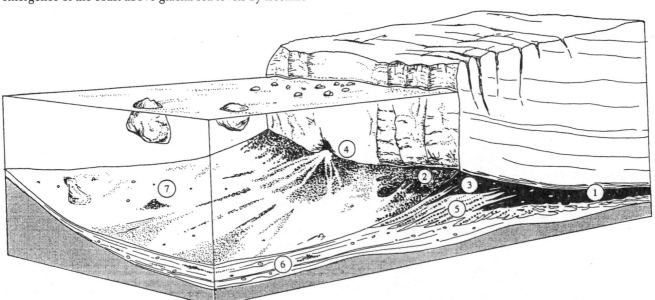

Figure 13.13 Reconstruction of the western margin of the Strath Bran Lobe, Achnasheen. 1. Saturated deforming till; 2. Debris flows onto the lake floor; 3. Bedded debris flow deposits; 4. Outwash emerging onto the lake floor; 5. Subaqueous outwash deposits; 6. Fine-grained laminated sediments; 7. Sediment dumped from icebergs. (Reprinted from 'Subglacial and subaqueous processes near a glacier grounding line: sedimentological evidence from a former ice-dammed lake, Achnasheen, Scotland' by D.1 Benn, from *Boreas,* 25, 1996, 23-36, by permission of Scandinavian University Press.)

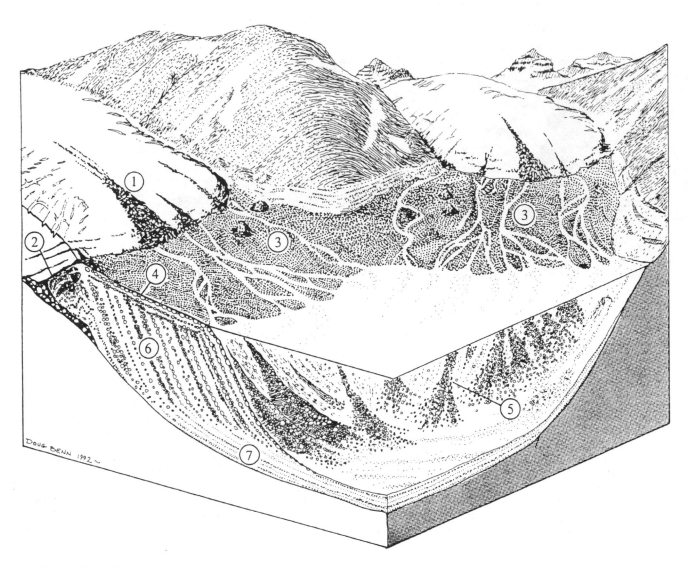

Figure 13.14 Formation of deltas, based on examples at Achnasheen. 1. Glacier margin; 2. Ice-pushed sediment; 3. Outwash plain; 4. Topsets; 5. Sediment avalanching down the delta front; 6. Foresets; 7. Bottomsets, formed on the lake floor and then buried by the advancing delta front. (Reprinted from 'The Achnasheen terraces' by D.I. Benn, from *Scottish Geographical Magazine,* 108, 1992, 128-131, by permission of the Royal Scottish Geographical Society.)

although these can be difficult to distinguish from sediments deposited over shorter timescales. Lacustrine sediments sometimes contain dropstones, dumped from floating icebergs. Laminated sediments with dropstones can be seen near Achnasheen and along the floor of Glen Roy near Spean Bridge. Glen Roy is most famous for the Parallel Roads, three extensive horizontal benches that mark successive levels of an ice-dammed lake ponded up against glaciers advancing from the high mountains to the south and west (Sissons, 1981; Gordon, 1993e).

Glacial marine deposits are similar in many ways to those deposited in glacial lakes. They generally consist of silts and muds with dropstones, but are often less obviously bedded than glacial lake deposits. Good examples of glacial marine sediments survive in parts of the west coast of Scotland, including the Isle of Islay and outer Loch Creran (Benn and Dawson, 1987; Peacock *et al.,* 1989). They are also represented in the estuaries of eastern and western Scotland where the Errol Beds and the Clyde Beds are partly glacial marine in origin (Chapter 12). In addition, glacial marine deposits are widespread on the continental shelves around Scotland, where they have been identified in cores recovered from the sea bed *(e.g.* Stoker and Bent, 1985; Stoker, 1988).

13.5 Conclusion

The Quaternary glaciations have left a strong imprint on the landscape of Scotland in the form of glacial landforms and sediments. Glacial erosion has extensively modified large areas of the pre-glacial landscape, particularly in the mountains and in the west, producing a range of features at a variety of scales from large troughs and corries to small striated rock surfaces. Most of the larger erosional landforms have probably evolved over several glacial cycles and they provide information on the style of glaciation *(e.g.* mountain glacier or ice sheet), as well as subglacial processes and thermal conditions. In contrast, glacial sediments and depositional landforms in the Lowlands and Highland glens are predominantly the product of the last glaciation. Their composition, form and distribution allow insights into the characteristics of the former glaciers and glacier processes, as well as reconstruction of the patterns of ice wastage and recession.

References

Alley, R.B., Blankenship, D.D., Bentley, C.R. and Rooney, S.T. 1986. Deformation of till beneath Ice Stream B, West Antarctica. *Nature, 322,* 57-59.

Auton, C.A. 1992. The Flemington eskers. *Scottish Geographical Magazine, 108,* 190-196.

Atkinson, T.C., Briffa, K. D. and Coope, G.R. 1987. Seasonal temperatures in Britain during the past 22,000 years, reconstructed using beetle remains. *Nature, 325,* 587-593.

Ballantyne, C.K. 1989. The Loch Lomond Readvance on the Isle of Skye, Scotland: glacier reconstruction and palaeoclimatic implications. *Journal of Quaternary Science, 4,* 95-108.

Ballantyne, C.K. and Benn, D.I. 1994. Paraglacial slope adjustment and resedimentation following recent glacier retreat, Fåbergstølsdalen, Norway. *Arctic and Alpine Research, 26,* 255-269.

Ballantyne, C.K. and Benn, D.I. 1996. Paraglacial slope adjustment during recent deglaciation: implications for slope evolution in formerly glaciated terrain. In: Anderson, M.G. and Brooks, S.M. (Eds.), *Advances in Hillslope Processes.* Vol. 2. Wiley, Chichester, 1173-1193.

Ballantyne, C.K. and McCarroll, D. 1995. The vertical dimensions of Late Devensian glaciation on the mountains of Harris and southeast Lewis, Outer Hebrides, Scotland. *Journal of Quaternary Science, 10,* 211-223.

Benn, D.I. 1989. Controls on sedimentation in a Late Devensian ice-dammed lake, Achnasheen, Scotland. *Boreas, 18,* 31-42.

Benn, D.I. 1991a. Glacial sediments and landforms on Skye. In: Ballantyne, C.K., Benn, D.I., Lowe, J.J. and Walker, M.J.C. (Eds), *The Quaternary of the Isle of Skye: Field Guide.* Quaternary Research Association, Cambridge, 35-67.

Benn, D.I. 1991b. Raised shorelines on Skye. In: Ballantyne, C.K., Benn, D.I., Lowe, J.J. and Walker, M.J.C. (Eds), *The Quaternary of the Isle of Skye: Field Guide.* Quaternary Research Association, Cambridge, 90-97.

Benn, D.I. 1992a. The genesis and significance of 'hummocky moraine': evidence from the Isle of Skye, Scotland. *Quaternary Science Reviews, 11,* 781-799.

Benn, D.I. 1992b. The Achnasheen terraces. *Scottish Geographical Magazine, 108,* 128-131.

Benn, D.I. 1993. Moraines in Coire na Creiche, Isle of Skye. *Scottish Geographical Magazine, 109,* 187-191.

Benn, D.I. 1994. Fluted moraine formation and till genesis below a temperate glacier: Slettmarkbreen, Jotunheimen, Norway. *Sedimentology, 41,* 279-292.

Benn, D.I. 1995. Fabric signature of subglacial till deformation, Breidamerkurjökull, Iceland. *Sedimentology, 42,* 735-747.

Benn, D.I. 1996. Subglacial and subaqueous processes near a glacier grounding line: sedimentological evidence from a former ice-dammed lake, Achnasheen, Scotland. *Boreas, 25,* 23-36.

Benn, D.I. 1997. Glacier fluctuations in western Scotland. *Quaternary International, 38/39,* 119-136.

Benn, D.I. and Dawson, A.G. 1987. A Devensian glaciomarine sequence in western Islay, Inner Hebrides. *Scottish Journal of Geology, 23,* 175-87.

Benn, D.I. and Evans, D.J.A. 1993. Glaciomarine deltaic deposition and ice-marginal tectonics: the 'Loch Don Sand Moraine', Isle of Mull, Scotland. *Journal of Quaternary Science, 8,* 279-291.

Benn, D.I. and Evans, D.J.A. 1996. The recognition and interpretation of subglacially-deformed materials. *Quaternary Science Reviews, 15,* 23-52.

Benn, D.I., Lowe, J.J. and Walker, M.J.C. 1992. Glacier response to climatic change during the Loch Lomond Stadial and early Flandrian: geomorphological and palynological evidence from the Isle of Skye, Scotland. *Journal of Quaternary Science, 7,* 125-144.

Bennett, M.R. 1994. Morphological evidence as a guide to deglaciation following the Loch Lomond Readvance: a review of research approaches and models. *Scottish Geographical Magazine, 110,* 24-32.

Bennett, M.R. 1995. The morphology of glacially fluted terrain: examples from the Northwest Highlands of Scotland. *Proceedings of the Geologists' Association, 106,* 27-38.

Bennett, M.R. and Boulton, G.S. 1993. A reinterpretation of Scottish 'hummocky moraine' and its significance for the deglaciation of the Scottish Highlands during the Younger Dryas or Loch Lomond Stadial. *Geological Magazine, 130,* 301-318.

Bennett, M.R. and Glasser, M.F. 1991. The glacial landforms of Glen Geusachan, Cairngorms: a reinterpretation. *Scottish Geographical Magazine, 107,* 116-123.

Boulton, G.S. 1976. The origin of glacially-fluted surfaces - observations and theory. *Journal of Glaciology, 17,* 287-309.

Boulton, G.S. 1979. Processes of glacier erosion on different substrata. *Journal of Glaciology, 23,* 15-38.

Boulton, G. S. 1987: A theory of drumlin formation by subglacial sediment deformation. In: Menzies, J. and Rose, J. (Eds), *Drumlin Symposium.* Balkema, Rotterdam, 25-80.

Dahl, R. 1965. Plastically sculptured detail forms on rock surfaces in northern Nordland, Norway. *Geografiska Annaler, 47,* 83-140.

Dawson. A.G. 1979. A Devensian medial moraine in Jura. *Scottish Journal of Geology, 15,* 43-48.

Eklund, A. and Hart, J.K. 1996. Glaciotectonic deformation within a flute from the Isfallsglaciaren, Sweden. *Journal of Quaternary Science, 11,* 299-310.

Forbes, J.D. 1846. Notes on the topography and geology of the Cuchullin Hills in Skye, and on the traces of ancient glaciers which they present. *Edinburgh New Philosophical Journal, 40,* 76-99.

Gordon, J.E. 1977. Morphometry of cirques in the Kintail-Affric-Cannich area of northwest Scotland. *Geografiska Annaler, 59A,* 177-194.

Gordon, J.E. 1981. Ice-scoured topography and its relationships to bedrock structure and ice movement in parts of northern Scotland and west Greenland. *Geografiska Annaler, 63A,* 55-65.

Gordon, J.E. 1993a. The Cairngorms. In: Gordon, J.E. and Sutherland, D.G. (Eds), *Quaternary of Scotland.* Chapman and Hall, London, 259-276.

Gordon, J.E. 1993b. Leavad. In: Gordon, J.E. and Sutherland, D.G. (Eds), *Quaternary of Scotland.* Chapman and Hall, London, 94-95.

Gordon, J.E. 1993c. Gartness. In: Gordon, J.E. and Sutherland, D.G. (Eds), *Quaternary of Scotland.* Chapman and Hall, London, 444-448.

Gordon, J.E. 1993d. Carstairs Kames. In: Gordon, J.E. and Sutherland, D.G. (Eds), *Quaternary of Scotland.* Chapman and Hall, London, 544-549.

Gordon, J.E. 1993e. Glen Roy and the Parallel Roads of Lochaber. In: Gordon, J.E. and Sutherland, D.G. (Eds), *Quaternary of Scotland.* Chapman and Hall, London, 328-343.

Gordon, J.E. and Sutherland, D.G. 1993. Carlops. In: Gordon, J.E. and Sutherland, D.G. (Eds), *Quaternary of Scotland.* Chapman and Hall, London, 573-575.

Gordon, J.E., Whalley, W.B., Gellatly, A.F. and Vere, D.M. 1992. The formation of glacial flutes: assessment of models with evidence from Lyngsdalen, north Norway. *Quaternary Science Reviews,* 11, 709-731.

Gray, J.M. 1981. P-forms from the Isle of Mull. *Scottish Journal of Geology,* 17, 39-47.

Gray. J.M. 1984. A p-form site on the Isle of Islay, Scottish Inner Hebrides. *Quaternary Newsletter,* 42, 17-20.

Gray, J.M. 1993. Scarisdale. In: Gordon, J.E. and Sutherland, D.G. (Eds), *Quaternary of Scotland.* Chapman and Hall, London, 369-373.

Gray, J.M. and Brooks, C.L. 1972. The Loch Lomond Readvance moraines of Mull and Menteith. *Scottish Journal of Geology,* 8, 95-103.

Gray, J.M. and Coxon, P. 1991. The Loch Lomond Stadial glaciation in Britain and Ireland. In: Ehlers J., Gibbard P.L. and Rose J. (Eds), *Glacial Deposits in Great Britain and Ireland.* Balkema, Rotterdam, 89-105.

Gustavson, T.C. and Boothroyd, J.C. 1987. A depositional model for outwash, sediment sources, and hydrologic characteristics, Malaspina Glacier, Alaska: a modern analog of the southeastern margin of the Laurentide Ice Sheet. *Geological Society of America Bulletin,* 99, 187-200.

Hall, A.M. 1986. Deep weathering patterns in north-east Scotland and their geomorphological significance. *Zeitschrift für Geomorphologie,* 30, 407-422.

Hall, A. M. and Bent, A.J.A. 1990. The limits of the last British ice sheet in northern Scotland and the adjacent shelf. *Quaternary Newsletter,* 61, 2-12.

Hall, A.M. and Connell, E.R. 1991. The glacial deposits of Buchan, north-east Scotland. In: Ehlers J., Gibbard P.L. and Rose J. (Eds), *Glacial Deposits in Great Britain and Ireland.* Balkema, Rotterdam, 129-136.

Hall, A.M. and Sugden, D.E. 1987. Limited modification of mid-latitude landscapes by ice sheets: the case of northeast Scotland. *Earth Surface Processes and Landforms,* 12, 531-542.

Hallet, B. 1996. Glacial quarrying: a simple theoretical model. *Annals of Glaciology,* 22, 1-8.

Harbor, J.M. 1992. Numerical modelling of the development of U-shaped valleys by glacial erosion. *Geological Society of America Bulletin,* 104, 1364-1375.

Hart, J.K. and Boulton, G.S. 1991. The inter-relation of glaciotectonic and glaciodepositional processes within the glacial environment. *Quaternary Science Reviews,* 10, 335-350.

Hart, J.K., Hindmarsh, R.C.A. and Boulton, G.S. 1990. Styles of subglacial glaciotectonic deformation within the context of the Anglian Ice Sheet. *Earth Surface Processes and Landforms,* 15, 227-241.

Haynes, V.M. 1968. The influence of glacial erosion and rock structure on corries in *Scotland. Geografiska Annaler,* 50A, 221-234.

Haynes, V.M. 1977. The modification of valley patterns by ice-sheet activity. *Geografiska Annaler,* 59A, 195-207.

Haynes, V.M. 1983. Scotland's landforms. In: Clapperton, C.M. (Ed.), *Scotland: a New Study.* David and Charles, Newton Abbot, 28-63.

Iverson, N. 1991. Potential effects of subglacial water pressure fluctuations on quarrying. *Journal of Glaciology,* 37, 27-3 6.

Iverson, N.R., Hanson, B., Hooke, R. LeB. and Jansson, P. 1995. Flow mechanism of glaciers on soft beds. *Science,* 267, 80-8 1.

Menzies, J. 1981. Investigations into the Quaternary deposits and bedrock topography of central Glasgow. *Scottish Journal of Geology,* 17, 155-168.

Menzies, J. 1996. Glasgow's drumlins. *Scottish Geographical Magazine,* 112, 188-193.

Merritt, J.W. 1993. The high-level marine shell-bearing deposits of Clava, Inverness-shire, and their origin as glacial rafts. *Quaternary Science Reviews,* 11, 759-779.

Peacock, J.D. Harkness, D.D., Housley, R.A., Little, J.A. and Paul, M.A. 1989. Radiocarbon ages for a glaciomarine bed associated with the maximum of the Loch Lomond Readvance in west Benderloch, Argyll. *Scottish Journal of Geology,* 25, 69-79.

Porter, S.C. 1989. Some geological implications of average Quaternary glacial conditions. *Quaternary Research,* 32, 245-261.

Price, R.J. 1969. Moraines, sandar, kames and eskers near Breidamerkurjökull, Iceland. *Transactions of the Institute of British Geographers,* 46, 17-43.

Rea, B.R. and Evans, D.J.A. 1996. Landscapes of areal scouring in N.W. Scotland. *Scottish Geographical Magazine,* 112, 47-50.

Rea, B.R. and Whalley, W.B. 1996. The role of bedrock topography, structure, ice dynamics and pre-glacial weathering in controlling subglacial erosion beneath a high-latitude, maritime ice field. *Annals of Glaciology,* 22, 121-125.

Richardson, C. and Holmlund, P. 1996. Glacial cirque formation in northern Scandinavia. *Annals of Glaciology,* 22, 102-106.

Robinson, M. and Ballantyne, C.K. 1979. Evidence for a glacial advance pre-dating the Loch Lomond Readvance in Wester Ross. *Scottish Journal of Geology,* 15, 271-277.

Rose, J. 1981. Field guide to the Quaternary geology of the south-eastern part of the Loch Lomond basin. *Proceedings of the Geological Society of Glasgow, 1980-81,* 1-19.

Rose, J. 1987. Drumlins as part of a glacier bedform continuum. In: Menzies, J. and Rose, J. (Eds), *Drumlin Symposium.* Balkema, Rotterdam, 103-116.

Rose, J. and Letzer, J.M. 1977. Superimposed drumlins. *Journal of Glaciology,* 18, 471-480.

Sissons, J.B. 1967. *The Evolution of Scotland's Scenery.* Oliver and Boyd, Edinburgh.

Sissons, J.B. 1977. Former ice-dammed lakes in Glen Moriston, Inverness-shire, and their significance in upland Britain. *Transactions of the Institute of British Geographers,* NS 2, 224-242.

Sissons, J.B. 1981. Ice dammed lakes in Glen Roy and vicinity: a summary. In: Neale, J. and Flenley, J. (Eds), *The Quaternary in Britain.* Pergamon Press, Oxford, 174-183.

Sissons, J.B. 1982. A former ice-dammed lake and associated glacier limits in the Achnasheen area, central Ross-shire. *Transactions of the Institute of British Geographers,* NS 7, 98-116.

Stoker, M.S. 1988. Pleistocene ice-proximal glaciomarine sediments in boreholes from the Hebrides shelf and Wyville-Thomson Ridge, NW UK Continental Shelf *Scottish Journal of Geology,* 24, 249-262.

Stoker, M.S. and Bent, A.J.A. 1985. Middle Pleistocene glacial and glaciomarine sediments in the west-central North Sea. *Boreas,* 14, 325-332.

Sugden, D.E. 1969. The age and form of corries in the Cairngorm Mountains, Scotland. *Scottish Geographical Magazine,* 85, 34-46.

Sugden, D.E. 1968. The selectivity of glacial erosion in the Cairngorm Mountains, *Scotland. Transactions of the Institute of British Geographers,* 45, 79-92.

Sugden, D.E. and John, B.S. 1976. *Glaciers and Landscape.* Edward Arnold, London.

Sugden, D.E., Glasser, N.F. and Clapperton, C.M. 1992. Evolution of large roches moutonnées. *Geografiska Annaler,* **74A,** 253-264.

Sutherland, D. 1984. The Quaternary deposits and landforms of Scotland and the neighbouring shelves: a review. *Quaternary Science Reviews,* **3,** 157-254.

Sutherland, D.G. and Gordon, J.E. 1993. The Quaternary in Scotland. In: Gordon, J.E. and Sutherland, D.G. (Eds), *Quaternary of Scotland.* Chapman and Hall, London, 11-47.

Thorp, P.W. 1981. A trimline method for defining the upper limit of Loch Lomond Readvance glaciers: examples from the Loch Leven and Glencoe areas. *Scottish Journal of Geology,* **17,** 49-64.

14. The Periglacial Geomorphology of Scotland

Colin K. Ballantyne

> The key themes covered in this chapter are:
>
> - relict periglacial features in the lowlands;
> - relict periglacial features in the uplands;
> - reconstructing past climates from periglacial features;
> - present-day periglacial activitiy on Scottish mountains.

14.1 Introduction

The term **periglacial** is used to describe the geomorphological processes that operate in cold, non-glacial environments, together with the landforms, sediments and soil structures produced by such processes. Although glaciation constituted the dominant influence on the development of the Scottish landscape during the Quaternary, periglacial processes have influenced or modified this glacial landscape in a variety of ways. Such processes operated during periods of cold climate before and after each invasion of glacier ice, and the resulting landforms and sediments often provide useful clues regarding the nature of the climate at the time of their formation.

Because of the effectiveness of glacial erosion and deposition, few periglacial features in Scotland survived the expansion of the last (Late Devensian) ice sheet, which covered almost all of the present land surface prior to about 18 ka BP. In consequence, most periglacial phenomena in Scotland developed during and after the waning of this ice sheet. Very cold conditions persisted until the end of the Dimlington Stadial at *c.* 13 ka BP (Atkinson *et al.*, 1987), permitting the operation of periglacial processes on land exposed by the retreating ice. Following a relatively brief period of temperate climate during the Windermere (or Late-glacial) Interstadial of *c.* 13-11 ka BP, very cold conditions returned during the Loch Lomond Stadial of *c.* 11-10 ka BP, and areas that lay outside the reach of glaciers at this time experienced widespread renewal of periglacial activity. With the onset of milder interglacial conditions around 10 ka BP, periglacial activity retreated to the higher parts of Scottish mountains, where it persists to the present day (Figure 14.1). This review considers first the effects of former periglacial processes on lowland areas of Scotland, then the legacy of Late Devensian periglacial activity on Scottish mountains. The palaeoclimatic implications of relict periglacial features are then discussed, and the review concludes with an outline of present-day periglacial activity on high ground.

14.2 Relict periglacial features in the Scottish Lowlands

A characteristic feature of many present-day periglacial environments is the presence at shallow depths of **permafrost** (ground that remains below 0°C), which may extend deep under the soil or drift cover to depths of hundreds of metres in the underlying bedrock. Even in the coldest environments, however, permafrost does not reach the ground surface, but is overlain by an **active layer** that thaws during the summer and refreezes each winter. Some of the relict periglacial features present on low ground in Scotland developed in former permafrost, whereas others reflect seasonal freeze-thaw of the former active layer.

One of the most striking features of permafrost terrain is the presence of extensive polygonal networks comprising shallow troughs in the ground surface (Figure 14.2). These **ice-wedge polygons** (**tundra polygons**), range from a few metres to several tens of metres in diameter, and the surface

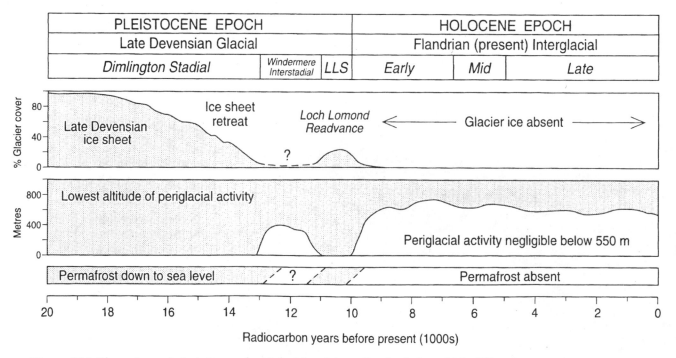

Figure 14.1 Chronology of glaciation and periglacial activity in Scotland, from 20 ka BP to the present.

Figure 14.2 Ice wedge polygons 10-20 m in diameter, Ellesmere Island, arctic Canada. (Photo: C. Harris).

troughs mark the locations of buried **ice wedges** that taper downwards into the permafrost from the base of the active layer. The polygons and their component ice wedges result from contraction cracking of permafrost in winter. Meltwater entering the open cracks freezes against the permafrost, forming first a thin vertical vein of ice, then, as the crack reopens from year to year, extending laterally to form a mature ice wedge (Figure 14.3). When the climate warms and the permafrost thaws, the voids created by melting ice wedges are filled by sediment slumping in from above, so that the former locations of ice wedges (and thus permafrost) are marked by wedge-shaped sediment infills known as **ice-wedge casts**. In some localities a faint polygonal pattern may also survive at the surface, and may be visible on aerial photographs in the form of vegetation contrasts between the polygon centres and the network of wedge casts.

Ice wedge casts have been located at numerous sites in Scotland, particularly in the Midland Valley, Angus and the North-East. All well-documented examples occur outside the limits of the glaciers that developed during the Loch Lomond Stadial (Figure 14.4). The great majority have been located in gravel pits excavated in outwash deposits laid down as the last ice sheet retreated, though a few are found in till or weathered bedrock. The affinity between ice-wedge casts and stratified outwash gravels probably reflects the availability of fresh exposures in gravel pits, combined with the fact that such wedges are easily identified where they interrupt horizontally-bedded strata, which may exhibit buckling or slump structures along the margins of wedges (Figure 14.5). Wedge casts in Scotland are up to 5m long, though the majority are 1-3m in length (Galloway, 1961). Centuries of ploughing have obliterated the polygonal networks in most areas, though a few examples have been

detected, particularly in NE Scotland, where Gemmell and Ralston (1984) have identified eight areas of relict ice wedge polygons 20-90m in diameter developed in outwash and alluvium.

The age of these features is open to debate. Most examples probably reflect the establishment of permafrost during the retreat of the last ice sheet prior to *c*. 13 ka BP. Some authors, such as Rose (1975) and Gemmell and Ralston (1984), have argued that renewed ice wedge formation took place during the Loch Lomond Stadial of *c*.11-10 ka BP. Although this seems likely, at present there appears to be no unequivocal stratigraphic or dating evidence for ice-wedge formation at this time. There is also very limited evidence in Scotland for ice-wedge development prior to the build-up of the last ice sheet, though at Kirkhill and at Oldmill Quarry in NE Scotland ice-wedge casts are developed in deposits that underlie an upper till, and hence demonstrate the existence of permafrost prior to the last glaciation at these sites. In this area there is some evidence that this final glaciation may have occurred during the Early Devensian rather than the Late Devensian, and indeed the widespread occurrence of ice-wedge casts and other periglacial phenomena in NE Scotland has been interpreted as favouring the argument that part of this area may have escaped glaciation during the Late Devensian (Connell and Hall, 1987; FitzPatrick, 1987) (see Chapter 6).

In the active layer above permafrost, soils mantling hillslopes are often subject to **solifluction**, a term used to describe the slow downslope movement of soil under conditions of seasonal freezing and thawing. Solifluction has two components: **frost creep**, which is a rachet-like descent of the soil due to expansion during freezing and contraction during thaw; and **gelifluction**, which is the localised flow of liquefied soil due to the melting of ice lenses. The resulting

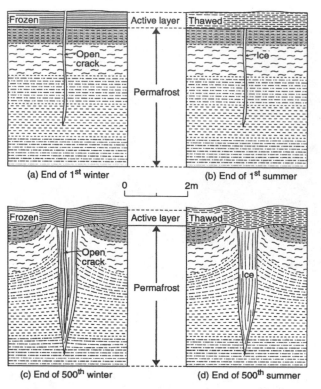

(a) End of 1st winter   (b) End of 1st summer

(c) End of 500th winter   (d) End of 500th summer

Figure 14.3 Formation of ice wedges by thermal contraction cracking of permafrost (schematic). Reprinted from C.K. Ballantyne and C. Harris 1994. *(The Periglaciation of Great Britain,* Cambridge University Press, Cambridge).

comprise reworked till or weathered regolith. On slopes in lowland Scotland, solifluction has often affected only a superficial layer 1-2 m thick, though deeper accumulations of gelifluctate are present on valley floors, particularly in the Southern Uplands (*cf.* Douglas and Harrison, 1987). Solifluction in lowland areas has rarely left any distinct surface morphology, but is evident in superficial sediments in the form of a preferred downslope orientation of elongate clasts, sometimes accompanied by crude stratification parallel to the slope, disturbance of underlying bedrock and internal discontinuities that mark former shear planes (FitzPatrick, 1987). Gelifluctate both underlies and overlies organic deposits of Windermere Interstadial age, implying that solifluction affected lowland slopes both prior to *c.* 13 ka BP and during the Loch Lomond Stadial. In the Glasgow area, for example, excavations on the flanks of drumlins deposited by the last ice sheet have revealed over 4 m of solifluction till overlying Windermere Interstadial peat deposits (Dickson *et al.,* 1976). The operation of solifluction over a much longer timescale is attested by the presence of gelifluctates that both underlie and overlie glacial and interglacial deposits in Quaternary exposures, indicating that periglacial episodes both preceded and succeeded each advance of glacier ice. At Kirkhill in NE Scotland, for example, no fewer than five gelifluctate horizons are intercalated with tills, glacifluvial gravels and interglacial soils. The oldest of these may relate to the cooling during the Anglian Glacial Stage, some half a million years ago (Connell and Hall, 1987).

A further common feature of the active layer in permafrost environments is the presence of disturbed soil horizons known as **cryoturbations** or **periglacial involutions**. Common forms include flame-structures or diapirs of soil that have intruded overlying horizons, bowl-shaped masses of soil that have sunk into the underlying layers, convoluted folds and isolated 'teardrop' masses of detached soil (Figure 14.6). Such features may form in a variety of ways. Many probably represent 'load structures' that formed during thaw of frozen ground, with liquefied sediment at depth being injected into denser overlying horizons. Alternatively, some cryoturbations may reflect upwards squeezing of unfrozen soil during winter freezeback, particularly in stratified sediments that generate differential frost heaving pressures. Not all involuted structures reflect freezing and thawing of the ground, however, and care is necessary in the interpretation of such disturbed soil horizons.

In Scotland, cryoturbations representing former periglacial conditions occur at depth in a number of Quaternary exposures. At Dalcharn, 23 km east of Inverness, cryoturbated sediments occur below a peat horizon that is overlain by two distinct glacial tills, and indicate periglacial soil modification prior to at least the last interglacial (Walker *et al.,* 1992). At Kirkhill in NE Scotland, cryoturbated or geliflucted sediments are overlain by three different till units and, like the lowest till at this site, may relate to the Anglian Glacial Stage (Connell and Hall, 1987). Most cryoturbations in Scotland, however, are developed at shallow depths in Devensian sediments, and hence post-date the last ice-sheet maximum (Figure 14.4). The majority have an amplitude of 0.8-1.8 m, and may represent the depth of the former active layer, though their precise age is uncertain: some may have formed during ice-sheet retreat prior to *c.* 13 ka BP, whilst it is likely that others developed during the Loch Lomond Stadial. The concentration of involutions in the Buchan area of NE Scotland has been inferred by some authors as indicating glacier-free conditions in this area during the Late Devensian (Galloway, 1961; FitzPatrick, 1987).

Another feature that reflects former permafrost conditions in lowland Scotland is the presence of near-surface **indurated horizons** or **fragipans** in many soils. In present permafrost environments, translocated silt and clay particles accumulate at the base of the active layer. There they become consolidated by intense freezing and thawing, forming a hard, dense layer, often with a platy or lenticular structure. In Scotland, such indurated layers occur in many freely-drained, fine-textured soils, generally 0.4-0.6 m below the surface, and have sharply-defined upper boundaries but diffuse lower ones. They have been interpreted as representing permafrost development and aggradation in the interval between retreat of the last ice sheet and the end of the Loch Lomond Stadial (FitzPatrick, 1987).

14.3 Relict periglacial features on Scottish mountains

The most widespread indication of former periglacial activity on Scottish mountains is the mantle of frost-weathered debris that covers plateaux and upper slopes. Although frost-shattered bedrock and debris is not confined to high ground (*cf.* FitzPatrick, 1987), it is on driftless mountain summits that frost-weathered regolith is most conspicuous. Significantly, *in situ* frost debris does not occur within the limits of the glaciers that developed during the Loch Lomond Stadial, implying that frost shattering of rock has been very limited under the milder conditions of the present interglacial, and that most frost-weathered debris is a relict of climates much colder than that of the present. The nature of frost detritus on Scottish mountains is closely related to bedrock type. Three basic types can be identified. Well-jointed but resistant rocks such as quartzite and microgranite have broken up under freeze-thaw action to form distinctive **blockfields** and **blockslopes,** which consist of openwork covers of boulders with little or no soil at the

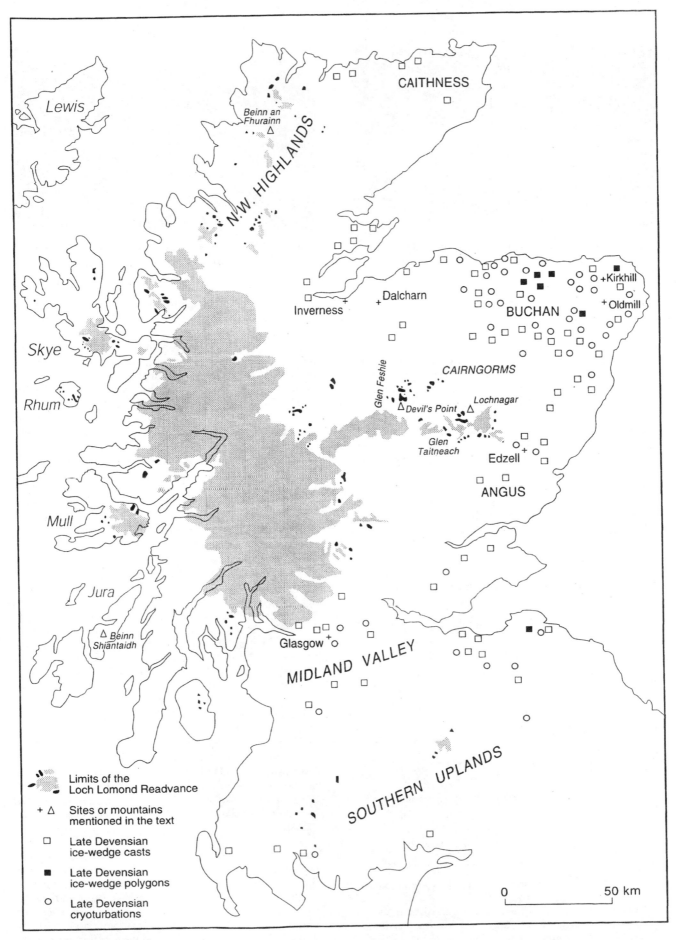

Figure 14.4 Distribution of Late Devensian ice-wedge polygons, ice-wedge casts and cryoturbations in Scotland, showing location of sites mentioned in the text.

Legend within figure:

Limits of the Loch Lomond Readvance

+ △ Sites or mountains mentioned in the text

□ Late Devensian ice-wedge casts

■ Late Devensian ice-wedge polygons

○ Late Devensian cryoturbations

0   50 km

Labels on map: Lewis, CAITHNESS, N.W. HIGHLANDS, Beinn an Fhurainn, Skye, Rhum, Inverness, Dalcharn, Kirkhill, Oldmill, BUCHAN, Glen Feshie, CAIRNGORMS, Devil's Point, Lochnagar, Glen Taitneach, Edzell, ANGUS, Mull, Jura, Beinn Shiantaidh, Glasgow, MIDLAND VALLEY, SOUTHERN UPLANDS

Figure 14.5 Ice wedge cast developed in Late Devensian outwash deposits near Edzell. (Photo: C.M. Clapperton).

Figure 14.7 Cambrian Quartzite blockslope, Sàil Mhór, near An Teallach, NW Highlands. (Photo: C.K. Ballantyne).

of openwork covers of boulders with little or no soil at the surface. Fine examples occur on Cambrian Quartzite in the NW Highlands (Figure 14.7) and on the quartzite summits in the Grampians, as well as on some granite summits in the Cairngorms, such as Derry Cairngorm and the south summit of Cairn Toul. On most granite mountains and on the Torridon Sandstone summits of the NW Highlands, the debris mantle takes the form of clasts embedded in a matrix of coarse sand derived from granular disaggregation of bedrock. The most widespread type of frost debris on Scottish mountains, however, consists of clasts embedded in a silty-sand matrix, again produced by disintegration of rock into finer particles. This final type is locally frost-sorted, so that clasts may be concentrated at or near the ground surface, and is typical of summits and plateaux underlain by mica-schists or shales. Each of these three types of frost debris supports a distinctive assemblage of relict and active periglacial features. In general, blockfields and blockslopes (type 1) support only large relict solifluction features and patterned ground; debris mantles with a coarse sandy matrix (type 2) carry a restricted range of frost-action landforms,

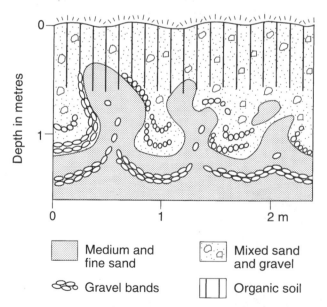

Figure 14.6 Cryoturbations developed near the surface of a Late Devensian outwash terrace in the Ythan Valley, Aberdeenshire. The lower limit of the pockets of sand and gravel may represent the depth of the active layer over former permafrost.

but a variety of aeolian landforms and sediments; and the final category of debris (type 3) supports a wide range of both active and relict frost-action features. The difference between types 2 and 3 above is that the matrix of the former is cohesionless, and thus readily entrained by wind, whereas the matrix of the latter is conducive to the development of ice lenses during freezing, and this favours both solifluction and patterned ground formation (Ballantyne, 1984).

For many years it was believed that the last ice sheet extended over the summits of all Scottish mountains, implying that upland debris mantles formed in the interval between ice-sheet deglaciation and the end of the Loch Lomond Stadial. Recent research in the Hebrides and the NW Highlands, however, has demonstrated that thick *in situ* frost debris on some rock types has a clear lower limit that declines in altitude along former directions of glacier movement. This lower limit to *in situ* debris has been interpreted as a **periglacial trimline** cut by the last ice sheet, making it possible to reconstruct the former profile of the ice sheet at its maximum thickness (*e.g.* Ballantyne, 1990; Ballantyne and McCarroll, 1995; McCarroll *et al.*, 1995; Figure 14.8). This implies that the frost debris above the ice-sheet trimline in these areas partly pre-dates the Late Devensian. In other areas, such as the Cairngorm plateaux, it is likely that frost-weathered debris survived Late Devensian glaciation under a cover of cold-based glacier ice that was frozen to the underlying surface and hence incapable of substantial erosion (see Chapter 4). However, other rock types, such as quartzite, have weathered to form debris mantles since ice-sheet downwastage. It thus appears that not all frost debris is of the same age. Some pre-dates the last glacial maximum, and survived Late Devensian glaciation on nunataks that rose above the ice surface (especially in the NW Highlands and Hebrides), or under a protective cover of cold-based ice. On summits eroded by the last ice sheet, frost debris formed in the period between ice-sheet deglaciation and the end of the Loch Lomond Stadial.

A variety of relict periglacial landforms has developed on the frost debris of Scottish mountains. Amongst the most conspicuous are solifluction features produced by the slow downslope movement of debris. Such movement has resulted in the development of step-like risers and gentler treads of debris. On convex upper slopes, such risers run parallel or oblique to the slope contours, and mark the downslope termination of individual **solifluction sheets**. With increasing gradient downslope, however, risers become increasingly crenulate, forming lines of relict the

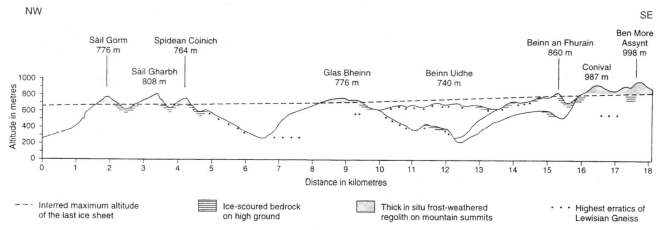

Figure 14.8 Periglacial trimline cut across the mountains of Assynt by the last ice sheet. Those summits above the trimline are characterised by frost-shattered rock outcrops and a cover of *in situ* frost debris, and are interpreted as former nunataks that remained above the level of the ice sheet. The dots represent the highest locations at which Lewisian Gneiss erratics occur. (After McCarroll *et al.*, 1995).

sheets and lobes are present on high ground: **nonsorted lobes** are those, often found on mica-schists, that display no horizontal or vertical sorting of clasts; **sorted lobes** are those in which a layer of boulders has been moved to the surface and margins of the feature, and are typical of more massive lithologies; and **boulder lobes** represent an extreme form of the latter, and have developed on rocks like granite and quartzite where weathering has produced an abundance of boulders but only a thin matrix of fine soil (Ballantyne and Harris, 1994). The treads of relict solifluction sheets and lobes usually rise 1-3 m above the adjacent slope, but are often degraded, and most are now completely vegetation-covered. The margins of boulder lobes, however, remain particularly conspicuous. These are widespread on the granite of the Cairngorms and Lochnagar, where they festoon the slopes of mountains over an altitudinal range of 540-1220 m. All varieties of relict solifluction features are absent from ground occupied by glacier ice during the Loch Lomond Stadial, demonstrating that they became inactive under the milder conditions of the present interglacial, though smaller-scale solifluction features are still active on high ground in some areas (see below).

Large-scale relict sorted patterned ground also occurs on Scottish mountains. Such patterns are defined by concentrations of clasts that define the margins of **sorted nets, sorted circles** and (less frequently) **sorted polygons**, or by alternating lines of coarse and fine debris that form **sorted stripes** on slopes of 5-20°. Such features are typically 1-4 m wide. Excavations have shown that clasts occupy troughs between cells or stripes of predominantly fine material, that the clasts in the troughs tend to coarsen upwards and that the cells or stripes of fines tend to be updomed above the level of the adjacent concentrations of clasts (Figure 14.10). Such characteristics are typical of patterned ground produced by lateral sorting of coarse debris by freeze-thaw action, though opinion is divided on how this occurs. One school of thought attributes lateral sorting to the formation of oblique freezing planes in the ground during winter freezeback, causing clasts to migrate laterally towards zones of less frost-susceptible (*i.e.* less ice-rich) soil. Alternatively, pattern development may result from 'convection' of soil during summer thaw, with density inversion causing slow overturning of soil, resulting in a concentration of clasts at the margins of convection cells (*cf.* Ballantyne and Harris, 1994, pp. 92-94). Whatever the origin of these fascinating microforms, the coarseness of

debris and the depth of sorting (often over 0.5 m) strongly suggests that they developed in the active layer above former permafrost. Most examples have certainly developed since ice-sheet downwastage, though it is possible that some formed on nunataks above the level of the last ice sheet, or may in some places (such as the Cairngorms) have survived the last glacial stage under a protective cover of cold-based glacier ice. Many areas of sorted patterned ground are now obscured or partly obscured by vegetation cover, but nets and stripes of boulders can sometimes be distinguished on plateaux and upper slopes, for example on Beinn an Fhurain in the NW Highlands, on Sròn an t-Saighdeir on Rum and on the Lochnagar plateau of the Eastern Grampians.

Three types of nonsorted patterned ground also occur on Scottish mountains. The most common are **earth hummocks**, which form domes of predominantly fine soil separated by a network of depressions (Figure 14.11). On slight gradients, such hummocks sometimes become aligned downslope in parallel bands to form **hummock stripes**, and with further increases in gradient individual hummocks may merge to form **relief stripes** consisting of alternating ridges and furrows aligned downslope. Individual hummocks are typically 10-50 cm high and 30-150 cm in diameter, but relief stripes tend to be generally flatter and wider. Superb examples occupy the upper slopes of Ben Wyvis in Easter Ross and Glas Maol in the SE Grampians. The presence of undisturbed podzolic horizons within such features indicates that they are essentially inactive and of considerable antiquity, though their age and origin remain uncertain. Ballantyne (1986a) has suggested that they developed from vegetation patterns during the Late Devensian, but this hypothesis remains untested.

Whilst plateaux and upper slopes experienced modification by freeze-thaw weathering, solifluction and frost sorting during the Late Devensian, the steep rockwalls exposed by the retreat of the last ice sheet were also affected by periglacial processes in a variety of ways. Freeze-thaw action operating on glacially-steepened cliffs resulted in the formation of extensive **talus slopes** of rockfall debris. Taluses of Late-glacial age, which accumulated in the interval between the retreat of the last ice sheet and the end of the Loch Lomond Stadial, are typically mature forms that extend high against the source rockwall, are extensively vegetated, and have often been eroded and modified by the operation of other processes (particularly debris flows) during the Holocene (Figure 14.12). Conversely, talus slopes

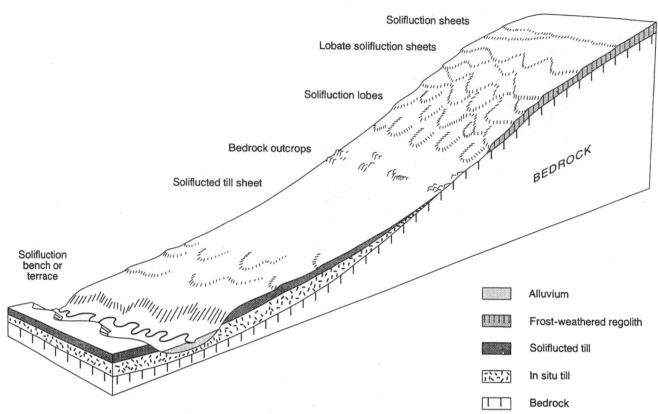

Figure 14.9 A catena of solifluction features found on Scottish mountains (schematic). (Reprinted from C.K. Ballantyne and C. Harris 1994. *The Periglaciation of Great Britain*. Cambridge University Press, Cambridge).

and talus cones that have accumulated during the Holocene, since the final retreat of glacier ice at the end of the Loch Lomond Stadial, are often immature features on which rockfall activity is still fairly active. It has been calculated that average rates of rockwall retreat during the Loch Lomond Stadial were within the range 1.5-3.0 mm a⁻¹, similar to those of alpine environments at present, but two orders of magnitude greater than recent rockwall retreat rates in Scotland (Ballantyne and Kirkbride, 1987). Such rapid rockwall retreat certainly reflects much more effective freeze-thaw activity under the cold conditions of the Late-glacial period, but may also be due in part to the inherent instability of rockwalls exposed by ice-sheet retreat.

During the Loch Lomond Stadial, talus accumulations were affected by a number of distinctive periglacial effects. In some locations, the development of banks of perennial firn against taluses resulted in the development of **protalus**

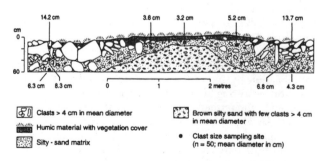

Figure 14.10 Cross-section through a relict sorted circle on Beinn an Fhurain, Assynt. The figures in centimetres refer to the mean diameters of samples of 50 clasts from the locations shown, and illustrate the vertical sorting of the coarse borders and the horizontal sorting from the cell to the borders.

ramparts, which are ridges or ramps of predominantly coarse detritus, formed by the accumulation of debris at the foot of former firn fields (Figure 14.13). Good examples occur at the foot of Conachair, on St Kilda, and on the southern flank of the Devil's Point in the Cairngorms. The Late-glacial protalus ramparts of the Scottish Highlands are arcuate or linear in planform, usually less than 300 m long, have steep outer slopes and are located within 15-25 m of the adjacent talus. They display an interesting altitudinal trend, being located near sea-level on St Kilda, at around 500 m in the western Highlands, but no lower than 650 m in the Cairngorms. This trend has been interpreted as indicating a pronounced eastwards decline in precipitation during the stadial (Ballantyne and Kirkbride, 1986).

Even more spectacular are the **protalus rock glaciers** that formed during the Loch Lomond Stadial. These are lobate extensions of the foot of talus slopes, and developed through the downslope deformation of ice or ice-rich sediment within the talus. There is some debate concerning the origin of such internal ice, but general consensus that it indicates former permafrost. Only a small number of protalus rock glaciers exists in Scotland. Particularly fine examples occur below Beinn Shiantaidh on Jura and in Coire Beanaidh in the western Cairngorms. That on Jura is 0.38 km wide (across-slope) and 0.18 km long (Dawson, 1977), whilst the Coire Beanaidh rock glacier is *c.* 0.6 km wide, up to 0.2 km long, and contains some 200,000 m³ of rock debris (Chattopadhyay, 1984). Even larger is the Strath Nethy rock glacier, also in the Cairngorms, which is 2.4 km wide and 0.35 km long (Figure 14.14). These remarkable features terminate in steep bouldery slopes and contain tranverse ridges, indicative of former deformation, and enclosed hollows produced by the melt-out of internal ice. Their scarcity seems to reflect the fact that many sites suitable for rock glacier development were invaded by glacier ice during the Loch Lomond Stadial, so that protalus rock glaciers

Figure 14.11 Earth hummocks near the summit of Glas Maol (1068 m) in the SE Grampian Highlands. (Photo: C.K. Ballantyne)

Loch Lomond Stadial, so that protalus rock glaciers occur only in locations peripheral to the main centres of ice accumulation at that time. Another constraint was the need for a rapid input of debris to generate the stresses required for the deformation of internal ice, and for this reason they are often located below steep cliffs or at sites of rock slope failure.

Under the periglacial conditions of the Late Devensian Late-glacial it is likely that snow avalanches were much more frequent and powerful than those that affect the Scottish mountains at present. Relict, overgrown **avalanche boulder tongues**, comprising lobes of debris swept beyond the downslope limits of talus slopes, occur at a number of

Figure 14.12 Vegetated Late-glacial talus slopes on the Trotternish Peninsula, Skye. Such slopes are now extensively gullied and modified by debris flow activity. (Photo: C.K. Ballantyne)

locations, such as upper Glen Feshie, Glen Taitneach in the SE Grampians, the Red Hills on Skye and the Cairngorms, but these forms have received little attention, and it is possible that some at least developed under snowier conditions during the 'Little Ice Age' of the 16th-19th centuries AD rather than during the Late-glacial.

14.4 Palaeoclimatic implications of relict periglacial features

Although several of the periglacial phenomena described above provide indications of the climate under which they developed, two problems beset the use of periglacial features as palaeoclimatic indicators. The first is uncertainty as to their age. As noted above, many surface or near-surface features, such as ice-wedge casts, ice-wedge polygons and cryoturbations, may have developed either during the period of ice-sheet retreat prior to *c.* 13 ka BP, or during the Loch Lomond Stadial (Figure 14.1). Similarly, frost debris, patterned ground and relict gelifluction features on Scottish mountains probably developed during both of these periods, but some of these features may be older, having survived Late Devensian glaciation on nunataks or under a protective cover of cold-based ice. Of the features considered, only protalus ramparts and protalus rock glaciers can be dated with any confidence, both being attributed to the Loch Lomond Stadial. The second problem arises from the use of periglacial landforms as palaeotemperature indicators. Such landforms reflect the thermal regime at the ground surface and subsurface, which owing to such factors as snowcover, shading, insolation and the thermal conductivity of surficial sediments may differ markedly from the ambient air temperature regime.

Ice wedge casts and ice-wedge polygons provide definite

Figure 14.13 Active protalus rampart on the Lyngen Peninsula, northern Norway. (Photo: C.K. Ballantyne).

evidence for former permafrost, and are thought to form where mean annual air temperature (MAAT) is lower than -3°C to -4°C, and probably lower than -6°C where such features are developed in coarse sand and gravel. They also indicate severe winter ground cooling, probably to temperatures lower than -20°C, and their development is thus favoured in fairly arid areas where the ground is not insulated by a thick cover of snow. The presence of ice-wedge casts under a layer of till in NE Scotland (Connell and Hall, 1987) thus confirms that such conditions existed in Scotland prior to the last glaciation of that area.

There is convincing faunal evidence that the progressive contraction of the Late Devensian ice sheet took place under sustained cold conditions (Peacock, 1981; Atkinson *et al.*, 1987), and probably reflected snowfall starvation rather than climatic warming. Of particular interest in this respect are the numerous ice-wedge casts and polygons that have been found in central and eastern Scotland. Though some of these may be of Loch Lomond Stadial age, most probably developed during ice-sheet retreat (Armstrong and Paterson, 1985). As these areas appear to have been deglaciated between 16-14 ka BP, the development of ice-wedges in Late Devensian sediments implies establishment of continuous permafrost down to sea level in the wake of the retreating ice sheet, thus supporting the notion that increased aridity rather than thermal amelioration was the prime cause of glacier retreat at this time. Moreover, these features suggest that the ice sheet had withdrawn to the central and western Highlands before the onset of the rapid warming that marked the beginning of the Windermere Interstadial around 13 ka BP.

Rather more can be inferred about the climate of Scotland during the Loch Lomond Stadial. Though definite evidence for ice-wedge formation in Scotland at this time remains elusive, the presence of securely dated examples of permafrost phenomena of Loch Lomond Stadial age in England implies widespread permafrost in Scotland also. This inference is supported by the development of protalus rock glaciers, which indicates the formation of at least discontinuous permafrost (MAAT -2°C or lower). The evidence of Loch Lomond Stadial permafrost features in England has been interpreted by Ballantyne and Harris (1994, pp. 286-292) as indicating a MAAT of -5°C for central England during the coldest part of the stadial. From this they inferred that permafrost probably extended down to sea level in Scotland at the same time, and that MAAT in NE Scotland declined to *c.* -8°C. When combined with reconstructed ablation season temperatures for Loch Lomond Stadial glaciers, this figure implies that mean January temperatures during the thermal nadir of the stadial were of the order of -22°C (Figure 14.15). Such a regime was almost certainly sufficiently severe for permafrost cracking and the formation of ice wedges and ice-wedge polygons.

Periglacial phenomena also provide some information on precipitation patterns during the Loch Lomond Stadial. As noted earlier, the altitudes of protalus ramparts formed at this time rise eastwards and northwards towards the Cairngorms. These landforms imply the development of firn fields with fairly constant dimensions, and hence maintenance of a delicate balance between snow accumulation and snowmelt. As snowmelt must have been much greater on low ground in the west of Scotland than on high ground in the Cairngorms, it follows that the supply of snow to the western ramparts was also much greater, implying a pronounced eastwards decline in snowfall during the stadial. This pattern is supported by calculations based on the altitudes of protalus rock glaciers, which form under extremely cold conditions only when precipitation (snowfall) is sufficiently low to inhibit the development of ice glaciers. Calculations based on an assumed MAAT of -7°C to -9°C for NE Scotland at sea level suggest that ground at around 900 m in the Cairngorms experienced no more than 375-550 mm a⁻¹ of precipitation during the period of rock glacier formation, only 19-27% of present values. In contrast, similar calculations carried out for the protalus rock glacier on Jura

Figure 14.14 The Strath Nethy rock glacier in the Cairngorm Mountains, which extends for 2.4 km along the foot of the slope. Crescentic failure scars in the granite rockwall above the rock glacier suggest that rockslides provided a large proportion of the rock glacier debris. (Photo: C.K. Ballantyne).

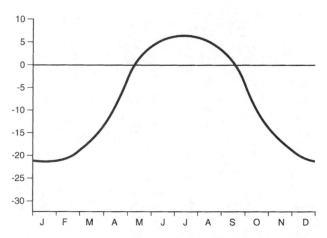

Figure 14.15 Conjectural range of mean monthly temperatures in NE Scotland during the coldest part of the Loch Lomond Stadial. This range is based on a mean July sea-level temperature of +6°C, derived from glaciological evidence, and a mean annual air temperature of -8°C (see text).

yield a maximum annual average precipitation in the range 800-1250 mm, 50-78% of present values (Ballantyne and Harris, 1994, p. 291). Despite the uncertainties inherent in these calculations, they suggest very pronounced eastwards reduction in precipitation during the Loch Lomond Stadial. This appears to have been due to the scavenging effect of the extensive icefield that occupied the Western Highlands at this time (Figure 14.4). Cooling of moist westerly airstreams that were forced to rise over this icefield must have caused heavy precipitation over the Western Highlands, whilst areas in the lee of the icefield experienced pronounced aridity. Under such circumstances, much of NE Scotland may have been an arid tundra landscape, with perhaps only 100-200 mm of precipitation per year.

14.5 Present-day periglacial activity on Scottish mountains

A very rapid increase in temperatures at the beginning of the Holocene (present) Interglacial (Atkinson *et al.*, 1987) effectively terminated periglacial activity in the Scottish lowlands, but on high ground a restricted range of periglacial processes continued to operate. Our knowledge of the periglacial activity on Scottish mountains during most of the Holocene is scant, and restricted to dated evidence for intermittent shallow solifluction over the past 5500 years (Sugden, 1971; Motterhead, 1978), wind erosion and redeposition of aeolian sediment since early Holocene times (Ballantyne and Whittington, 1987) and erosion of talus and other steep slopes by debris flows (Brazier *et al.*, 1988; Brazier and Ballantyne, 1989). However, in view of the relatively limited amplitude of climate change during the Holocene, it is likely that periglacial processes now active on high ground are fairly typical of those that have operated throughout the Holocene, though the lower limit of activity may have varied with changes in climate and vegetation cover.

The present climate on high ground in Scotland is characterised by wetness and strong winds rather than extreme cold. Even on the highest summits, MAAT is slightly above 0°C, and temperatures below -10°C are infrequent. Permafrost is consequently absent, though annual ground freezing occasionally reaches depths of 0.5 m or more. Above 600 m, all but the most easterly summits experience mean annual precipitation of over 2000 mm,

and some western mountains receive twice that figure. Average snow-lie (>50% cover) generally exceeds 100 days above 600 m in the Highlands, and strong winds are frequent, with gusts over 200 km/hr on the highest summits. This wet and windy **maritime periglacial** regime is very different from those of the Late Devensian, so it is not surprising that the range of periglacial features now active also differs in many respects. Three sets of periglacial processes are currently operative: those relating to frost action and late-lying snow, those resulting from wind action, and those that modify talus and other steep debris-mantled slopes (Ballantyne, 1987, 1991a).

The present operation of freeze-thaw activity on Scottish hills is manifest in three ways: rock weathering, the development of frost-sorted patterned ground, and solifluction. All three, however, operate on a much reduced scale to that of similar effects during the Late Devensian. Frost weathering of rock on high ground is largely restricted to superficial granular disaggregation of certain lithologies, particularly sandstone and granite, and small-scale flaking of fissile rocks such as mica-schists and shales. Active patterned ground in the form of miniature sorted nets and sorted stripes occurs on unvegetated surfaces (Figure 14.16), but patterns rarely exceed 0.6 m in width and sorting rarely extends deeper than 0.2 m, a reflection of the shallowness of soil freezing under present conditions. Such features, moreover, tend to be restricted to silt-rich soil containing clasts less than 15 cm in diameter, and are thus absent from coarse regolith. Active solifluction sheets and lobes are fairly widespread above 550 m in the Highlands, particularly on schists, but are much smaller than their relict counterparts, with risers less than 1m high. Only vegetation-covered nonsorted sheets and lobes are currently active, and are distinguishable from relict forms by the steepness of their risers, and by the fact that they often overlie organic soil or peat fragments containing Holocene pollen assemblages. Dating of such organic materials suggests that shallow solifluction has been at least intermittently active throughout the late Holocene (and probably earlier), and at one site in the NW Highlands it appears to have accelerated during

Figure 14.16 Miniature active sorted stripes on granite regolith, Beinn a' Bhuird, Eastern Cairngorms. Rucksack in background gives scale. (Photo: R. Goodier).

the past few centuries (Ballantyne, 1986b). Commonly associated with active solifluction lobes and sheets are **ploughing boulders**, which are boulders located at the downslope end of a furrow or depression in vegetated soil. These are amongst the most common manifestations of present periglacial activity on Scottish hills, and in places extend downslope to an altitude of 450 m. They are believed to move through the surrounding regolith when underlying ice lenses melt in spring, reducing the frictional strength of the contact between the boulder and the soil. Rates of boulder movement are generally a few millimetres a year; present activity is indicated by a deep niche immediately upslope of individual boulders.

The current effectiveness of **nivation** (erosion associated with late-lying snowbeds) is uncertain. Observations at snowpatch sites in the northern Highlands suggest that the geomorphic role of late-lying snow is limited to localised redistribution of fine sediment by surface wash during snowmelt (Ballantyne, 1985), though there is some evidence that the presence of late-lying snowbeds may also enhance the weathering of underlying boulders (Ballantyne *et al.*, 1989).

The second major agent of current periglacial activity on Scottish mountains is wind action. Erosion by strong winds has created extensive **deflation surfaces** on many high plateaux from which vegetation and fine sediment have been removed, leaving a lag deposit of clasts embedded in soil and fine gravel. Outstanding examples occupy the granite plateaux of the Cairngorms and the Torridon Sandstone summits of the NW Highlands. On some hills, 'islands' of vegetated soil or windblown sand survive amid widespread areas of deflation, suggesting that such surfaces were once mantled by a stable vegetated soil cover, and that opening up of the closed vegetation mat has resulted in drastic soil erosion by wind. On some mountains, soil eroded from cols or plateaux upwind has been redeposited as vegetated sheets of windblown sand on lee slopes. Research on the sandstone massif of An Teallach in the NW Highlands has shown that such deposits are currently accumulating through sand from plateaux upwind becoming trapped in the winter snowpack on sheltered lee sites. As the snow melts, the sand is lowered on to the underlying vegetation, which grows through the accumulating deposit and thus stabilises it. Such deposits are thus at least partly **niveo-aeolian** in origin, and have accumulated in this way since the beginning of the Holocene, reaching thicknesses of up to 4 m (Ballantyne and Whittington, 1987).

Associated with many deflation surfaces are three types of wind-patterned ground: deflation scars (patches of bare ground on vegetated terrain), wind stripes (straight or wavy lines of vegetation that alternate with unvegetated soil) and wind crescents (arcuate patterns of vegetation across otherwise unvegetated surfaces). Deflation scars result from selective opening up of vegetation cover by the combined action of frost and wind, but the origin of regular wind patterns (Figure 14.17) remains uncertain (Bayfield, 1984). Equally enigmatic is the origin of **turf-banked terraces**, which occupy moderate slopes and have steep vegetated risers but sparsely vegetated treads, though these appear to form through the accumulation of mobile debris behind 'dams' of vegetation (Ballantyne and Harris, 1994, pp. 261-267).

Talus slopes have accumulated during the Holocene in areas that were occupied by glacier ice during the Loch Lomond Stadial, but in comparison with Late-glacial taluses these are often immature features, indicating that rockfall rates have diminished markedly since the end of the stadial. Many taluses are now dominated by erosion and reworking

Figure 14.17 Wind stripes consisting of alternating band of heather *(Calluna vulgaris)* and bare ground, Beinn a' Bhuird, Eastern Cairngorms. (Photo: R. Goodier).

of debris rather than rockfall accumulation. In a few areas, such as the Lairig Ghru in the Cairngorms, snow avalanches have played a prominent role in stripping debris from the upper parts of talus slopes and redistributing it downslope, locally in the form of **avalanche boulder tongues** that are still intermittently active (Ballantyne, 1989; Luckman, 1992). The most widespread agent of sediment transfer on talus and other steep slopes, however, is debris flow activity. **Debris flows** are rapid flows of poorly sorted debris mixed with water, and are mainly triggered by high intensity rainstorms. Most originate in shallow gullies upslope, and flow paths are marked by the deposition of parallel levées and terminal lobes of debris (Figure 14.18). They are particularly abundant on debris with a coarse sandy matrix, and in some areas are the most effective form of present-day debris transport: over 70 debris flows were mobilised in the Lairg Ghru between 1970 and 1980. The majority of flows carry less than 30 m³ of sediment (Innes, 1985), but over time repeated debris flows have constructed substantial · fan-shaped **debris cones**, such as those that line the flanks of Glen Etive and Glencoe in the Western Grampians. One fascinating aspect of debris flow activity in the Scottish Highlands is that rates appear to have increased markedly over the past three centuries (Innes, 1983); Brazier and Ballantyne, 1989). Indeed, there is a growing body of evidence to suggest that various forms of erosion in the Highlands have intensified during this period. Whether this increase in erosion is climatically induced or results from anthropogenic causes, such as burning or overgrazing of vegetation, is currently unknown (Ballantyne, 1991b), and the cause of such accelerated erosion constitutes an urgent priority for future research on the mountain environments of Scotland.

14.6 Conclusion

Periglacial processes have extensively modified the landscape of Scotland during the Quaternary, both in the lowlands and in the mountains, producing a distinctive suite of landforms and deposits. These features not only provide a record of former geomorphological activity, but also allow

Figure 14.18 A recent debris flow in the Lairig Ghru, Cairngorms. Such debris flows constitute the most effective mode of sediment transport in some parts of the Scottish Highlands. Most occur as a result of intensive rainstorms inducing soil failure at the top of the slope. The debris then flows downslope as a slurry. (Photo: C.K. Ballantyne).

a valuable means of reconstructing past climatic conditions. Periglacial processes continue to operate on Scottish mountains under wet and windy climatic conditions, in contrast with much colder and drier conditions at the end of the last ice age.

References

Armstrong, M. and Paterson, I.B. 1985. Some recent discoveries of ice-wedge cast networks in north-east Scotland - a comment. *Scottish Journal of Geology*, **21**, 107-108.

Atkinson, T.C., Briffa, K.R. and Coope, G.R. 1987. Seasonal temperatures in Britain during the past 22,000 years, reconstructed using beetle remains. *Nature*, **325**, 587-592.

Ballantyne, C.K. 1984. The Late Devensian periglaciation of upland Scotland. *Quaternary Science Reviews*, **3**, 311-343.

Ballantyne, C.K. 1985. Nivation landforms and snowpatch erosion on two massifs in the Northern Highlands of Scotland. *Scottish Geographical Magazine*, **102**, 40-49.

Ballantyne, C.K. 1986a. Nonsorted patterned ground on mountains in the Northern Highlands of Scotland. *Biuletyn Peryglacjalny*, **30**,15-34.

Ballantyne, C.K. 1986b. Late Flandrian solifluction on the Fannich Mountains, Ross-shire. *Scottish Journal of Geology*, **22**, 395-406.

Ballantyne, C.K. 1987. The present-day periglaciation of upland Britain. In: Boardman, J. (Ed.), *Periglacial Processes and Landforms in Britain and Ireland*. Cambridge University Press, Cambridge, 113-126.

Ballantyne, C.K. 1989. Avalanche impact landforms on Ben Nevis, Scotland. *Scottish Geographical Magazine*, **105**, 38-42.

Ballantyne, C.K. 1990. The Late Quaternary glacial history of the Trotternish Escarpment, Isle of Skye, Scotland, and its implications for ice-sheet reconstruction. *Proceedings of the Geologists' Association*, **101**, 171-186.

Ballantyne, C.K. 1991a. Holocene geomorphic activity in the Scottish Highlands. *Scottish Geographical Magazine*, **107**, 84-98.

Ballantyne, C.K. 1991b. Late Holocene erosion in upland Britain: climatic deterioration or human influence? *The Holocene*, **1**, 81-85.

Ballantyne, C.K., Black, N.M. and Finlay, D.P. 1989. Enhanced boulder weathering under late-lying snowpatches. *Earth Surface Processes and Landforms*, **14**, 745-750.

Ballantyne, C.K. and Harris, C. 1994. *The Periglaciation of Great Britain*. Cambridge University Press, Cambridge.

Ballantyne, C.K. and Kirkbride, M.P. 1986. The characteristics and significance of some Lateglacial protalus ramparts in upland Britain. *Earth Surface Processes and Landforms*, **11**, 659-671.

Ballantyne, C.K. and Kirkbride, M.P. 1987. Rockfall activity in upland Britain during the Loch Lomond Stadial. *Geographical Journal*, **153**, 86-92.

Ballantyne, C.K. and McCarroll, D. 1995. The vertical dimensions of Late Devensian glaciation on the mountains of Harris and southeast Lewis, Outer Hebrides, Scotland. *Journal of Quaternary Science*, **10**, 211-223.

Ballantyne, C.K. and Whittington, G.W. 1987. Niveo-aeolian sand deposits on An Teallach, Wester Ross, Scotland. *Transactions of the Royal Society of Edinburgh: Earth Sciences*, **78**, 51-63.

Bayfield, N.G. 1984. The dynamics of heather *(Calluna vulgaris)* stripes in the Cairngorm Mountains, Scotland. *Journal of Ecology*, **72**, 515-527.

Brazier, V. and Ballantyne, C.K. 1989. Late Holocene debris cone evolution in Glen Feshie, western Cairngorm Mountains, Scotland. *Transactions of the Royal Society of Edinburgh: Earth Sciences*, **80**, 17-24.

Brazier, V. Whittington, G.W. and Ballantyne, C.K. 1988. Holocene debris cone evolution in Glen Etive, Western Grampian Highlands, Scotland. *Earth Surface Processes and Landforms*, **13**, 525-531.

Chattopadhyay, G.P. 1984. A fossil valley-wall rock glacier in the Cairngorm Mountains. *Scottish Journal of Geology*, **20**, 121-125.

Connell, E.R. and Hall, A.M. 1987. The periglacial history of Buchan, north-east Scotland. In: Boardman, J. (Ed.), *Periglacial Processes and Landforms in Britain and Ireland*. Cambridge University Press, Cambridge, 277-285.

Dawson, A.G. 1977. A fossil lobate rock glacier in Jura. *Scottish Journal of Geology*, **13**, 37-42.

Dickson, J.H., Jardine, W.G. and Price, R.J. 1976. Three late-Devensian sites in west-central Scotland. *Nature*, **262**, 43-44.

Douglas, T.D. and Harrison, S. 1987. Late Devensian periglacial slope deposits in the Cheviot Hills. In: Boardman, J. (Ed.), *Periglacial Processes and Landforms in Britain and Ireland*. Cambridge University Press,

FitzPatrick, E.A. 1987. Periglacial features in the soils of North-East Scotland. In: Boardman, J. (Ed.), *Periglacial Processes and Landforms in Britain and Ireland*. Cambridge University Press, Cambridge,153-162.

Galloway, R.W. 1961. Ice wedges and involutions in Scotland. *Biuletyn Peryglacjalny,* **10,** 169-193.

Gemmell, A.M.D. and Ralston, I.B.M. 1984. Some recent discoveries of ice-wedge cast networks in north-east Scotland. *Scottish Journal of Geology,* **20,** 115-118.

Innes, J.L. 1983. Lichenometric dating of debris flow deposits in the Scottish Highlands. *Earth Surface Processes and Landforms,* **8,** 579-588.

Innes, J.L. 1985. Magnitude-frequency relations of debris flows in north-west Europe. *Geografiska Annaler,* **67A,** 23-32.

Luckman, B.H. 1992. Debris flows and snow avalanche landforms in the Lairig Ghru, Cairngorm Mountains, Scotland. *Geografiska Annaler,* **74A,** 109-121.

McCarroll, D., Ballantyne, C.K., Nesje, A. and Dahl, S.-O. 1995. Nunataks of the last ice sheet in north-west Scotland. *Boreas,* **24,** 305-323.

Mottershead, D.N. 1978. High altitude solifluction and Postglacial vegetation, Arkle, Sutherland. *Transactions of the Botanical Society of Edinburgh,* **43,** 17-24.

Peacock, J.D. 1981. Scottish late-glacial marine deposits and their environmental significance. In: Neale, J. and Flenley, J. (Eds), *The Quaternary in Britain,* Pergamon Press, Oxford, 222-236.

Rose, J. 1975. Raised beach gravels and ice-wedge casts at Old Kilpatrick, near Glasgow. *Scottish Journal of Geology,* **11,** 15-21.

Sugden, D.E. 1971. The significance of periglacial activity on some Scottish mountains. *Geographical Journal,* **13,** 388-392.

Walker, M.J.C., Merritt, J.W., Auton, C.A., Coope, G.R., Field, M.H., Heijnis, H. and Taylor, B.J. 1992. Allt Odhar and Dalcharn: two pre-Late Devensian/Late Weichselian sites in northern Scotland. *Journal of Quaternary Science,* **7,** 69-86.

Further Reading

Ballantyne, C.K. 1991. Holocene geomorphic activity in the Scottish Highlands. *Scottish Geographical Magazine,* **107,** 84-98.

Ballantyne, C.K. and Harris, C. 1994. *The Periglaciation of Great Britain*. Cambridge University Press, Cambridge.

Boardman, J. (Ed.) 1987. *Periglacial Landforms and Processes in Great Britain and Ireland*. Cambridge University Press, Cambridge.

Clark, M.J. (Ed.) 1988. *Advances in Periglacial Geomorphology*. Wiley, Chichester.

15. Quaternary Landforms and Deposits as Part of Scotland's Natural Heritage

John E. Gordon and Alan P. McKirdy

> The key themes covered in this chapter are:
>
> - Quaternary sites and the natural heritage;
> - the Geological Conservation Review;
> - Regionally Important Geological/ Geomorphological Sites (RIGS);
> - impacts of human activities;
> - Quaternary studies and integrated landscape management;
> - Natural Heritage Zones;
> - environmental education.

15.1 Introduction

The Earth sciences have an important contribution to make to the sustainable management of Scotland's natural heritage which includes a rich diversity of geomorphological features, landscapes and habitats. This diversity reflects the cumulative inheritance of a long and varied geological history, dating back to Precambrian times, which has provided not only a fundamental structural and tectonic framework at a broad scale, but also strong underlying geological controls for many landscape features (Chapters 2 and 3). The Quaternary ice ages have also left a clear signature on the landscape, both directly in the form of glacial, glaciofluvial and periglacial landforms (Chapters 4, 5, 6, 8, 13 and 14) and indirectly through changes in the relative levels of the land and sea (Chapter 12). The history of Scotland's geomorphological evolution and the accompanying environmental changes is preserved in a variety of fossil landforms as well as in terrestrial, lacustrine and marine sedimentary records (Chapters 7, 9, 10 and 11). Modern coastal, fluvial and slope processes are also continuing to shape the landscape, and during the latter part of the present interglacial, human activity has increasingly contributed to landscape change (Chapter 10).

Quaternary interests form an important element of Scotland's natural heritage in several respects. First, there is the intrinsic scientific interest of landforms, environmental change and landscape evolution for purposes of scientific research and education. Second, Quaternary geomorphology and geomorphological processes provide the physical underpinning of habitats and their associated biota, landscape character and natural heritage zones, for example through controls on landforms, soils, hydrology and nutrient cycling. Moreover, the invaluable records of Quaternary landscape evolution and environmental change, preserved in a range of sedimentary environments, provide a critical temporal dimension to many present day phenomena, for example allowing the evolution of particular types of habitat to be determined. Third, Quaternary studies and geomorphology are significant in a wider context through helping to understand the dynamics and history of the landscape. Such understanding can make a significant contribution to developing an integrated approach to sustainable land management, environmental monitoring and landscape interpretation. Finally, from an aesthetic and cultural viewpoint, Quaternary interests form an integral part of Scotland's natural heritage.

Scottish Natural Heritage (SNH) is the statutory body responsible for the conservation of Scotland's natural assets. Its aims are first, to secure the conservation and enhancement of the natural heritage of Scotland; and second, to foster understanding and facilitate the enjoyment of that heritage. The fundamental principle underlying the work of SNH is that anything done in relation to the natural heritage of Scotland is carried out in a manner which is sustainable. Furthermore, the focus is on the whole landscape, not only protected sites.

Most of the landscape of Scotland is modified to varying degrees by human activity, resulting in a range of impacts on the Quaternary interests and geomorphology. It is therefore not surprising that the focus in the past in Earth science conservation has been 'protectionist', following a site-based approach as epitomised in the Geological Conservation Review (GCR) (Ellis *et al.*, 1996). However, Earth science conservation can also be viewed in the broader framework of sustainable and integrated management of the whole countryside. Quaternary studies and geomorphology have a significant role to play in an integrated and multidisciplinary approach to the management of Scotland's landscapes, particularly in developing a better understanding of physical processes, their sensitivity to change, their spatial and temporal variability and their interactions with habitat ecology. In addition, the more dynamic elements of the landscape are subject to natural perturbations of varying magnitude and frequency (*e.g.* floods and sea-level changes) which may impact adversely on human activities, land use and ecological systems. Such impacts, however, can be mitigated through better understanding of the physical processes and how they have varied in the past.

SNH also has an important educational role in helping to foster wider awareness and enjoyment of our natural heritage. This is particularly critical in the Earth sciences which intrinsically lack the immediate appeal of, say, birds and plants. However, geology and geomorphology form the very essence of the physical landscape in which nature and humans interact. Furthermore, as the preceding chapters in this volume have illustrated, the evolution of Scotland's landscape is a remarkable story of plate tectonics, mountain building and erosion, ice ages, sea-level changes, rapid environmental changes and dynamic geomorphological processes. It is a story to excite the imagination and one that deserves to be more widely known.

The aim of this chapter is to review recent advances in Earth science conservation and to outline the important role of Quaternary studies and geomorphology within the integrated approach to sustainable management of Scotland's natural heritage that is being developed by SNH. This is taking place against a background of wider developments in Earth science conservation, as reflected in the publications arising from several recent conferences (O'Halloran *et al.*, 1994; Stevens *et al.*, 1994; Taylor *et al.*, 1996).

15.2 Quaternary sites and the natural heritage

15.2.1 The Geological Conservation Review (GCR)

The traditional approach to Earth science, or Earth heritage, conservation in Britain has focused on the protection of special or representative sites selected on the basis of scientific criteria. The underlying rationale is that national networks of key sites are necessary to support new research and education in the future. This is essential to allow testing of existing ideas, development of new models and application of new research methods. These networks of sites together represent the principal spatial and temporal components of the geological evolution of the present landscape, the patterns of environmental change and the current landform and process domains. These networks of sites also have a significant educational role in the field training of new generations of Earth scientists and can provide a valuable resource for applied research and teaching, as in natural hazards mapping and prediction (for some applications of Quaternary research, see Gray, 1992). They also ensure protection of important elements of our Earth heritage, such as classic landforms.

The GCR provides the basis for the site-based approach to conservation of our Earth heritage. This major exercise, which began in 1977, involved a review of all the main aspects of Earth science interests in Britain from the Precambrian to the Quaternary. The aim was to identify the key sites for conservation that represented the geology and geomorphology of Britain. Site selection was completed in 1989, with over 3000 individual localities identified. Publication of the results and scientific descriptions of the sites selected is currently in progress through a series of thematic volumes aimed at the specialist reader. The principles behind the GCR and the general criteria for site selection are described in an introductory volume written for a wider audience (Ellis *et al.,* 1996). Broadly, sites have to be of international importance, contain exceptional features or be representative of a feature, event or process fundamental to Britain's Earth history. Various guidelines were employed to inform the site selection process and to minimise duplication (Ellis *et al.,* 1996): preference was given to sites that -

- display an assemblage of interests;
- show an extended or relatively complete record of the features of interest;
- have been studied in detail and which have a long history of research and reinterpretation;
- have potential for future study;
- are of historical interest through having played a significant part in the development of the Earth sciences.

These guidelines are explained further, with examples, in the introduction to each volume in the GCR Series *(e.g.* Gordon and Sutherland, 1993).

Selection of Quaternary sites for the GCR was organised on a regional basis, reflecting the different patterns of geology, glaciation and palaeoenvironmental gradients (for example in Scotland, Wales and East Anglia) and the distinctive contribution that each region makes to the overall picture of Quaternary landscapes and environments in Britain. A prime aim of site selection was to reflect this diversity and to select networks of sites representing the major regional variations in landscape evolution and the history of environmental change during the Quaternary in Britain. These 'regions' also provided a practical basis for site selection.

The concept of site **networks** is fundamental to the GCR. Within the general regional framework, the approach adopted was to identify networks of sites that represent the main landscape features, the distinctive aspects of Quaternary history and the principal research themes. For the Quaternary of Scotland (Gordon and Sutherland, 1993), the site networks represent the following themes:

- aspects of long-term landscape evolution;
- glacial landforms and deposits;
- periglacial landforms and deposits;
- sea-level changes;
- key sequences of deposits for interpreting the distinctive Quaternary history of Scotland;
- Late-glacial and Holocene vegetation history and environmental change.

Potential sites representing the key elements of these networks were identified from extensive consultations and then compared to ensure selection of the 'best' sites and to minimise duplication of similar features within each regional block. Site selection decisions were made on the basis of the guidelines outlined above. Particular emphasis was given to: uniqueness; classic examples; representativeness; being part of a site network; providing understanding of present environments; historical importance; and research potential and educational value. Individual sites may fall into one or more of these categories. In total, 139 sites (or groups of sites) were selected for the Quaternary of Scotland (Figure 15.1).

Unique sites may be either the only known representatives of particular parts of the geological record or they may be features with no comparable equivalents elsewhere in Scotland or Britain. The pre-Late Devensian sequences at Fugla Ness and Kirkhill (Chapter 6) are examples of the former; Glen Roy and the Cairngorms of the latter.

Some sites are nationally or internationally recognized as being classic examples of particular features and are quoted in standard textbooks. Examples include the Parallel Roads of Glen Roy, the raised shore platforms of Northern Islay, the raised shingle beaches of the West Coast of Jura and the eskers of Carstairs Kames.

Other sites are representative of important aspects of geomorphology, landscape evolution or environmental change during the Quaternary in Scotland. Some sites have therefore been selected because they are the best studied, are the best preserved and/or have the most complete local representation of phenomena that are quite widespread. They are therefore important reference sites for the particular feature, event or area concerned, such as glacial deposits or landforms (*e.g.* the hummocky moraines of Glen Torridon, the meltwater channels at Carlops, south-west of Edinburgh, the eskers at Kildrummie Kames near Nairn and the Gairloch Moraine which forms part of the Wester Ross Readvance). Others are representative or informally recognized reference sites for Quaternary stratigraphy (*e.g.* the till deposits at Nigg Bay, south of Aberdeen, which reflect the interaction of ice masses from different sources, and the deposits at Croftamie, near Drymen, which help to define the Loch Lomond Stadial in its type area).

Where the scientific interests have a strong geographical component, networks of sites were chosen to incorporate significant regional variations in the characteristics of the feature or event concerned, for example in relation to factors such as geology, climate or relief. Such networks may comprise unique, classic or representative sites. A good example is the case of Late-glacial and Holocene vegetational change where no single site in any part of the country can represent the complex patterns of plant colonisation and succession at the end of the Late Devensian and during the early Holocene (Chapter 9). Other examples include networks of sites for mountain-top periglacial landforms and deposits (Chapter 14), and Late-glacial and Holocene changes in sea level (Chapter 12).

Certain sites are of particular importance because they provide palaeoecological or geomorphological evidence for

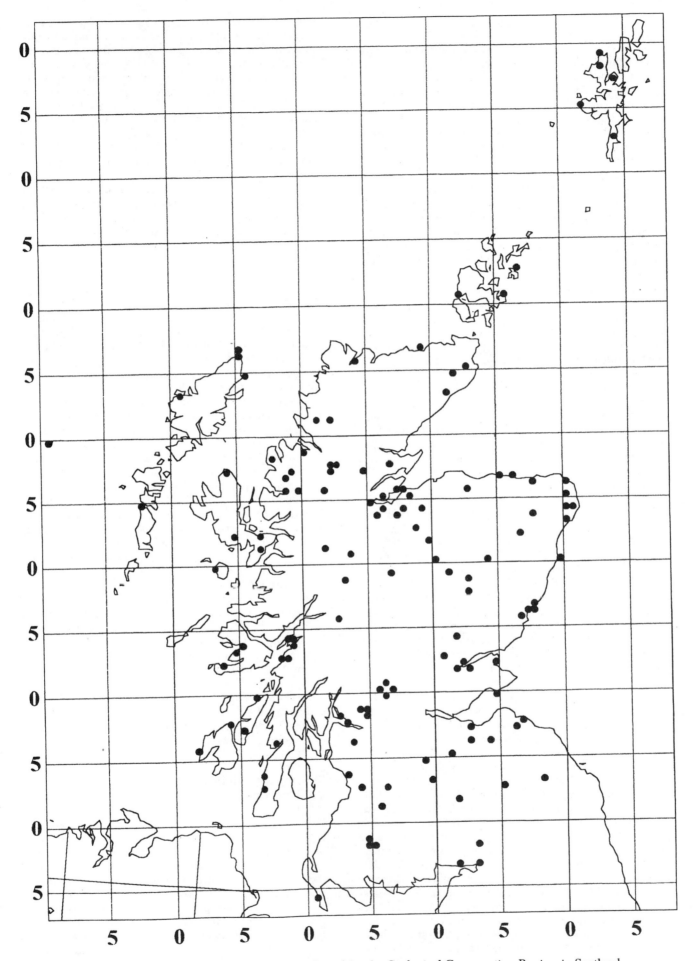

Figure 15.1 Distribution map of Quaternary sites selected for the Geological Conservation Review in Scotland

interpreting present landscape patterns or changes. An example is a group of sites which illustrate the palaeoecological development of rare or distinctive modern plant communities, such as the arctic-alpine plant species on certain mountains, the nearest equivalents of which may be in Norway. Sites such as Corrie Fee in Glen Clova, part of Caenlochan National Nature Reserve (NNR), and Morrone NNR, near Braemar, demonstrate that montane species have survived on Scottish mountains since the Late Devensian, when they were much more widespread in their occurrence. A very different example is that where palaeoecological records provide baseline measurements for assessing the levels of modern environmental pollutants. The diatom records from sites such as the Round Loch of Glenhead in Galloway have allowed an assessment of the extent of recent acidification of lochs through the reconstruction of pH levels before the start of modern industrial emissions. Other sites may demonstrate the sensitivity of certain parts of the environment to change through natural processes and human activities. Sites such as Glen Feshie have provided information on rates of change in upland geomorphological processes and river channel movements that have occurred during the Holocene. Comparison of modern rates and past rates may reveal whether significant changes have occurred (see Chapter 11) and give cause for concern.

A number of sites also have notable historical interest or associations. As outlined in Chapter 1, Scotland has played a significant role in the development of Quaternary studies. The glacial theory was more widely accepted during the middle of the last century by the Earth science community in Scotland than in Britain in general, and over the 50-year period between 1840 (when the glacial theory was introduced by Louis Agassiz) and 1890, many of the concepts related to glacial landforms, sediments and the interaction between solar radiation, climate, ice sheets and sea-level change were developed from field evidence in Scotland. Certain of the Quaternary sites in Scotland are therefore of major significance in the history of geology and deserve to be conserved on this basis alone; examples include the Glen Roy-Glen Spean area which was fundamental in influencing the development of Agassiz' ideas, Agassiz Rock in Edinburgh, a striated rock surface named after the principal proponent of the glacial theory, the Cuillin Hills which were the location of Forbes' (1846) early study of mountain glaciation, and Rhu Point, near Dumbarton, where Maclaren (1845, 1846) first identified links between glaciation and raised shorelines. Other sites have had a long history of research and have played a fundamental role in the development of new ideas and interpretations of Quaternary events, chronology or landscape processes; for example the raft of glacially transported marine sediments at Clava, near Inverness, the glaciomarine sediments at Ardersier and the quartzite gravels at Windy Hills near Fyvie.

A final justification of many sites is the interpretation or interpretations, frequently controversial, that have been placed upon them. Such sites may illustrate the development of scientific thinking on the subject of landscape history and the debates, for example about process or chronology, that characterize certain areas of Quaternary science. It is important that such sites continue to be available for further study and to stimulate active scientific debate. Other sites provide fundamental baselines, for example in dating or as stratigraphical markers, and must remain accessible for reference (e.g. Kirkhill and Teindland - see Chapter 6). There are many outstanding questions not yet resolved in the Quaternary of Scotland, but in many respects this is a

strength and not a weakness of the science and will hopefully stimulate future generations to enquire in depth about the evolution of Scotland during the Quaternary. Although new sites will become available through further research, it is important that existing sites are maintained to allow the application of new research techniques. The long-term research potential of many sites is therefore a key factor in their selection. Finally, the educational importance of many of the sites should not be overlooked, and in total the coverage provides a history of the evolution of the Scottish landscape as recorded in its constituent landforms and sediments.

Many of the sites selected for the GCR have been designated as Sites of Special Scientific Interest (SSSIs). Following designation, SSSIs are accorded statutory protection through planning legislation and the Wildlife and Countryside Act (see Gordon and Campbell, 1992; Ellis et al., 1996).

15.2.2 Regionally Important Geological/Geomorphological Sites (RIGS)

Since 1990, a system has been developed to recognise the value of sites that lie outwith the GCR (Harley and Robinson, 1991). The identification and protection of Regionally Important Geological/Geomorphological Sites (RIGS) has been undertaken by voluntary groups, involving museums, wildlife trusts, local geologists and interested amateurs. Such sites have no statutory status but are notified to local planning authorities which often accord them discretionary protection and recognise their interest in Local and Structure Plans. RIGS groups have been formed in most areas of England and Wales (Harley, 1994), but in Scotland their development has been more hesitant; RIGS groups now exist for Lothian and Borders (Butcher, 1994), Fife, Tayside and the Highlands, but few sites have been selected. Criteria for the selection of RIGS include scientific and educational importance, historic interest and aesthetic and cultural value. Generally in England, emphasis has been placed on the first of these (Harley, 1994).

The SNH approach to RIGS has been to lend support and to foster interest, rather than to take the lead in what is perceived to be a 'grass-roots' movement. RIGS should not be viewed as simply another layer of site designation. Rather, we propose that RIGS should reflect local features that form a significant part of the natural heritage of local communities. Where possible they should form a community resource for multiple uses including recreation, education and interpretation. The local community should feel a strong sense of ownership and involvement through participation, provision of interpretation and publicity. Within this approach, there is clearly a place for the close involvement of schools and teachers in RIGS activities.

15.3 Impacts of human activities

The principal sources of human impact on Quaternary interests are summarised in Table 15.1 (Gordon and Campbell, 1992; Werritty et al., 1994). Several principal types of effect may result. First, the interest may suffer physical damage or destruction; for example the loss of an esker system through quarrying for sand and gravel. Second, the integrity of the interest may be adversely affected. This may occur through removal of part of the interest by quarrying or the disruption of sediment supply to a beach system by construction of coastal defences. Third, the naturalness of the interest may be lost. In some cases, as in a sediment succession in a quarry section, this may be relatively unimportant providing that access is maintained;

Table 15.1 Human activities and possible impacts on Quaternary features

Activity	Possible Impacts
1. Mineral extraction (including peat)	- destruction of relict landforms, sedimentary records and palaeoenvironmental archives - changes in sediment supply to active process systems - disruption of drainage network - may have positive benefits in creating new sedimentary sections
2. Restoration of gravel pits	- loss of sedimentary exposures
3. Landfill	- loss of sedimentary exposures
4. Commercial and industrial developments	- large scale damage and disruption of surface and sub-surface features - changes to geomorphological processes downstream or downslope
5. Coast protection	- loss of coastal exposures - changes to sediment circulation and processes downdrift
6. River management and engineering	- destruction of active and relict landforms - disruption of active processes
7. Afforestation	- loss of landform visibility - physical damage to small scale landforms - temporary changes in sediment yield and runoff
8. Agriculture	- landform damage through ploughing, ground levelling and drainage - changes in runoff response times arising from drainage - episodic soil erosion, leading to increased sedimentation in lochs and lowland river systems
9. Other land management changes (*eg.* drainage, dumping, construction of tracks)	- degradation of landforms and palaeoenvironmental records in peat bogs - changes in runoff and sediment supply
10. Recreation (infrastructure, footpath development, use of all-terrain vehicles)	- physical damage to small-scale landforms

in other cases the effect may be significant as in the loss of visibility of features arising from afforestation or through the proliferation of small scale building development across an assemblage of glaciofluvial landforms. Fourth, the impact may alter the state of the interest; for example, river channel engineering may stabilise an active fluvial environment, 'fossilising' an assemblage of shifting gravel bars and channels. Conversely, inappropriate development may reactivate formerly stable slopes or initiate landslips. Fifth, developments may produce geomorphological impacts beyond their immediate area; for example coastal erosion downdrift of sea defences. Essentially these impacts are on specific features identified for their conservation value, although they may also have wider economic and social implications, for example on patterns of river discharge and flooding or coastal erosion. Also in the wider context of landscape management, human activities may produce other adverse geomorphological impacts such as enhanced soil erosion and changes to hydrological systems.

Not all impacts are negative, however; for example quarrying may produce new sections revealing the three-dimensional sedimentary architecture of glacial deposits. Equally, activities may vary in their degree of impact. In assessing impacts, therefore, geomorphological sensitivity is a potentially useful concept. In relation to static sites or features, sensitivity evaluation may be based on a qualitative scale of impact assessment in relation to specific activities (Werritty and Brazier, 1994) and the site or area zoned accordingly. For example an area of kame terraces with kettle holes and palaeochannels will be generally sensitive to extraction of sand and gravel and afforestation, and locally sensitive to road and track construction or building development where small-scale landforms occur. In the case of dynamic systems or in assessing wider landscape impacts, the situation is more complex, involving the need to understand thresholds, process-response activity, carrying capacity and other factors that determine the sensitivity of process systems (Schumm, 1991; Werritty and Brazier, 1994; see Chapter 10). Prediction of how such systems will respond to a given change in land use or land management is an aspect that requires greater awareness and research. There is also an additional complication of separating the effects of human impacts from those of natural changes that are either intrinsic within the system or the product of external changes, for example in climate or sea level. Nevertheless, from the existing body of geomorphological theory and observations it should be possible to provide land managers and planners with guidance as to best land management practice, based on understanding of current and past processes of landscape evolution.

15.4 Towards integrated management

15.4.1 Changing the approach to natural heritage conservation

Nature conservation in Great Britain in the past has principally been concerned with the protection of wildlife and physical features for scientific reasons (cf. Ratcliffe, 1977a). The approach, be it in relation to landforms, landscapes, habitats or individual species, has conventionally been site-based, and a network of SSSIs, NNRs and National Scenic Areas (NSAs) has been developed to safeguard the best and most representative aspects of our natural heritage. Earth science conservation has essentially fitted into this mould, as reflected in the emphasis on the GCR. The Nature Conservation Review (NCR) (Ratcliffe, 1977b), is the biological analogue to the GCR and describes the key sites of habitat and species interest throughout Great Britain. Together, these reviews of the Earth science and nature conservation resource have informed and directed much of the work of the statutory conservation agencies to date. However, our natural heritage comprises not only these protected sites but also the wider landscape and, moreover, human activities also impact not only on sites but also on the wider landscape. The SNH approach, therefore, places much greater emphasis on sustainability and integrated management of the whole landscape. Site conservation now forms only one element in a broader strategy. Such an approach opens up new opportunities both to enhance the wider conservation of Quaternary features as well as to develop the contribution of Quaternary studies to a broader multidisciplinary approach to landscape conservation.

This approach has several advantages from a Quaternary/geomorphological perspective. First, it incorporates the concept of spatial scales, allowing focus on an integrated

hierarchy of landscape elements ranging from whole landscapes with a common origin or set of characteristics down through landform assemblages to individual landforms and their constituent sediment sequences. Second, it permits the development of a structured management framework across such a range of spatial scales. Third, it provides a means of integrating site management with the wider landscape, allowing individual features to be managed in the context of their wider relationships with other components of the landscape. Fourth, the focus on systems emphasises both temporal and spatial scales, and it allows the incorporation of the vitally important palaeoenvironmental dimension.

In Scotland much, if not all, of the landscape is already modified by human activities, so that conservation is not as much concerned with protection of undisturbed features or landscapes, but rather with ensuring sustainable management of the natural heritage. Where appropriate, however, a sustainable approach will still involve protection of unique or exceptional features, particularly at a site-specific scale.

15.4.2 Quaternary studies and integrated management

Quaternary studies have a potentially important contribution to make to integrated management. This arises through the physical underpinning of habitats and ecosystems, the value of palaeoenvironmental records and the shaping of landscape characteristics.

Geomorphology and landscape evolution are closely interwoven with habitats and ecosystem development; for example, geomorphological processes play a significant role in vegetation stability and change, particularly through small-scale interactions with topography, soils, hydrology and micro-climates. In particular, four areas of interaction between geomorphology and ecosystems have been identified (Swanson et al., 1988):

- the influence of landforms on environmental gradients, e.g. the relationships between elevation, aspect, solar energy and water balances;
- the influence of landforms on movements of materials, organisms, propagules and energy;
- the influence of landforms on the frequencies and patterns of non-geomorphologically induced disturbances, e.g. fire, snow accumulation, floods;
- the influence of geomorphological processes on ecosystems, e.g. river channel dynamics.

Understanding such interactions is an important element in explaining the physical basis of ecosystems.

In sensitive ecosystems, small scale changes in geomorphological processes may produce significant effects, for example through expansion of upland deflation surfaces where vegetation cover is broken and the soil exposed to wind erosion. Large-scale effects will occur where geomorphological changes are of high magnitude, for example on landslides. Understanding geomorphological processes and their responses to change during the Quaternary is therefore an important consideration in the sustainable management of sensitive ecosystems.

Geomorphological systems are important for many key aspects of monitoring change in the natural environment. Such change may be a response to natural processes (e.g. climate change or change in river sediment supply) or human impacts (e.g. afforestation or deforestation) and may be manifested through variations in geomorphic process activity, energy transfers or sediment and solute movement. For example, upland areas are generally sensitive to change on account of steep slopes, high relief and steep environmental gradients. Vegetation and soil systems are frequently fragile and susceptible to low-magnitude disturbance. Slope stability thresholds are therefore more likely to be crossed, so that sudden slope failures (*e.g.* debris flows), as well as responses of a more gradual nature, may be detected. Further, using palaeoenvironmental records, the components of environmental change can be investigated at different temporal and spatial scales and the impact, for example, of high-magnitude but often localised effects can be placed in a wider perspective of changes during, say, the Holocene.

The present landscape holds subtle clues about its past evolution and the changing patterns of climate, geomorphological processes and environmental conditions, as revealed in the earlier chapters. These clues are preserved in landforms and sediment sequences, both in terrestrial situations in lochs and bogs and in the marine environment. The application of powerful analytical techniques for the analysis of sediment chemistry and the biogenic material contained in the sediments has proved particularly valuable when combined with advances in dating methods (*e.g.* Chapters 9 and 11). Parallel investigations of landforms have included dating their times of formation, and analysis of the sediment sequences they contain (*e.g.* Chapters 6, 8, 13 and 14).

Such studies are significant in several respects. They allow the pace, direction and magnitude of current geomorphological change to be placed in a longer time perspective (*e.g.* river channel changes - Chapter 10). Such evaluation of longer-term relationships between process magnitude and frequency is essential to a proper understanding and assessment of the implications of current landscape changes taking place through natural processes and human activities, for example peat erosion in the uplands (Stevenson *et al.*, 1990). Palaeoenvironmental reconstructions can provide useful models for predicting the long-term impacts of current changes and offer opportunities for testing deductive models. From an ecological perspective, palaeoenvironmental records have allowed reconstruction of vegetation change at the end of the last glaciation (Chapter 9), the pattern of spread of different tree species across Scotland during the early and middle Holocene (Chapters 9 and 11) and the impact of human activities on the landscape (Chapter 11). Such records allow contemporary ecological patterns and changes to be placed in their historical context (*e.g.* the decline of heather moorland in the uplands - Stevenson and Thompson, 1993) and they show how plant communities might respond to future environmental changes (Huntley, 1991). Palaeoecological studies may also contribute to nature conservation in a number of significant ways (Birks, 1996): assessment of the naturalness and fragility of ecosystems, the conservation status of rare species, ecosystem responses to human activities and effects such as acidification. Palaeoenvironmental records are often a valuable (sometimes the only) source of baseline information for monitoring environmental change or undertaking ecosystem restoration.

Landforms, their evolution and the geomorphological processes currently active are core elements in determining the particular character of landscapes. The landforms and surface deposits define much of the detail that is seen and appreciated in the landscape today. They form an essential part of recent geological history and are an integral component of landscape character. The physical features of the landscape and its dynamic processes are therefore as much a part of our natural heritage as is the pattern of vegetation or the distribution of the flora and fauna. The landscape also serves a vital function in providing the wider context for the GCR site networks which often represent only selected and narrowly defined parts of a wider continuum of features. In upland and coastal areas, the relationships between geomorphology and landscape are often most clearly or spectacularly evident. Such areas can therefore provide an important setting for interpreting and fostering a greater public awareness of how landscapes have evolved, how they function and how human activity interacts with natural processes. Furthermore, the physical characteristics and history of landscapes are significant for the manner in which they interact with the biological and socio-economic components, forming an integrated whole; for example, the geomorphology and surface deposits provide the foundations for soils, vegetation, habitats and energy pathways, but at the same time they can also underpin a resource suitable for economic or social exploitation (*e.g.* forestry, recreation, water supply). Landscape provides a focus to promote the integration of wider conservation and environmental studies and to realise a more holistic approach to the conservation of Scotland's natural heritage. Such a contribution can usefully encompass landscape classification, assessment, interpretation, history and dynamics, integrated with sustainable landscape management that recognises the value of the Quaternary legacy.

15.5 Natural Heritage Zones

SNH is preparing a major new approach to its work in Scotland with the introduction of **Natural Heritage Zones.** The primary purpose of this shift in emphasis is to ensure that our perception of the natural heritage is not only focused on special places; rather that we recognise that the protection of SSSIs or NSAs is part of a broader conservation strategy that addresses the whole landscape. This type of whole country philosophy is also reflected in the UK Biodiversity Action Plan which states that "if we are to maintain and enrich the characteristic biological diversity and natural features of the UK across their traditional ranges, the countryside as a whole must be managed in a way which will support and complement our best areas" (Anon, 1994, p. 74). Only 11% or 893,000 hectares of the land surface of Scotland is currently covered by SSSI designation, and this necessarily leads to the exclusion of many areas of very high conservation quality.

"Ours is essentially a working landscape largely created and managed by people making their living directly from the land. Natural heritage interest must be seen in that context. To achieve multiple objectives in a landscape which 'works for its living', the needs of the natural heritage will best be served through **integrated land management.** The goal of economically viable and environmentally sustainable land use can only be attained through an integrated approach. Other approaches tend simply to tinker around the edges, leaving conservation areas divorced from productive areas." These are Roger Crofts' words, spoken at a Heritage Conference at Robert Gordon's University in October 1995. They capture the new approach, which has now been formally adopted by SNH and will guide our work for many years to come.

The development of natural heritage zonation in Scotland is entirely consistent with approaches in many other countries around the world where steps have been taken to bring together management of environmental resources with social needs, economic opportunities and cultural heritage. It also provides many other partner organisations, such as local government, the voluntary bodies and industry, the opportunity to share our vision for the management of the natural heritage and to identify a common agenda for action.

Twenty Natural Heritage Zones have been identified. The definition of these zones was guided principally by landscape character and an appreciation of the biogeographical distribution of some key species, refined on the basis of soils and climate data. In detail, the attributes considered were as follows:

- landform - topography, soils, geology, drainage;
- climate - rainfall, temperature range, exposure, maritime influence;
- landcover - land cover type, land use type, linear features, 'natural' type;
- artifacts - buildings, settlement pattern.

There are clearly many relationships that exist between these attributes, but no one factor or dependency was given an overriding weighting. The way in which these attributes interact to create consistent or divergent patterns across the countryside was used to define the distribution of zones. This process inevitably involves some elements of subjectivity and a requirement for informed judgement to be exercised. Consequently, there may be a need to refine the zone boundaries as the implementation process proceeds.

SNH's programme of implementing Natural Heritage Zones will involve three distinct phases. The first phase will concentrate on the development of a prospectus for each of the Natural Heritage Zones. This will draw together all the existing information on all aspects of the natural heritage to describe the character of each zone and to identify the trends and issues influencing it. However, it is important to stress that the prospectus will not establish a blueprint for the future of the natural heritage; rather it will indicate how the present condition can be improved upon in partnership with all the other interested parties.

Analysis of the natural heritage will take place both within the local and national context. The local dimension will involve the identification of the component 'countryside types' within each of the zones. Taking the Western Isles NHZ as an example, six countryside types can be identified to characterise the zone:

- machair;
- crofting inbye and outbye land;
- rocky moor and lochans;
- peaty moorland;
- mountain massif;
- the coastal edge.

Other factors that influence this local analysis include the degree to which the natural heritage is in harmony with current land uses, the 'intactness' of the countryside types and the key issues (both threats and opportunities) relating to each specific area. In the light of both the local and national analyses, the final prospectus for each zone will include:

- a description of the natural heritage of the entire zone, characterised by the combination of the countryside types, incorporating its nationally important attributes and designations (SSSIs, EU designations and NSAs);
- a statement on its relative 'state' based on current trends (declining, sustaining, enhancing) and the associated key issues, mainly land use, affecting these trends;
- the principle natural heritage needs to be addressed to establish and sustain a beneficial trend, forming the environmental agenda for each zone into the foreseeable future.

Each prospectus could be published to provide a public statement on the natural heritage character of each zone and to provide information for others.

The second phase will establish a general 'strategy for action' within each zone, and SNH will have an important role in facilitating the delivery of the range of activities identified in the prospectus. SNH's research programme will also in future be geared to addressing the research needs highlighted through the zonal programme. The zonal approach will also facilitate SNH's environmental audit role, as 'state of the natural heritage' monitoring will be undertaken within each zone.

The third phase envisages a co-ordinated approach to ensure delivery of the strategy for action. SNH will seek to engage partners in planning and land use decision-making as a whole, so that over time, there is a shared vision for each zone. Clear roles and responsibilities for all concerned will be identified to ensure that these environmental improvements are delivered.

At the time of writing, SNH's Main Board has just approved the decision to move forward with the Natural Heritage Zones initiative and, over the next few years, it should take shape along the lines outlined above. The Earth sciences will have an important part to play in the characterisation of these zones, the development of environmental auditing and in advising on management options based on an understanding of the physical environment and the palaeoenvironmental record.

15.6 Environmental education in relation to Quaternary issues

Raising awareness of the natural heritage through environmental education forms an important component of SNH's remit. The numerous publications produced for the earth sciences in recent years were reviewed in a previous issue of this journal (McKirdy, 1995). Since then, a number of new developments have occurred.

The **Landscape Fashioned by Geology** series has continued to grow and six titles have now been published:

- *Edinburgh* (1993)
- *Skye* (1993)
- *Cairngorms* - with accompanying worksheets for Standard and Higher grade work (1994)
- *Loch Lomond to Stirling* (1995)
- *Orkney and Shetland* (1996)
- *East Lothian and The Borders* (1997)

The Quaternary legacy of the landscape is described in each publication. Additional titles on *Arran and Bute, North West Highlands* and a series overview, *Scotland - A Landscape Fashioned by Geology,* are currently in preparation. Each publication has sold around two thousand copies per year, testimony to the fact that geology and geomorphology can create interest amongst the general public if the subject is attractively presented.

During the last year, significant advances have been made in the planning of the proposed visitor centre at **Knockan Crag** near Ullapool (see McKirdy, 1995). Following research by the Scottish Tourist Board, which confirms that most visitors come to Scotland for its combination of landscape and history, a new approach is being developed that will largely focus on an appreciation of the landscape. Here we have the opportunity to interpret the dramatic landscape of the Assynt area and beyond using innovative interpretive techniques, including amongst other media, interactive CD-ROMs, poetry and people (countryside rangers being the most interactive of media!). Story-telling techniques will also be used to involve the visitor - **provoking** their interest in subjects regarded as difficult to communicate to the general public, **relating** the stories to issues in their everyday lives, and **revealing** a web of interconnections that link us to the natural world. Discussion of the Quaternary history of the area will be a key feature of the interpretation offered at Knockan Crag.

Whilst Knockan Crag is one of the most accessible geological sites in Assynt, the area is rich in striking sites and impressive landscapes. Most visitors to Knockan will come by car, so a self-guided car trail will be prepared to introduce visitors to the geological and geomorphological highlights of the area, including Loch Glencoul, with its section through the Moine Thrust, the impressive Torridonian Sandstone peak of Stac Pollaidh, the striking ice-scoured 'cnoc-and-lochan' topography near Lochinver and the glaciated karst landscapes of Inchnadamph NNR. Landscape change through geological time is one of the key themes that the interpretation will address, so the events of the Ice Age, the legacy of erosional and depositional landforms, and subsequent changes during the Holocene will figure prominently. The interaction of human activity and landscape change is another important theme which will be explored. Appropriate teaching material will also be produced.

Development of the **Dynamic Earth** exhibition, which is to be built in Holyrood Park in Edinburgh, continues to make exciting progress. The project was recently awarded over £15 million by the Millennium Commission. SNH has funded a series of initiatives that have made a considerable contribution towards the overall interpretive story that the exhibition will deliver. Projects funded to date include ten interactive multimedia CD-ROMs on various aspects of the exhibition, including glaciation and plate tectonics. The main benefit that SNH will derive from this close association with Dynamic Earth is in relating processes that operate on a global scale, such as glaciation and volcanic activity, to locations in Scotland where examples of these phenomena can be demonstrated. So the anticipated half million visitors that will pass through the exhibition each year will gain a clearer understanding of the processes that have created and shaped Planet Earth and will be able to relate this appreciation to geological and landform sites throughout Scotland. This is an important fulfilment of one of SNH's guiding principles - that of 'fostering an understanding of the natural heritage of Scotland.'

Continuing the theme of public involvement and understanding, SNH organised the first **Scottish Geology Week** in August 1997 (Figure 15.2). This initiative included over a hundred events, ranging from talks to guided fieldtrips, exhibitions with 'hands on' workshops and competitions for schools and community groups. These events took place all over Scotland in villages, towns and cities.

15.7 Conclusion

With a secure basis for site protection established through the GCR, Earth heritage conservation is well placed to reflect the changing balance of priorities in SNH, with a new emphasis on the whole landscape. Although protection of statutory sites will continue to be an important part of Earth heritage conservation, the wider focus and objectives of Scottish Natural Heritage will provide new opportunities to contribute to integrated management based on a sound understanding of landscape evolution during the Quaternary, as well as to raise wider public awareness of this dynamic period of landscape history.

Acknowledgements
We thank Kath Leys for reviewing the manuscript.

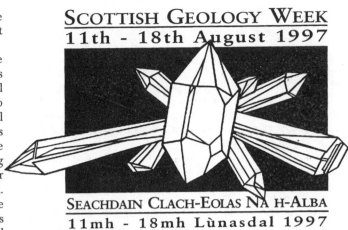

Figure 15.2 The logo for Scottish Geology Week.

References
Anon 1994. *Biodiversity: the UK Action Plan.* HMSO, London.

Birks, H.J.B. 1996. Contributions of Quaternary palaeoecology to nature conservation. *Journal of Vegetation Science,* 7, 89-98.

Butcher, N. 1994. The work of the Lothian and Borders RIGS Group in Scotland. In: O'Halloran, D., Green, C., Harley, M., Stanley, M. and Knill, J. 1994. *Geological and Landscape Conservation.* The Geological Society, London, 343-345.

Ellis, N.V., Bowen, D.Q., Campbell, S., Knill, J.L., McKirdy, A.P., Prosser, C.D., Vincent, M.A. and Wilson, R.C.L. 1996. *An Introduction to the Geological Conservation Review.* Joint Nature Conservation Committee, Peterborough.

Forbes, J.D. 1846. Notes on the topography and geology of the Cuchullin Hills in Skye, and on the traces of ancient glaciers which they present. *Edinburgh New Philosophical Journal,* 40, 76-99.

Gordon, J.E. and Campbell, S. 1992. Conservation of glacial deposits in Great Britain: a framework for assessment and protection of Sites of Special Scientific Interest. *Geomorphology,* 6, 89-97.

Gordon, J.E. and Sutherland, D.G. (Eds) 1993. *Quaternary of Scotland.* Chapman & Hall, London.

Gray, J.M. (Ed.) 1992. *Applications of Quaternary Research.* Quaternary Proceedings, No. 2. Quaternary Research Association, Cambridge.

Harley, M. 1994. The RIGS (Regionally Important Geological/geomorphological Sites) challenge - involving local volunteers in conserving England's geological heritage. In: O'Halloran, D., Green, C., Harley, M., Stanley, M. and Knill, J. 1994. *Geological and Landscape Conservation.* The Geological Society, London, 313-317.

Harley, M. and Robinson, J.E. 1991. RIGS - a local earth science conservation initiative. *Geology Today,* 7, 47-50.

Huntley, B. 1991. Historical lessons for the future. In: Spellerberg, I.F., Goldsmith, F.B. and Morris, M.G. (Eds), *Scientific Management of Temperate Communities for Conservation.* Blackwell, Oxford, 473-503.

Maclaren, C. 1845. Glaciers and icebergs in Scotland in ancient times. *The Scotsman,* 29(2685), 2.

Maclaren, C. 1846. Further evidence of the existence of glaciers in Scotland in ancient times. *The Scotsman,* 30(2798), 2.

McKirdy, A.P. 1995. Reading the landscape. A role for Scottish Natural Heritage. *SAGT Journal,* No. 24, 11-17.

O'Halloran, D., Green, C., Harley, M., Stanley, M. and Knill, J. 1994. *Geological and Landscape Conservation.* Geological Society, London.

Ratcliffe, D.A. 1977a. Nature conservation: aims, methods and achievements. *Proceedings of the Royal Society of London,* **197B,** 11-29.

Ratcliffe, D.A. 1977b. *A Nature Conservation Review.* 2 vols. Cambridge University Press, Cambridge.

Schumm, S.A. 1991. *To Interpret the Earth. Ten Ways to be Wrong.* Cambridge University Press, Cambridge.

Stevens, C., Gordon, J.E., Green, C.P. and Macklin, M.G. 1994. *Conserving Our Landscape. Evolving landforms and Ice-age Heritage.* Peterborough.

Stevenson, A.C. and Thompson, D.B.A. 1993. Long-term changes in the extent of heather moorland in upland Britain and Ireland: palaeoecological evidence for the importance of grazing. *The Holocene,* **3,** 70-76.

Stevenson, A.C., Jones, V.J. and Battarbee, R.W. 1990. The cause of peat erosion: a palaeolimnological approach. *New Phytologist,* **114,** 727-735.

Swanson, F.J., Dratz, T.K., Caine, N. and Woodmansee, R.G. 1988. Landform effects on ecosystem patterns and processes. *BioScience,* **38,** 92-98.

Taylor, A.G., Gordon, J.E. and Usher, M.B. 1996. *Soils, Sustainability and the Natural Heritage.* HMSO, Edinburgh.

Werritty, A. and Brazier, V. 1994. Geomorphic sensitivity and the conservation of fluvial SSSIs. In: Stevens, C., Green, C.P., Gordon, J.E. and Macklin, M.G. (Eds), *Conserving Our Landscape: Evolving Landforms and Ice-age Heritage.* Peterborough, 100-109.

Werritty, A., Brazier, V., Gordon, J.E. and McManus, J. 1994. Geomorphology. In Maitland, P.S., Boon, P.J. and McLusky, D.S. (Eds), *The Freshwaters of Scotland. A Resource of International Significance.* Wiley, Chichester, 65-88.